Thomas Klier
East Lansing Fall '88

THE EMPIRICAL RENAISSANCE IN INDUSTRIAL ECONOMICS

THE EMPIRICAL RENAISSANCE IN INDUSTRIAL ECONOMICS

Edited by

TIMOTHY F. BRESNAHAN
RICHARD SCHMALENSEE

Basil Blackwell

published in cooperation with

The Journal of Industrial Economics

First published 1987
First published in USA 1987

Basil Blackwell Ltd
108 Cowley Road, Oxford, OX4 1JF, UK

Basil Blackwell Inc.
432 Park Avenue South, Suite 1503
New York, NY 10016, USA

British Library Cataloguing in Publication Data applied for.
Library of Congress Cataloging in Publication Data applied for.

ISBN 0-631-15743-3

Typeset by Advanced Filmsetters (Glasgow) Limited
Printed in Great Britain by Whitstable Litho and bound by
Standard Bookbinding Company Limited, London

CONTENTS

THE EMPIRICAL RENAISSANCE IN INDUSTRIAL ECONOMICS: AN OVERVIEW

TIMOTHY F. BRESNAHAN AND RICHARD SCHMALENSEE

This brief essay introduces a special issue of *The Journal of Industrial Economics* devoted to the recent burst of empirical work in industrial organization. Trends in empirical research in this field are discussed, emphasizing the ways in which recent work builds upon and departs from earlier traditions. The papers in the special issue, which exemplify these developments, are briefly discussed.

I. INTRODUCTION

THE 1980s have seen a rebirth of interest and activity on the empirical side of industrial economics, stimulated in part by the wide-ranging and fundamental theoretical advances of the preceding decade. The papers in this collection exemplify the interrelated set of developments that have revitalized empirical work in industrial economics in recent years. While each study makes significant contributions to knowledge, these contributions are quite diverse. These essays are unified by style and approach rather than by topic, method, or findings. A brief history of styles of empirical work in industrial economics (section II) serves to set the stage for a discussion of these unifying themes.[1]

This collection of essays was easy to assemble because many able industrial economists are now doing interesting empirical work. Our task would have been considerably harder at the start of this decade, since much less was then happening on the empirical front. And a collection of empirical work assembled in 1980 would have differed in several basic respects from this one.

Recent studies do follow the earlier cross-section tradition by relying primarily on systematic statistical evidence. But the recent literature reflects the growing importance of formal theory in industrial economics; there is more interest in testing a specific hypothesis in the context of explicit maintained hypotheses. In addition, reflecting the case study tradition, recent studies are likely to involve collection of new data and analysis of a small group of firms or industries. In sections III and IV of this essay we attempt to articulate some of the unifying themes running through the new work and to relate them to the papers in this collection.

[1] The knowledgeable reader will recognize that we have glossed over much in section II in the interest of brevity. We hope we will be forgiven for not calling attention to a number of important contributions that do not conform to the generalizations we advance.

II. HISTORICAL BACKGROUND

Grether [1970] and other writers (particularly in the United States) date the emergence of Industrial Economics (or Industrial Organization) as a distinct field of economics from the work of Edward Chamberlin and Edward Mason at Harvard in the early 1930s. The "Harvard School" initially stressed detailed, book-length case studies of particular industries; see Wallace [1937] for an influential early example. The research program led by Mason sought to learn about imperfectly competitive markets by induction from careful studies of particular examples. These studies made relatively little use of formal economic theory or of econometric techniques.

In the early 1950s, Joe Bain [1951], [1956] changed the focus of empirical research in industrial economics by showing the apparent power of statistical studies of industry-level cross-section data. Bain's approach seemed to promise rapid and objective development of general relations based on large samples of markets. While few followed Bain's lead immediately, the journals began to fill with cross-section work in the 1960s as computation costs fell and government-supplied data became more widely available.

As economics as a whole shifted from a book-oriented discipline, like history, to a journal-oriented discipline, like mathematics, in this same period, shorter case studies began to become more common. Instead of examining all aspects of an industry's structure, conduct, and performance, these studies generally focused on particular aspects of conduct. And, under the influence of George Stigler and others identified with the "Chicago School", increasing use was made of the tools of Marshallian price theory.[2] But little explicit modeling of imperfect competition was done, and econometric techniques were not heavily employed.

In a survey of "Quantitative Studies of Industrial Organization" presented in 1970, Leonard Weiss [1971] concentrated almost exclusively on cross-section econometric work. As William Comanor [1971, pp. 403–4] noted in his favorable comment on Weiss' paper:

> Despite the original prescription of Edward Mason, practitioners in this area have moved away from an early reliance on case studies and toward the use of econometric methods of analysis. To a large extent, therefore, a review of econometric studies of industrial organization is a review of much of the content of the field.

At the end of his survey, Weiss [1971, p. 398] opined that "perhaps the right next step is back to the industry study, but this time with regression in hand".

While some econometric industry studies were done in the 1970s, the early part of that decade saw the publication of many more cross-section studies of industry-level, government-supplied data. But critics of this approach became

[2] For examples of both current and contemporary interest, see the essays collected in Stigler [1968]

more vocal and persuasive during the 1970s. They argued that industry-level cross-section data could not be used to identify and estimate structural relationships of interest. And, by the end of the decade, the critics had generally prevailed. The study of industry-level cross-section data had fallen from fashion, and fewer studies of this sort appeared in leading journals.[3]

The journal space thus made available was filled not by industry studies but by reports on a burst of theoretical activity, begun by Michael Spence and others in the early 1970s, involving the formal analysis of imperfectly competitive markets. This activity continues unabated, with recent work making heavy use of the developing tools of noncooperative game theory.

At the start of the 1980s, then, relatively little exciting empirical work was being done in industrial organization: industry-level cross-section work was suspect, and case studies were no more attractive than they had been a decade earlier. The main action was on the theoretical front.

III. THE RECENT RENAISSANCE

As the papers in this collection demonstrate, a good deal of exciting empirical work has been done in industrial economics in the last few years. As in the earlier cross-section tradition, this work stresses systematic statistical analysis rather than anecdotes. Similarly, the turn of much recent work toward single industries or groups of closely related industries is a continuation of the case study tradition. Recent studies, however, tend to differ from much of the earlier work in the mainstream case study and cross-section traditions in three interrelated ways. In retrospect, at least, all three of the new trends discussed in this section and exemplified in this collection are natural responses to the dissatisfaction with the two earlier traditions, a dissatisfaction that solidified in the late 1970s.[4]

First, a large fraction of recent work employs new sources of data or data sets constructed in new ways from traditional sources. The field has moved well away from the heavy reliance on Census-provided industry-level data acknowledged by Weiss [1971] and Comanor [1971] at the start of the 1970s.

There is, of course, nothing really new in this. The careful collection of new evidence was always central to the case study tradition in both its "Harvard School" and "Chicago School" variants. But data collection is not a terribly exciting activity, and as traditional case studies fell from fashion, so did the construction of new data sets.

Data set construction is more popular now partly because developments in computer hardware and software have reduced the associated costs and partly because the shortcomings of traditional data sets have become clear. Just as new experiments are central to advances in most natural sciences, so it

[3] For general discussions of these developments, see Schmalensee [1982, 1988].

[4] Schmalensee [1982] provides a vintage-1980 view of then-emerging trends in empirical research.

is becoming clear that new data are important to progress in industrial economics. But the main reason for a renewed interest in data is probably the widespread perception that new tools and approaches permit one to perform new and interesting empirical analyses. The personal, professional payoff to data set construction has risen.

A second trend visible in recent work is the growing tendency to exploit contemporary advances in economic theory and econometric methods. The theoretical developments that began in the 1970s produced a rich set of hypotheses, along with a powerful set of modeling techniques for use in imperfectly competitive markets and a generation of scholars familiar with those techniques. Similarly, as the general analytical level of work in industrial economics has risen, empirical researchers in the field have become more willing and able to exploit the latest advances in econometric method and thus to move well beyond exclusive reliance on ordinary least squares.

But the best recent work is not just a showcase for technique; rather it lets new data tell interesting stories simply and clearly. Several of the papers in this collection use nothing more than ordinary least squares and simple tables to allow new data to speak clearly to the reader. Others use relatively exotic techniques because they are necessary to reveal what the data have to say about the issues addressed.

A third trend apparent in the recent empirical literature is a shift toward the firm, rather than the industry, as the unit of observation. Again, there is nothing really new in this; industry studies have always necessarily treated individual firms as separate observations. But the work of Demsetz [1973] and others in the early 1970s began to focus attention on the importance of intra-industry differences and thus to shift attention away from industries and toward firms. In the same period, Iwata [1974] showed that formal theory and sophisticated econometric techniques could be used to analyze seller conduct in new and interesting ways.

Following Iwata [1974], many authors have responded to Weiss' [1971] call to go "back to the industry study, but this time with regression in hand". Econometric industry studies are a growth area, with new analytical techniques being developed to cope with problems that arise in these studies.[5] Like the earlier "Chicago-style" industry studies, recent efforts generally focus on particular aspects of conduct. But, in a departure from the earlier traditions, the tools of imperfect competition theory are now routinely used to construct explicit structural models, and the latest econometric techniques are used to estimate structural parameters and to test structural hypotheses.

IV. THIS COLLECTION

Six of the essays assembled here follow the cross-section tradition insofar as they are based on data covering many industries. But none closely resembles

[5] For a detailed survey of this area, see Bresnahan [1988].

the cross-section studies that dominated the empirical literature in the late 1960s and 1970s. Though several use data from traditional sources, none limits attention to a single industry-level cross-section, and only the study by Domowitz, Hubbard, and Petersen takes the industry, rather than the firm or business unit, as the fundamental unit of observations. And the influence of recent developments in economic theory and econometrics is quite clear in this set of papers.

Profitability differences

Three of the papers that study multiple industries deal with a phenomenon that was the focus of the cross-section tradition: sources of differences in profitability among firms and industries.

Domowitz, Hubbard, and Petersen use a panel data set they constructed from US Census data. These data allow them to focus on differences in the cyclical behavior of prices and price-cost margins among industries with different structures and different average margin levels. They relate the observed differences to recent dynamic models of collusive behavior.

Schmalensee's essay is based on traditional US data sources: the Internal Revenue Service and the Census of Manufactures. But he uses intra-industry data for two different years, along with a set of formal models and non-standard econometric techniques, in an attempt to evaluate the collusive (Bain [1951]) and differential efficiency (Demsetz [1973]) explanations of intra- and inter-industry differences in measured profitability.

Finally, the paper by Cubbin and Geroski uses a newly-constructed panel data set on large UK firms to study the relative importance of firm-specific and industry-wide determinants of profitability changes over time. The results of this study strongly support the importance of firm-level analysis.

Oligopoly pricing

Much attention has been recently paid to empirical analysis of individual markets, rather than of the broad sweep of industries. Half of the essays in this collection concentrate on individual industries or markets, and five of these are primarily focused on the measurement of power over price. But these are not traditional case studies. They are all firmly grounded in recent theoretical work on imperfectly competitive markets, and several of them employ novel econometric methods.

The essay by Panzar and Rosse has circulated in working paper form since 1977 and has had a considerable influence on recent studies of individual industries. Panzar and Rosse use microeconomic theory to derive tools for interpreting reduced form relations between revenue and input prices that were encountered in research on the US newspaper industry.

Bresnahan's essay, earlier versions of which have circulated since 1980, applies maximum likelihood methods to estimate structural models of markets with differentiated products using data on the US automobile industry. Bresnahan compares the empirical implications of alternative behavioral assumptions and argues that a sharp, temporary increase in competition occurred in this industry in 1955.

Ashenfelter and Sullivan advance the work of Panzar and Rosse by developing nonparametric techniques for studying the relationship between cost shifts and industry equilibrium. They apply these techniques to data on the US cigarette industry. Their work has interesting implications both about behavior in this industry and for the study of firm behavior in other settings.

Slade analyzes data she collected on day-by-day changes in retail prices and wholesale costs of gasoline for a set of filling stations in Vancouver, British Columbia, during and after a price war. She estimates demand and reaction functions for these stations and uses her results to shed light on the validity of competing theories of price wars.

Hendricks, Porter, and Boudreau analyze data on auctions for the rights to extract oil from particular undersea tracts off the US coast, along with information on the subsequent returns from those tracts. Their analysis has implications for the validity of recent theoretical models of auctions and shows the power of simple statistical methods when carefully applied to rich data.

Competition in the long run

The remaining four studies in this collection treat questions of industry structure and firm conduct from a somewhat longer-run perspective. Of these, three of the four use broad cross-sections of firms in different industries. Lieberman's study, however, is based on his database of closely-related chemical processing industries.

Cohen, Levin, and Mowery employ the Line-of-Business data collected by the US Federal Trade Commission (FTC) along with the results of a large-scale survey. The FTC data relate to individual business units within diversified firms, and thus permit one to disentangle the influences of firm, business unit, and industry characteristics. Cohen and his co-authors use these data to test the Schumpeterian hypothesis that large firms are more research intensive, all else equal.

The papers by Evans and Hall are concerned with the classic Gibrat's Law hypothesis that average firm growth rates are independent of firm size. Both papers use large, new data sets. Evans concentrates on industry-specific patterns and on the effects of firm age on growth; Hall develops new econometric techniques to deal with problems posed by the non-random disappearance of firms in the sample over time.

Finally, Lieberman analyzes data on additions to capacity in the chemical industry. He uses recently-developed techniques for the estimation of qualitative choice models along with traditional case-study methods to shed light on the empirical relevance of theoretical models in which investment in long-lived capacity is undertaken to deter entry.

V. CONCLUDING REMARKS

As we noted at the start of this essay, the studies that follow are indeed diverse. They address a wide range of issues, ranging from traditional concerns to the implications of very recent theoretical work. But they share elements of style and approach that clearly mark them as work of the 1980s. And many of them will serve as important points of departure for future research—both empirical and theoretical.

TIMOTHY F. BRESNAHAN,
Department of Economics,
Stanford University,
Stanford,
California 94305,
USA.

RICHARD SCHMALENSEE,
Sloan School of Management,
Massachusetts Institute of Technology,
Cambridge,
Massachusetts 02139,
USA.

REFERENCES

BAIN, J. S., 1951, 'Relation of Profit Rate to Industry Concentration: American Manufacturing, 1936–1940', *Quarterly Journal of Economics*, 65 (August), pp. 293–324.

BAIN, J. S., 1956, *Barriers to New Competition* (Harvard University Press, Cambridge).

BRESNAHAN, T. F., 1988, 'Empirical Studies of Industries with Market Power', in R. SCHMALENSEE and R. D. WILLIG (eds.), *Handbook of Industrial Organization* (North-Holland, Amsterdam).

COMANOR, W. S., 1971, 'Comments [on Weiss (1971)]', in M. D. INTRILIGATOR (ed.), *Frontiers of Quantitative Economics* (North-Holland, Amsterdam).

DEMSETZ, H., 1973, 'Industry Structure, Market Rivalry, and Public Policy', *Journal of Law and Economics*, 16 (April), pp. 1–10.

GRETHER, E. T., 1970, 'Industrial Organization: Past History and Future Prospects', *American Economic Review*, 60 (May), pp. 83–89.

IWATA, G., 1974, 'Measurement of Conjectural Variations in Oligopoly', *Econometrica*, 42 (September), pp. 947–966.

SCHMALENSEE, R., 1982, 'The New Industrial Organization and the Economic Analysis of Modern Markets', in W. HILDENBRAND (ed.), *Advances in Economic Theory* (Cambridge University Press, Cambridge).

SCHMALENSEE, R., 1988, 'Inter-Industry Studies of Structure and Performance', in R. SCHMALENSEE and R. D. WILLIG (eds.), *Handbook of Industrial Organization* (North-Holland, Amsterdam).

STIGLER, G. J., 1968, *The Organization of Industry* (Richard D. Irwin, Homewood, Illinois).

WALLACE, D. H., 1937, *Market Control in the Aluminum Industry* (Harvard University Press, Cambridge).

WEISS, L. W., 1971, 'Quantitative Studies of Industrial Organization', in M. D. INTRILIGATOR (ed.), *Frontiers of Quantitative Economics* (North-Holland, Amsterdam).

OLIGOPOLY SUPERGAMES: SOME EMPIRICAL EVIDENCE ON PRICES AND MARGINS*

IAN DOMOWITZ, R. GLENN HUBBARD and BRUCE C. PETERSEN

This paper is a panel data study on the behavior of prices and margins of oligopolies involved in repeated games. We examine the predictions of Green and Porter [1984] and Rotemberg and Saloner [1986], two supergame models which generate very different predictions about the cyclical behavior of prices and margins. Our evidence on the levels of price-cost margins indicates that oligopolies achieve equilibria that more closely resemble a one-shot Cournot–Nash outcome than monopoly. We find, however, that industries with "high" price-cost margins exhibit cyclical price behavior which is quite different from that of unconcentrated industries. We find little evidence of price wars during either recessions or booms.

I. INTRODUCTION

WHETHER OLIGOPOLISTS are able to achieve collective outcomes approaching that of a monopolist is an issue of considerable debate in theoretical industrial economics; its relevance for public policy is clear. Recent theoretical work on oligopoly supergames has demonstrated that, for a wide range of situations, oligopolists may be able to approximate cooperative outcomes in games which are (structurally) noncooperative.[1]

In this paper we focus on two recent and innovative supergames models involving trigger strategies and generating predictions about the cyclical behavior of prices. In the model of Green and Porter [1984], demand shifts are imperfectly observed by oligopolists and output does not vary as long as price remains above the trigger price. Since all adjustments occur through price unless a reversion occurs, prices and price-cost margins should be procyclical with the possibility of occasional very sharp price declines. In contrast, Rotemberg and Saloner [1986] assume that demand shifts are perfectly observable and versions of their model predict that price-cost margins should be countercyclical. The assumptions and predictions of these two models are further described in the next section of the paper.

An empirical test of the predictions of these models in particular, and

* We are grateful to Timothy Bresnahan, Dennis Carlton, Kenneth Judd, John Panzar, Robert Porter, Richard Schmalensee, Lawrence J. White, and members of the NBER Working Group on Macroeconomics and Industrial Organization for helpful comments, and to Craig Paxton and John Simpson for excellent research assistance. The usual disclaimer applies. Financial support from the National Science Foundation (SES-8420152) is acknowledged.

[1] Until recently, it was generally thought that finitely repeated games of the "Prisoners' Dilemma" variety were inherently similar to a single-period game (see the review in Friedman [1986]).

oligopoly supergames in general, is best undertaken with panel data. Using information on four-digit-SIC level manufacturing industries over the period from 1958 to 1981, we focus on a subset of industries having structural characteristics closely resembling those cited by Green and Porter and Rotemberg and Saloner. While oligopoly supergames predict that prices and margins will on average be above the Cournot levels, this need not be true for all time periods (see for example Green and Porter [1984]). It is desirable, therefore, to examine several years of data for any given industry. The use of longitudinal data also allows for tests that distinguish between individual models employing trigger strategies.

In section III we examine whether the price-cost margins of any industry ever approach collusive levels in any time period covered by the available data. We find that margins for our sample of highly concentrated industries are on average higher than margins in unconcentrated industries, but they more closely resemble the predicted levels of a single-period Cournot equilibrium than that of monopoly. This finding alone, however, is not conclusive evidence that oligopolists never engage in the quasi-cooperative arrangements implied by trigger equilibria strategies. There are many reasons why the sustainable outcomes in such games may not be on the profit-possibility frontier.

In section IV we examine the cyclical behavior of margins and prices for a subset of highly concentrated oligopolistic industries exhibiting above average price-cost margins over the 1958–1981 period. Census price-cost margins are procyclical for concentrated industries, although less so for high-margin than low-margin industries. We find no evidence for reversions from cooperative to Cournot behavior as in Green and Porter. Finally, price movements among highly concentrated, high price-cost margin industries are countercyclical.

II. TRIGGER STRATEGY EQUILIBRIUM

The basic concept of trigger strategies was first discussed by Luce and Raiffa [1957] with respect to repeated games based on the Prisoners' Dilemma. An excellent overview of the literature that followed and a description of the conditions for trigger-strategy equilibria are given by Friedman [1986, chapter 3]. Simply put, these equilibria are agreements, possibly including the joint-profit maximizing outcome, which can be enforced by the threat of retaliation in the event of defection. That is, in response to a violation, all players agree to revert to a (single-period) noncooperative equilibrium. Because the threat involves playing noncooperative strategies, it must be credible; the equilibrium is subgame-perfect (in the sense described by Selten [1975]).

Recent work involving infinite and finite-horizon supergames has demonstrated that trigger strategies are viable under a wide range of conditions. Friedman [1985] derives the conditions under which finite-horizon trigger strategies exist. He also shows that where trigger strategies do not exist, the discontinuity between infinite and finite horizons can be smoothed if the players no longer seek perfect optimization in their strategies. Furthermore, if players are "close" to behaving optimally, then trigger-strategy "epsilon-equilibria" are possible if games have sufficiently long but finite horizons (see Radner [1980]).

We now turn to two well known models involving trigger strategies. Green and Porter [1984] examine an oligopoly situation where the industry is presumed to be stable (mature), products are homogeneous, and all available information is public knowledge except for each firm's knowledge about its own present and past output levels. Firms cannot perfectly observe the level of industry demand in each period and the output choices of their competitors; they agree on a "trigger price" to which they compare the market price when they make their production decision. If the market price remains above the trigger price, all firms agree to produce at a collusive level. If, however, the price drops below the trigger price, all firms agree to revert to the one-shot (Cournot) equilibrium for some fixed period of time. A firm which considers a secret expansion of output above the collusive level must trade off immediate profit gains with the increased probability that the market price might fall below the trigger price, thereby increasing the likelihood of an industry reversion and lower profits.[2] Alternatively, Porter [1985] describes how firms could focus on market shares instead of a trigger price; in this case, large enough deviations of actual from allocated market shares would trigger a price war.

In the Green–Porter model, reversionary episodes sometimes will occur simply because of low demand. They emphasize that such reversions are not defections by any of the participants from the supergame. Rather, in the uncertain environment of their model, reversions are necessary to keep the equilibrium subgame-perfect; that is, to provide incentives for all firms to choose rationally to produce at collusive levels in normal times.

One testable prediction of the Green–Porter model involves the cyclical behavior of prices and price-cost margins. Output is fixed in their model unless a reversion occurs. If all demand shocks are unobservable, prices and margins should be procyclical.[3] While changes in cost are not considered by Green and Porter, economy-wide inflation should not affect the collusive output level. All that has to be updated is the nominal value of the trigger price. Shocks which increase costs will reduce profit margins until the collusive output is updated, but prices will continue to be procyclical. If,

[2] For each firm's cooperative output level to be the noncooperative action, the marginal expected loss in future profits from triggering a reversion to Cournot behavior must exactly balance the marginal gain from cheating on the agreement.

[3] Assuming that demand shifts are so imperfectly observed that output changes never occur unless there is a reversion is extreme. Relaxing this assumption, however, and permitting a partial response (i.e., by allowing output to be somewhat procyclical) would not change the basic prediction that prices should be procyclical with periodic sharp declines.

however, some demand shocks are observable and others are not, a definitive test of the Green–Porter model with respect to the cyclical behavior of prices may not be possible.

A second testable prediction of the Green–Porter model is that of periodic sharp declines in industry price, something not contained in earlier trigger-strategy models where the incentives were so perfect that the deterrent mechanisms were never observed. Green and Porter [1984, p. 94] emphasize that, according to their model, industries having the appropriate characteristics will exhibit price instability if oligopoly members are colluding and that such episodes play an essential role in the maintenance of an ongoing scheme of collusive incentives.

Rotemberg and Saloner [1986] present a second supergame model employing trigger strategies and generating predictions about oligopoly price behavior over the business cycle. As in Green and Porter, the major departure of this model from the earlier literature is allowing for industry shifts in demand. The major distinction between the two models is that Rotemberg and Saloner assume that demand shifts are observable. In most other respects, including the set of industry characteristics (homogeneous products, etc.) the models are alike.

Changes in industry demand cause firm payoffs to be nonstationary. It is this nonstationarity that Rotemberg and Saloner exploit. They do so by assuming that firms know the new level of demand before selecting their level of the choice variable in each period. Once choice variables are selected, they cannot be adjusted until the following period.

In this environment, the rewards for cheating on a collusive agreement will be different from period to period, in general varying positively with the state of demand. The future punishment that can be inflicted on a cheater, however, is independent of current demand if variations in demand are assumed to be independently and identically distributed. Thus, in periods of sufficiently high demand, the rewards from cheating on at least some collusive agreements may exceed any future punishments. The likelihood of such an episode, of course, depends on the length of the period for which a firm can cheat on its competitors before retaliation can begin.[4]

Rotemberg and Saloner suggest a method by which oligopolies may keep firms from defecting. For periods of high demand, firms agree to choose a price (quantity) low enough (high enough) such that the rewards from defection are sufficiently reduced to keep cooperation the optimal strategy. This is possible since industry demand is observable to the oligopoly. Their strongest results are for the case in which prices are the strategic variable and marginal costs are constant. In this case, increases in demand beyond a certain point actually lower the oligopoly's prices monotonically. Their results are somewhat weaker when quantity is the strategic variable, but they

[4] If such a period were very short, defection would never be desirable.

do present examples where increases in demand again lead to more competitive behavior.

The testable prediction of the Rotemberg and Saloner model is that the Lerner index is countercyclical; in booms oligopolies reduce the spread between price and marginal cost to lower the per unit gain from cheating. They present some rudimentary evidence that this may in fact be the case in some industries. They also point out the practical difficulties in testing their hypothesis using traditional measures of the price-cost margin if movements in marginal cost and average variable cost over the business cycle are not highly correlated. An alternative test is to assume that marginal cost is procyclical and to test for the cyclical behavior of price.

In the sections which follow, we provide some simple tests of the predictions of these models for industry price-cost margins and prices for a selected sample of manufacturing industries.

III. LEVELS OF PRICE-COST MARGINS FOR SELECTED INDUSTRIES

One straightforward test of trigger-strategy models is to examine whether the Census price-cost margin of any industry ever approaches collusive levels in any time period covered by our panel. For industries producing undifferentiated products, expressions can be derived relating the price-cost margin (Lerner index) to industry structural conditions for different types of industry behavior.

It is well known that[5] for a given industry, a firm's price-cost margin (PCM) can be expressed as:

$$\frac{P-MC_i}{P}=\frac{s_i(1+v_i)}{\varepsilon} \tag{1}$$

where s_i is the ith firms market share, v_i is its conjectural variation (the ith firm's guess about the output response of all other firms), and ε is the industry demand elasticity. Reference points of interest are the monopoly outcome, $PCM = 1/\varepsilon$, and the Cournot outcome, $PCM = s_i/\varepsilon$.

We do not have firm data and it is extremely difficult to estimate marginal cost. However, industry expressions can be derived by aggregating equation (1) across firms. If marginal cost is assumed to equal average variable cost for each firm, then such an aggregation will yield[6]

[5] See for example Waterson [1984, pp. 18–20].

[6] Multiplying equation (1) by q_i/Q and summing across all firms in the industry yields:

$$\frac{\sum P\cdot q_i-\sum MC_i\cdot q_i}{PQ}=\frac{\sum s_i^2(1+v_i)}{\varepsilon}$$

If marginal cost equals average variable cost, then the above expression can be rewritten as:

$$\frac{\pi+F}{PQ}=\frac{H}{\varepsilon}$$

where F is fixed cost and the left-hand side of the equation is the ratio of gross profits to sales.

$$\frac{P-AVC}{P}=\frac{\sum s_i^2(1+v_i)}{\varepsilon} \tag{2}$$

where AVC is the industry-weighted average variable cost. The left-hand side of equation (2) can also be expressed as the ratio of gross profits to revenue. The interesting reference points again are the monopoly outcome,

$$\frac{P-AVC}{P}=\frac{1}{\varepsilon} \tag{3}$$

and the Cournot outcome,

$$\frac{P-AVC}{P}=\frac{\sum s_i^2}{\varepsilon}=\frac{H}{\varepsilon} \tag{4}$$

where H is the Herfindahl index of concentration.

Three points should be made about equations (3) and (4). First, the difference between the predicted margins in equations (3) and (4) (collusion versus Cournot) is very large. In manufacturing industries, Herfindahl indices above 0.35 are rare, while values much above 0.4 are no longer observed.[7]

TABLE I

IMPLIED *PCM*s FOR SELECTED DEMAND ELASTICITIES AND HERFINDAHL INDICES

			*Monopoly Outcome**		
ε	1.00	1.25	1.50	1.75	2.00
PCM	1.00	0.80	0.67	0.57	0.50
			Cournot Outcome†		
ε	1.00	1.25	1.50	1.75	2.00
H					
0.15	0.15	0.12	0.10	0.09	0.08
0.20	0.20	0.16	0.13	0.11	0.10
0.25	0.25	0.20	0.17	0.14	0.13
0.30	0.30	0.24	0.20	0.17	0.15
0.35	0.35	0.28	0.23	0.20	0.18

Notes: * Based on equation (3) in text.
† Based on equation (4) in text; entries in the matrix are *PCM* values; *H* denotes the Herfindahl index.

[7] Consider as an example the automobile industry, one of the most concentrated industries in the United States. The approximate market shares of General Motors, Ford, Chrysler and American Motors are: 0.5, 0.25, 0.20 and 0.05. The Herfindahl index for this configuration of market shares is 0.355. Nelson [1963] reports Herfindahl values for most of the existing four-digit Census industries between 1947–1956. None of the Herfindahl values exceed 0.30. Nelson was unable, however, to report *H* values for a few of the most concentrated industries (e.g., aluminum).

Secondly if MC differs from AVC, $(P-AVC)/P$ will result in a biased estimate of market power; this estimate will be biased upward if marginal cost exceeds average variable cost, but the opposite bias is theoretically also possible. Finally, if ε is large enough, then values of $(P-AVC)/P$ considerably less than unity are consistent with collusion.

This final point, as well as the differences between predicted margins in equations (3) and (4), are illustrated in Table I. For both the Cournot outcome and the monopoly outcome, margins are calculated for selected values of the Herfindahl index and the demand elasticity ε. It is apparent that elasticities must be quite high for the monopoly PCM to be less than 0.50. It is also apparent that for the Cournot outcome, PCMs are not likely to exceed 0.30.

We now turn to an examination of actual price-cost margins for four-digit-SIC-level Census manufacturing industries.[8] While Census price-cost margins are only approximations to the Lerner index, they are flow measures that are relatively free of accounting distortions. Detailed descriptions of the data can be found in Domowitz, Hubbard, and Petersen [1986a], [1986b].[9] The full data set contains information on 312 manufacturing industries over the period from 1958 to 1981. To focus on trigger-strategy models, we delineate a subsample of fifty-seven industries in Table II. The common characteristics of these industries are: (i) they are "producer-goods" industries;[10] (ii) they have been recognized as Census industries at least since 1958; (iii) they have four-firm concentration ratios[11] above 0.50 in 1972; and (iv) they are not listed as "miscellaneous" or as "not elsewhere classified". The object of (i)–(iv) was to select mature, homogeneous-goods oligopolies operating in well defined

[8] The PCM is defined as

$$PCM = \frac{Value\ of\ Sales + \Delta Inventories - Payroll - Cost\ of\ Materials}{Value\ of\ Sales + \Delta Inventories}$$

which is identical to (Value Added − Payroll)/(Value Added + Cost of Materials) given the Census's definition of value added.

[9] The *Census of Manufactures* and the *Annual Survey of Manufactures* (published by the US Bureau of the Census) are the primary sources of information used in constructing the panel data base. Other possible sources were not used because of definitional problems, the short time period covered, or stringent confidentiality restrictions. Data for most industries go back to at least 1958, and for some industries even as far back as 1947, allowing for a panel of substantial length. Census definitional issues are discussed in Domowitz, Hubbard, and Petersen [1986a], [1986b]. The data are described therein, with the exception of the capital stock series, which has been modified to reflect a more realistic depreciation schedule.

[10] The producer-goods/consumer-goods classification is taken from Ornstein [1975]. Ornstein's classification is based on the percentage of shipments of output for final demand in four categories: consumption, investment, materials, and government. If fifty percent or more of an industry's output went to consumption, it was classified as a consumer-goods industry, if fifty percent or more went to investment plus materials, it was classified as a producer-goods industry.

[11] We used the four-firm concentration ratios constructed by Weiss and Pasco [1981]. They adjusted the concentration ratio for all Census industries for 1972 for inappropriate product groupings and geographic fragmentation.

TABLE II
PRICE-COST MARGINS FOR CONCENTRATED PRODUCER-GOODS INDUSTRIES

Industry (SIC)	C4	Adjusted C4	Average PCM	Standard Deviation of PCM	Minimum PCM (Year)	Maximum PCM (Year)
High-PCM Industries:						
Flour (2045)	68	62	0.306	0.030	0.232 (1978)	0.348 (1970)
Corn Wet Milling (2046)	63	63	0.290	0.042	0.191 (1973)	0.345 (1960)
Flavoring Extracts (2087)	66	62	0.483	0.033	0.413 (1975)	0.528 (1979)
Manufactured Ice (2097)	32	86	0.392	0.030	0.317 (1971)	0.444 (1973)
Pressed and Molded Pulp Goods (2646)	75	75	0.332	0.049	0.165 (1980)	0.389 (1977)
Alkalines and Chlorine (2812)	72	60	0.369	0.038	0.299 (1980)	0.422 (1975)
Industrial Gases (2813)	65	78	0.503	0.059	0.423 (1958)	0.605 (1970)
Inorganic Pigments (2816)	52	52	0.365	0.063	0.269 (1978)	0.447 (1964)
Synthetic Rubber (2822)	62	54	0.279	0.057	0.170 (1981)	0.356 (1969)
Organic Fibers (2824)	74	70	0.380	0.093	0.231 (1975)	0.493 (1958)
Explosives (2892)	67	69	0.272	0.077	0.126 (1970)	0.380 (1980)
Carbon Black (2895)	74	74	0.393	0.114	0.160 (1980)	0.514 (1968)
Tires & Tubes (3011)	73	73	0.273	0.030	0.227 (1964)	0.334 (1973)
Reclaimed Rubber (3031)	78	74	0.277	0.068	0.171 (1970)	0.500 (1979)
Flat Glass (3211)	92	83	0.362	0.042	0.296 (1981)	0.446 (1972)
Products of Purchased Glass (3231)	43	54	0.270	0.019	0.242 (1970)	0.318 (1960)
Cement, Hydraulic (3241)	26	73	0.436	0.045	0.339 (1981)	0.490 (1959)
Brick and Structural Tile (3251)	17	65	0.292	0.037	0.217 (1960)	0.352 (1977)
Gypsum Products (3275)	80	79	0.356	0.068	0.237 (1976)	0.446 (1963)
Mineral Wool (3296)	71	72	0.337	0.032	0.291 (1963)	0.413 (1977)
Primary Aluminum (3334)	79	69	0.315	0.047	0.208 (1981)	0.390 (1968)
Turbines (3511)	90	80	0.276	0.041	0.206 (1969)	0.340 (1960)
Internal Combustion Engines (3519)	50	74	0.251	0.021	0.197 (1960)	0.276 (1971)
Elevators (3534)	55	52	0.323	0.069	0.186 (1980)	0.421 (1969)
Ball Bearings (3562)	53	70	0.274	0.014	0.239 (1969)	0.295 (1981)
Scales, Balances (3576)	50	63	0.335	0.055	0.267 (1962)	0.436 (1980)
Transformers (3612)	59	69	0.271	0.022	0.231 (1972)	0.313 (1959)
Switchgear (3613)	51	62	0.321	0.031	0.261 (1961)	0.384 (1981)
Motors & Generators (3621)	47	55	0.270	0.026	0.230 (1961)	0.316 (1977)
Carbon and Graphite Product (3624)	80	79	0.350	0.019	0.314 (1972)	0.398 (1975)
Sewing Machines (3636)	84	80	0.306	0.082	0.128 (1958)	0.433 (1972)
Electric Lamps (3641)	90	87	0.450	0.016	0.416 (1958)	0.474 (1975)
Telephone Apparatus (3661)	89	88	0.266	0.030	0.178 (1968)	0.308 (1978)
Storage Batteries (3691)	57	58	0.260	0.040	0.194 (1960)	0.350 (1966)
Primary Batteries (3692)	92	91	0.373	0.043	0.288 (1981)	0.446 (1972)
X-Ray Apparatus (3693)	54	52	0.324	0.044	0.251 (1961)	0.415 (1972)
Engine Electrical Equipment (3694)	65	76	0.284	0.016	0.244 (1980)	0.315 (1976)
Environmental Controls (3822)	57	57	0.333	0.028	0.287 (1979)	0.377 (1961)
Photographic Equipment (3861)	74	86	0.458	0.053	0.350 (1958)	0.537 (1971)

TABLE II—*continued*
PRICE-COST MARGINS FOR CONCENTRATED PRODUCER-GOODS INDUSTRIES

Industry (SIC)	*C4*	*Adjusted C4*	*Average PCM*	*Standard Deviation PCM*	*Minimum PCM (Year)*	*Maximum PCM (Year)*
Low-PCM Industries:						
Tobacco, Drying (2141)	67	66	0.051	0.014	0.031 (1963)	0.078 (1978)
Man-Made Fiber, Finishing Plants (2262)	56	56	0.195	0.021	0.161 (1974)	0.232 (1968)
Thread Mills (2284)	62	58	0.192	0.027	0.155 (1978)	0.255 (1974)
Tire Cord and Fabric (2296)	84	81	0.111	0.022	0.073 (1959)	0.153 (1974)
Sanitary Food Containers (2654)	46	56	0.250	0.019	0.203 (1980)	0.276 (1968)
Fiber Cans (2655)	54	52	0.213	0.013	0.190 (1960)	0.238 (1974)
Cellulosic Fiber (2823)	96	70	0.250	0.090	0.109 (1978)	0.361 (1966)
Ready-Mix Concrete (3273)	6	51	0.233	0.013	0.207 (1961)	0.258 (1969)
Electrometallurgical Product (3313)	74	88	0.216	0.050	0.105 (1958)	0.326 (1974)
Malleable-Iron Foundries (3322)	52	51	0.212	0.306	0.126 (1958)	0.265 (1976)
Primary Copper (3331)	72	60	0.138	0.044	0.047 (1975)	0.281 (1969)
Primary Zinc (3333)	66	57	0.160	0.047	0.074 (1971)	0.276 (1964)
Copper Rolling and Drawing (3351)	39	51	0.143	0.024	0.108 (1975)	0.202 (1966)
Metal Coating (3479)	15	72	0.248	0.032	0.192 (1972)	0.306 (1981)
Construction Machinery (3531)	43	63	0.244	0.033	0.133 (1960)	0.280 (1978)
Blast Furnaces and Steel Mills (3312)	45	51	0.202	0.026	0.151 (1981)	0.238 (1965)
Aircraft (3721)	66	82	0.218	0.059	0.130 (1959)	0.328 (1976)
Aircraft Engines (3722)	60	60	0.226	0.042	0.157 (1960)	0.303 (1979)

Note: The adjusted concentration ratio is that reported in Weiss and Pascoe [1981].

markets. These industries approximate the structural characteristics cited by Green and Porter and Rotemberg and Saloner.

For each industry, Table II reports the following information: (i) the Census four-firm concentration ratio and the Weiss–Pascoe adjusted concentration ratio in 1972, (ii) the average value and the standard deviation of the Census price-cost margin over the period from 1958 to 1981, and (iii) the minimum and maximum values of the price-cost margin. In addition, Table II is divided into "high *PCM*" industries—those with average *PCM*s greater than the mean for producer-goods industries, and corresponding "low *PCM*" industries. We will make use of this division of industries by level of *PCM* later in the paper. One would expect that the high-*PCM* industries are the ones most likely to be collusive—and thus to behave as per trigger-strategy models.

Unfortunately, we are unable to include Herfindahl values for the industries in Table II. Nelson [1963] reports Herfindahl indices for many of the Table II industries, but they are out of date. As a point of reference, Nelson's numbers indicate that industries with four-firm concentration ratios between 0.80 and 0.90 (highly concentrated) have Herfindahl indices that cluster between 0.25 and 0.30.

The average *PCM* for the fifty-seven industries in Table II is 0.290, compared to an average *PCM* of 0.240 for all unconcentrated producer-goods industries and to an average *PCM* of 0.250 for all producer-goods industries.[12] While these differences are not great, the differential between the average *PCM* of concentrated and unconcentrated industries is significant at the 0.005 level, based upon a simple t test for sample means. If we divide Table II into high-*PCM* and low-*PCM* industries, thirty-nine fall into the former category, with an average *PCM* of 0.333. Within this high-*PCM* group, only five have averages over 0.400 (flavoring extracts, industrial gases, hydraulic cement, electric lamps, and photographic equipment). The largest average *PCM* is 0.506. Even an examination of each industry's maximum *PCM* over the 1958–81 time period does not reveal many particularly large margins; in only five instances does a maximum *PCM* exceed 0.500, the largest recorded margin being 0.605.

There are several explanations for the patterns in Table II. One possibility is that oligopolists are rarely able to engage in quasi-cooperative arrangements such as trigger strategies. A second explanation is that credible punishments are not large enough to permit margins much above a one-shot equilibrium level; that is, trigger strategies may not generally permit outcomes near the profit frontier.[13] Oligopolists may also face much more elastic industry demand curves than generally believed. A final explanation is, of course, that the threat of entry, perhaps from import competition or from the backward integration of major buyers of producer goods, may keep margins at levels close to Cournot–Nash levels for even very concentrated industries.

IV. RESPONSES OF MARGINS AND PRICES TO DEMAND CHANGES

We turn now to tests of the cyclical predictions of the trigger-strategy models described in section II. The Green–Porter model predicts that oligopoly prices and margins will be procyclical while the Rotemberg–Saloner model predicts that price-cost margins will be countercyclical. We therefore present evidence on the cyclical behavior of both price and the price-cost margin for several categories of industries, including highly concentrated producer-goods industries having comparatively high margins.

[12] This result is consistent with the findings of several cross-sectional studies of small differences in measures of profitability between concentrated and unconcentrated industries. For recent examples, see Salinger [1984] and Alberts [1984].

[13] A necessary condition in the Rotemberg–Saloner model is that the magnitude of the punishment be a binding constraint on margins and prices. Oligopolists then have to lower prices to keep cheating incentives in line with punishments when industry demand increases.

While we present evidence on the cyclical behavior of price-cost margins, we place much greater emphasis on the corresponding cyclical behavior of prices. The reasons for this are as follows. With respect to the Green–Porter model, the cyclical behavior of the price-cost margin is probably a poor indicator of the cyclical behavior of price if in fact output and average variable cost are not constant. With respect to the Rotemberg–Saloner model, there are a number of reasons why the cyclical behavior of $(P-AVC)/P$ may be a misleading indicator of the cyclical behavior of $(P-MC)/P$. During industry downturns, marginal cost may fall below AVC because of labor hoarding. Rotemberg and Saloner (p. 400) point out that measurements of labor costs may include a fixed cost component. Finally, concentrated industries tend to be more unionized, and most of the evidence indicates that the union–non-union wage differential is countercyclical.[14]

Cyclical movements in price-cost margins

In previous studies (see Domowitz, Hubbard and Petersen [1986a], [1986b]), we found that *PCM*s were more "procyclical" in concentrated industries and in producer-goods industries than in consumer-goods industries. In this paper, we extend our previous work by examining the cyclical behavior of margins across several categories of industries as outlined in section III. These categories are: (i) all industries, (ii) industries for which $C4 < 50$, (iii) consumer-goods industries for which $C4 > 50$, (iv) producer-goods industries for which $C4 > 50$, (v) above-average *PCM* producer-goods industries for which $C4 > 50$, and (vi) below-average *PCM* producer-goods industries for which $C4 > 50$. This partitioning of our sample by concentration is sensible given the models we are interested in testing.[15]

For each category of industries, we model the *PCM* as a function of industry measures of concentration, capital-output ratio, advertising-sales ratio, and capacity utilization in manufacturing[16] (as a measure of aggregate demand). That is,

$$PCM_{it} = \beta_0 + \beta_1 C4_{it} + \beta_2 (K/Q)_{it} + \beta_3 (A/S)_{it} + \beta_4 CU_t + \varepsilon_{it} \quad (5)$$

where i and t denote the industry and time period, respectively. OLS and fixed-effects[17] estimation results for equation (5) appear in Table III.

The effects of industry variables on the price-cost margin are consistent

[14] For an overview of the evidence, see chapter three of Freeman and Medoff [1984].

[15] Rotemberg and Saloner note that their theory says nothing about the volatility of price as concentration increases, only that once an industry becomes an oligopoly it becomes more likely that it will cut prices in a boom.

[16] Data on capacity utilization in manufacturing are taken from the *Economic Report of the President* [1986].

[17] An important potential qualification of the OLS results is that the coefficient estimates may be biased by the omission of individual industry effects. With panel data, we can account for unobservable persistent industry differences; here we interpret "persistent" as time-invariant and re-estimate the model using the standard fixed-effects within-group estimator.

TABLE III
CYCLICAL SENSITIVITY OF *PCM*s BY CATEGORY OF INDUSTRY
(DEPENDENT VARIABLE: *PCM*)

	Industries					
	All	$C4 \leqslant 50$	$C4 > 50(C)$	$C4 > 50(P)$	$C4 > 50(PH)$	$C4 > 50(PL)$
OLS Results						
Constant	0.107	0.131	0.173	−0.040	0.087	−0.032
	(0.017)	(0.019)	(0.061)	(0.048)	(0.051)	(0.058)
C4	0.110	0.092	0.143	0.185	0.127	−0.006
	(0.0005)	(0.008)	(0.029)	(0.020)	(0.023)	(0.023)
A/S	1.064	1.106	1.125	0.433	0.224	1.755
	(0.031)	(0.052)	(0.053)	(0.088)	(0.077)	(0.380)
K/Q	0.030	0.027	−0.041	0.055	0.024	0.065
	(0.002)	(0.003)	(0.013)	(0.005)	(0.005)	(0.010)
CU	0.096	0.077	0.039	0.197	0.165	0.227
	(0.021)	(0.022)	(0.070)	(0.056)	(0.059)	(0.067)
$\bar{R}^2$	0.275	0.169	0.467	0.183	0.086	0.147
Fixed-Effects Results						
C4	0.123	0.136	0.133	0.122	0.199	0.007
	(0.010)	(0.012)	(0.030)	(0.029)	(0.041)	(0.032)
A/S	0.003	−0.327	0.077	0.225	0.208	1.010
	(0.054)	(0.084)	(0.089)	(0.121)	(0.133)	(0.840)
K/Q	−0.017	−0.007	−0.003	−0.044	−0.051	−0.008
	(0.003)	(0.004)	(0.010)	(0.007)	(0.008)	(0.012)
CU	0.078	0.066	0.118	0.116	0.103	0.161
	(0.010)	(0.012)	(0.034)	(0.028)	(0.039)	(0.038)
$\bar{R}^2$	0.037	0.041	0.059	0.065	0.080	0.047

Note: *C*, *P*, *PH*, and *PL* denote consumer-goods industries, producer-goods industries, high-*PCM* producer-goods industries, and low-*PCM* producer-goods industries, respectively. *C4* refers to the Weiss–Pascoe adjusted measure (see footnote 7). Standard errors are in parentheses.

with our previous results (see the interpretation there in light of standard structure-conduct-performance models). With respect to the impact of changes in capacity utilization on margins, our principal findings are two. First, margins are procyclical in all categories, though demand effects in unconcentrated industries are negligible, with more pronounced cyclical impacts in concentrated and producer-goods industries. Second, price-cost margins in concentrated, high-*PCM* industries ("trigger-strategy" industries) are less procyclical than margins in concentrated, low-*PCM* industries. It will be easier to interpret this result after the evidence on the cyclical behavior of price and cost is presented.

Price wars and the cyclical responses of industry prices

For reasons discussed in section II, we are interested in both the cyclical behavior of industry prices and in any evidence for the existence of price wars, either during recessions or otherwise. We begin with the latter issue.

It is straightforward to compute expressions for both the percentage change in the Lerner index and in the industry price following a reversion from monopoly to Cournot behavior. Using equations (3) and (4) and

TABLE IV
PRICE CHANGES IN HIGH-*PCM* INDUSTRIES

Industry (SIC)	*Maximum Price Decrease (Year)*	%ΔP			
		1961	*1970*	*1975*	*1980*
Flour (2045)	−10.4 (1976)	0.9	0.4	7.6	−5.5
Corn Wet Milling (2046)	−22.2 (1976)	3.5	4.0	2.9	2.4
Flavoring Extracts (2087)	−19.4 (1976)	0.1	−2.0	3.9	2.3
Manufactured Ice (2097)	−9.7 (1980)	0.2	1.0	0.8	−9.7
Pressed and Molded Pulp Goods (2646)	−3.9 (1974)	−2.6	0.2	−3.0	−2.2
Alkalines & Chlorine (2812)	−10.0 (1979)	−0.6	−3.0	35.1	1.2
Industrial Gases (2813)	−11.6 (1977)	0.0	4.6	11.3	0.1
Inorganic Pigments (2816)	−4.8 (1980)	−0.6	−3.3	3.0	−4.8
Synthetic Rubber (2822)	−6.4 (1974)	0.2	−3.2	0.1	4.6
Organic Fibers (2824)	−14.2 (1974)	−1.4	−3.9	−13.3	−3.1
Explosives (2892)	−3.9 (1959)	3.3	−1.7	6.0	−3.7
Carbon Black (2895)	−7.5 (1978)	−3.0	−2.5	27.6	8.0
Tires and Tubes (3011)	−4.8 (1962)	−0.4	2.6	0.6	−1.0
Reclaimed Rubber (3031)	−6.8 (1980)	0.5	−3.5	−1.7	−6.8
Flat Glass (3211)	−15.3 (1974)	−2.5	1.9	−5.5	−7.7
Products of Purchased Glass (3231)	−16.2 (1959)	−1.1	−0.7	−1.0	−6.2
Cement, Hydraulic (3241)	−9.1 (1959)	0.4	5.5	7.2	−5.9
Brick and Structural Tile (3251)	−10.7 (1959)	1.1	0.6	−0.1	−7.8
Ceramic Tile (3253)	−13.6 (1974)	0.6	−3.4	−2.4	−10.2
Gypsum Products (3275)	−12.7 (1980)	2.6	−6.9	−6.1	−12.7
Mineral Wool (3296)	−9.4 (1979)	−5.4	2.9	13.0	−3.8
Primary Aluminum (3334)	−19.1 (1972)	−4.3	1.8	−5.0	5.5
Turbines (3511)	−9.5 (1974)	−9.1	5.6	15.0	3.5
Elevators (3534)	−6.5 (1974)	1.2	5.6	7.8	−4.6
Ball Bearings (3562)	−7.6 (1965)	−1.5	1.7	4.0	0.5
Scales, Balances (3576)	−9.6 (1974)	0.8	−0.2	0.0	−5.7
Transformers (3612)	−8.3 (1969)	−4.4	2.0	5.7	−6.4
Switchgear (3613)	−5.4 (1972)	0.8	2.0	5.9	−1.9
Motors and Generators (3621)	−6.1 (1974)	−2.7	3.3	4.1	−3.8
Carbon and Graphite Product (3624)	−5.0 (1976)	−0.4	0.5	17.6	−0.9
Sewing Machines (3636)	−9.4 (1974)	1.4	1.3	4.9	−8.6
Electric Lamps (3641)	−8.8 (1974)	0.3	0.4	10.7	−5.0
Telephone Apparatus (3661)	−11.2 (1974)	−1.7	1.1	11.8	−6.0
Storage Batteries (3691)	−10.6 (1980)	0.9	3.2	3.1	−10.6
Primary Batteries (3692)	−15.4 (1974)	−0.8	−1.7	5.8	−10.6
X-Ray Apparatus (3693)	−20.0 (1959)	−0.6	3.0	4.5	−1.5
Engine Electrical Equipment (3694)	−11.9 (1959)	−0.2	1.6	7.0	−4.4
Environmental Controls (3822)	−18.1 (1959)	2.0	12.4	0.8	−7.4
Photographic Equipment (3861)	−12.8 (1974)	1.1	−1.5	−1.1	4.9

Note: Price increases and decreases are relative to those for all industries on average.

assuming constant marginal cost, the predicted percentage change in the PCM is $(1-H)*100$ and the predicted change in industry price is $[(1-H)/(\varepsilon-H)]*100$. These expressions imply quite dramatic changes following a reversion. For example, if $H = 0.30$ and $\varepsilon = 2$, the predicted percentage change in price is approximately forty percent.

To analyze the prediction of the Green–Porter model of large, discrete price decreases in periods of low demand, we report in Table IV price changes[18] for thirty-nine "high-*PCM*" industries for 1961, 1970, 1975, and 1980, the four points in time when capacity utilization in manufacturing fell below eighty percent. The sharpest declines occurred in 1970 and 1975, when capacity utilization fell by ten percent and thirteen percent respectively. These price changes are all expressed relative to the rate of change for all manufacturing industries on average in 1961, 1970, 1975, and 1980. While many industries do indeed exhibit declines (fifteen in 1970 and ten in 1975), these relative price decreases are quite small—certainly less than what would normally be expected from an industry reverting from a collusive to either a Cournot or a Bertrand outcome in the middle of a recession.

Of course, we cannot be sure how an economy-wide recession affects demand in any given industry; that is, output movements in individual industries could "lead" or "lag" the business cycle. Large declines in demand also occur for some industries in non-recession years. Such demand shocks may be more difficult to observe and therefore more likely to trigger the sort of reversion predicted by the Green–Porter model. We therefore report in Table IV maximum price declines (and the years they occurred) for the thirty-nine "high-*PCM*" industries. Incidences of large price declines appear to be quite rare. In only two instances (corn wet milling and X-ray apparatus) were there relative price declines exceeding twenty percent.

The evidence in Table IV does not lend much support for oligopoly price wars, at least not at the Census four-digit level of disaggregation. We should point out, however, some qualifications. Our data are annual, so that price wars of short duration would not show up in Table IV. Punishments resulting from such short reversions, however, would be very small and probably would not deter cheating. Another consideration is that if margins are not greatly elevated by trigger strategies for any of the reasons mentioned in the previous section, then a price war (or a reversion to a one-shot equilibrium) may result in only a modest decline in price.

We turn now to an assessment of the cyclical behavior of prices. In the Green–Porter model, prices increase continuously with increases in industry demand, although prices could fall discontinuously during downturns in demand if a reversion occurs. In the Rotemberg–Saloner model, prices fall continuously when demand increases beyond a certain point.

[18] Industry output price deflators are obtained from the four-digit-SIC-level data base constructed by the Penn-SRI-Census project and updated and extended at the National Bureau of Economic Research.

To pursue differences across categories of industries in response of price changes to cyclical fluctuations, we begin with a simple markup model of pricing. The target industry price P^* is determined as a markup over unit cost C:

$$P_{it}^* = (1+\lambda_{it})C_{it} \tag{6}$$

Variation in P^* arises both from changes in unit cost and from the cyclical nature of the markup, λ. This simple formulation does not violate any of the main features of either the Green–Porter or the Rotemberg–Saloner model. The average markup, $\bar{\lambda}_i$, presumably depends on such industry specific features as the magnitude of credible punishments.

Letting lower case variables denote logs, we can re-express equation (6) as:

$$p_{it}^* \simeq \lambda_{it} + c_{it} \tag{7}$$

Taking first differences of equation (7), we obtain:

$$\Delta p_{it}^* \simeq \Delta\lambda_{it} + \Delta c_{it} \tag{8}$$

We assume that the markup λ can be expressed as:

$$\lambda_{it} = \gamma_i + \gamma_1 t + \gamma_2 CU_t \tag{9}$$

where γ_i is the time-invariant industry component, γ_1 allows for the possibility of a secular time trend and γ_2 is the cyclical component. Differencing equation (9) and substituting into equation (8) we obtain:[19]

$$\Delta p_{it}^* = \gamma_1 + \gamma_2 \Delta CU_t + \gamma_3 \Delta c_{it} + \varepsilon_{it} \tag{10}$$

We note that differencing cost removes any fixed-cost component that may inadvertently be entering into the computation of variable cost.[20] The coefficient on cost in equation (10) is unrestricted in the empirical work reported below, rather than set to unity, as in equation (8). Although this may entail a loss of efficiency in estimation if the restriction indeed holds, our measure of cost is not perfect, and a unit coefficient may not be appropriate.

We can extend this cyclical markup model to capture the idea that differences in price adjustment across industries may also reflect sticky prices due to costs of adjustment (Rotemberg [1982]) or nominal contracts

[19] Since the equation is in first differences, fixed unobservable industry effects in setting prices have been removed. A natural way to interpret equation (10) statistically, as well as equation (11) which follows, is to view the original equation as one in the log levels of the variables, which also includes a time-invariant industry component and a secular time trend. Equations (10) and (11) are then the estimating equations for the fixed-effects differencing estimator.

[20] The percentage change in unit labor costs is defined as the excess of the percentage growth in wage rates over the percentage growth in output per worker-hour. Industry specific data on the materials prices are not available. Assuming a constant ratio of materials to output, the percentage change in unit materials costs can be expressed as the percentage change in the total cost of materials less the percentage change in industry output.

TABLE V
CYCLICAL SENSITIVITY OF PRICES BY CATEGORY OF INDUSTRY
(DEPENDENT VARIABLE: $\%\Delta p_{it}$)

	Constant	$\%\Delta p_{it-1}$	$\%\Delta c_{it}$	ΔCU_t	$\bar{R}^2$
All Industries	0.010	—	0.817	−0.034	0.820
	(0.0007)		(0.012)	(0.011)	
	0.005	0.227	0.718	0.016	0.812
	(0.001)	(0.007)	(0.013)	(0.012)	
C4 < 50	0.009	—	0.864	−0.021	0.839
	(0.0008)		(0.014)	(0.013)	
	0.004	0.184	0.781	0.028	0.831
	(0.001)	(0.009)	(0.016)	(0.014)	
C4 > 50(C)	0.009	—	0.810	−0.047	0.788
	(0.003)		(0.053)	(0.040)	
	0.005	0.455	0.503	−0.074	0.777
	(0.003)	(0.033)	(0.060)	(0.042)	
C4 > 50(P)	0.011	—	0.718	−0.053	0.782
	(0.002)		(0.033)	(0.031)	
	0.006	0.284	0.584	−0.032	0.776
	(0.002)	(0.019)	(0.035)	(0.032)	
C4 > 50(PH)	0.012	—	0.685	−0.106	0.764
	(0.002)		(0.040)	(0.040)	
	0.005	0.347	0.518	−0.127	0.768
	(0.002)	(0.023)	(0.042)	(0.040)	
C4 > 50(PL)	0.011	—	0.768	0.039	0.828
	(0.003)		(0.056)	(0.048)	
	0.008	0.174	0.672	0.098	0.814
	(0.004)	(0.032)	(0.062)	(0.052)	

Note: C, P, PH, and *PL* denote consumer-goods industries, producer-goods industries, high-*PCM* producer-goods industries, and low-*PCM* producer-goods industries, respectively. Standard errors are in parentheses.

(Hubbard and Weiner [1985]). If Δp_{it}^* is the target industry price adjustment, and $\Delta p_{it} = (1-\gamma_4)\Delta p_{it}^* + \gamma_4 \Delta p_{it-1}$, then equation (10) can be rewritten as:[21]

$$(11) \qquad \Delta p_{it} = \alpha_1 + \alpha_2 \Delta CU + \alpha_3 \Delta c_{it} + \alpha_4 \Delta p_{it-1} + \varepsilon_{it}$$

Results from estimating (10) and (11) using instrumental variables[22] appear in Table V.

With respect to all concentrated producer-goods industries (high-*PCM* as

[21] Given the interpretation of (11) as a fixed-effects estimating equation, we note the problems associated with the use of a lagged dependent variable, as exposited, for example, in Nickell [1986]. The bias in coefficient estimates is sharply reduced as the number of time-periods grows, and may be considered negligible for the case here, given the length of our sample in the time-dimension.

[22] The endogenous variable is cost, of course. The instrument list included the (current-period) percentage change in the aggregate industrial production index, as well as percentage changes in cost and output prices lagged two periods. The first lag of the last two variables was not used, due to the nature of the error term under the fixed-effects interpretation given in footnote 13. Ordinary least squares estimation of (6) and (7) yielded results which were quite similar to those reported here. The main effect of using an instrumental-variables scheme was to enlarge the standard errors of the estimated coefficient on the percentage change in cost.

well as low-*PCM* industries) price movements are countercyclical. That is, the coefficient on ΔCU is negative, although only marginally statistically significant. If we partition the sample into high- and low-*PCM* industries, however, differences appear. It is the high-*PCM* ("trigger-strategy") subsample for which countercyclical price movements are statistically significant and economically important. Concentrated producer-goods industries with low average *PCM*s have procyclical price movements although the coefficient on ΔCU is measured with a large standard error. This pattern is robust to whether or not a lagged dependent variable is included. The coefficients on ΔCU in the specifications including the lagged rate of change of prices imply that a 10-percentage-point increase in the aggregate rate of capacity utilization lowers the rate of change of prices in the high-*PCM*, concentrated, producer-goods industries by approximately 1.3 percentage points, and raises the rate of change of prices in the low-*PCM* counterparts by 1 percentage point.

We considered two tests of the robustness of the results presented in Table V. The first was to add an industry-specific measure of demand variation to equations (10) and (11). Demand variation coming from ΔCU is quite in keeping with the flavor of the Rotemberg–Saloner model and is consistent with a strict interpretation of the imperfectly observed demand assumption in the Green–Porter model. While it is difficult to construct good proxies for industry specific demand variation, we entered such a measure in equations (10) and (11). The coefficient on this variable was estimated with large standard errors across categories, while the qualitative conclusions reported above went unchanged.[23]

As a supplementary test, we examined the cyclical behavior of cost itself. We have found that concentrated producer-goods industries have more procyclical price-cost margins and that concentrated high *PCM* industries have countercyclical prices. These results lead one to expect that costs must be more countercyclical for concentrated, producer-goods industries, and in

[23] We constructed the percentage rate of change in industry output (Q/Q) as a proxy for industry demand fluctuations. Industry output Q was constructed as the quotient of the sum of current-dollar value added and cost of materials and the industry-specific output deflator. The percentage rate of change of output was orthogonalized with respect to changes in the aggregate rate of capacity utilization. An instrumental variables procedure was employed to eliminate the potential simultaneous equations bias inherent in regressing the change in prices on change in output.

The results from adding $\dot{Q}/Q$ to the model in equation (11) are given below. The result for all unconcentrated industries ($C4 < C50$), concentrated low-*PCM* industries, and concentrated, high-*PCM* industries, respectively, are:

$$\Delta p_{it} = \underset{(0.001)}{0.007} + \underset{(0.016)}{0.021}\Delta CU_t + \underset{(0.016)}{0.807}\Delta c_{it} + \underset{(0.009)}{0.143}\Delta p_{it-1} - \underset{(0.012)}{0.068}(\dot{Q}/Q)_{it}; \qquad \bar{R}^2 = 0.84$$

$$\Delta p_{it} = \underset{(0.002)}{0.003} + \underset{(0.065)}{0.118}\Delta CU_t + \underset{(0.071)}{0.786}\Delta c_{it} + \underset{(0.033)}{0.112}\Delta p_{it-1} + \underset{(0.060)}{0.051}(\dot{Q}/Q)_{it}; \qquad \bar{R}^2 = 0.80$$

$$\Delta p_{it} = \underset{(0.003)}{0.005} - \underset{(0.043)}{0.129}\Delta CU_t + \underset{(0.040)}{0.551}\Delta c_{it} + \underset{(0.022)}{0.313}\Delta p_{it-1} + \underset{(0.030)}{0.027}(\dot{Q}/Q)_{it}; \qquad \bar{R}^2 = 0.77$$

particular for the high-*PCM* category. While a formal study of cost behavior is well beyond the scope of this paper, preliminary results indicate that average variable cost is considerably more countercyclical for our concentrated, high-*PCM* category of industries.[24]

The results in Tables II–V shed some light on the two trigger-strategy models described in the paper. The absence of large discrete price declines during the period covered by our data combined with the countercyclical price findings casts some doubt on the empirical validity of the Green–Porter model. Our price findings are qualitatively consistent with the predictions of the Rotemberg–Saloner model, as long as marginal cost is not countercyclical. However, the movements in prices estimated here cannot be described as large.

Interestingly, prices are "stickier" for the trigger-pricing subsample as well (in the sense of a significantly higher coefficient on the lagged rate of change in prices), indicating the need for additional research on sources of possible differences in dynamic price adjustment. That source of price rigidity may well be quantitatively more important than the differences in contemporaneous adjustment to cyclical movements.

V. CONCLUSIONS AND IMPLICATIONS

There has been a significant interest on a theoretical level in the application of supergames to oligopoly behavior. Implications for pricing behavior in trigger-strategy models in response to demand changes are of particular importance for public policy considerations. We contrast the predictions of two such models put forth by Green and Porter [1984] and Rotemberg and Saloner [1986], and test the predictions using a panel data set of US manufacturing industries.

Our principal findings are four. First, the levels of price-cost margins of concentrated, producer-goods industries, while higher than those of unconcentrated counterparts, appear to be closer to those predicted by a single-period Cournot–Nash equilibrium than monopoly. Second, there is little evidence to support the idea that price-cost margins of these industries have different cyclical patterns from other industries apart from effects by level of industry concentration. Maximum price declines for concentrated industries

[24] We estimated Δc as a linear function of the lagged percentage change in cost and ΔCU. The results for all unconcentrated industries ($C4 < 50$), concentrated, low-*PCM* industries, and concentrated, high-*PCM* industries, respectively, are:

$$\underset{}{\Delta c_{it}} = \underset{(0.001)}{0.036} + \underset{(0.015)}{0.169}\Delta c_{it-1} - \underset{(0.030)}{0.217}\Delta CU_t; \qquad \bar{R}^2 = 0.07$$

$$\Delta c_{it} = \underset{(0.005)}{0.044} + \underset{(0.051)}{0.086}\Delta c_{it-1} - \underset{(0.111)}{0.404}\Delta CU_t; \qquad \bar{R}^2 = 0.06$$

$$\Delta c_{it} = \underset{(0.003)}{0.038} + \underset{(0.030)}{0.129}\Delta c_{it-1} - \underset{(0.065)}{0.644}\Delta CU_t; \qquad \bar{R}^2 = 0.14$$

give little support for the occurrence of price wars during either recessions or booms. Finally, consistent with the predictions of the Rotemberg–Saloner model, the industries with high price-cost margins have more countercyclical price movements than those exhibited by other industries. That gradual price adjustment is quantitatively important for those industries, suggests, however, that other factors may lie behind the apparent rigidity of prices.

These conclusions suggest two promising extensions for future research. First, the results for inter-industry differences in responses of *PCM*s and prices to changes in aggregate demand suggest that countercyclical cost movements are likely to be important in producer-goods industries (say sticky real wages traceable to union bargaining agreements). Second, decomposing manufacturing industries into subgroups based on industry concentration or type of good produced, it is possible to test whether predictions of models of price adjustment based on costs of adjustment, contracting, or strategic considerations are consistent with the data. These extensions overlap substantially with recent theoretical concerns of both industrial economists and macroeconomists.

IAN DOMOWITZ,
Department of Economics,
Northwestern University,
Evanston,
Illinois 60201,
USA.

R. GLENN HUBBARD,
Department of Economics and Center for Urban Affairs and Policy,
Northwestern University; and *The National Bureau of Economic Research.*

BRUCE C. PETERSEN,
Department of Economics,
Northwestern University; and *The Federal Reserve Bank of Chicago.*

REFERENCES

ALBERTS, W. W., 1984, 'Do Oligopolists Earn "Noncompetitive" Rates of Return?', *The American Economic Review*, 74, 4, pp. 624–632.

DOMOWITZ, I., HUBBARD, R. G. and PETERSEN, B. C., 1986a, 'Business Cycles and the Relationship Between Concentration and Price-Cost Margins', *Rand Journal of Economics*, 17, pp. 1–17.

DOMOWITZ, I., HUBBARD, R. G. and PETERSEN, B. C., 1986b, 'The Intertemporal Stability of the Concentration-Margins Relationship', *Journal of Industrial Economics*, 35, 1, pp. 13–34.

FREEMAN, R. B. and MEDOFF, J. L., 1984, *What Do Unions Do?* (Basic Books, Inc., Publishers, New York).

FRIEDMAN, J. W., 1985, 'Cooperative Equilibria in Finite Horizon Noncooperative Supergames', *Journal of Economic Theory*, 35, pp. 390–398.

FRIEDMAN, J. W., 1986, *Game Theory with Applications to Economics* (Oxford University Press, New York).

GREEN, E. J. and PORTER, R. H., 1984, 'Noncooperative Collusion Under Imperfect Price Information', *Econometrica*, 52, pp. 87–100.

HUBBARD, R. G. and WEINER, R. J., 1985, 'Nominal Contracting and Price Flexibility in Product Markets', Working Paper No. 1738, National Bureau of Economic Research.

LUCE, D. and RAIFFA, H., 1957, *Games and Decisions* (Wiley and Sons, New York).

ORNSTEIN, S. I., 1975, 'Empirical Uses of the Price-Cost Margin', *Journal of Industrial Economics*, 24, pp. 105–117.

NELSON, R. L., 1963, *Concentration in the Manufacturing Industries of the United States* (Yale University Press, New Haven).

NICKELL, S., 1986, 'Biases in Dynamic Models with Fixed Effects', *Econometrica*, 45, pp. 1417–1426.

PORTER, R. H., 1985, 'Incidence and Duration of Price Wars', *Journal of Industrial Economics*, 33, 4, pp. 415–426.

RADNER, R., 1980, 'Collusive Behavior in Noncooperative Epsilon-Equilibria of Oligopolies with Long but Finite Lives', *Journal of Economic Theory*, 22, pp. 136–154.

ROTEMBERG, J. J., 1982, 'Sticky Prices in the United States', *Journal of Political Economy*, 90, pp. 1187–1212.

ROTEMBERG, J. J. and SALONER, G., 1986, 'A Supergame-Theoretic Model of Price Wars During Booms', *American Economic Review*, 76, pp. 390–407.

SALINGER, M., 1984, 'Tobin's *q*, Unionization, and the Concentration-Profits Relationship', *Rand Journal of Economics*, 15, pp. 159–170.

SELTEN, R., 1975, 'Reexamination of the Perfectness Concept for Equilibrium Points in Extensive Games', *International Journal of Game Theory*, 4, pp. 25–55.

WATERSON, M., 1984, *Economic Theory of the Industry* (Cambridge University Press, Cambridge).

WEISS, L. W. and PASCOE, G., 1981, 'Adjusted Concentration Ratios in Manufacturing', mimeograph.

COLLUSION VERSUS DIFFERENTIAL EFFICIENCY: TESTING ALTERNATIVE HYPOTHESES*

RICHARD SCHMALENSEE

The predictions of collusion- and efficiency-based static equilibrium explanations of inter-industry profitability differences are formally developed and tested, using appropriate econometric techniques, with intra-industry data on 70 US Internal Revenue Service minor manufacturing industries in 1963 and 1972. None of the explanations has much explanatory power. The 1963 data are consistent with collusion-based models, while the 1972 data are inconsistent with all non-null hypotheses considered. Patterns of profitability are sharply different (in complex ways apparently unrelated to cyclical forces or the Phase II price controls) in these two years. Implications of these results are discussed.

I. INTRODUCTION

SINCE THE pioneering work of Joe Bain [1951], a positive correlation between industry concentration and accounting measures of industry-average profitability has generally been accepted as a stylized fact. Until recently, this fact was almost universally rationalized by the *Differential Collusion Hypothesis* (DCH):

> Industries differ in the effectiveness with which sellers are able to limit competition by tacit or explicit collusion. Collusion is more likely to be effective, and profitability is more likely to be above competitive levels, the higher is seller concentration.

A decade ago, Harold Demsetz [1973], [1974] proposed an alternative explanation of the positive correlation between concentration and profitability, the *Differential Efficiency Hypothesis* (DEH):[1]

* I am indebted to the National Science Foundation for financial support, to Alan J. Daskin and the PICA project at the Harvard Graduate School of Business Administration (especially Michael Spence and Marilyn Shesko) for providing most of the data used in this study, and to Steven Postrel and, especially, Ian Ayres for excellent research assistance. I am grateful to Ian Ayres, William Long, Tom Stoker, Tim Bresnahan, Larry White, anonymous referees, and audiences at Johns Hopkins, the Federal Trade Commission, Southampton, Nuffield, *SIOP* (Belgium), and the 1985 Econometric Society World Congress for helpful comments on earlier versions of this essay. Only I can be held responsible for sins of omission or commission embodied in this paper, however.

[1] There is important common ground between the DCH and the DEH. Under the DEH, one should attempt to understand the obstacles to diffusion of knowledge that must be present if intra-industry efficiency differences are to persist. Under the DCH, obstacles of this sort are a subset of what Caves and Porter [1977] have termed "barriers to mobility". See also Weiss and Pascoe [1985].

Effective collusion is rare or nonexistent. In some industries, long-lived efficiency differences are unimportant, and both concentration and accounting profitability are generally low. Where efficiency differences are important, efficient firms obtain large market shares and earn rents, and both concentration and industry-level profitability are thus high.

This essay considers the consistency of these hypotheses with observed patterns of profitability in US manufacturing. Demsetz [1973], [1974] conducted the first study of this sort, using data on Internal Revenue Service (IRS) minor industries. He was followed by a host of others, including Carter [1978], Caves and Pugel [1980], Clarke, Davies and Waterson [1984], Daskin [1983], Long [1982], Porter [1979], Round [1975], Ravenscraft [1983], Schmalensee [1985], and Weiss and Pascoe [1985]. The strategy in much of this work, which is also employed here, is to focus on the inter-industry relation between seller concentration and various parameters of industry-specific distributions of profitability and market share.[2] (Scherer [1980, ch. 9], Brozen [1982], and Daskin [1983] discuss this literature.) This study differs from most previous work in three major respects.

First, most previous empirical comparisons of the DEH and the DCH have not employed formal models of industry behavior under alternative hypotheses. Section II analyzes simple equilibrium models that clarify the intra-industry and inter-industry implications of the DEH, the DCH, and hybrid hypotheses combining key features of both. This analysis does not attempt to develop a complete structural model of the determinants of accounting profitability. The goal is rather to use simple models to identify critical testable predictions of these alternative world-views. The focus is on empirical regularities and stylized facts, not structural coefficients.

Second, most inter-industry work in industrial economics is based on a single year's data. In this study the same industries are examined in 1963 and 1972, two cyclically comparable years. This design permits both evaluation of the stability of key relationships and analysis of industry-level changes over time. Section III describes the data set employed.

[2] The interesting work of Peltzman [1977], [1979] and Lustgarten [1979], [1984] on the relation between changes in concentration and improvements in productivity (see also Scherer [1979]) was designed to test the DEH in a rather different fashion. The main finding of these studies is that large increases *or* decreases in concentration are associated with above-average increases in productivity. While this is certainly consistent with the DEH, and inconsistent with the *pure* DCH, it is not inconsistent with hybrid DEH/DCH models. (See section II for definitions.) After all, one does not generally expect to see major changes in seller concentration except in response to major alterations in competitive relationships. Major innovations, which are likely to be followed by an increase in the innovator's market share under the DEH or a DEH/DCH hybrid, are an important source of such alterations. Innovations by market leaders should thus tend to be associated with increases in both concentration and industry productivity under either the DEH or the DEH/DCH. Innovations by new entrants or small firms should tend to lower concentration while raising average productivity. Industries in which little process or product innovation occurs are likely to exhibit stable concentration along with below-average gains in measured productivity. (Note also that Peltzman [1977] finds evidence in support of the DCH assertion that increases in concentration lead to increases in price—cost margins.)

Third, the use of IRS size-class data and of estimated coefficients instead of true parameters raises a set of econometric problems that have not generally been treated explicitly in previous work in this area. These problems and their treatment are discussed in section IV.

Section V presents statistical findings and discusses their consistency with the DEH and the DCH. Section VI summarizes the main implications of this study. To preview, the results obtained here provide little comfort to those who believe in the general applicability of any of the hypotheses examined in this study.

II. IMPLICATIONS OF ALTERNATIVE HYPOTHESES

Two central features of the DEH, which should be present in any formal model designed to reveal the implications of that hypothesis, are the dependence of market shares on efficiency differences and the independence of seller behavior and market concentration. In contrast, a central feature of the DCH is the dependence of seller behavior on market concentration. I also take as a central feature of what I term the "pure" DCH the lack of a general relation between market share and differential efficiency within industries. In at least some textbook versions of the DCH, mergers, historical accidents, and random shocks are stressed as sources of share differences, rather than differential efficiency or, except for very small firms, economies of scale. (See, for instance, the discussion in Scherer [1980, ch. 4].)

II(i). *The pure DEH*

The relation between market share and differential efficiency under the DEH must refer to the long run, since an efficiency-enhancing innovation's full impact on the innovator's market share is usually not felt until capacity has been expanded or modified. To explore the inter-industry implications of the DEH, it is thus natural to focus on long-run equilibria that reflect the presence of efficiency differences. Moreover, while one cannot expect all industries in any data set to be in long-run equilibrium, it seems reasonable in the absence of a suitable model of disequilibrium to follow standard practice in industrial economics by treating deviations from long-run equilibrium as random in cross-section data.

I thus consider an industry in long-run equilibrium with N sellers. Suppose that all have attained minimum efficient scale and hence face constant long-run average costs. (Most studies of scale economies have concluded that US manufacturing firms generally need relatively small market shares to be in this position; see Scherer [1980, ch. 4] for a survey.) Let there be long-lived efficiency differences among these firms, so that $c_1 \leqslant c_2 \leqslant \ldots \leqslant c_N$, with at least one inequality strict, where c_i is firm i's unit cost.[3] Unit cost should not be interpreted in narrow process efficiency terms here. A firm with a superior product may simply be more efficient in the production of the Lancastrian characteristics it supplies to an existing market. While major product innovations that yield substantial differentiation and create something approaching a new market cannot be sensibly modeled as simply reducing costs, it seems reasonable to simplify formal analysis of profitability by treating minor product innovations as cost reductions. I thus make the convenient assumption of product homogeneity.

Adoption of the DEH as a working assumption rules out collusive behavior. But it does not necessarily require pure price-taking behavior. It is hard to see why firms with large shares of industry capacity or output should be assumed to ignore the effects of their actions on market price. (Though admittedly this may well be what Demsetz [1973] had in mind.) It seems much more plausible to begin with the basic assumption of non-cooperative behavior, under which each firm simply makes its best (most profitable) response to its rivals' actions. As we are concerned with long-run equilibria, investment in productive capacity becomes a central decision variable. This is in effect an output choice, which suggests that Cournot equilibria are the most relevant. More formally, Kreps and Scheinkman [1983] have recently shown that non-cooperative capacity decisions, followed by non-cooperative (Bertrand) price competition yield Cournot outcomes under some reasonably plausible assumptions.

Accordingly, I explore the implications of the DEH by examining Cournot equilibria with cost differences. (As the discussion of equation (6), below, indicates, the assumption of Cournot equilibria is not essential. The analysis goes through essentially unchanged as long as the extent of collusion is uncorrelated with concentration across industries.) The economic profit of a typical firm is given by

$$(1) \qquad \pi_i = [P(q_i + \bar{q}_i) - c_i]q_i$$

where P is market price, $P(Q)$ is the inverse demand function, and $\bar{q}_i \equiv Q - q_i$ is the total output of firm i's rivals. Firm i's first-order condition, with rivals' output treated as exogenous, can be written as follows:

$$(2) \qquad (P - c_i) = ePq_i/Q$$

[3] This model has been used by Clarke and Davies [1982] to analyze the determinants of equilibrium concentration in the presence of efficiency differences; see also Long [1982], Clarke, Davies, and Waterson [1984], and Kwoka and Ravenscraft [1986] for further development and empirical applications. The more complex DEH models of Jovanovic [1982], Lippman and Rumelt [1982], and Telser [1982] stress the dynamic mechanisms determining N and the c_i rather than equilibrium and do not lend themselves readily to use in empirical analysis. In the Cournot model in the text, the larger is N, the smaller the differences among the c_i that are consistent with non-negative market shares. If the market demand curve is $P = a - bQ$, for instance, non-negative shares require $c_i \leqslant [a + (N-1)\bar{c}_i]/N$ for all i, where $\bar{c}_i$ is the average of all c's except c_i.

where $e \equiv -1/[(\partial Q/\partial P)(P/Q)]$ is the reciprocal of the industry elasticity of demand. Multiplication of (2) by q_i yields firm i's *economic* profit in equilibrium. If firm i employs assets worth K_i, and if the normal, competitive rate of return on invested capital relevant to the industry is ρ, firm i's *accounting* profit is given by

$$\pi a_i = \rho K_i + e(q_i/Q)(Pq_i) \tag{3}$$

Finally, letting $s_i \equiv q_i/Q$ be firm i's market share and $v_i \equiv Pq_i/K_i$ be its revenue/capital ratio, one can divide (3) by K_i to obtain a simple equation involving the accounting rate of return on assets:

$$r_i = A + B(s_i v_i) \tag{4}$$

where, under the DEH, $A = \rho$, the competitive rate of return, and $B = e$, the reciprocal of the market elasticity of demand. One can think of A as the rate of return corresponding to a zero market share. The smallest firms actually operating in any industry will thus generally have rates of return in excess of A under the DEH. The size of this excess may even be positively related to concentration.[4] While equation (4) flows directly from the DEH, one need not accept that hypothesis to view (4) as a natural specification to employ in investigations of intra-industry profitability differences. (Note in particular that the presence of v_i gives the independent and dependent variables the same units.) It is employed as such in what follows.

Under the pure DEH, as described above, both A and B should be positive for all industries. Further, neither parameter should be correlated (positively or negatively) with seller concentration across industries. Under the pure DEH, variations of A across industries ought mainly to reflect differences in risk and in accounting biases, while variations in B should mainly reflect differences in demand elasticities. To obtain an alternative measure of large-firm profitability advantage that should be correlated with concentration under the DEH, define RA as the difference between an industry's average rate of return, R, and its intercept parameter, A. Then, using equation (4), the DEH implies

$$RA \equiv \left(\sum_{i=1}^{N} \pi a_i \bigg/ \sum_{i=1}^{N} K_i \right) - A = veH \tag{5}$$

where $v \equiv (PQ/\sum K_i)$ and $H \equiv \sum (s_i)^2$ is the Hirschman–Herfindahl index

[4] To see this last point, suppose, in the spirit of the more complex DEH models cited in footnote 3, that in order to enter any particular industry, firms must spend some industry-specific amount on research and development. This allows them in effect to draw a value of c from the industry-specific distribution of possible unit costs. Firms that draw a high c will elect not to start up production, while lucky firms with low c's will enter and earn positive rents on their luck. Depending on the pattern of differences in R & D costs and distributions of possible c's across industries, one might expect industries that attract relatively few firms to draw costs or to enter (and are thus concentrated *ex post*) to produce substantial rents to all those lucky enough to be able to operate profitably.

of seller concentration. RA should be positive for all industries under the DEH, and it should be positively correlated with most concentration measures, especially when differences in capital intensity are controlled for. Since e varies across industries, however, one cannot expect the correlation between RA and concentration to be particularly strong.

II(ii). *The pure DCH*

Under what I label the pure DCH, market shares are not determined by differences in efficiency. Under this hypothesis, estimation of (4) should still yield positive values of A. But, since share and profitability are not systematically related, the distribution of B and RA across industries should have a mean of approximately zero. Inter-industry differences in these parameters would reflect accounting quirks and historical accidents.

There is no reason why B should be correlated with concentration under the DCH, but the implications regarding A and RA are less clear. On the one hand, if industries differ in the importance of barriers to entry, but barriers to mobility (Caves and Porter [1977]) are generally unimportant, collusive behavior will raise the profits of all firms together. With market shares and concentration unrelated to efficiency differences, A will be positively correlated with concentration in cross-section, but RA (which may be positive or negative in any particular industry) will not be.

On the other hand, a positive correlation between RA and seller concentration is also consistent with the pure DCH. To see this, suppose (following Porter [1979]) that an industry has two strategic groups: one in which market shares are small and into which entry is free, and one in which established sellers are protected by barriers to entry and mobility. Sellers in the first group will earn only competitive returns, while the DCH implies that if (and only if) the second group is concentrated, its members will earn monopoly rents, and the industry average rate of return will be supracompetitive. If this two-group structure is typical, RA will be positively related to concentration in cross-section, while A will not be. Thus the pure DCH predicts that either A or RA, or possibly both, will be positively correlated with concentration in cross-section.

II(iii). *DEH/DCH Hybrids*

Since the pure versions of the DEH and the DCH describe polar cases, it is important to investigate the implications of DEH/DCH hybrids, in which shares are related to differential efficiency *and* seller concentration facilities collusion. To do this, I generalize the Cournot model developed above, using the conjectural variation formalism to describe possible collusive equilibria. If λ_i is firm i's conjectural derivative, $\partial \bar{q}_i/\partial q_i$, equation (4) can be written as

$$r_i = \rho + [(1+\lambda_i)e](s_i v_i) \tag{6}$$

It is easy to show that all else (including rivals' total output) equal, the higher is λ_i, the lower is firm i's output. In other words, the higher is λ_i, the more firm i restricts output in equilibrium. Under the DEH/DCH, one would expect the λ_i to be positive and to be generally larger the more concentrated is the industry considered.

If $\lambda_i = \lambda$ for all firms in some industry, equation (6) implies immediately that estimation of (4) should yield $A = \rho$, $B = e(1+\lambda)$, and $RA = evH(1+\lambda)$, all of which are positive as long as $\lambda > -1$. (If, in addition, λ is constant across industries or uncorrelated with concentration, equation (6) becomes empirically indistinguishable from the Cournot version of the pure DEH developed above.) If λ is positively correlated with concentration across industries, A should be independent of concentration, and both B and RA should be positively correlated with concentration.

But there is no obvious reason to suspect that the λ_i are in fact equal within industries. Clarke and Davies [1982] have proposed the alternative assumption $\lambda_i = \alpha(1-s_i)/s_i$, with α positively correlated with concentration. (See also Long [1982], Clark, Davies, and Waterson [1984], and Kwoka and Ravenscraft [1986].) Under this assumption, equation (6) becomes

$$r_i = [\rho + \alpha e v_i] + [(1-\alpha)e](s_i v_i) \tag{7}$$

This version of the DEH/DCH thus implies that greater seller concentration should be associated with higher estimates of A and *lower* estimates of B.

The main rationale for the Clarke–Davies assumption appears to be that as $\alpha \rightarrow 1$ (with rising marginal cost), the equilibrium described by (7) converges to the maximization of total industry profit. But total industry profit is not an especially plausible cartel objective function when side payments are impossible. Moreover, maximization of total industry profit requires small, inefficient firms to be the main restrictors of output, and the inverse relation between s_i and λ_i in the Clarke–Davies assumption imposes this pattern on all imperfectly collusive equilibria (i.e., those with $\alpha < 1$). But this pattern seems inconsistent with most descriptions of the actual behavior of imperfect cartels. (See almost any discussion of behavioral differences within OPEC, for instance.[5]) The Clarke–Davies assumption is also inconsistent with Stigler's [1964] model of oligopoly, which implies that small firms run a lower risk of detection and punishment than large firms if they fail to do their "fair share" of output restriction. I thus conclude that a positive relation between s_i and λ_i is more plausible than a negative relation of the sort postulated by Clarke and Davies.

To explore the implications of such a relation, suppose that the DEH/DCH holds for some industry, so that equation (6), with the addition of a disturbance distributed independently of the λ_i and $(s_i v_i)$, is the correct specification. To focus on the influence of concentration, suppose that $v_i = v$ for all i.

[5] But see Spiller and Favaro [1984] for an apparent counterexample.

Finally, assume that the λ_i have mean λ and are linear in the s_i, so that $\lambda_i = \lambda + \gamma[s_i - (1/N)]$, where N is the number of firms in the industry, and γ is some constant. Then if least squares is employed to estimate equation (4), a bit of algebra yields the following expectations of the estimated parameters:

(8a) $$E(A) = \rho + ev\gamma[H^2 - \sum(s_i)^3]/[NH-1]$$

(8b) $$E(B) = e(1+\lambda) + e\gamma[N^2\sum(s_i)^3 - 2NH + 1]/[N(NH-1)]$$

(8c) $$E(RA) = \rho + evH(1+\lambda) + ev\gamma[\sum(s_i)^3 - (H/N)] - E(A)$$

If the distribution of the s_i can be adequately approximated by the lognormal, which is commonly treated as a workable approximation to firm size distributions, it is easy to show (using results from Aitcheson and Brown [1963, ch. 2]) that the expected value of $\sum(s_i)^3$ is NH^3. Making this substitution in equations (8) yields

(9a) $$E(A) = \rho - ev\gamma H^2$$

(9b) $$E(B) = e(1+\lambda) + e\gamma[N^3H^3 - 2NH + 1]/[N(NH-1)]$$

(9c) $$E(RA) = evH(1+\lambda) + ev\gamma[NH^3 + H^2 - (H/N)]$$

As an empirical matter, N is at best weakly (negatively) correlated with concentration. (See, for instance, Schmalensee [1977, esp. footnote 1].) And it is easy to show that the second terms on the right of (9b) and (9c) are positive and increasing in H for $H > 1/N$, its lower bound.

Equations (9) thus imply that if γ is generally positive and non-negatively correlated with concentration, A should be *negatively* correlated with concentration in cross-section, though the correlation may be weak, while the positive correlation between concentration and both B and RA will be stronger than if $\gamma = 0$. If γ is large, A could be negative for highly concentrated industries, but B and RA should be positive in all cases. On the other hand, negative values of γ, which I have argued are relatively implausible, will tend to induce a positive correlation between concentration and A and to weaken the positive correlations between concentration and B and between concentration and RA. If γ is generally negative and large, these latter correlations could become negative, producing results like those implied by equation (7). If $\gamma < 0$ is the norm, A should be positive in all cases, but negative values of B and RA could be observed in highly concentrated industries. Finally, since e may vary substantially among industries (along with v and γ), one cannot expect any of the correlations predicted by this hybrid DEH/DCH model to be particularly strong.

III. DATA EMPLOYED

The data employed in this study cover US Internal Revenue Service (IRS) minor manufacturing industries, which are frequently studied in this context, for 1963 and 1972. I chose to use years for which Census of Manufactures data could be used to measure seller concentration. These particular Census years were selected because data for them were readily available, they were far enough apart in time for changes in industry-level variables to reflect changes in their fundamental determinants, and because they were comparable in terms of the business cycle.[6]

The overall unemployment rate was 5.5% in both years, while the civilian unemployment rate was 5.7% in 1963 and 5.6% in 1972.[7] The Federal Reserve Board's measure of capacity utilization in manufacturing was 83.5% in both periods. Real GNP originating in manufacturing rose 7.7% in 1963 and 10.4% in 1972. The corresponding implicit deflator *fell* 1.1% during 1963 and rose only 0.3% during 1972. Almost all the inflation that worried policy-makers during 1972 occurred outside the manufacturing sector.

Perhaps the most obvious difference between 1963 and 1972 is the operation of Phase II price controls during 1972. But there are at least four reasons for concluding that this is unimportant for the present study. First, the macroeconomic literature suggests that these controls did not have large effects on the economy as a whole; see, for instance, Dornbusch and Fischer [1981, pp. 566–567] and the references they cite. Second, Appendix C (available from the author on request) reports the results of a time-series analysis indicating that the Phase II controls had an insignificant effect on manufacturing profits. Third, Appendix C also reports the results of a small-scale study of the time-series behavior of the relation between firm size and profitability in US manufacturing. This study, undertaken to test for the possibility that the Phase II controls were enforced mainly against leading firms, giving their smaller rivals artificial competitive advantages, does not find 1972 to be an outlier in any relevant sense. (But it does point to substantial changes over time in the relation between firm size and profitability that deserve further study.) Fourth, neither 1963 nor 1972 appears as an outlier in the recent analysis of the relation between concentration and industry price-cost margins over the 1958–1981 period by Domowitz, Hubbard, and Petersen [1986].

Data by industry and by industry-specific asset size-class for Internal Revenue Service minor industries for 1972 were mainly obtained from the Project on Industry and Company Analysis (PICA) at the Harvard Graduate

[6] On the necessity of using substantial inter-period gaps in the analysis of structural change, see, for instance, the discussion of concentration changes by Caves and Porter [1980, esp. p. 9]. It should be noted that Demsetz [1974] has argued that 1963 is an outlier that is somewhat less consistent with the DEH than surrounding years, though the statistical analysis that supports his argument is suspect because it is based on absolute firm size rather than market share. (See Daskin [1983] for a general discussion of this issue.)

[7] All data used in this paragraph come from the 1984 *Economic Report of the President*. Growth rates reported for any year T are the annual rates of growth experienced between $(T-1)$ and $(T+1)$. This procedure better reflects growth during the second half year T than the usual approach of reporting changes between $(T-1)$ and T.

School of Business Administration. In order to reduce well-known measurement problems associated with very small firms and to reduce the importance of scale-related cost differences (the presence of which would tend to bias our results against the pure DCH) in the data, size-classes with assets below $500 000 were excluded. In order to have at least four usable size classes for each industry, five IRS industries (2380, 2398, 2899, 3860, and 3870) were then dropped from the sample. Many of the remaining industries are sufficiently broadly defined that they should be thought of as including several markets with at least some supply-side links. A final industry (3990, miscellaneous manufactured products, except ordinance, manufacturing not allocable) was dropped because the markets it included seemed unlikely to be at all closely linked. Our final sample consisted of 70 IRS minor industries, each with at least four usable size classes. The maximum number of usable classes was eight; the mean number was 6.8.

Data for 1963 IRS industries was provided by Alan J. Daskin, from the data set assembled for use in his dissertation (Daskin [1983]). These data were aggregated (size-class by size-class) to conform to the 1972 industry definitions, following the 1968 IRS *Sourcebook of Statistics of Income.* All 1963 industries had between five and nine usable size classes, with a mean of 8.3 classes per industry.

For each size-class for each industry, I compiled the number of firms, total assets, pre-tax profits plus interest payments, and business receipts. The ratio of total pre-tax returns (profits plus interest) to total assets employed was used as the accounting rate of return, r. This measure avoids the distorting effects of differences in leverage and effective income taxation. (Daskin [1983] reports that the effects in this context of using after-tax returns are negligible.) Like all accounting measures of profitability, r contains measurement error. Random errors in the dependent variable make estimation less precise but do not induce bias, of course. The inter-industry equations discussed below include controls (crude ones, to be sure) for some frequently-discussed accounting biases. A recent study by Salamon [1985] suggests that while accounting measurement error may bias estimates of B and RA upward, and thus induce a bias against the pure DCH, relations involving concentration

TABLE I
MAIN INDUSTRY-LEVEL VARIABLES

Variable	1963 Mean	1963 Std. Dev.	1972 Mean	1972 Std. Dev.	1963–1972 Correlation
R	0.1028	0.0352	0.0995	0.0299	0.5802
CONC	0.3353	0.1572	0.3606	0.1511	0.7602
AD/K	0.0270	0.0326	0.0197	0.0226	0.8302
PQ/K	1.5837	0.6310	1.4086	0.4502	0.8764

Note: See text for sources and definitions.

are unlikely to be biased. (Note, however, that Salamon [1985] employs published financial reports, not, as here, tax returns.) Similarly, the conglomerate merger wave of the late 1960s undoubtedly serves to lower the quality of the 1972 data, but it is not clear why it should bias estimates of relations involving concentration.

The following variables were computed for each IRS minor manufacturing industry in 1963 and 1972:

R = Ratio of pre-tax profits plus interest payments to total assets for all firms with assets above $500 000.
$CONC$ = Weighted average, using value-added weights, of four-firm concentration ratios of constituent 4-digit Census industries.
AD/K = Ratio of advertising outlays to total assets.
PQ/K = Ratio of business receipts to total assets.
$DDUR = 1-DNDR = 1$ for durable goods industries, zero otherwise.
$DCON = 1-DPRO = 1$ for consumer goods industries, zero otherwise.

The means, standard deviations, and inter-year correlations of the first four of these variables are shown in Table I. Those figures seem generally consistent with the presumption that 1963 and 1972 are comparable years. They also indicate that dramatic changes between these years were relatively rare.[8]

The correlations between R and the corresponding industry-wide rates of return were above 0.99 in both years; the exclusion of small firms is not terribly important in these data. If one thinks of IRS minor industries as including multiple markets, observed rates of return must be thought of as asset-weighted averages of rates of return in those markets. Thus $CONC$ should ideally also be computed using (net) asset weights; value-added weights seemed the closest readily available substitute. The advertising-sales ratio, AD/PQ, is often treated as a proxy for product differentiation under the DCH. The correlations between AD/K, which seems slightly preferable because it has the same units as the other variables, and AD/PQ exceeded 0.96 in both years. AD/K is also the more natural variable to use as a rough correction for advertising-related accounting biases; see Demsetz [1979]. The variable PQ/K serves both to control for differences in capital intensity and as a rough correction for accounting biases in asset valuation during

[8] To investigate the intertemporal stability of R and $CONC$, equations of the form $[X(1972)-X(1963)] = \gamma[\alpha - X(1963)]$ were estimated for each variable. (More complex specifications, in which γ, α, or both were functions of other variables, generally did not perform noticeably better.) Estimates of γ indicate a half-life of deviations of R from the mean ($= 9.0 \times [\ln(0.5)/\ln(1-\gamma)]$, the equation's median lag in years) of 8.8 years, with an asymptotic standard error of 2.1 years. $CONC$ also tends to regress towards the mean in these data, but the process seems much slower; the estimated half-life of deviations from the mean is 19.9 years, with an asymptotic standard error of 6.6 years. It is unclear exactly how to interpret this difference in adjustment speeds, especially in light of the differences in patterns of profitability between the 1963 and 1972 samples discussed in section V.

inflation. I do not attempt to provide structural interpretations of the coefficients of AD/K and PQ/K; these variables are included as controls and for descriptive purposes.

Similarly, in the interests of providing an adequate description of the data, it seemed desirable to examine differences between industries producing durable and nondurable goods and between industries producing consumer and producer goods. I used Ornstein's [1977, Appendix B] classification of four-digit Census industries in 1967, along with 1963 value-added weights and the correspondence between 1963 and 1972 IRS definitions to classify the sample industries along these lines. Seventeen of the 70 industries in the sample were found to produce mainly durable goods, and 22 were classified as consumer goods industries by this procedure.[9]

IV. ECONOMETRIC PROBLEMS

In order to compare values of A, B, and RA across industries, equation (4) must be estimated for each industry in the sample. This is not a completely straightforward task, since (4) relates to individual firms, while the data are for groups of firms within asset-based size-classes. Only Daskin [1983] seems to have recognized that one cannot obtain consistent estimates by simply substituting size-class averages into equations like (4) He dealt with the problem by estimating an intra-industry equation linear in profits and assets, for which there is no problem of aggregation bias. Unfortunately, it is difficult to interpret the parameters of Daskin's equation in terms of the hypotheses of interest here.

The approach taken in this study is to aggregate (4) from firm to size-class data explicitly and to substitute estimates of the unobservable quantities (defined below) that appear as a consequence of aggregation. Consider size class c in some industry. Suppose it has N_c firms, and let the subscript "ci" denote the ith firm in class c. Multiplying equation (4) by the firm's total assets and adding a disturbance term yields

$$(10) \qquad \pi a_{ci} = AK_{ci} + BP(q_{ci})^2 + \varepsilon_{ci}$$

The basic equation for size-class average rates of return is then obtained by summing over the firms in class c and dividing by total assets in the class:

$$(11) \qquad r_c \equiv \sum_{i=1}^{N_c} \pi a_{ci} \bigg/ \sum_{i=1}^{N_c} K_{ci} \equiv \pi a_c / K_c = A + B(f_c \bar{s}_c v_c) + u_c$$

[9] Previous studies using IRS data from the early 1960s (e.g., Comanor and Wilson [1974] and Porter [1979]) typically have many more consumer goods industries. A good deal of the difference is accounted for by aggregation from 1963 to 1972 industries and the deletion of some of the latter. But a detailed comparison reveals that a number of industries generally classified as producing mainly consumer goods in earlier studies in fact generate the majority of their value-added in four-digit industries that Ornstein [1977, Appendix B] classifies as producer goods industries. Examples include IRS minor industries 2850 (Paints and allied products), 3010 (Rubber products), and 3420 (Cutlery, hand tools, and hardware).

The new variables in this equation are defined as follows:

(12a) $$f_c \equiv N_c \sum_{i=1}^{N_c} (q_{ci})^2 \bigg/ \left(\sum_{i=1}^{N_c} q_{ci} \right)^2 \equiv N_c \sum_{i=1}^{N_c} (q_{ci})^2/(q_c)^2$$

(12b) $$\bar{s}_c \equiv (q_c/N_c)/Q$$

(12c) $$v_c \equiv Pq_c/K_c$$

(12d) $$u_c \equiv \sum_{i=1}^{N_c} \varepsilon_{ci}/K_c$$

The unobservable quantity f_c equals one if and only if all firms in size class c have the same sales. In general, f_c equals one plus the ratio of the sample variance of the q_{ci} to the square of their sample mean. It thus is an indicator of the importance of intra-class differences in market share.

In order to handle the unobservability of the f_c, I assume that intra-class differences in assets are as important as those in sales:

(13) $$f_c = N_c \sum_{i=1}^{N_c} (K_{ci})^2/(K_c)^2$$

This assumption is needed here because size-class boundaries relate to assets, not sales. A sufficient (but not necessary) condition for (13) to be satisfied is that within a given industry, all firms in each size class have the same revenue/capital ratio. Given (13), the f_c are estimated using N_c, K_c, and the values of size-class boundaries. The procedure employed is based on the assumption that assets of firms within each class are drawn from a class-specific density function linear in assets. Details are given (and an alternative approach based on the lognormal distribution is discussed) in Appendix A.

A second problem in estimating (11) with size-class data is that aggregation is likely to produce differences in the variances of the u_c within industries. To deal with this heteroskedasticity problem, I employ two alternative, bounding assumptions about the distribution of the ε_{ci} in (10). (Given the small number of observations on each industry, this seems preferable to relying on heteroskedasticity-consistent estimators of coefficient standard errors.) The most natural assumption is that the standard deviation of ε_{ci} is σK_{ci} for all i and c, where σ is an industry-specific constant. Under this assumption, the variance of u_c is given by

(14) $$\sigma^2(u_c) = \sigma^2 \sum_{i=1}^{N_c} (K_{ci})^2/(K_c)^2 = \sigma^2(f_c/N_c)$$

Division of (11) by $(f_c/N_c)^{\frac{1}{2}}$ yields what is referred to below as the CRS estimating equation, because it embodies the assumption of stochastic constant returns to scale:

(15) $$r_c(N_c/f_c)^{\frac{1}{2}} = A(N_c/f_c)^{\frac{1}{2}} + B[\bar{s}_c v_c (f_c N_c)^{\frac{1}{2}}] + \xi_c$$

The variance of ξ_c is σ^2 for all classes in a given industry if (14) holds.

The literature on the effects of scale on the time-series and cross-section variability of firms' rates of return suggests an alternative to the CRS specification. These studies generally find that the standard deviation of rates of return declines with firm size, with the decline less rapid than that of $(K_i)^{-\frac{1}{2}}$. (See Prais [1976, pp. 92–98] and Daskin [1983] for overviews of this literature.) This suggests that the standard deviation of ε_{ci} is generally equal to $\sigma(K_{ci})^b$, where σ is as before and $1/2 < b < 1$. The CRS specification assumes $b = 1$. Since b is unknown and may vary from industry to industry and from year to year, I deal with the possibility that b is less than unity by exploring the implications of the alternative bounding assumption $b = 1/2$. Under this assumption the variance of u_c is simply σ^2/K_c. Division of (11) by $(K_c)^{-\frac{1}{2}}$ yields the IRS estimating equation, which embodies the assumption of stochastic increasing returns to scale:

$$(16) \qquad r_c(K_c)^{\frac{1}{2}} = A(K_c)^{\frac{1}{2}} + B[\bar{s}_c v_c f_c(K_c)^{\frac{1}{2}}] + \xi_c$$

Even if the true values of A and B were the same for all industries, estimates would differ because of sampling error. Following, for instance, Swamy [1970, esp. Sect. 5], one can nevertheless make inferences about the distributions of the true parameter values. If b_j is the estimate of some true parameter, β_j, for industry j, one can write

$$(17) \qquad b_j = \beta_j + \eta_j = \mu + v_j + \eta_j$$

Here η_j is the sampling error associated with b_j. It is unobservable, but it can be treated as having mean zero and standard deviation equal to the standard error of b_j, which we denote $\sigma(\eta_j)$. If μ is the mean of the population from which the β_j are drawn, so that the v_j have mean zero, an unbiased estimator of the variance of the population distribution of the β_j is

$$(18) \qquad \sigma^2(v) = \sum_{j=1}^{M} (b_j - \bar{b})^2/(M-1) - \sum_{j=1}^{M} \sigma^2(\eta_j)/M$$

where $\bar{b}$ is the sample mean of the b_j, and M is the number of industries. Given $\sigma^2(v)$, the precision-weighted average of the b_j provides an efficient estimate of μ:

$$(19) \qquad \mu = \sum_{j=1}^{M} \{b_j/[\sigma^2(v) + \sigma^2(\eta_j)]\} \Big/ \sum_{j=1}^{M} \{1/[\sigma^2(v) + \sigma^2(\eta_j)]\}$$

A comparison of μ with its large-sample variance, $1/\sum\{1/[\sigma^2(v) + \sigma^2(\eta_j)]\}$, yields a large-sample χ^2 test of the null hypothesis that the population mean of the β_j is zero.

Finally, in order to estimate cross-section relations involving A, B, and RA efficiently, one must again take explicit account of the fact that the estimates from intra-industry regressions measure the true underlying parameters with error. If β_j is the true value of some such parameter for industry j, and Z_j and

δ are vectors of industry-specific explanatory variables and inter-industry coefficients, respectively, a typical inter-industry equation can be written as follows:

$$b_j = \beta_j + \eta_j = Z_j'\delta + (\zeta_j + \eta_j) \tag{20}$$

The ζ_j and the η_j are assumed to be independent. If the ζ_j have common variance $\sigma^2(\zeta)$, the variance of the jth error term in equation (21) is $[\sigma^2(\zeta)+\sigma^2(\eta_j)]$. Since the sampling variances of the b_j differ in general, application of ordinary least squares to (20) would yield inefficient estimates of δ.

This problem has been treated in general terms by Hanushek [1974] and Saxonhouse [1977]; Long [1982] and Daskin [1983] have previously allowed for this source of heteroskedasticity in this context. In order to obtain efficient estimates of δ, one needs a consistent estimate of $\sigma^2(\zeta)$. Since the standard errors of the b_j can be treated as known, such estimates can be obtained by applying least squares to (20), either as it stands or after division by the $\sigma(\eta_j)$. Because these two regressions often yield rather different estimates of $\sigma^2(\zeta)$ and because estimates of δ in many cases appear sensitive to the estimate of $\sigma^2(\zeta)$ employed, I used an iterative fixed-point approach to the estimation of that variance, the details of which are presented in Appendix B. Weighted least squares was then used to obtain efficient estimates of δ.

V. EMPIRICAL RESULTS

V(i). *Intra-industry estimates*

The parameter estimates obtained by employing the CRS and IRS specifications with 1963 and 1972 data are summarized in Table II. The statistics given under the heading "Sample Coefficients" are self-explanatory.[10] Those statistics indicate that essentially all estimates of A are positive in both years, while estimates of B and RA have both signs in both years. The majority of estimates of B (59%) and RA (56%) are positive in 1963, while negative values (66% of B's and 69% RA's) are the rule in 1972. (The means of t-statistics and their absolute values indicate that some negative (positive) B's and RA's have t's large in absolute value in 1963 (1972).) Perhaps the most striking feature of this Table is the sharp difference between the 1963 and 1972 estimates. Table I shows that on average $R(=RA+A)$ changed little between these years, but Table II reveals that A rose broadly and substantially, while B and RA generally fell.

The first two statistics given under the heading "Probability Levels" are the

[10] Since R is known, the sampling variance of RA ($\equiv R-A$) is equal to the square of the standard error of A. Similarly, since 1963 and 1972 can be treated as providing independent observations, sampling variances of changes in parameters between these two years are sums of the corresponding squared standard errors.

significance levels obtained in standard χ^2 tests of the indicated null hypotheses. Except for estimates of B under the CRS specification, these indicate that the null hypotheses that the underlying parameters or their 1963–1972

TABLE II
SUMMARY STATISTICS FROM INTRA-INDUSTRY REGRESSIONS

	Coefficient/Specification					
	A/CRS	*A/IRS*	*RA/CRS*	*RA/IRS*	*B/CRS*	*B/IRS*
Statistics for 1963						
Sample Coefficients						
Sample Mean	0.0910	0.0955	0.0118	0.0077	0.4823	0.1747
Standard Deviation	0.0322	0.0296	0.0416	0.0322	1.7599	0.9397
Number Positive	69	70	39	40	42	40
Mean t-Statistic	11.2	7.27	1.27	0.64	0.31	0.89
Mean |t|-Statistic	11.2	7.27	3.35	1.68	0.76	2.29
Population Estimates						
Estimated Mean	0.0919	0.0929	0.0114	0.0077	*	0.1359
Standard Deviation	0.0275	0.0220	0.0381	0.0254	*	0.4391
Probability Levels						
Coefficients = 0	<0.01	<0.01	<0.01	<0.01	0.18	<0.01
Coefficients Equal	<0.01	<0.01	<0.01	<0.01	0.29	<0.01
Population Mean = 0	<0.01	<0.01	0.02	0.03	*	0.03
Statistics for 1972						
Sample Coefficients						
Sample Mean	0.1118	0.1079	−0.0123	−0.0084	−0.3554	−0.3532
Standard Deviation	0.0253	0.0273	0.0350	0.0325	0.8492	1.0839
Number Positive	70	70	19	24	23	24
Mean t-Statistic	18.0	12.8	−2.00	−0.99	−0.32	−1.18
Mean |t|-Statistic	18.0	12.8	4.31	2.83	0.83	3.45
Population Estimates						
Estimated Mean	0.1121	0.1077	−0.1249	−0.0079	*	−0.2586
Standard Deviation	0.0228	0.0242	0.0332	0.0300	*	1.0119
Probability Levels						
Coefficients = 0	<0.01	<0.01	<0.01	<0.01	0.08	<0.01
Coefficients Equal	<0.01	<0.01	<0.01	<0.01	0.08	<0.01
Population Mean = 0	<0.01	<0.01	<0.01	0.04	*	0.04
Changes, 1963 to 1972						
Sample Coefficients						
Sample Mean	0.0208	0.0128	−0.0241	−0.0162	−0.8377	−0.5279
Standard Deviation	0.0323	0.0336	0.0372	0.0330	1.8832	1.5400
Number Positive	53	49	15	20	18	19
Mean t-Statistic	1.86	0.87	−2.06	−1.09	−0.45	−1.44
Mean |t|-Statistic	2.34	1.50	2.04	1.69	0.67	2.29
Population Estimates						
Estimated Mean	0.0211	0.0135	−0.0245	−0.0170	*	−0.3731
Standard Deviation	0.0253	0.0241	0.0314	0.0289	*	1.2373
Probability Levels						
Coefficients = 0	<0.01	<0.01	<0.01	<0.01	0.97	<0.01
Coefficients Equal	<0.01	<0.01	<0.01	<0.01	0.99	<0.01
Population Mean = 0	<0.01	<0.01	<0.01	<0.01	*	0.02

* Could not be computed because estimated population variance was negative.

changes are the same across industries can be confidently rejected. That is, the intra-industry estimates of the coefficients of equation (4) provide information on what seem to be real inter-industry differences.[11]

The statistics under the heading "Population Estimates" in Table II provide summary information on the importance of those differences, based on equations (18) and (19) above. (Equation (18) yielded a negative estimate of $\sigma(v)$ for B under the CRS specification, reflecting the large standard errors of the corresponding parameter estimates.) Population standard deviations are large relative to population means, especially for RA and B. Comparing sample and population standard deviations indicates that in all but two cases (A/IRS and B/IRS in 1963), less than 40% of the variance of coefficient estimates can be attributed to sampling error. The last line under "Probability Levels" indicates that population means differ significantly from zero and that changes in estimated values between 1963 and 1972 reflect real changes in underlying population means.

V(ii). *Inter-industry estimates*

Table III presents weighted least squares estimates of the cross-section relations between concentration and A, B, and RA. For comparison purposes, estimates of the relation between concentration and R are also presented. The statistics labeled "Basic Model" refer to a simple bivariate model in which $CONC$ is the only independent variable, while in the "Full Model" the variables AD/K and PQ/K are added to control for advertising and capital-intensity differences. All equations estimated included intercept terms, which are of little interest and hence are not reported. The null hypothesis that CRS and IRS equations had identical coefficients was never rejected at conventional significance levels using a (heteroskedasticity-corrected) Chow test. Since the CRS and IRS samples are not independent, however, visual inspection of coefficients and standard errors probably provides more convincing evidence that the choice of stochastic specification is not crucial here. Similarly, Chow tests for coefficient stability applied to equations involving A, B, or RA provided no evidence of significant coefficient differences between durable goods and nondurable goods industries or between consumer goods industries and producer goods industries.[12]

[11] A number of authors including Ravenscraft [1983] and Schmalensee [1985] have found highly significant relations between share and profitability in models in which the coefficient of share is constrained to be the same across industries. (See Scherer [1980, ch. 9] for a discussion of earlier work of this sort.) The tests of coefficient equality in Table II indicate that this constraint is highly suspect. Profitability is apparently strongly related to market share in some industries, but not in all.

[12] The equations involving R (Table III) and ΔR (Table 5 in Appendix D, available from the author on request) showed signs of coefficient instability between consumer and producer goods industries. But since these equations play no direct role in our comparisons of the DEH and the DCH, the sources of this instability were not explored.

The first measure of goodness of fit presented in Table III, R^2-Wtd., is the R^2 statistic of the weighted regression used to estimate δ. A second measure, R^2-Raw, is based on the variances of actual and predicted values of b_j. The second measure can be negative; the first must lie between zero and one. Both measures make it clear that these equations have little ability to explain

TABLE III
RESULTS OF INTER-INDUSTRY WEIGHTED REGRESSIONS

	Dependent Variable						
	R	*A/CRS*	*A/IRS*	*B/CRS*	*B/IRS*	*RA/CRS*	*RA/IRS*
Basic Model							
1963:							
CONC	0.0631	0.0360	0.0326	0.1675	−0.3425	0.0316	0.0399
	(2.42)	(1.72)	(1.42)	(0.34)	(0.68)	(1.05)	(1.61)
R^2-Wtd.	—	0.042	0.029	0.002	0.007	0.016	0.037
-Raw	0.079	0.082	0.037	−0.044	0.006	0.017	0.007
1972:							
CONC	−0.0131	−0.0165	−0.0266	0.5339	0.9172	0.0043	0.0175
	(0.55)	(0.82)	(1.27)	(1.08)	(1.52)	(0.15)	(0.68)
R^2-Wtd.	—	0.010	0.023	0.017	0.033	0.0003	0.007
-Raw	0.044	0.017	0.018	−0.007	0.048	0.001	0.001
Prob. Level: Slope Equal	0.08	0.07	0.06	0.83	0.15	0.51	0.53
Full Model							
1963:							
CONC	0.0463	0.0317	0.0208	0.1948	−0.3804	0.0215	0.0331
	(1.97)	(1.44)	(0.91)	(0.40)	(0.75)	(0.76)	(1.29)
AD/K	0.5438	0.0154	0.3281	5.3232	2.0313	0.5267	0.2178
	(4.85)	(0.15)	(2.90)	(2.52)	(0.93)	(4.03)	(1.75)
PQ/K	−0.0094	−0.0036	−0.0044	−0.0068	−0.0191	−0.0055	−0.0028
	(1.58)	(0.73)	(0.90)	(0.07)	(0.16)	(0.82)	(0.50)
R^2-Wtd.	—	0.049	0.138	0.091	0.020	0.214	0.080
-Raw	0.324	0.079	0.154	−0.055	0.012	0.150	0.059
1972:							
CONC	−0.0211	−0.0325	−0.0332	0.7131	0.8478	0.0001	0.0156
	(0.96)	(1.53)	(1.45)	(1.53)	(1.39)	(0.35)	(0.61)
AD/K	0.7101	0.0425	0.1702	8.4427	8.8881	0.6657	0.5445
	(5.05)	(0.32)	(1.19)	(3.16)	(2.40)	(4.14)	(3.39)
PQ/K	0.0031	−0.0154	−0.0035	0.2966	0.1011	0.0165	0.0062
	(0.42)	(2.14)	(0.45)	(1.85)	(0.50)	(1.89)	(0.70)
R^2-Wtd.	—	0.074	0.044	0.215	0.123	0.280	0.180
-Raw	0.303	0.055	0.033	0.163	0.097	0.253	0.168
Prob. Level: Slopes Equal	<0.01	0.17	0.23	0.26	0.19	0.11	0.21

Note: Figures in parentheses are absolute values of t-statistics.

inter-industry differences in *A*, *B*, or *RA* in these data. That is, most of the variation in these parameters seems to be unrelated to concentration, the central variable in all the competing hypotheses.

The "Prob. Level" statistics in Table III are the significance levels of F-tests of the null hypotheses of equal slope coefficients in 1963 and 1972, with intercepts allowed to differ in light of the results shown in Table II. The clear instability in the *R* equations has obvious and disturbing implications for the reliability of conclusions drawn from single-year cross-section studies of profitability. (See also Domowitz, Hubbard, and Petersen [1986] on this general point.)

The "Prob. Level" statistics also cast some doubt on the null hypothesis of stability for equations involving *A*, *B*, and *RA*. Moreover, an examination of the coefficient estimates and t-statistics in those equations indicates that failure to reject this null hypothesis convincingly can generally be attributed in large measure to imprecision of the parameter estimates in at least one of the two years. In the *B/CRS* Basic Model estimates, for instance, the 1963 estimate has such a large standard error (the two-σ range is from -0.81 to 1.15) that it can hardly be statistically inconsistent with the 1972 estimate. The t-statistics on the key concentration coefficients do differ noticeably between years, however, though not between CRS and IRS specifications or between Basic and Full Models. Thus not only do the average values of *A*, *B*, and *RA* differ between 1963 and 1972, but their correlations with concentration and other industry characteristics (themselves relatively stable, as Table I indicates) appear to differ as well. The instability detected in Table II seems quite fundamental. On the other hand, key results are insensitive to choice of stochastic specification or to the presence or absence of control variables.

Since all competing hypotheses predict only the existence of statistically weak relations (if only because of inter-industry variation in *e*), it is probably appropriate to apply looser than usual standards for rejecting null hypotheses of no relation. With this in mind, *A* and *RA* appear to be positively correlated with concentration in 1963. In 1972, *A* appears to be negatively correlated with concentration, while the correlation between concentration and *B* appears to be positive. There is not a hint here of a non-zero correlation between *B* and concentration in 1963 or between *RA* and concentration in 1972.

V(iii). *Findings vs. predictions*

Table IV summarizes the predictions of the DEH, the DCH, and the DEH/DCH models developed in section II, along with the corresponding statistical findings from Tables II and III. All models except the pure DEH and the DEH/DCH hybrid with $\gamma < 0$ predict that *B* and *RA* will be positive in all industries. But this prediction is clearly contradicted by the data for

TABLE IV
SUMMARY OF THEORETICAL PREDICTIONS AND EMPIRICAL FINDINGS

	Parameter Value*			Correlation with *CONC*†		
	A	*B*	*RA*	*A*	*B*	*RA*
Predictions: Pure DEH	>0	>0	>0	0	0	>0
Predictions: Pure DCH‡	>0	Both noise, mean $\simeq 0$		$\geqslant 0$	0	$\geqslant 0$
Predictions: DEH/DCH, $\gamma > 0$	Mostly >0	>0	>0	<0	>0	>0
Predictions: DEH/DCH, $\gamma = 0$	>0	>0	>0	0	>0	>0
Predictions: DEH/DCH, $\gamma < 0$	>0	Both mostly >0		>0	?	?
Findings: 1963	>0	59% >0	56% >0	1.37	−0.17	1.18
(μ, σ)		(0.14, 0.44)	(0.01, 0.03)			
Findings: 1972	>0	66% <0	69% <0	−1.27	1.38	0.45
(μ, σ)		(−0.26, 1.01)	(−0.07, 0.03)			

Notes: Predictions are from section II; Findings summarize Tables II and III.

* Values of μ and σ are IRS population estimates for *B* and the average of the CRS and IRS population estimates for *RA*. Percentages positive or negative are averages over both specifications.

† Figures shown on the last two lines are averages of the four relevant t-statistics from Table III.

‡ Either *A*, *RA*, or both should be positively correlated with *CONC*.

both 1963 and 1972. Broadly similar results have been reported by a host of previous authors, including Caves and Pugel [1980], Clark, Davies, and Waterson [1984], Comanor and Wilson [1974], Daskin [1983], Long [1982], Marcus [1969], Porter [1979], and Weiss and Pascoe [1985], using a variety of specifications and data sets. It is thus clear, especially in light of Salamon's [1985] recent work, that one cannot treat the positive intra-industry relation between profitability and market share predicted by the pure DEH and the two most plausible DEH/DCH hybrids as a stylized fact in US manufacturing.

Taken as a whole, the 1963 results can be argued to be consistent with the pure DCH and with the DEH/DCH hybrid assuming $\gamma < 0$. (Note in particular the lack of any support for the positive relation between *CONC* and *B* predicted by the DEH/DCH for non-negative γ.) But, as I argued above, neither of these hypotheses is especially plausible. When one adds to the information in Table IV the very low explanatory power of the regressions reported in Table III, the null hypothesis that the 1963 data support none of the competing hypotheses becomes very attractive.

The results obtained for 1972 are very clearly inconsistent with all the hypotheses developed in section II. Negative values of *B* and *RA* are the norm; the null hypotheses that the corresponding population means are zero are decisively rejected. The estimated population mean of *B* is small relative to the corresponding standard deviation, however, so that the estimated distribution of *B* could perhaps be described as approximately symmetric around zero and thus consistent with the pure DCH. But the statistics for *RA* describe a distribution with most of its mass below zero, and this is consistent with none of the non-null hypotheses. The apparent negative relation between concentration and *A* is consistent only with the DEH/DCH hybrid with $\gamma > 0$, but that hypothesis predicts a positive relation between concentration and *RA* that is clearly not present in these data.

Perhaps the most disturbing aspect of the findings summarized in Table IV is the striking difference between the 1963 and 1972 estimates for identically defined industries in cyclically comparable years. This difference casts considerable doubt on the stability assumption implicit in single-year cross-section work in industrial economics.

V(iv). *Postscript: Changes over time*

I had originally intended to use industry-specific changes between 1963 and 1972 to test a variety of dynamic hypotheses based on the DEH and the DCH. But the evidence of basic differences between these two years presented above and the results of a few attempts to estimate dynamic models made it clear that the stationarity conditions necessary for such an exercise to be sensible were not satisfied. It nonetheless seemed worthwhile to summarize the pattern of parameter change between 1963 and 1972 by computing weighted least-squares estimates of the Basic and Full Models using average values of *CONC*, *AD*/*K*, and *PQ*/*K* as independent variables.

This exercise (which is described in more detail in Appendix D, available from the author on request) revealed a complex pattern of parameter changes that casts further doubt on the hypothesis that the 1963/1972 differences have anything to do with the Phase II price controls. No evidence of coefficient differences between consumer goods industries and producer goods industries was encountered, but most versions of the Full Model (though not of the Basic Model) showed instability between durable goods and nondurable goods industries. Durable goods industries experienced smaller increases in *A* and smaller decreases in *B* and *RA* than nondurable goods industries, all else equal. *CONC* was unrelated to changes in *A*, positively related to changes in *B* for durables industries, and negatively related to changes in *RA* for nondurables. Capital intensity was negatively related to changes in *A* and positively related to changes in *B* and *RA* in the durables subsample. I have no good explanation for these findings or the related details reported in Appendix D.

VI. CONCLUSIONS AND IMPLICATIONS

This essay has derived a set of testable implications of the DEH, the DCH, and a hybrid DEH/DCH model and employed appropriate econometric techniques to test those implications with data on 70 identically-defined Internal Revenue Service minor manufacturing industries in 1963 and 1972. The results are discouraging in a number of respects. The 1963 data can be interpreted as supporting the pure DCH or a (relatively implausible) DEH/DCH hybrid. But they are also consistent with the null hypothesis that none of the models developed in section II can explain observed profitability differences. Moreover, the 1972 data seem consistent only with this null hypothesis. Finally, the results for these two cyclically comparable years differ significantly in a number of important respects, and the pattern of changes in industry-level parameters is quite complex.

Since the DEH and the pure DCH reflect polar opposite, and thus extreme, views of the world, it may not be surprising that the data are not consistent with either. It is perhaps more of a surprise that the more plausible DEH/DCH hybrids fare no better. At any rate, there is no support here for the use of the DEH, the DCH, or the DEH/DCH hybrids as maintained hypotheses in policy analysis or the study of individual industries. It would appear likely that the relative importance of collusion and differential efficiency vary considerably among industries and over time.

The instability found here between two cyclically comparable years casts a good deal of doubt on the quality of evidence provided by inter-industry studies that use data for a single point in time. Two years of data provided a useful check on stability in this study. But two years are not enough to yield estimates reliable enough to serve as stylized facts in the process of theory construction. This work thus supports the view that empirical research in industrial economics should make more use of panel data.

RICHARD SCHMALENSEE,
Sloan School of Management,
Massachusetts Institute of Technology,
Cambridge,
Massachusetts 02139,
USA.

APPENDIX A

Consider a size class including N firms with assets between a and b, and let m be reported mean assets per firm. Let K be the assets of a typical firm in this class, assumed to be a draw from the density function $g(K)$ with mean μ. Taking the expectation of the second-order Taylor series expansion of the right-hand side of equation (13) about the point at which all the $K_{ci} = \mu$, one obtains the asymptotic approximation employed to estimate the f_c:

(A1) $$f^* = [1+(N-1)R]/N$$

where the quantity R, which equals or exceeds unity and reflects the population dispersion in $g(K)$, is given by

(A2) $$R = E(K^2)/\mu^2$$

Note that for $N = 1$, both the true f and the approximation f^* equal one for any distribution, as there are no intra-class differences. As $N \rightarrow \infty$, both f and f^* approach the population value R. The mechanics of estimating the population ratio R depend on whether b is known or unknown.

In the largest size class in each industry, the upper bound on firm size, b, is unknown. I deal with this by assuming that $g(K)$ is a linear decreasing function of K and reaches zero at $K = b$. For such a triangular distribution it is easy to show that

(A3) $$\mu = (2a+b)/3$$

(A4) $$E(K^2) = (3a^2+2ab+b^2)/6$$

Setting $\mu = m$ in (A3) yields an estimate of b. Substitution into (A4) and division by m^2 then produces an estimate of R.

When b is known, I assume initially that $g(a) = \alpha$, $g(b) = \beta$, with $\alpha, \beta \geqslant 0$, and that $g(K)$ is a linear function of K between these points. For such a trapezoidal distribution,

(A5) $$\mu = [\omega(2a+b)+(1-\omega)(a+2b)]/3$$

where $\omega = \alpha/(\alpha+\beta)$, and

(A6) $$E(K^2) = [6(a+b)\mu-(a^2+4ab+b^2)]/6$$

For $(2a+b)/3 \leqslant m \leqslant (a+2b)/3$, R is estimated by setting $\mu = m$ in (A6) and dividing by m^2. For $m < (2a+b)/3$, the triangular distribution of the preceding paragraph is employed. For $m > (a+2b)/3$, $g(K)$ is assumed to be triangular with $g(b) > 0$ and $g(x) = 0$ for some $x > a$.

I experimented at some length with an alternative approach that involved assuming a lognormal distribution of firms' assets within each industry. This approach should be more efficient than that described above for industries with approximately lognormal size distributions. Parameter estimates were computed using variants of the basic maximum likelihood method for estimating the parameters of truncated lognormal distributions; see Aitcheson and Brown [1963, Sects. 9.2 and 9.6]. Exact formulae for conditional expectations then produced class-specific estimates of R. For most industries this approach gave f^*'s and estimates of A and B that were very close to those produced by the method described above. In a few cases, however, involving industries with size distributions that seemed far from lognormality, this alternative approach yielded implausible estimates of the f_c. The technique described above was employed because of its apparently greater robustness to substantial departures from lognormality.

APPENDIX B

Consider estimating equation (20) in the text by weighted regression, dividing the jth observation by $(w_j)^{\frac{1}{2}}$. For any set of positive w_j, a consistent estimate of $\sigma^2(\zeta)$, the unknown variance of the ζ_j, is given by

$$\text{(B1)} \qquad v = \left[SSR - \sum_{j=1}^{M} (\sigma^2(\eta_j)/w_j) \right] \Big/ \sum_{j=1}^{M} (1/w_j)$$

where M is the number of industries, and SSR is the sum of squared residuals from the weighted regression. Interest attaches here to weights of the form

$$\text{(B2)} \qquad w_j = [v + \sigma^2(\eta_j)]$$

Let D equal the coefficient of variation of the w_j, the ratio of the standard deviation of these weights to their mean. For weights given by (B2), D varies between 0 and s/m, where m is the mean of the $\sigma^2(h_j)$ and s is their standard deviation.

Now consider the function F, from $[0, s/m]$ to the real line, defined constructively as follows. Pick a non-negative initial value of v, v^0. Use (B2) to compute the corresponding vector of weights, w^0, and directly calculate the initial value of D, D^0. Run a weighted regression with weight vector w^0 and use (B1) to obtain a new value of v, which need not be non-negative. Finally, use (B2) to compute new weights and a new value of D, $D^1 \equiv F(D^0)$. Iterated weighted least squares is simply a search for a fixed point of F.

In this study it proved very efficient computationally to employ a linear approximation to the function F. OLS estimation of (20) yields $F(0)$; estimation with $w_j = \sigma^2(\eta_j)$ yields $F(s/m)$. Let SSR_0 be the sum of squared residuals from the first regression, and let SSR_w be the sum of squared residuals from the second. A bit of algebra establishes that if F is linear and has a fixed point, the corresponding value of v is given by

$$\text{(B3)} \qquad v^* = (SSR_0/M)[(SSR_w/M) - 1]/[(SSR_w/M) - 1 + \gamma]$$

where

$$\text{(B4)} \qquad \gamma \equiv \left[\sum_{j=1}^{M} \sigma^2(\eta_j) \right] \left[\sum_{j=1}^{M} 1/\sigma^2(\eta_j) \right] \Big/ N^2$$

Given an estimate of $\sigma^2(\zeta)$ from (B3), one can use (B2) to compute weights for a third weighted regression. If a fixed point of F has been found, it follows from (B1) and (B2) that the sum of squared residuals from this regression will equal M.

This technique could not be applied to equations involving estimates of B computed using the CRS specification; because these estimates differed little relative to their standard errors, (B3) produced negative values of v^*. (See the discussion of Table II in section IV of the text.) Instead, estimates of $\sigma^2(\zeta)$ derived from the IRS specification were used for all equations involving estimates of B. (In equations involving estimates of A and RA, the CRS and IRS estimates of $\sigma^2(\zeta)$ were generally nearly identical.) Otherwise, the approach described above either yielded an approximate fixed point directly or made it easy to obtain such a point with one additional iteration.

REFERENCES

AITCHESON, J. and BROWN, J. A. C., 1963, *The Lognormal Distribution* (Cambridge University Press, Cambridge).

BAIN, J. S., 1951, 'Relation of Profit Rate to Industry Concentration: American Manufacturing, 1936–1940', *Quarterly Journal of Economics*, 65 (August), pp. 293–324.

BROZEN, Y., 1982, *Concentration, Mergers, and Public Policy* (Macmillan, New York).

CARTER, J. R., 1978, 'Collusion, Efficiency, and Antitrust', *Journal of Law and Economics*, 21 (October), pp. 435–444.

CAVES, R. E. and PORTER, M. E., 1977, 'From Entry Barriers to Mobility Barriers: Conjectural Decisions and Contrived Deterrence to New Competition', *Quarterly Journal of Economics*, 91 (May), pp. 241–261.

CAVES, R. E. and PORTER, M. E., 1980, 'The Dynamics of Changing Seller Concentration', *Journal of Industrial Economics*, 29 (September), pp. 1–15.

CAVES, R. E. and PUGEL, T. A., 1980, *Intraindustry Differences in Conduct and Performance: Viable Strategies in U.S. Manufacturing Industries* (New York University Graduate School of Business Administration, Salomon Brothers Center for the Study of Financial Institutions, New York).

CLARKE, R. and DAVIES, S. W., 1982, 'Market Structure and Price-Cost Margins', *Economica* 49 (August 1982), pp. 277–287.

CLARKE, R., DAVIES, S. W. and WATERSON, M., 1984, 'The Profitability—Concentration Relation: Market Power or Efficiency?', *Journal of Industrial Economics*, 32 (June), pp. 435–450.

COMANOR, W. S. and WILSON, T. A., 1974, *Advertising and Market Power* (Harvard University Press, Cambridge).

DASKIN, A. J., 1983, 'Essays on Firm Diversification and Market Concentration', Ph.D. dissertation, M.I.T.

DEMSETZ, H., 1973, 'Industry Structure, Market Rivalry, and Public Policy', *Journal of Law and Economics*, 16 (April), pp. 1–10.

DEMSETZ, H., 1974, 'Two Systems of Belief about Monopoly', in H. GOLDSCHMIDT, H. M. MANN and J. F. WESTON (eds.), *Industrial Concentration: The New Learning* (Little-Brown, Boston).

DEMSETZ, H., 1979, 'Accounting for Advertising as a Barrier to Entry', *Journal of Business*, 52 (July), pp. 345–360.

DOMOWITZ, I., HUBBARD, R. G. and PETERSEN, B. C., 1986, 'Business Cycles and the Relationship Between Concentration and Price-Cost Margins', *Rand Journal of Economics*, 17 (Spring), pp. 1–17.

Dornbusch, R. and Fischer, S., 1981, *Macroeconomics*, 2nd Ed. (McGraw-Hill, New York).

Hanushek, E. A., 1974, 'Efficient Estimators for Regressing Regression Coefficients', *American Statistician*, 28 (May), pp. 66–67.

Jovanovic, B., 1982, 'Selection and the Evolution of Industry', *Econometrica*, 50 (May), pp. 649–670.

Kreps, D. M. and Scheinkman, J. A., 1983, 'Quantity Precommitment and Bertrand Competition Yield Cournot Outcomes', *Bell Journal of Economics*, 14 (Autumn), pp. 326–337.

Kwoka, J. E., Jr. and Ravenscraft, D. J., 1986, 'Cooperation vs. Rivalry: Price-Cost Margins by Line of Business', *Economica*, 53 (August), pp. 351–363.

Lippman, S. A. and Rumelt, R. P., 1982, 'Uncertain Imitability: An Analysis of Interfirm Differences in Efficiency under Competition', *Bell Journal of Economics*, 13 (Autumn), pp. 418–438.

Long, W. F., 1982, 'Market Share, Concentration and Profits: Intra-Industry and Inter-industry Evidence', mimeographed, US Federal Trade Commission, October.

Lustgarten, S., 1979, 'Gains and Losses from Industrial Concentration: A Comment', *Journal of Law and Economics*, 22 (April), pp. 183–190.

Lustgarten, S., 1984, *Productivity and Prices: The Consequences of Industrial Concentration* (American Enterprise Institute, Washington).

Marcus, M., 1969, 'Profitability and Size of Firm: Some Further Evidence', *Review of Economics and Statistics*, 51 (February), pp. 104–107.

Ornstein, S. I., 1977, *Industrial Concentration and Advertising Intensity* (American Enterprise Institute, Washington).

Peltzman, S., 1977, 'The Gains and Losses from Industrial Concentration', *Journal of Law and Economics*, 20 (October), pp. 229–263.

Peltzman, S., 1979, 'The Causes and Consequences of Rising Industrial Concentration: A Reply', *Journal of Law and Economics*, 22 (April), pp. 209–211.

Porter, M. E., 1979, 'The Structure Within Industries and Companies' Performance', *Review of Economics and Statistics*, 61 (May), pp. 214–227.

Prais, S. J., 1976, *The Evolution of Giant Firms in Britain* (Cambridge University Press, Cambridge).

Ravenscraft, D. J., 1983, 'Structure-Profit Relationships at the Line of Business and Industry Level', *Review of Economics and Statistics*, 65 (February), pp. 22–31.

Round, D. K., 1975, 'Industry Structure, Market Rivalry and Public Policy: Some Australian Evidence', *Journal of Law and Economics*, 18 (April), pp. 273–281.

Salamon, G. L., 1985, 'Accounting Rates of Return', *American Economic Review*, 75 (June), pp. 495–504.

Saxonhouse, G. R., 1977, 'Regressions from Samples Having Different Characteristics', *Review of Economics and Statistics*, 59 (May), pp. 234–237.

Scherer, F. M., 1979, 'The Causes and Consequences of Rising Industrial Concentration', *Journal of Law and Economics*, 22 (April), pp. 191–208.

Scherer, F. M., 1980, *Industrial Market Structure and Economic Performance*, 2nd Ed. (Rand-McNally, Chicago).

Schmalensee, R., 1977, 'Using the *H*-Index of Concentration with Published Data', *Review of Economics and Statistics*, 59 (May), pp. 186–193.

Schmalensee, R., 1985, 'Do Markets Differ Much?', *American Economic Review*, 75 (June), pp. 341–351.

Spiller, P. T. and Favaro, E., 1984, 'The Effects of Banking Regulation on Oligopolistic Interaction: The Uruguayan Banking Sector', *Rand Journal of Economics*, 15 (Summer), pp. 244–254.

Stigler, G. J., 1964, 'A Theory of Oligopoly', *Journal of Political Economy*, 72 (February), 44–61.

SWAMY, P. A. V. B., 1970, 'Efficient Inference in a Random Coefficient Regression Model', *Econometrica*, 38 (March), pp. 311–323.

TELSER, L., 1982, 'A Theory of Innovation and its Effects', *Bell Journal of Economics*, 13 (Spring), pp. 69–92.

WEISS, L. W. and PASCOE, G., 1985, 'Concentration, X-Inefficiency and Mr. Peltzman's Superior Firms', University of Wisconsin—Madison, Social Systems Research Institute, Workshop Series Paper 8501.

THE CONVERGENCE OF PROFITS IN THE LONG RUN: INTER-FIRM AND INTER-INDUSTRY COMPARISONS*

J. CUBBIN AND P. GEROSKI

This paper considers the extent to which the short run dynamic behaviour and long run equilibrium levels of profitability differ amongst firms within the same industry. Movements in profits are modelled in terms of firm specific deviations from average industry profits, and industry specific deviations from economy wide average returns. Applied to a sample of 217 large UK firms, 1951–1977, the results suggest that considerable heterogeneities exist within most industries. That is, most firms' profitability experience differs considerably from those of their closest rivals.

I. INTRODUCTION

IT HAS long been conventional to treat the industry as a basic unit of analysis when considering the performance of firms and markets. Under the presumption of what Porter [1979] calls the "shared asset" theory of profit determination, industrial economists have compared average levels of profitability across industries, looking for significant differences associated with variations in the level of industry concentration, and other market structure variables. A vast body of results have persuaded most scholars that such differences do exist, and are important. However, a concern with industry averages implicitly assumes that intra-industry variations in profits are small and uncorrelated with market structure. If this assumption is not true, then it is no longer obvious that analysis at the industry level is interesting or important.[1]

In fact, it does seem to be the case that the "shared asset" theory may have missed the mark. Porter's [1979] examination of traditional profits—concentration models for leaders (large firms) and followers (small firms) shows clear differences between the two groups, and a variety of studies have suggested that the gains to market power are not evenly distributed amongst small and

* We are obliged to D. Allard, T. Mahmood, R. Masson, J. Schwalbach, R. Schmalensee, H. Yamawaki, J. Watters and participants at seminars at Southampton, Sheffield, KUL Leuven, the EEC Commission, and the IIM, Berlin for helpful remarks. Dennis Mueller and the Editors provided extensive comments which helped us to substantially improve the first draft. Financial assistance from the IIM and the Office of Fair Trading is gratefully acknowledged. The usual disclaimer applies.

[1] Needless to say, there are other reasons for shifting away from "the industry" as the central unit of analysis, including the increasing diversification across markets of large firms. Further, the notion of "the industry" has always generated unease when applied to markets where goods are extensively differentiated.

large firms in different industries (e.g. Caves and Pugel [1980]; Clarke *et al.* [1984]; Schmalensee [1986]; and others cited therein). In a similar vein, several scholars have found market share to be an important determinant of relative firm profitability, and frequently to be more important than industry wide structural traits such as concentration (e.g. Martin [1983]; Ravenscraft [1983]; Gale [1972]; Shepherd [1972]; and others). Quite how to interpret these "revisionist" studies (the term is due to Schmalensee [1985]) is sometimes a little problematic, but it seems clear that much significant variation in performance occurs within industries.

There are several ways to assess the relative importance of firm specific and industry wide factors in determining any particular firm's profitability. Intra and inter-industry "effects" on profitability are sometimes deduced from co-efficients on variables like market share and industry concentration. Whilst appeal to explicit structural models can sharpen this interpretation, there always exist some doubts with this procedure at a purely statistical level. An ingenious alternative (he calls it a "descriptive" rather than a "structural" approach) has been proposed by Schmalensee [1985], who uses an analysis of variance framework to decompose variation in performance into "industry", "firm", and "market share" effects. Somewhat surprisingly, he finds the first to be overwhelmingly important in a sample of US industries in the mid-1970s. In this paper, we propose to explore a third route. All of the work discussed thus far is cross-section in nature, and, following Mueller [1977], [1986], we shall work with an explicitly dynamic model applied to times series data.[2] In a kindred spirit to Schmalensee, we will examine the co-variance between profit paths across firms in a given industry. To the extent that there are important correlations between the movements in profitability of firms in the same industry, then clearly "industry effects" are present and important. However, to the extent that the profit experiences of firms in the same industry over time are unrelated, then "industry effects" diminish in importance. Our major concern is to discover how important "industry effects" are in the UK.

The plan of the paper is as follows. In section II, we develop our empirical model. Its essence is an equation in which a firm's current profits are decomposed into firm and industry specific components, each of which are assumed to follow their own separate dynamic path. In section III, we develop interpretations of the parameters of the model, treating the question of the relative importance of "firm" and "industry" effects as a model selection

[2] There are several reasons for this choice (discussed more extensively in Geroski [1985]). The main one is our concern that exogenous events which affect large and small firms unequally can make cross-sections of particular years difficult to interpret. For example, negative correlations between profits and concentration using the 1975 Line of Business data have been attributed to the effects of recession and energy price shocks particularly on capital intensive, highly concentrated sectors. See, for example, Martin [1983]; Ravenscraft [1983]; this effect also seems present in Schmalensee [1985].

problem. Section IV presents some results from applying the model to a sample of 217 UK firms, 1951–1977, and section V contains a few final thoughts.

II. THE MODEL

Consider some firm i in industry I. Suppose that i's current profit rate is $\pi_i(t)$, and that there is, in principle, a long run equilibrium profit rate, $\pi^*(t)$, common to all firms in all industries. In general one is unlikely to observe $\pi_i(t) = \pi^*(t)$. This can arise either because i is not in long run equilibrium at t, or because i's long run equilibrium profit rate differs from $\pi^*(t)$. Thus, entry barriers and other industry specific factors may drive a wedge between $\pi^*(t)$ and the average profit rate earned by members of industry I, $\pi_I(t)$. Further, mobility barriers and a host of firm specific factors may also allow individual firms in I to earn returns different from $\pi_I(t)$, even in the long run. Our maintained hypothesis is that i's current profit rate is determined by $\pi^*(t)$ and $\pi_I(t)$, and the dynamic forces that generate adjustment towards them within and between industries. Defining

$$\rho(t) \equiv \pi_i(t) - \pi^*(t) = [\pi_i(t) - \pi_I(t)] + [\pi_I(t) - \pi^*(t)] \equiv \rho(i, t) + \rho(I, t) \tag{1}$$

we propose to model $\rho(t)$ by directly modelling movements in $\rho(i, t)$ and $\rho(I, t)$.

The main problem with modelling $\rho(i, t)$ and $\rho(I, t)$ is that many of the factors which induce adjustment towards equilibrium are almost impossible to measure. Not only is it the case that actual flows of entry into industries or into strategic groups within industries are often difficult to observe, but entry need not actually occur to have an effect on profits. That is, the mere threat of entry may lead to pre-emptive moves (such as limit pricing). Other dynamic forces, such as imitation or capacity expansion by incumbents, can also have a potent effect on market performance before they actually occur. Hence, dynamic empirical models of profitability must come to terms with a basic latent variables problem that affects the equations which describe movements in profitability out of equilibrium. Our solution to this problem is as follows.

Consider first $\rho(I, t)$. The difference between average industry profits and the long run rate $\pi^*(t)$ declines towards zero as new firms enter the industry, as incumbents expand, and as competitors initiate each other's strategies and attempt to pre-empt rivals. Let us collectively refer to these actions as "entry". While the precise mechanism of how "entry" operates to affect performance is generally illuminated by a wave of the hand, what lies at the base of most arguments is a proportional error control mechanism in which profits and "entry" interact. In this spirit, we assume that "entry" occurs whenever $\rho(I, t) > 0$, and that "entry" affects both the long run level of $\rho(I, t)$ as well as the speed of adjustment towards that long run. Thus,

(2) $$E(t) = \alpha_I \rho(I, t-1) + \mu(I, t)$$

(3) $$\Delta\rho(I, t) = \beta_I E(t) + \theta_I \rho(I, t-1) + \varepsilon(I, t)$$

where $E(t)$ is "entry" and $\Delta\rho(I, t) \equiv \rho(I, t) - \rho(I, t-1)$.[3] By construction, $\mu(I, t)$ and $\varepsilon(I, t)$ are orthogonal to $\rho(I, t-1)$ and $E(t)$ respectively, and they represent "all other forces".[4] Since $E(t)$ is latent, it is impossible to estimate α_I, β_I, and θ_I. It is, however, possible to assess their combined effects by substituting (2) into (3) to get

(4) $$\begin{aligned}\rho(I, t) &= (1 + \alpha_I \beta_I + \theta_I)\rho(I, t-1) + \beta_I \mu(I, t) + \varepsilon(I, t) \\ &\equiv \lambda_I \rho(I, t-1) + v(I, t)\end{aligned}$$

If "entry" is strongly attracted by $\rho(I, t) > 0$ and, in turn, has a strong impact on average industry profitability, and if, in addition, this process is stable, then $\lambda_I \rightarrow 0$. This implies that $\rho(I, t)$ is always at or near its long run level, varying only in response to unsystematic factors. In contrast, if dynamic forces are weak, then $\lambda_I \rightarrow 1$ and profits can persist out of equilibrium for long periods of time.

Consider now $\rho(i, t)$. Here things are more complex. Imagine that firm i occupies some niche or strategic position i in industry I. Then $\rho(i, t) > 0$ signals that firm i is earning returns above those earned on average in the industry, and this can be expected to set in motion a response directed at i's strategic position. New firms may threaten or attempt to enter, incumbents in other market niches may contemplate diversification, and firm i may choose to expand capacity and/or pre-empt rivals. Let us refer to all of this activity collectively as "mobility", $M_i(t)$. It is also possible that when $\rho(i, t) > 0$, these forces set in motion by $\rho(I, t) > 0$ (i.e. "entry") may particularly affect i. Hence, the analogue of (2) and (3) for $\rho(i, t)$ takes the form

(5) $$M_i(t) = \alpha_i \rho(i, t-1) + \mu(i, t)$$

(6) $$\Delta\rho(i, t) = \beta_i M(i, t) + \gamma_i E(t) + \varepsilon(i, t) + \theta_i \rho(i, t-1)$$

[3] It is conventional to write entry equations in the form $E(t) = \alpha[\pi(t) - \bar{\pi}]$, where $\bar{\pi}$ is some level of "limit profits" (for a survey, see Geroski [1983]). This is consistent with (2), given suitable interpretation of $\mu(I, t)$. In (3), if $\theta_I = 0$, then at $E(t) = 0$, $\Delta\rho(I, t)$ is a random walk. Since, in this case, there is a non-zero probability that $\rho(I, t) \rightarrow \pm\infty$ at some $t < \infty$, then $\theta_I \neq 0$ is necessary to insure a satisfactory specification of long run $\rho(I, t)$. (3) is the reduced form of a two step process: "entry" changes market structure, and changes in structure change performance. For a fuller discussion of this structural model (and a survey of the empirical work done on it), see Geroski and Masson [1986].

[4] Since we have defined "entry" broadly to include all systematic dynamic forces interacting with profits, it is natural to assume that the factors summarized by $\mu(I, t)$ and $\varepsilon(I, t)$ are unsystematic. A firm might "get lucky" and earn high profits for several years running, but evidently this kind of "luck" requires weak competitive reactions from rivals if it is to persist. There is nothing in this, however, that rules out a non-zero mean for either $\mu(I, t)$ or $\varepsilon(I, t)$, insuring $\pi_I(t) \neq \pi^*(t)$ even in the long run.

where $\mu(i, t)$ and $\varepsilon(i, t)$ capture unsystematic forces in the manner of $\mu(I, t)$ and $\varepsilon(I, t)$. Since $M_i(t)$ is clearly latent, we follow the same procedure as before, yielding

$$(7) \qquad \rho(i, t) = (1 - \alpha_i\beta_i + \theta_i)\rho(i, t-1) + \gamma_i E(t) + \beta_i\mu(i, t) + \varepsilon(i, t)$$
$$\equiv \lambda_i\rho(i, t-1) + \gamma_i E(t) + v(i, t)$$

Equation (7) describes firm specific deviations from average industry profitability as a simple autoregressive process like (4), augmented by possible additional feedback as inter-industry forces generated by $\rho(I, t) \neq 0$ concentrate particularly on firm i's niche in industry I. That is, the process describing $\rho(i, t)$ differs from that describing $\rho(I, t)$ to the extent that i is more or less vulnerable than average to the effects of "entry". The speeds of the two processes differ according to the relative strength of "entry" and "mobility".

Using (2) and then substituting (7) and (4) into (1), we arrive at the basic model describing $\rho(t)$,

$$(8) \qquad \rho(t) = \lambda_i\rho(i, t-1) + \phi_i\rho(I, t-1) + \eta(i, t)$$

as a first order process defined on its two components plus an unknown, unsystematic term $\eta(i, t)$, where $\lambda_i \equiv (1 + \alpha_i\beta_i + \theta_i)$ and $\phi_i \equiv (\gamma_i\alpha_i + \lambda_I) = (\gamma_i\alpha_i + 1 + \alpha_I\beta_I + \theta_I)$. The mean of $\eta(i, t)$ is the sum of the means of $v(I, t)$ and $v(i, t)$ which serve to determine the long run departures of average profits in I from that common to all industries, and of i's profits from those of rivals in I. The two components of $\rho(t)$ which determine its motion are firm and industry specific, and to each there is a firm specific response. The response λ_i to the firm specific component of motion $\rho(i, t-1)$ depends on the firm specific factors α_i, β_i, and θ_i which govern "mobility" into i's market niche. The response ϕ_i to the industry specific component of motion $\rho(I, t-1)$ depends on the factors describing how "entry" bids down profits on average in the industry, α_I, β_I and θ_I, and takes on a firm specific value only if i's strategic position in the industry is unusually vulnerable to "entry" (that is $\gamma_i \neq \gamma$).

III. INTERPRETING THE MODEL

There are several types of question that (8) can be used to illuminate. Our major interest is to assess the relative importance of firm and industry effects in explaining movements in $\rho(t)$ over time. This requires that one assess the extent to which equations like (8) share common parameters when applied to individual members i of some industry I. For example, in the limit all i in I may exhibit identical parameters and innovations $\eta(i, t)$, in which case aggregating (8) and examining dynamics at industry level involves no sacrifice of information. Conversely, a collection of firms that are not affected by similar dynamic forces will reveal no common parameter values, and aggregation is likely to be worse than useless. The best way to proceed is to structure a set of nested tests in which one moves towards models in which all

i in I have more unknown parameters in common. Essentially, this converts the assessment of firm and industry effects into a model selection problem.

Consider, for example, an industry I with two members, $i = 1, 2$. A regression model of (8) is a system

$$(9) \qquad \begin{cases} \rho_1(t) = \delta_1 + \lambda_1 \rho(1, t-1) + \phi_1 \rho(I, t-1) + \omega(1, t) \\ \rho_2(t) = \delta_2 + \lambda_2 \rho(2, t-2) + \phi \rho_2(I, t-1) + \omega(2, t) \end{cases}$$

where $\eta(i, t) \equiv \delta_i + \omega(i, t)$, and so $\omega(i, t)$ is a zero-mean white noise process. Now, it is evident that $\rho_1(t)$ and $\rho_2(t)$ share a common term, $v(I, t)$, and so are not fully independent. This is reflected in a non-zero covariance between $\omega(1, t)$ and $\omega(2, t)$ in (9). There are two parameter restrictions that can be applied to (9) which weaken even this limited interdependence between $\rho_1(t)$ and $\rho_2(t)$. First, they may be stochastically independent, so that there are virtually no unsystematic factors (like macroeconomic events or industry changes unrelated to "entry") that have a common effect on both firms. This restriction yields

(10) (9) plus $\text{cov}\,[\omega(1, t), \omega(2, t)] = 0$

Further, their response to industry wide factors $\rho(I, t-1)$ may be the same as their response to firm specific factors $\rho(i, t-1)$, yielding

(11) (10) plus $\lambda_i = \phi_i$

This second restriction reduces (9) to a first order autoregression in $\rho(t)$, suggesting that $\pi_i(t)$ moves with reference only to $\pi^*(t)$ and not $\pi_I(t)$. In this event, firm i's profits follow a dynamic path truly independent of those rivals in I. Hence, as we move from model (9) to model (11), firms i in industry I reveal themselves to be increasingly unrelated. Information about the movement in profits of any of i's rivals is less helpful in predicting movements in i's own profits.

Now consider the alternative possibility that firms respond in a similar fashion to the systematic forces that affect them. If $\gamma_i = \gamma$, then "entry" affects all industry members in the same way, and so all $\rho(t)$ react in a similar fashion to the common value $\rho(I, t-1)$. In this case, (9) becomes

(12) (9) plus $\phi_1 = \phi_2 = \phi$

Somewhat stronger is the notion that firms may also respond to firm specific forces in the same manner. This arises if "mobility" affects all firms i in I to the same degree, and can be represented with restrictions on (9) that transform it into

(13) (12) plus $\lambda_1 = \lambda_2 = \lambda$

Finally, firms may respond in the same fashion to both $\rho(i, t-1)$ and $\rho(I, t-1)$, thus eliminating the distinction between firm and industry specific effects. This final possibility is

(14) (13) plus $\lambda = \phi$

Like (11), (14), reduces (9) to a first order autoregression in $\rho(t)$. However, unlike (11), the system (14) models firms as experiencing common effects from the occurrence of unsystematic factors ($\text{cov}\,[\omega(1,\text{t}), \omega(2,\text{t})] \neq 0$), and as responding in identical fashion to $\rho(t-1)$. If, in addition to (14), $\delta_1 = \delta_2$, then firms i in I differ only randomly. Clearly, in this case aggregation of (14) to industry level would involve no sacrifice in information and, in this sense,

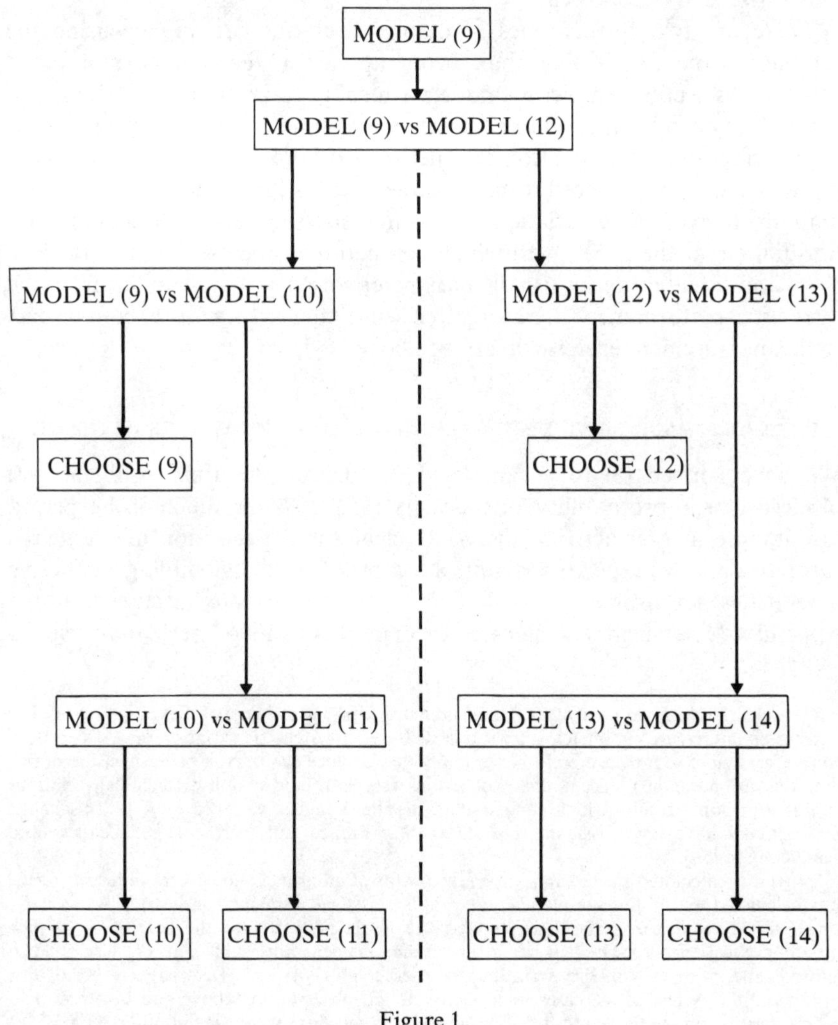

Figure 1
The Decision Tree

only the industry matters in describing movements in $\pi_i(t)$. The consequence is that information on movements in the profits of any of i's rivals will be useful in predicting movements in i's profits.

Thus, we can rank industries according to the inter-dependence of their member firms. Those industries that provide the weakest forces binding firms' profits together are represented by systems (11) and (10); those industries in which firms are clearly interdependent are represented by systems (14), (13), (12) and (9). The obvious nesting of these possibilities suggests that an appropriate testing procedure is to start with (9) and simplify as appropriate, allocating industries to one of the six possible models. Figure 1 shows the decision tree to be followed.

There are two further lines of inquiry that one can pursue using the estimates from (9). Rather than being applied to explain current profit rates, cross-section empirical models which purport to explain long run profitability can be applied to explaining variations in δ_i across firms (this is the methodological innovation of Mueller [1986]). Further, variations in the parameters, λ_i and ϕ_i need to be explained across firms and industries. This amounts to explaining variations across industries in the duration of disequilibrium; i.e. in the speed with which competitive processes occur.[5] Both of these additional exercises use the parameters of (9) in ways familiar from the "structure-performance" literature. In a sense, they are a natural counterpart to the measurement exercise described above.

IV. SOME MEASUREMENT TESTING: INDUSTRY AND FIRM EFFECTS IN THE UK

We have applied (8) to a sample of 217 large UK firms, using annual observations in profitability for the years 1951–1977. As much of this period saw intense merger activity, there is a clear sample selection bias towards survivors, and we experienced quite a few problems in assembling a cohesive data series on profits for each firm. These issues are discussed in the Appendix.[6] Each firm was allocated to an industry and, of the 48 industries so

[5] It is clear that the variance of $\eta(i, t)$ in (8) is an upper bound estimate of that of $\varepsilon(i, t)$ in (6). The latter is an interesting parameter, since it reflects the non-systematic variation in $\rho(t)$. This is, of course, very close to a measure of risk: certainly the variance of $\varepsilon(i, t)$ is a better measure of risk than the variance of $\rho(t)$, since it reflects only non-systematic (and so non-predictable) variations in $\rho(t)$. For some results which suggest that, despite a higher variance of $\rho(t)$, firms in the UK actually have lower risk (in this sense) than France and Germany, see Geroski and Jacquemin [1986].

[6] $\pi_I(t)$ was calculated as the sample average profits of all firms i allocated to industry I; $\pi^*(t)$ was calculated as the full sample average profits across all firms and industries. At an early stage in the empirical analysis we entered the levels of $\pi_I(t)$ into the regression to pick up any cyclical effects. Neither it nor a time trend was generally significant. We also tried to allow λ_i and ϕ_i to vary in size according to whether $\rho(i, t-1)$ and $\rho(I, t-1)$ were positive or negative. In very few of the cases were there enough observations above and below zero to satisfactorily estimate these additional parameters. When there were, we did observe signs that adjustment to profits above "the norm" differs from adjustment below "the norm".

chosen, 10 contained only one firm (which, automatically, meant selection of model (11) for these 10 industries). The remaining 38 industries were allocated to models (9)–(14) using Likelihood Ratio tests on the parameter restrictions discussed in section III. The cross-equation constraints and correlations between errors led us to estimate models (9), (12)–(14) using Full Information Maximum Likelihood methods, while (10) and (11) were estimated using OLS.[7]

Of the 38 multi-firm industries, 12 were best explained by (9), 8 by (12), 5 by (13), 12 by (14) and 1 by (10). In making this classification, we used conservative criteria. Whenever an industry allocation was marginal between two models, we allocated it to the more general model.[8] Models (12)–(14) are those where "the industry matters" in the sense that values of λ_i, ϕ_i or both are common to all i in I. In models (9)–(11), there are no common responses to firm or industry effects even when these can be distinguished. Further, in (10)–(11), there are even no common responses to unsystematic factors. Thus, these numbers imply that the firms in just under 35% of our 38 industries showed no systematic cohesion in the sense of common responses to industry or firm specific forces.[9] Since the number of firms per industry varies, another way to summarize these results is the following. Roughly 39% of the 217 firms covered were best described by (9), 24% by (12), 6% by (13), 25% by (14), 1% by (10), and 5% by (11). Hence, about only 55% of the firms covered exhibited at least *some* dynamic communality with rivals in the same industry, and very few, if any, appeared capable of being subsumed into an "average" or "representative' firm along the lines of the "shared asset" theory.

Roughly 70% of the firms in our sample showed differences in response to firm and industry forces (i.e. those allocated models (9), (10), (12), (13)). Of these 153 firms, about 90 (or about 59%) exhibited more sensitivity to $\rho(i, t-1)$ than to $\rho(I, t-1)$. Of the 207 firms in the 38 industries with more than one firm, 24 firms in 17 industries (or, about 12% and 45% respectively) showed λ_i not significantly different from zero, while 76 firms in 19 industries (or, about 37% and 50% respectively) showed ϕ_i not significantly different

[7] Although (8) does not involve a lag dependent variable, it is easy to see departures from white noise generating bias because of the way $\rho(t)$ is constructed from $\rho(i, t)$ and $\rho(I, t)$. Further, departures from white noise correspond to the persistence of "luck", an interesting hypothesis in its own right (as mentioned in footnote 4). All regressions were examined for serial correlation, and this proved not to be a cause for concern; see also Geroski and Jacquemin [1986] for further and more elaborate testing on a different sample which, nonetheless, yielded similar results.

[8] Seven industries were found to be marginal at various stages of the decision tree, and they were allocated as follows: 3 to (9), 2 to (12) and 2 to (13).

[9] A further observation is in order. There was a tendency for industries allocated to (9) and (12) to have also a larger number of constituent members (7 or so on average, as compared to an average of 3 or 4 for the others). Closer inspection suggests that, in the larger population industries allocated to (9) and (12), there were subsets of firms that could have been simplified (on their own) down to models (12)–(14). To us, this kind of result suggests that "strategic groups" (Caves and Porter [1977]) are, perhaps, the most appropriate unit of analysis.

from zero. Thus, industry specific forces frequently provoked a more substantial response than firm specific ones, suggesting that "entry" is stronger and more effective than "mobility", or (roughly) that "mobility" barriers are higher than "entry" barriers. Many firms seem to inhabit market niches better protected than those on average in their industry.

The estimated values of λ_i and ϕ_i exhibited quite a bit of variation in size across the sample, although 50% of both the λ_i and the ϕ_i exceeded 0.500. While there is some reason to believe that these understate the true values of ϕ_i and λ_i for purely statistical reasons,[10] these values are nonetheless of interest. For a process $\rho(t) = \beta\rho(t-1)+\mu(t)$, a value of $\beta = 0.0500$ implies that an initial departure of π_i from π^* of 10% will take about three years to return to within 1% of π^*. While there were firms in the sample whose profits persistently exceeded "the norm" for long periods of time, the dynamic forces operating on the "median" firm appear to be fairly strong. This is particularly the case with the industry wide adjustment associated with "entry".

Finally, about 66% of firms in our sample exhibited a constant not significantly different from zero, with about 17% showing positive values. This is evidence pointing towards the notion that returns are not equalized across all firms and sectors even in the long run. Whilst two thirds of our sample converged towards a common profitability level, a solid core of firms appear able to maintain some independence from market forces more or less indefinitely.

There are a number of ways to describe the observed inter-firm and inter-industry heterogeneity in these estimated parameters. Perhaps the simplest is to regress the estimated parameters on various structural variables of interest, looking for simple patterns of association or broad tendencies within the data. It should be emphasized that this is largely a descriptive exercise, and the results are limited to the 60% or so of the 38 industries for which we could get satisfactory data. While any familiar structural variable (relating, as appropriate, to firm or industry) will prove informative in an exercise like this, it is worth focusing attention on those that seem to be putative candidates for explaining how fast market dynamics work.

Consider first explaining variations in the response to industry effects. It proved to be almost impossible to account for variations in ϕ at all. Somewhat more success was achieved when we tried to account for which model the various industries were allocated to. In particular, it proved to be possible to differentiate industries allocated to model (9) from the rest. The first equation on Table I shows that these industries differ from the rest largely in being high advertising, high import, low growth and low export

[10] See, for example, Johnston [1972, p. 305]. A statistical model $x(t) = \beta x(t-1)+\mu(t)$ produces an estimate of β, $E\{\beta\}$, which depends on the number of observations used. Thus, $E\{\beta\} = \beta(1-2/T) < \beta$, where T is the number of observations. For $t = 26$, our sample size, $E\{\beta\} = (0.923)\beta$, so that an 8% upward correction of the estimates might be appropriate.

TABLE I

Dependent Variable	Constant	GR	SF	CON	DV	LF	AS	ES	IS	$\bar{R}^2$
M1	−0.1856 (−0.6822)	−0.1433 (−2.049)	0.1740 (0.2821)	0.8363 (1.872)	0.0194 (1.733)	−0.7731 (1.9211)	11.845 (3.106)	−0.6405 (−2.347)	1.324 (3.315)	0.2517
M2	0.1421 (0.4264)	−0.0696 (−0.8121)	−0.6147 (−0.8127)	−0.0909 (−0.1660)	0.00006 (0.0047)	0.5854 (1.184)	−0.2185 (−0.0461)	0.2663 (0.7959)	−0.3221 (0.6577)	−0.1248
M234	0.5496 (1.425)	−0.322 (−0.3244)	−1.459 (−1.667)	−0.4342 (−0.6830)	0.0032 (0.2096)	0.9332 (1.616)	−2.8705 (−0.5304)	0.3541 (0.9145)	−0.3926 (−0.6927)	−0.0338

M1 = 1 if industry is allocated to (9); zero otherwise.
M2 = 1 if industry is allocated to (12); zero otherwise.
M234 = 1 if industry is allocated to (12), (13), or (14); zero otherwise.
GR = average industry (sales) growth, 1968–1973.
SF = % of industry output accounted for by foreign owned firms, 1968.
CON = 5-firm industry concentration ratio, 1968.
DV = index of diversification.
LF = % industry output accounted for by firms in *Times* top 200.
AS = advertising intensity, 1968.
GS = export intensity, 1968.
IS = import intensity, 1968.
t-statistics in brackets under estimated coefficients.

TABLE II

	"Industry" Variables						"Company" Variables							
	Constant	SF	CON	DV	AS	GS	IS	ASSETS	M5	ACQ	PROD	GROW	CAPINT	$\bar{R}^2$	N
(1)	60.00 (6.04)	−0.154 (−0.676)	0.185 (1.53)	−0.480 (−1.21)	−775 (2.25)	1.27 (0.35)	−42.9 (−1.67)							0.097	88
(2)	45.366 (4.78)							−0.000006 (−0.474)	−0.00035 (−0.401)	−0.152 (−0.971)	−0.028 (1.09)	15.29 (1.35)	0.491 (1.69)	0.0046	133
(3)	37.22 (2.52)	−0.432 (−1.35)	0.379 (2.17)	0.020 (0.033)	40.7 (0.426)	−24.6 (0.457)	−12.8 (−0.398)	−0.000009 (−0.573)	0.0018 (−1.30)	−0.1679 (0.877)	−0.0004 (0.011)	4.11 (0.274)	0.184 (0.489)	0.0082	83
(4)	0.075 (0.054)	−0.021 (−0.626)	−0.0027 (0.161)	0.0071 (0.126)	18.86 (0.419)	4.64 (0.949)	−3.27 (−0.810)							−0.045	88
(5)	−0.462 (−3.42)							0.000005 (2.51)	0.000028 (0.296)	−0.033 (−2.16)	0.0013 (4.04)	5.92 (3.67)	−0.085 (−2.27)	0.119	132
(6)	−4.37 (−0.35)	−0.081 (−2.08)	−0.0024 (−0.124)	0.060 (0.853)	−2.17 (−0.196)	−1.62 (−0.268)	0.270 (0.063)	0.000004 (3.11)	0.00004 (3.45)	−0.031 (−1.78)	0.0065 (1.56)	5.73 (2.94)	−0.092 (−2.01)	0.154	83

ASSETS = Assets in 1973, £'000.
MS = "Market share" = company sales (1973)/industry sales (1968) at SIC level.
ACQ = Number of acquisitions, 1951–1973.
PROD = Increase in productivity (rate of change of sales per employee), 1968–73.
GROW = (ASSETS 1973 − ASSETS 1951)/ASSETS 1973.
CAPINT = ASSETS/EMPLOYEE, 1973.
The dependent variable is λ_i in the first three regressions, and the constant from (8) in the second three. All regressions are weighted to correct for the heteroscedasticity arising from using an estimated coefficient as a dependent variable; see Saxonhouse [1977].

industries.[11] If one takes the view that much trade is intra-industry trade in brand variants of several basic goods, then the first two correlations point to industries which exhibit considerable product heterogeneity. It is easy to believe that firms in such industries will often differ from each other. It is rather less obvious why they might be slow growing or less export intensive. The second and third equations on Table I illustrate the kinds of results that we uncovered in trying to explain allocation into any of the other models, or into groups of them. The strongest and, unhappily, rather negative conclusion that one can draw from Table I is that the kinds of factors which often explain average industry profits seem much less suited to accounting for the speed of industry dynamics.

Much the same conclusion seems warranted when we look at the possible determinants of the company adjustment rates, λ_i, and the determinants of long run equilibria. Table II reports the results of regression analysis of these coefficients against the same industry variables as in Table I plus company specific variables calculated from published information. The first three equations explore the determinants of λ_i. It seems clear that most of the rather small explanation achieved is due to industry characteristics, particularly industry concentration (and, somewhat less, advertising and imports). Firms in highly concentrated industries adjust much more slowly towards long run equilibrium profit rates. The second three equations on Table II explore some of the characteristics of these long run equilibria. Here industry characteristics play almost no role (barring, perhaps, the extent of foreign ownership). Large, productive and fast growing firms all earn higher profits in the long run; acquisition oriented firms in highly capital intensive industries earn lower returns in the long run. None of these correlations (barring, perhaps, that relating to size) are very novel or surprising. The lack of significance of industry variables is slightly extreme, but is loosely consistent with the results in much of the literature cited in the Introduction, and by Mueller [1986].

Tables I and II give little reason for thinking that conventional market structure variables are capable of explaining most of the variation in dynamic disequilibrium behaviour that one observes in different firms in different industries. Of most importance are variables like concentration, advertising and import intensity, but even these appear to leave most of the story untold. In view of the importance of firm specific factors, it is probably the case that variables relating to the structure of firms and the quality of their management will prove useful here. Further gains are to be reaped from additional work in this direction.

[11] The regressions on Table I were estimated using OLS. Since the dependent variable is (1, 0), OLS is inefficient. In view of the quality of the results, it did not seem worthwhile doing a GLS or a LOGIT or PROBIT estimation. The coefficient estimates on Table I can be transformed into LOGIT or PROBIT coefficients in a straightforward manner for those interested.

V. CONCLUSIONS

Our main concern in this paper has been with the question of whether the industry is an appropriate unit of analysis when considering the performance of firms and markets. While not exactly a new concern, we have departed from previous work on this subject by conducting our analysis entirely within the framework of a dynamic model of profitability. This has given our analysis what are, perhaps, its two most unusual characteristics. First, the forces of "entry" and "mobility" are not, in general, easy to observe, and this has forced us to treat market dynamics using latent variable techniques. Since market dynamics are often thought to work as simple proportional control feedback mechanisms, the consequence of this latent variables formulation has been empirical models that are essentially autoregressive representations of profitability. Second, while we have followed previous work in using an analysis of variance framework to examine the question at issue, we have been concerned to try to measure the *extent* to which industry and firm effects matter and to relate this to the basic parameters of our simple structural models of market dynamics. This concern gave rise to six models with nested parameter restrictions which provide descriptions of industries ranging from those for which "only the industry matters" to those for which "the industry does not matter".

We have applied these ideas to a sample of medium to large UK firms that were allocated among 48 three-digit industries. Our results are fairly clear and reasonably consistent with the literature cited in the Introduction (save, perhaps, the work of Schmalensee [1985]). Nearly half the firms (or, alternatively, firms in nearly a third of the sample industries) showed no common, industry-wide response to dynamic forces. To be sure, there are factors and forces to which these apparently strange bedfellows all responded, but these were largely stochastic. Our results are also not inconsistent with the notion that "entry" barriers are, perhaps, less formidable on average than "mobility" barriers. Certainly, the systematic persistence of profitability that we do observe arises primarily from persistence in the firm specific component of above average profits rather than from the industry specific component. Finally, a not entirely satisfactory attempt to account for variations across firms and industries in the character of their dynamic behaviour yielded little more than the firm feeling that more work was needed.

It is our view that the research described here is no more than a first step toward a full understanding of market dynamics. We have made a start on a somewhat technical front by confronting and then proposing at least one solution to the classic latent variables problem we believe to be endemic to this area. Perhaps far more substantively, we have found fairly clear reasons to believe that market dynamics within industries are likely to be rather heterogeneous, with differences between firms often persisting for long periods of time. Market power may indeed be a shared asset, but some firms certainly seem to enjoy a good deal more of it for a good deal longer than others.

J. CUBBIN,
Department of Economics,
Queen Mary College,
Mile End Road,
London E1 4NS,
UK.

P. GEROSKI,
Department of Economics,
The University,
Southampton SO9 5NH,
UK.

APPENDIX

The data used in this study were extracted from the databank of company accounts produced jointly by the UK Department of Trade and Industry and the Department of Applied Economics, Cambridge University. These accounts have been standardised to permit more sensible comparisons across different companies and different years than are possible with the raw accounts. The population consists of British quoted companies operating principally in the UK. Certain additional criteria, principally relating to minimum size, were also imposed at various points in the construction of the data set.

The principal problem in using a long series for this population is disappearance through merger, owing to the UK's liberal merger laws. In addition to disappearance of one of the parties to a merger, the surviving company will experience a swelling of both assets and profits. In order to minimise the effects of this, the following procedure was followed:

(1) All companies surviving in the databank from 1951–1977 were identified and used as the basis of the analysis.

(2) A "merger" tree was derived from the databank showing which companies took over which others, making it possible to identify the final location of any disappearing company's assets, where this final location was one of the surviving companies.

(3) This tree was then used to aggregate the accounts of all the companies that ended up together. This eliminates the effect of different gearing ratios (or "leverage") on the volatility of profit rates.

The economy-wide rate of return was based on a similar ratio defined for all firms in the sample, whether they survived for the whole period or not. Both profits and assets were aggregated across the sample and the ratio then used as our indicator. The "industry rate of return" was calculated in the same way, except that the averaging was done across companies classified to the same three-digit industry, (in fact, the classification system of this data is slightly more aggregated than the SIC Minimum List Heading level). Companies are classified to an industry according to their principal activity. A fortunate consequence of the liberal merger laws is that, for the period to which this study relates, horizontal mergers were the preferred variety, so that the possible problems arising from the presence of many highly diversified companies were largely avoided.

REFERENCES

CAVES, R. and PORTER, M., 1977, 'From Entry Barriers to Mobility Barriers', *Quarterly Journal of Economics*, 91, pp. 241–262.

CAVES, R. and PUGEL, T., 1980, 'Intra-industry Differences in Conduct and Performance: Viable Strategies in U.S. Manufacturing Industries', *Monograph Series in Finance and Economics* (NYU Graduate School of Business Administration).

CLARKE, R., DAVIES, S. and WATERSON, M., 1984, 'The Profitability-Concentration Relation: Market Power or Efficiency?', *Journal of Industrial Economics*, 32 (June), pp. 435–450.

GALE, B., 1972, 'Market Share and Rate of Return', *Review of Economics and Statistics*, 54 (November), pp. 412–423.

GEROSKI, P., 1983b, 'The Empirical Analysis of Entry: A Survey', mimeo, University of Southampton.

GEROSKI, P., 1985, 'The Persistence of Profits: Some Methodological Remarks on Measurement and Explanation', mimeo, University of Southampton.

GEROSKI, P. and MASSON, R., 1986, 'Dynamic Market Models in Industrial Organization', forthcoming, *International Journal of Industrial Organization.*

GEROSKI, P. and JACQUEMIN, A., 1986, 'The Persistence of Profits: A European Comparison', mimeo, Louvain-la-Neuve.

JOHNSTON, J., 1972, *Econometric Methods* (McGraw-Hill, New York).

MARTIN, S., 1983, *Market, Firms, and Economic Performance* (NTU Graduate School of Business Administration).

MUELLER, D., 1977, 'The Persistence of Profits Above the Norm', *Economica*, 44 (November), pp. 369–380.

MUELLER, D., 1986, *Profits in the Long Run* (Cambridge University Press, Cambridge).

ORR, D., 1974, 'The Determinants of Entry: A Study of the Canadian Manufacturing Industries', *Review of Economics and Statistics*, 61 (February), pp. 58–66.

PORTER, M., 1979, 'The Structure within Industries and Companies Performance', *Review of Economics and Statistics*, 61 (May), pp. 214–228.

RAVENSCRAFT, D., 1983, 'Structure-Profit Relationships at the Line of Business and Industry Level', *Review of Economics and Statistics*, 61 (February), pp. 22–31.

SAXONHOUSE, G., 1977, 'Regressions from Samples Having Different Characteristics', *Review of Economics and Statistics*, 58 (May), pp. 234–237.

SCHMALENSEE, R., 1985, 'Do Markets Differ Much?', *American Economic Review*, 75 (June), pp. 341–351.

SCHMALENSEE, R., 1986, 'Collusion versus Differential Efficiency: Testing Alternative Hypotheses', *Journal of Industrial Economics*, this issue.

SHEPHERD, W. G., 1972, 'The Elements of Market Structure', *Review of Economics and Statistics*, 54 (February), pp. 25–37.

TESTING FOR "MONOPOLY" EQUILIBRIUM*

JOHN C. PANZAR AND JAMES N. ROSSE

This paper develops a very general test for "monopoly". Using standard comparative statics analysis, we derive testable restrictions on the firm's reduced form revenue equation which must be satisfied by any profit maximizing firm whose choices are not affected by either strategic interactions or the threat of entry. For such an unfettered monopolist, the sum of the factor price elasticities of the reduced form revenue equation must be nonpositive. The set of interesting alternative hypotheses is not empty. We develop simple models of oligopolistic, competitive and monopolistically competitive markets for which this test statistic may take on positive values.

I. INTRODUCTION

THE UNIFYING theme of this issue is empirical studies of firm and industry behavior. Unlike the other papers included here, we have no new empirical results to offer. However our analysis is a direct result of a puzzling empirical regularity we encountered over a decade ago. In attempting to find a theoretical explanation for that result, we derived a generally applicable testable implication of monopoly profit maximizing behavior. We think that both the test itself and the comparative statics approach used to derive it may be of interest to those, like ourselves, interested in investigating the performance of industrial markets using firm and industry level data. The tests are based on properties of reduced form revenue equations at the firm level, and the data requirements (revenues and factor prices) are relatively modest.

In the course of an investigation of the American daily newspaper industry, one of us (Rosse) noticed that the coefficients of newsprint and other factor prices were persistently positive in the reduced form revenue equations which he was estimating. Intuitively, this seemed very strange. The vast majority of newspapers are local monopolies, and the textbook theory of the unconstrained monopolist would suggest that an upward shift in its marginal cost curve would lead to a reduction of both equilibrium output and revenues. While the issue turns out to be somewhat more complex when dealing with multi-input, multi-output firms, we were clearly on the right track: the hypothesis of monopoly profit maximization does place testable restrictions

* We would like to thank all those, too numerous to mention, who have given us constructive criticism and encouragement over the years. Our greatest debts are to Tim Bresnahan, Dick Schmalensee and Larry White, both for their long term interest in the ideas presented here and, especially, for supplying the final "shove" required to get us to prepare a version suitable for publication. Any remaining errors are, of course, solely our responsibility. Research support from the National Science Foundation (SES-8409171) is gratefully acknowledged.

on the estimated parameters of firms' reduced form revenue equations. Section II provides a general analysis of this issue.

However that left our theoretical work only partially complete. For example, even if one found that the parameter estimates of daily newspapers' reduced form revenue equations were not consistent with the hypothesis of monopoly profit maximization, it would then be necessary to investigate whether or not there exist economically interesting alternative hypotheses which were consistent with the data. This issue is relevant to hypothesis testing generally, for if *all* interesting economic models lead to the same testable restrictions, what is learned from rejection?

Section III develops simple models of equilibrium in single product monopolistically competitive, oligopolistic and perfectly competitive markets. Then, using standard comparative static techniques, we demonstrate that these models yield testable restrictions on firms' reduced form revenue equations which are different from those implied by the monopoly model. In all cases, the implications are in terms of the response of the equilibrium values of firm revenues to changes in factor prices.

While the monopoly model is quite general, the models of oligopoly, monopolistic and perfect competition that we analyze are as simple and as devoid of complications as possible. We present these models primarily to provide economically interesting alternatives to the monopoly hypothesis and to illustrate the generality of our methodological approach. In an actual empirical application it would be desirable to incorporate more specific institutional details and prior information in order to obtain as sharp a statistical test as possible. However, from a purely positive standpoint, it is probably always a useful starting point to determine which simple "as if" model best explains the behavior of the firms under study.

Finally, we should explain why "monopoly" appears in quotation marks in the title of this paper. This was done to emphasize one of the most important aspects of our analysis. For the refutable implications derived in section II apply to any firm whose *structural* revenue function contains as *endogenous* variables *only* those under the direct control of the firm. While this certainly captures the traditional definition of monopoly, it also applies to price-taking competitive firms, as long as the prices they face are truly exogenous, that is, as long as their equilibrium values are unaffected by changes in the other exogenous variable in the model. Thus an empirical refutation of our "monopoly" equilibrium hypothesis constitutes a rejection of the assumption that the revenues of the firms in question are independent of the decisions of rivals, actual or potential.

II. A TESTABLE IMPLICATION OF "MONOPOLY" EQUILIBRIUM

Let $\mathbf{y}$ be a vector of decision variables which affect the firm's revenues, so that $R = R(\mathbf{y}, \mathbf{z})$, where $\mathbf{z}$ is a vector of exogenous variables that shift the firm's revenue function. In addition, we assume that the firm's costs also depend, directly or indirectly, on $\mathbf{y}$, so that $C = C(\mathbf{y}, \mathbf{w}, \mathbf{t})$. Here, $\mathbf{w}$ is a vector of m factor prices that are exogenous to the firm and $\mathbf{t}$ is a vector of exogenous variables that shift the firm's cost function. The vectors $\mathbf{t}$ and $\mathbf{z}$ may or may not have components in common. It is natural to think of $\mathbf{y}$ as representing a vector of output levels. However that interpretation is overly restrictive. The components of $\mathbf{y}$ could include prices, advertising expenditures or quality levels; i.e., any decision variables which *structurally* enter the monopolist's revenue function.[1]

Thus firm profits can be written as $\pi = R - C = \pi(\mathbf{y}, \mathbf{z}, \mathbf{w}, \mathbf{t})$. Let $\mathbf{y}^0 = \operatorname{argmax}_{\mathbf{y}}\{\pi(\mathbf{y}, \mathbf{z}, \mathbf{w}, \mathbf{t})\}$ and $\mathbf{y}^1 = \operatorname{argmax}_{\mathbf{y}}\{\pi(\mathbf{y}, \mathbf{z}, (1+h)\mathbf{w}, \mathbf{t})\}$, with the scalar $h \geqslant 0$. Also, let $R^0 = R(\mathbf{y}^0, \mathbf{z}) \equiv R^*(\mathbf{z}, \mathbf{w}, \mathbf{t})$ and $R^1 = R(\mathbf{y}^1, \mathbf{z}) \equiv R^*(\mathbf{z}, (1+h)\mathbf{w}, \mathbf{t})$, where R^* is the firm's reduced form revenue function. Then, by definition,

$$(1) \qquad R^1 - C(\mathbf{y}^1, (1+h)\mathbf{w}, \mathbf{t}) \geqslant R^0 - C(\mathbf{y}^0, (1+h)\mathbf{w}, \mathbf{t})$$

Because C is linearly homogeneous in $\mathbf{w}$, this can be written as

$$(2) \qquad R^1 - (1+h)C(\mathbf{y}^1, \mathbf{w}, \mathbf{t}) \geqslant R^0 - (1+h)C(\mathbf{y}^0, \mathbf{w}, \mathbf{t})$$

Similarly, it must also be the case that

$$(3) \qquad R^0 - C(\mathbf{y}^0, \mathbf{w}, \mathbf{t}) \geqslant R^1 - C(\mathbf{y}^1, \mathbf{w}, \mathbf{t})$$

Multiplying both sides of (3) by $1+h$ and adding the result to (2) yields

$$(4) \qquad -h(R^1 - R^0) \geqslant 0$$

Dividing both sides of (4) by $-h^2$, we obtain

$$(5) \qquad (R^1 - R^0)/h = [R^*(\mathbf{z}, (1+h)\mathbf{w}, \mathbf{t}) - R^*(\mathbf{z}, \mathbf{w}, \mathbf{t})]/h \leqslant 0$$

This nonparametric[2] version of our result simply states that a proportional cost increase always results in a decrease in the firm's revenues. Assuming that the reduced form revenue function is differentiable, taking the limit of (5) as $h \to 0$ and then dividing the result by R^* yields

$$(6) \qquad \psi^* \equiv \sum w_i(\partial R^*/\partial w_i)/R^* \leqslant 0$$

Thus we have established

Theorem 1: The sum of the factor price elasticities of a monopolist's reduced form revenue equation must be nonpositive.

[1] Care must be taken when interpreting the cost function when some or all of the components of $\mathbf{y}$ are prices. For example, if $\mathbf{y}$ is a price vector and $\mathbf{Q} = \mathbf{Q}(\mathbf{y}, \mathbf{z})$ is the associated system of market demand equations, then $C(\mathbf{y}, \mathbf{w}, \mathbf{t}) = \tilde{C}(\mathbf{Q}(\mathbf{y}, \mathbf{z}), \mathbf{w}, \boldsymbol{\tau})$, where $\tilde{C}$ is the conventional multi-product cost function, $\boldsymbol{\tau}$ is a vector of exogenous technological parameters (that do not enter the demand functions) and $\mathbf{t} = (\mathbf{z}, \boldsymbol{\tau})$. It is important to note in such cases that C (and its associated gradient) "inherit" linear homogeneity in $\mathbf{w}$ from the structural cost function $\tilde{C}$.

[2] We are indebted to Hal Varian for suggesting this line of proof. See Ashenfelter and Sullivan [1987] for a nonparametric analysis of the implications of oligopoly behavioral models.

Intuitively, it is easy to trace the source of the power of this result. For ψ can, alternatively, be defined as the elasticity of reduced form revenues $R^*(\mathbf{z}, k, \mathbf{w}, \mathbf{t})$ with respect to the scalar $k = 1+h$, evaluated at $k = 1$. In words, this asks the question: What will be the percentage change in equilibrium revenues resulting from a 1% change in all factor prices? We know from duality theory that a 1% increase in all factor prices leads to precisely a 1% upward shift in *all* of the firm's cost curves: average, total, and marginal. Thus we can rephrase the above question to read: What will happen to the monopolist's revenues if its costs increase by 1%? In effect, estimating ψ provides a way to empirically shift the firm's cost curves even though cost data are unavailable!

An illustration of the practical application of this analysis can be obtained from the analysis of a simple single product monopoly model. Suppose that the monopolist faces a demand curve of constant price elasticity $e > 1$, so that $R(y, z) = \gamma z^{\alpha} y^{(e-1)/e}$. For simplicity, assume also that the monopolist employs a constant returns to scale Cobb–Douglas technology, so that its cost function can be written as

$$(7) \qquad [\ln C(y, \mathbf{w}, t)] = [\ln y] + \beta[\ln t] + \sum a_i[\ln w_i]; \qquad a_i > 0 \text{ and } \sum a_i = 1$$

Then it is straightforward to show that the (nonstochastic version of the) firm's reduced form revenue equation is given by

$$(8) \qquad [\ln R^*(z, t, \mathbf{w})] = \gamma_0 + e\alpha\,[\ln z] - (e-1)\beta[\ln t] - (e-1)\sum a_i[\ln w_i]$$

where the intercept $\gamma_0 = e[\ln \gamma] - (1-e)[\ln(e-1)/e]$. Thus $\psi^* = -(e-1)\sum a_i = 1-e$, which must be negative if the marginal cost curve is to cut the marginal revenue curve from below as required by the second order conditions for monopoly profit maximization. Note that, because of the simple structure of the example, in this case estimation of the reduced form revenue equation not only allows one to test the hypothesis of monopoly profit maximization, it also provides the analyst with estimates of all of the structural parameters of interest when the hypothesis is maintained. In particular, this example indicates that the *magnitude*, as well as the sign, of ψ^* may be of interest. Here, because it provides an estimate of the price elasticity of demand, ψ^* also yields an estimate of the Lerner index of monopoly power $L = (e-1)/e = \psi^*/(\psi^* - 1)$.

Theorem 1 is a very general result, requiring little beyond the maximization hypothesis itself. For example, it does not require that the observations be generated by long-run equilibrium behavior. Components of **z** and **t** might be decision variables of the firm that it is reasonable to assume are fixed, or predetermined, over the relevant time frame. However, it is important to recognize a limitation of the analysis stemming from the very generality of our result: ψ^* must be nonpositive for all "monopolies", even those facing a perfectly elastic market demand curve!

To see this intuitively, note that nothing in the analysis prevents **z** from being an exogenously given world price vector, so that $R = \mathbf{z} \cdot \mathbf{y}$. To take a specific single product example, let $R(y, z) = zy$ and assume that the firm operates a decreasing returns Cobb–Douglas technology, so that its cost function can be written as

$$(9) \qquad [\ln C(y, \mathbf{w}, t)] = \theta + \delta[\ln y] + \beta[\ln t] + \sum a_i[\ln w_i]: \quad \delta > 1; \theta, a_i > 0 \text{ and } \sum a_i = 1$$

Then it is straightforward to show that the (nonstochastic version of the) firm's reduced form revenue equation is given by

$$(10) \qquad [\ln R^*(z, t, \mathbf{w})] = \{\delta[\ln z] - \theta_0 - \beta[\ln t] - \sum a_i[\ln w_i]\}/(\delta - 1)$$

where $\theta_0 = \theta + [\ln \delta]$. Thus $\psi^* = \sum a_i/(\delta - 1) = 1/(\delta - 1) < 0$. In this case, while the reduced form revenue equation again yields estimates of all the structural parameters of interest, the magnitude of ψ^* is totally unrelated to the degree of monopoly power, which is zero by hypothesis.

The above examples should convince the reader that, while both of the firms in question were monopolists in the strict sense of the term, what they have in common is not the degree of monopoly power that they enjoy. Rather, the common element in both cases is that they operate in isolation: their structural revenue functions do not depend on any other optimizing agents' decision variables. Thus a rejection of the hypothesis that $\psi \leqslant 0$ must mean that the revenue functions of the observed firms are influenced by the actions of others. This intuition is made precise in the models of the next section.

III. ALTERNATIVE MODELS AND THEIR TESTABLE IMPLICATIONS

The analysis of the preceding section has established that an empirical investigation yielding an estimate of ψ significantly greater than 0 constitutes grounds for rejecting the hypothesis that the data were generated by firms acting as independent "monopolists". The natural next question, then, is whether or not there exist *any* models of firm and industry equilibrium consistent with estimated values of $\psi > 0$. If not, the above hypothesis test is of little practical use. Fortunately, the answer is in the affirmative. In this section we show that three commonly employed simple models of industry equilibrium are consistent with values of $\psi > 0$. As one would expect, all three models have the property that the revenue function facing the individual firm depends either implicitly or explicitly upon the decisions of its actual or potential rivals. Finally, it is important to note that, unlike the monopoly model, the results for the models of perfect and monopolistic competition depend quite crucially on the assumption that the firms in question are observed in long-run equilibrium.

III(i). *Monopolistic competition*

Recall for a moment the practical problem which caused us to begin our theoretical analyses. The daily newspapers whose reduced form revenue equations did not conform to the predictions of the monopoly equilibrium hypothesis were, for the most part, the only newspapers in their market areas. Thus, in order to model their behavior interactively, it was natural to posit that they were in competition with other purveyors of *differentiated* information services such as magazines and radio and television stations. The theory of monopolistic competition is therefore the source of our first alternative hypothesis.

Chamberlin [1962] adamantly maintained that firms selling differentiated products were qualitatively indistinguishable from classical monopolists:

> The more substitutes controlled by any one seller, the higher he can put his price. But that is another matter. As long as the substitutes are to any degree imperfect, he still has a monopoly of his own product and control over its price within the limits imposed upon any monopolist—those of the demand. (page 67)

Thus it was his position that one could *not* distinguish between a monopolistic competitor and a pure monopolist from observation of the firm's decision variables. However, at the same time, Chamberlin insisted that *market* equilibria in the two models were vastly different:

> The theory of monopoly, although the opening wedge, is very soon discovered to be inadequate.... Within any group of closely related products (such as that ordinarily included in one imperfectly competitive market) the demand and cost conditions (and hence the price) of any one are defined only if the demand and cost conditions with respect to the others are taken as given. Partial solutions of this sort, yielded by the theory of monopoly, contribute nothing towards a solution of the whole problem, for each rests upon assumptions with respect to the others. (pages 68 and 69)

In sum, he writes:

> Monopolistic competition is evidently a different thing from either *pure* monopoly or *pure* competition. As for monopoly, *as ordinarily conceived and defined*, monopolistic competition embraces it and takes it as a starting point. (page 68)
>
> Monopolistic competition, then, concerns itself not only with the problem of an *individual* equilibrium (the theory of ordinary monopoly), but also with that of a *group* equilibrium (the adjustment of economic forces within a group of competing monopolists, ordinarily regarded as a group of competitors. (page 69)

A moment's reflection should reveal that the comparative statics approach is ideally, and perhaps uniquely, suited to the task of developing testable hypotheses capable of distinguishing between these two theories. For only by analyzing the market equilibrium as a whole can we expect to find any differences. Each firm, viewed in isolation, would, in both theories, behave exactly as a monopoly would, and its actions would satisfy all the conditions of monopoly profit maximization. Nevertheless, it may be hoped that by examining the effects of changes in exogenous variables the "hidden" forces of Chamberlin's "group equilibrium" condition may come into focus.

In the past half century a good deal of the criticism of Chamberlinian theory has focused upon its inability to yield empirically refutable hypotheses. (G. C. Archibald [1961] provides perhaps the most scathing critique.) The conventional wisdom is thus that Chamberlin's model, *in the absence of any additional assumptions*, has no predictive power. However, by adding some additional structure to the model that is both plausible and present in most theoretical treatments, we are able to derive testable restrictions on the reduced form revenue equation of the monopolistically competitive firm.

What follows is an analysis of the comparative statics properties of the "Chamberlinian tangency". S. P. Das [1981] has studied this problem and its implications for the long-run behavior of the monopolistic competitors' output supply and input demand functions and contrasted them with the results of Silberberg [1974] and others on the behavior of the perfectly competitive firm in long-run equilibrium. However, as in the monopoly case, our analysis of the firm's reduced form revenue equation does not require detailed observations on output levels or prices.

In the familiar large group Chamberlinian equilibrium, the firm sets its price so that it operates at an output where perceived marginal revenue equals marginal cost. The demand curve facing the individual firm depends upon the prices (quantities) of the substitute products in the market. For expositional convenience, Chamberlin began the practice, much beloved by modern analysts, of imposing symmetry so that, while the products are differentiated, the representative firm can be studied diagrammatically. The entry or exit of additional products in response to profits or losses will cause the perceived demand curve of the representative firm to shift in or out until, in long-run equilibrium, zero economic profits are achieved with said demand curve tangent to the average cost curve. Under symmetry, these conditions allow us to define two equations that determine the equilibrium number of firms and their level of output.

As in the monopoly case, the exogenous variables whose impact we study are factor prices. Intuitively, the immediate effect of an input price increase is to shift upward the firm's average and marginal cost curves and reduce its output. However, this would result in losses for the representative firm, inducing exit by some firms, which would, in turn, result in an upward shift in the demand curve facing the representative firm until the tangency equilibrium was re-established.

To capture this process analytically and derive its testable implications, we first define the representative firm's perceived inverse demand function $P(y, n, \mathbf{z})$ that, under symmetry, relates price P to firm output y, the number of rivals n, and a vector of exogenous variables $\mathbf{z}$. We assume, as usual, that $\partial P/\partial y \equiv P_y < 0$ and that $\partial P/\partial n \equiv P_n < 0$. In addition, we require the eminently plausible:

Assumption 1: The elasticity of perceived demand facing the individual firm, $e(y, n, \mathbf{z}) \equiv -P/[y\partial P/\partial y]$, is a nondecreasing function of the number of (symmetric) rivals. That is, $\partial e/\partial n \geqslant 0$.

That the elasticity of demand facing the firm increases with the number (and in a symmetric model, perforce) the closeness of the substitutes with which it competes seems almost a truism. However, it involves some assumptions about the structure of the product space that are difficult to test directly. Here, we accept it on faith, noting only that the most commonly used theoretical models of monopolistic competition satisfy this condition.[3]

We now proceed to an analysis of the comparative statics properties of Chamberlinian equilibrium. Letting $R(y, n, \mathbf{z}) = yP(y, n, \mathbf{z})$, this is characterized by the two equation system

$$R_y - C_y = 0 \tag{11}$$

$$R(y, \hat{n}, \mathbf{z}) - C(\hat{y}, \mathbf{w}, \mathbf{t}) = 0 \tag{12}$$

Equations (11) and (12) implicitly define the long-run equilibrium values of $\hat{y}$ and $\hat{n}$ as functions of the exogenous variables $\mathbf{z}$, $\mathbf{w}$, and $\mathbf{t}$. Totally differentiating (11) and (12) with respect to w_i and solving using Cramer's Rule yields:

$$\partial\hat{y}/\partial w_i = \{R_n(\partial\tilde{x}_i/\partial y) - R_{yn}\tilde{x}_i\}/\hat{D} \tag{13}$$

where the $\tilde{x}_i(y, \mathbf{w}, \mathbf{t})$ are conditional factor demand functions. We know that $\hat{D} \equiv (R_{yy} - C_{yy})R_n > 0$ from the second order conditions associated with (11). Since $\hat{R}(\mathbf{z}, \mathbf{w}, \mathbf{t}) = R(\hat{y}, \hat{n}, \mathbf{z})$, using (12) and the chain rule, we obtain

$$\partial\hat{R}/\partial w_i = C_y(\partial\hat{y}/\partial w_i) + \tilde{x}_i \tag{14}$$

Multiplying by $(w_i/\hat{R})$ and summing (14) over all inputs yields

$$\hat{\psi} = \sum w_i(\partial\hat{R}/\partial w_i)/\hat{R} = C/\hat{R} + (C_y/\hat{R})\sum w_i(\partial\hat{y}/\partial w_i) \tag{15}$$

Making use of (12) and (13), we have

$$\hat{\psi} = 1 + C_y\{R_n \sum w_i(\partial\tilde{x}_i/\partial y) - R_{yn}\sum w_i\tilde{x}_i\}/\hat{R}\hat{D} \tag{16}$$

But from the definition of the cost minimizing input vector $\tilde{\mathbf{x}}$, this becomes

$$\hat{\psi} = 1 + C_y\{R_n C_y - R_{yn} C\}/\hat{R}\hat{D} \tag{17}$$

[3] For example, the elasticity of the individual firm's perceived demand curve in the model of Dixit and Stiglitz [1977] is independent of the number of rivals, so that $\partial e/\partial n = 0$. This is also an implicit feature of the analysis of Spence [1976]. Those authors derive the firm's perceived demand curve under the assumption that the firm believes that total *industry* output will be unaffected by a change in its own output level. In the more general analysis of Koenker and Perry [1981], it can be shown that $\partial e/\partial n$ is positive when the firms hold less competitive (e.g. Cournot–Nash) conjectures about rivals' responses.

Substituting in the profit maximizing condition (11), the zero profit condition (12) and rearranging terms, we have

$$\hat{\psi} = 1 + R_y[R_n R_y - R R_{yn}]/\hat{R}\hat{D} \tag{18}$$

Rewriting the bracketed term in (18) in terms of the inverse demand function and cancelling terms yields

$$\hat{\psi} = 1 + R_y[y^2(P_n P_y - P P_{yn})]/\hat{R}\hat{D} \tag{19}$$

Since $\partial e/\partial n = (PP_{yn} - P_y P_n)/[y(P_y)^2]$, the bracketed term in (19) is non-positive by Assumption 1, and $\hat{\psi} \leqslant 1$. Thus we have established

Proposition 1: In symmetric Chamberlinian equilibrium, the sum of the elasticities of firm's reduced form revenues with respect to factor prices is less than or equal to unity.

The range of permissible values for $\hat{\psi}$ includes that of ψ^*(i.e., the negative real line) *plus* the unit interval. Thus the analyst can, in principle, observe data that are consistent with the hypothesis of monopolistic competition but *not* with that of profit maximizing monopoly.

III(ii). *Long-run competitive equilibrium*

A natural benchmark case to examine is that of perfect competition. However our analysis in section II makes it clear that price-taking behavior will lead to $\psi \leqslant 0$ unless some firm interactions are introduced into the model. Intuitively, the way to proceed is to formulate a model in which competitive entry makes the output price facing the firm an endogenous variable.

Over the last two decades there has arisen a literature on the theory of the competitive firm when observed in long-run equilibrium. The most elegant example of this literature is Silberberg [1974]. Briefly, it was found that the traditional Samuelsonian comparative statics of the firm must be modified when applied to long-run equilibrium behavior. This comes about for essentially the same reason as in the Chamberlinian case: changes in factor prices will, in the long-run, result in entry or exit and changes in the equilibrium output price, which will, in turn, affect the firm's input demand and output supply decisions. Here, we develop the implications of this long-run theory of the competitive firm in order to examine the properties of the associated reduced form revenue function.

The equilibrium price p^C and firm output level y^C in a perfectly competitive industry with free entry and a freely available technology is defined implicitly by the two equation system

$$p^C - C_y(y^C, \mathbf{w}, \mathbf{t}) = 0 \tag{20}$$

$$p^C y^C - C(y^C, \mathbf{w}, \mathbf{t}) = 0 \tag{21}$$

(A third equation, determining the equilibrium number of firms and aggregate industry output, is unnecessary for our present purposes.) Totally differentiating (20) and (21) with respect to w_i and solving via Cramer's Rule yields

$$(22) \qquad \partial y^C/\partial w_i = [\tilde{x}_i - y^C(\partial \tilde{x}_i/\partial y)]/y^C C_{yy}$$

Since $R^C(\mathbf{w}, \mathbf{t}) \equiv p^C(\mathbf{w}, \mathbf{t}) y^C(\mathbf{w}, \mathbf{t})$, we obtain, using (21),

$$(23) \qquad \partial R^C/\partial w_i = C_y(\partial y^C/\partial w_i) + \tilde{x}_i$$

Multiplying (23) through by w_i and summing over all factors yields

$$(24) \qquad \sum w_i(\partial R^C/\partial w_i) = (C_y/yC_{yy})\{\sum w_i \tilde{x}_i - y\sum w_i(\partial \tilde{x}_i/\partial y)\} + \sum w_i \tilde{x}_i$$

Using the definitions of the total and marginal cost functions, this becomes

$$(25) \qquad \sum w_i(\partial R^C/\partial w_i) = (C_y/yC_{yy})\{C - yC_y\} + C$$

Substituting in (20) and (21) and dividing by R^C, we have

$$(26) \qquad \psi^C = \sum (w_i/R^C)(\partial R^C/\partial w_i) = 1$$

allowing us to state

Proposition 2: For firms observed in long-run competitive equilibrium, the *sum* of the elasticities of reduced form revenues with respect to factor prices equals unity.

The intuition behind this result should by now be clear, since ψ^C measures the impact of a proportional increase in all factor prices. Suppose all factor prices rise by 1%. Because average cost is linearly homogeneous in **w**, such an increase will shift that curve upward by 1% for all output levels, leaving its minimum point unchanged. Since, in long-run competitive equilibrium firms always operate at said minimum , this means that y^C is unchanged. However, in equilibrium, p^C is equal to the level of AC at its minimum point, and this has increased by 1%. Thus equilibrium revenues also go up by 1%, the amount of the increase in factor prices. But this is precisely the condition that $\psi^C = 1$.

The astute reader will have noticed that there is another testable implication of this simple competitive model: reduced form revenues are not affected by shifts in the market demand curve; $\partial R^C/\partial z = 0$. This is due to the fact that we have been working with the simple textbook model of the long-run perfectly competitive industry which gives rise to a horizontal industry supply curve. In that model, equilibrium market price and output per firm are completely determined by technological variables and factor prices, so it should come as no surprise that equilibrium firm revenues are also unaffected by market demand conditions. However a simple extension of the model can handle the case of the competitive industry with a rising long-run supply curve.

Following standard textbook practice, suppose that the price of input 1 rises as the industry expands. That is, w_1 is exogenous to the firm but endogenous to the industry. Then, in addition to equations (16) and (17) we need to add conditions equating supply and demand in the output market ($Q(p^C, \mathbf{z}) = n^C y^C$) and in the market for input 1 (for example, $\hat{w}_1 = S[n^C \tilde{x}_1(y^C, \mathbf{w}, \mathbf{t}), \mathbf{s}]$). This would yield a system of four equations to determine the four endogenous variables p^C, y^C, n^C, and $\hat{w}_1$, where n^C is the long-run equilibrium number of firms in the industry. The firm's revenue equation, no longer a true reduced form, could be estimated as above, with the exogenous variables $\mathbf{z}$ and $\mathbf{s}$ available to construct an instrument for the endogenous variable $\hat{w}_1$.

Let us pause to review what has been accomplished thus far. We have analyzed three models of market equilibrium that yield distinctly different refutable implications with respect to the test statistic ψ. The "monopoly" equilibrium hypothesis requires that ψ be nonpositive, (symmetric) Chamberlinian equilibrium requires a $\psi \leqslant 1$, and in (symmetric) long-run competitive equilibrium it must be the case that $\psi = 1$. Thus, in any empirical application, rejecting the hypothesis of $\psi \leqslant 0$ rules out the "monopoly" model. Rejecting the hypothesis of $\psi \leqslant 1$ implies the rejection of all three models, while rejection of *both* the (hypothesis of $\psi \leqslant 0$ *and* the hypothesis of $\psi = 1$ (but not $\psi \leqslant 1$) means that, of the models considered so far, only the Chamberlinian model could be consistent with the data.[4]

III(iii). *Conjectural variation oligopoly*

The first two models in this section introduce interdependence (i.e., endogenous variables beyond the control of the firm) into firms' structural revenue functions via the hypothesis that free entry and exit result in zero profits in equilibrium. Next, we demonstrate that a model which exhibits strategic interactions among a *fixed* number of rivals may also be consistent with positive values of ψ.

Consider a simple, symmetric n firm homogeneous product oligopoly

[4] In the preliminary empirical analyses reported in Rosse and Panzar [1977], we were able to reject the "monopoly" hypothesis with t-levels ranging from 1.81 to 4.50, depending on the specification of the functional form of the reduced form revenue equation. For all but one specification, the hypothesis that $\psi = 1$ was rejected with t-levels greater than 2.5. The Chamberlinian hypothesis could not be rejected with any degree of confidence for any specification. (See tables IV and V.) Unfortunately these tests must be viewed as suggestive rather than conclusive. Since the firm data were reported anonymously, demographic data for the firms' local markets, such as population, *per capita* income, etc., were unavailable. Missing such important components of the vector $\mathbf{z}$, the reduced form revenue equation had no explanatory power. The impact of such missing variables were adequately reflected by the variation in the firms' circulation levels, and including circulation as an explanatory variable allowed us to obtain the estimates referred to above. However, for those specifications to yield valid results, circulation must be exogenously determined. Since the underlying structural model could not be identified, it was impossible to test this key assumption.

model. Each firm chooses its output level y_k to maximize its profits $\pi_k = P(Y, \mathbf{z})y_k - C(y_k, \mathbf{w}, \mathbf{t})$, where P is the market inverse demand curve and $Y = \sum y_k$ is total industry output. Then the first-order condition for profit maximization for the kth *producing* firm requires

(27) $$\partial\pi_k/\partial y_k = \lambda y_k P_Y + P - C_y = 0$$

where the conjectural variation $\lambda = dY/dy_k$ measures the change in industry output which the kth firm perceives will result from a marginal increase in y_k. (We assume that the second-order condition associated with (27) is also satisfied.) Typically, λ takes on values between 0 and n. If $\lambda = 0$, inspection of (27) reveals that the market behaves competitively. If $\lambda = n$, the collusive outcome is achieved. See Seade [1980] for a discussion of this class of oligopoly models.

Restricting attention to symmetric equilibria allows us to substitute the conditions $y_k = y^0$ and $Y^0 = ny^0$ into (27), obtaining

(28) $$\lambda y^0 P_Y(ny^0, \mathbf{z}) + P(ny^0, \mathbf{z}) - C_y(y^0, \mathbf{w}, \mathbf{t}) = 0$$

Equation (28) defines oligopolistic firm output y^0 as an implicit function of the variables λ, $\mathbf{z}$, $\mathbf{w}$, and $\mathbf{t}$. Then, *assuming that the degree of oligopolistic coordination, as measured by* λ, *is unaffected by changes in factor prices*, totally differentiating (28) with respect to w_i yields

(29) $$\partial y^0/\partial w_i = (\partial^2 C/\partial y \partial w_i)/D^0$$

where $D^0 = [ny^0\lambda P_{YY} + (n+\lambda)P_Y - C_{yy}]$. Seade [1980] has shown that $D^0 < 0$ is required for the stability of the symmetric equilibrium under study. Premultiplying both sides of (29) by w_i and summing over all i yields

(30) $$\sum w_i(\partial y^0/\partial w_i) = \sum w_i(\partial^2 C/\partial y \partial w_i)/D^0 = C_y/D^0 < 0$$

where the last equality, again, follows from the fact that marginal cost is linearly homogeneous in factor prices. Dividing by y^0 establishes

Proposition 3: For firms in a stable, symmetric, homogeneous product, conjectural variation oligopoly equilibrium, the *sum* of the factor price elasticities of the reduced form firm output equation, $y^0(\mathbf{z}, \mathbf{w}, \mathbf{t})$, is negative.

However the effects of factor prices on reduced form revenues will, in general, be indeterminate. Since $R^0(\mathbf{z}, \mathbf{w}, \mathbf{t}) = y^0 P(ny^0, \mathbf{z})$, applying the chain rule to (30) and dividing by R^0 yields

(31) $$\psi^0 = \sum w_i(\partial R^0/\partial w_i)/R^0 = (y^0 n P_Y + P)\sum w_i(\partial y^0/\partial w_i)/R^0 = R_Y C_y/D^0 R^0$$

where $R_Y = Y^0 P_Y + P$ is the equilibrium value of the *industry* marginal revenue curve. Now for an oligopoly which behaves sufficiently like a collusive monopoly (that is, $\lambda \approx n$), the first-order condition (31) will ensure that R_Y is positive. But, in general, there is nothing in this class of oligopoly models which restricts the industry's aggregate output to the elastic portion of the market demand curve.[5]

IV. CONCLUDING REMARKS

In this paper we have presented a methodology for uncovering some of the testable implications contained in models of firm and industry equilibrium. However it should be clear that we have not begun to exhaust the potential applications of positive, comparative statics approaches to industrial economics. We have assumed that the only firm specific data available are revenues and factor prices. It seems likely that much sharper tests would be possible if, as is sometimes the case, the analyst also has available data on equilibrium prices and quantities for the firm and/or industry.[6] The models examined here were selected for analysis because of their familiarity and tractability. However the cost minimization hypothesis and duality theory, the key ingredients in our comparative statics approach, can be employed in much the same way to virtually any system of well-defined equilibrium equations. The usefulness of focusing on the sum of the factor price elasticities of reduced form equations is that that statistic captures the effect of a proportional shift in the average, total, or marginal cost curve even when cost data themselves are unavailable. Thus the technique employed in this paper should prove useful whenever factor prices are observable but it is not possible to estimate cost functions.

JOHN C. PANZAR,
Northwestern University,
Evanston IL 60201,
USA.

JAMES N. ROSSE,
Stanford University,
Stanford CA 94305,
USA.

REFERENCES

ARCHIBALD, G. C., 1961, 'Chamberlin versus Chicago', *Review of Economic Studies*, 29 (July), pp. 2–28.

ASHENFELTER, O. and SULLIVAN, D., 1987, 'Nonparametric Tests of Market Structure:

[5] This is not to say that there are no testable restrictions on the comparative statics properties of the model for various values of λ and n. See Sullivan [1985] for an analysis which successfully places bounds on the Cournot equivalent number of firms, n/λ.

[6] See Bresnahan [1982] and Lau [1982] for discussions of the conditions required to identify the conjectural variation parameter λ when observations on industry prices and quantities are available.

An Application to the Cigarette Industry', *Journal of Industrial Economics*, this issue.

BRESNAHAN, T. F., 1982, 'The Oligopoly Solution Concept is Identified', *Economic Letters*, 10, pp. 87–92.

CHAMBERLIN, E. H., 1962, *The Theory of Monopolistic Competition*, 8th edition (Harvard University Press, Cambridge, Mass.).

DAS, S. P., 1981, 'Long-Run Behavior of a Monopolistically Competitive Firm', *International Economic Review*, 22 (February), pp. 159–165.

DIXIT, A. and STIGLITZ, J. E., 1977, 'Monopolistic Competition and Optimum Product Diversity', *American Economic Review*, 65 (June), pp. 297–308.

KOENKER, R. W. and PERRY, M. K., 1981, 'Product Differentiation, Monopolistic Competition, and Public Policy', *Bell Journal of Economics*, 12 (Spring), pp. 217–232.

LAU, L. J., 1982, 'On Identifying the Degree of Competitiveness from Industry Price and Output Data', *Economic Letters*, 10, pp. 93–99.

ROSSE, J. N. and PANZAR, J. C., 1977, 'Chamberlin versus Robinson: An Empirical Test for Monopoly Rents', Studies in Industry Economics, Research Paper no. 77, Stanford University, Stanford, California.

SEADE, J. E., 1980, 'On the Effects of Entry', *Econometrica*, 48 (March), pp. 479–489.

SILBERBERG, E., 1974, 'The Theory of the Firm in "Long Run" Equilibrium', *American Economic Review*, 84 (September), pp. 734–741.

SPENCE, A. M., 1976, 'Product Selection, Fixed Costs, and Monopolistic Competition', *Review of Economics Studies*, 43 (June), pp. 217–236.

SULLIVAN, D., 1985, 'Testing Hypotheses About Firm Behavior in the Cigarette Industry', *The Journal of Political Economy*, 93 (June), pp. 586–598.

COMPETITION AND COLLUSION IN THE AMERICAN AUTOMOBILE INDUSTRY: THE 1955 PRICE WAR*

TIMOTHY F. BRESNAHAN

Movements in total quantity and in quality-adjusted price suggest a supply-side shock in the American automobile market in 1955. This paper tests the hypothesis that the shock was a transitory change in industry conduct, a price war. The key ingredients of the test are equilibrium models of oligopoly under product differentiation. Explicit hypotheses about cost and demand are maintained while the oligopoly behavioral hypothesis is changed from collusive to competitive (Nash) equilibrium. In nonnested (Cox) tests of hypothesis, the collusive solution is sustained in 1954 and in 1956, while the competitive solution holds in 1955. The result does not appear to be an artifact, since it is robust in tests against alternative specifications.

IN 1955, American passenger automobile production was 45 percent greater than in the two surrounding years, while quality-adjusted prices were lower (see Table I). Many studies of aggregate automobile demand have had difficulty explaining the 1955 events.[1] Although 1955 saw a mild macroeconomic expansion, the size of the increase in auto sales was out of proportion to earlier and later experience. The decrease in price is unlikely to reflect a demand shock in any case. Paul Samuelson summarized the situation in his famous classroom remark that he "... would flunk any econometrics paper that claimed to provide an explanation of 1955 auto sales."[2] The alternative approach of searching for a supply shock is clearly attractive. This paper provides an explanation by testing the hypothesis that there was a supply shock of a very specific form, a one-year increase in the competitiveness of conduct in the industry. It provides a model of the non-price-taking supply of differentiated products under more and less cooperative behavior, and shows how the hypothesis of competition can be empirically distinguished from that of collusion. Thus the tests of economic hypotheses in the paper are cast in precise econometric form: conduct in 1955 comes from a competitive model, in nearby years, from a collusive one.

* This paper is a revision of Essay II of my 1980 Princeton University dissertation. The help of R. Quandt, G. Butters, R. Willig, G. Chow and K. Small is gratefully acknowledged. Comments on an earlier draft by R. Masson, M. Kamien, and R. Schmalensee were very helpful. Remaining error is mine.

[1] See, for example, Chow [1960] at pp. 168–169. "The year 1955 is an exception, [to the rule that residuals are small] where we find the residual to be twice as large as the standard error."

[2] I am grateful to R. E. Hall for this anecdote.

The basis for the empirical test of the price war hypothesis is a model of short-run equilibrium in an industry with differentiated products. Here the definition of short-run is taken to reflect an important feature of the US automobile market. It is the period within which prices and quantities are set, but also the period for which firms' product lines are predetermined. The model of product differentiation is spatial, with the product space having a "quality" rather than a "location" interpretation. With fixed costs, one would expect products to be less than perfect substitutes in equilibrium. Thus even the "competitive" model investigated here is one in which there is some market power; the label refers to noncooperative conduct rather than to price-taking. In the model, firms have multiple products.

The intuition of why competitive and collusive behaviors are distinct in such a model is straightforward. If firms compete on price, price will be near marginal cost for those products for which a close, competitive substitute exists. If firms are setting price by some (tacitly) collusive means, then $(P-MC)$ for one firm's products will not depend crucially on whether their close substitutes are sold by competitors or by the firm itself. This simple intuition is an example of a much more general point about the observable consequences of noncompetitive conduct. Hypotheses about conduct have implications for the *comparative statics of price and quantity with respect to demand elasticities.* Thus even when marginal costs are taken to be unobservable, competitive and collusive conduct can be discerned from the movements in industry and firm price and quantity.

The next section reviews the history of automobile market events in the mid-fifties to motivate the specific hypotheses tested in this paper. Sections II and III lay out the models, making specific functional form assumptions about cost, demand and product type. The model is solved under two different conduct hypotheses: competitive (Nash equilibrium with prices as strategic variables) and collusive (joint profit maximizing). Section IV presents the econometric evidence on the 1955 price war hypothesis, including a discussion of robustness of the results.

I. THE FACTS TO BE EXPLAINED

Tables I and II show some aggregate indicators of US automobile market events in the mid-1950s. This section reviews these data to establish the aggregate facts the later sections will explain. In the table, the time unit is the model year, so that a row labelled 1955 is (for example) actually 1954Q4–1955Q3. Nominal data are deflated using the GNP deflator.

The first two columns of Table I show 1955 to be a high quantity, low price model year in the auto industry. Nearly half again as many cars were made in that year as in either of the surrounding years. Superior quality adjustments in the price indexes do not change the inference that 1955 was a price trough. Column 3 shows the percentage price change on earlier years with the Cagan

TABLE I

Year	(1) Auto Production[a]	(2) Real Auto Price-CPI[b]	(3) % Change Auto Price-Cagan[c]	(4) Auto Sales[d]	(5) Auto Quantity Index[e]
1953	6.13	1.01	NA	14.5	86.8
1954	5.51	0.99	NA	13.9	84.9
1955	7.94	0.95	−2.5	18.4	117.2
1956	5.80	0.97	6.3	15.7	97.9
1957	6.12	0.98	6.1	16.2	100.0

Notes: [a] Millions of units over the model year. [Source: *Automotive News.*]
[b] (CPI New automobile component)/CPI. [Source: *Handbook of Labor Statistics.*]
[c] Adjusted for quality change. [See Cagan (1971), especially pp. 232–3.]
[d] Auto output in constant dollars, *QIV* of previous year through *QIII* of named year, in billions of 1957 dollars. [Source: *National Income and Product Accounts.*]
[e] (4)/(2), normalized so 1957 = 100.

TABLE II

Year	(6) Per Capita Disposable Personal Income[f]	(7) Interest Rate[g]	(8) Durables Expenditures (Non-Auto)[h]	(9) Automakers Profits[i]
1953	1623	1.9	14.5	2.58
1954	1609	0.9	14.5	2.25
1955	1659	1.7	16.1	3.91
1956	1717	2.6	17.1	2.21
1957	1732	3.2	17.0	2.38

Notes: [f] Billions of 1957 dollars, *QIV* of previous year through *QIII* of named year. [Source: *National Income and Product Accounts.*]
[g] Three-month *T*-bill rate. [Source: *Statistical Abstract.*]
[h] Durables component of consumer expenditures minus component for automobiles and parts, billions of 1957 dollars. [Source: *National Income and Product Accounts.*]

[1971] quality adjustment. Cagan's method is based only on physically unchanging automobile models, but the hedonic regression price index reported by Griliches [1964] is similar. Real sales of autos in value terms (Column 4) expanded substantially less than unit sales. This is not to be entirely attributed to the price trough for all autos. In Column 5, I report the implicit quantity index obtained by dividing sales by the price index in Column 2, which expands substantially more than Column 4 in 1955. What is going on here is a one-year shift during 1955 to smaller, lower value cars by consumers.[3] Clearly, the data in these first five columns suggest that the supply curve for automobiles shifted down in 1955. I shall return later to the point about the shift to smaller, lower-value cars.

[3] See production by "Price Group" in *Ward's Automotive Yearbook* for 1956, p. 49, and for 1957, p. 59.

Columns 6–8 (Table II) show data from outside the auto market. The income figure shows 1955 to be a year of mild macroeconomic expansion. Interest rates were also low that year. Both of these would tend to increase demand for automobiles, a durable good. Indeed, non-auto durables expand somewhat in 1955, though they do not contract the next year as the macroeconomic boom continues. This difference between auto and non-auto expansion is one way to think of the poor 1955 fit of automobile demand models.[4] Any explanation of all of the 1955 events from the demand side will need to be fairly fancy. However, it is clear that some fraction of the increase in 1955 auto quantity was due to demand factors.

Column 9 shows the accounting profits of the five largest operating automobile companies. The obvious, though wrong, inference is that there was a decrease in automobile competition in 1955. The technology of automobile manufacturing is characterized by large fixed costs: plant costs and product development costs are joint costs of production in many years. Standard accounting practice spreads these costs out smoothly over many years. As a result, there is no stable time-series relationship between accounting profit and price-cost margins in the economic sense. High unit sales years, like 1955, tend to be "profitable" in the accounting sense no matter what is going on in the economic sense.

Demand

Automobile purchasers typically buy one unit or none. The demand for automobiles is thus given by the number of buyers and not by the number bought by any hypothetical single consumer. Formally, we assume a continuum of potential buyers, differentiated by tastes. Each consumer chooses some automobile or decides to buy none. Aggregating the decisions of all consumers yields the demand functions for the automobile models. In this model, different consumers buy different autos because of differences in tastes. The heterogeneity in tastes are modelled in such a way as to yield a demand system for automobile models that is linear in prices. This requires strong assumptions. We assign every consumer a constant marginal rate of substitution between automobile quality and all other goods. Further, that marginal rate is distributed uniformly in the population of consumers. Each consumer, v, has tastes for automobile quality, x, and for money not spent on autos, $Y-P$;

$$U(x, Y, v) = vx + Y - P \qquad \text{if some auto is bought} \tag{1}$$

$$U(x, Y, v) = v\gamma + Y - E \qquad \text{otherwise} \tag{2}$$

[4] The quantitative extent to which standard auto demand models underpredict the 1955 expansion will be treated below.

The interpretation of γ and E in (2) will appear shortly. The interpretation of v is as willingness to pay for auto quality.

Consumers differ in their v, but there are equally many consumers with each v: v is distributed uniformly with density δ on $[0, V_{max}]$.[5] Both δ and V_{max} are parameters for econometric estimation. Consider first the auto product selection part of the demand behavior of a consumer with utility (1). Let there be several products, each with price P and quality x. Then the consumer of type v will select that product j which minimizes $P_j - vx_j$. Aggregating this selection rule across consumers yields the demand for all of the products.

To aggregate individual demand behavior into product demand functions, first calculate the v of the consumer who is just indifferent between two products. Let products h and i have (p_i, x_i) and (p_h, x_h) with $x_i > x_h$. Then consumer v_{hi} is indifferent between h and i if and only if:

$$P_i - x_i v_{hi} = P_h - x_h v_{hi} \tag{3}$$

Rearranging yields v_{hi} as a function of prices and qualities:

$$v_{hi} = \frac{P_i - P_h}{x_i - x_h} \tag{4}$$

All consumers with $v > V_{ni}$ strictly prefer product i, all with lower v, product h.

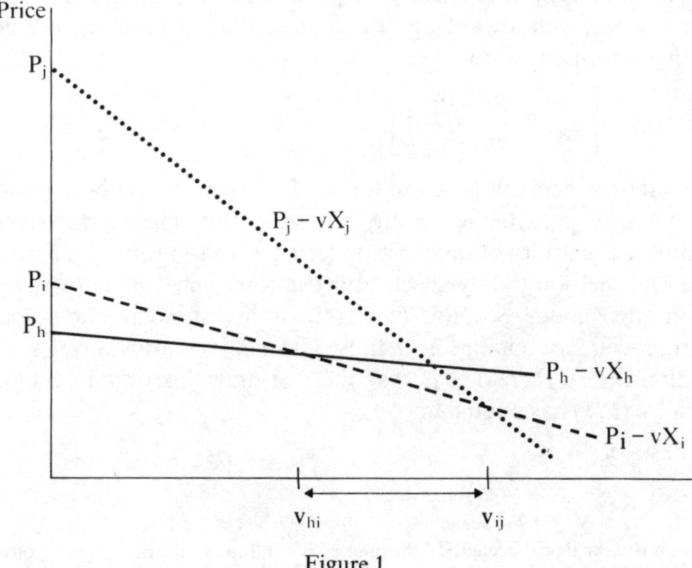

Figure 1

[5] The demand system is that of Prescott and Visscher [1977]. It has received considerable attention in the "Vertical Product Differentiation" literature, e.g. Shaked and Sutton [1983].

To find product i's demand function, let there be another product j with $x_j > x_i$. Calculate v_{ij} exactly as v_{hi}. Then product i is bought only by consumers in the interval $[v_{hi}, v_{ij}]$. Since the density of consumers is δ, the demand function is:

$$(5) \qquad q_i = \delta[v_{ij} - v_{hi}] = \delta\left[\frac{(P_j - P_i)}{(x_j - x_i)} - \frac{(P_i - P_h)}{(x_i - x_h)}\right]$$

Note that the difference in qualities, $x_i - x_h$, is an indicator of how close substitutes the products are. The smaller the difference in qualities, the closer the cross-price demand derivative, $(\delta/(x_i - x_h))$ is to own-price demand derivative $-(\delta/(x_i - x_h) - \delta/(x_j - x_i))$ in absolute value. The products are perfect substitutes in the limit as x_i goes to x_h.

The selection of consumers into product market segments is illustrated in Figure 1. The three products have their prices on the vertical axis. The slope of the line through each product's price is (minus) its quality. Thus, the lines trace the "total price" of each product to consumers as a function of tastes, v. Product i is bought by these consumers in the marked interval, since it is there that i has the lowest total price. If product i's price were higher, or either of its neighbors lower, the market interval for i would shrink.[6]

That completes discussion of selection of products by those consumers who buy some auto. The other part of the demand functions, the decision whether to buy any auto, is now treated. The first assumption is that the person most valuing auto quality, $v_{\max}$, always buys some auto. Since the equilibrium $v_{\max}$ will always buy the highest-quality auto, x_n, the demand for the highest-quality auto is

$$(6) \qquad q_n - \delta\left[v_{\max} - \frac{P_n - P_{n-1}}{x_n - x_{n-1}}\right]$$

To calculate the demand function for the lowest-quality good, consider the consumer's decision whether to buy any new auto. The rational consumer will compare the utility of the most-preferred auto to utility when no auto is bought. The decision to buy affects utility in three ways. First, there is less to spend on other goods. Second, there is the utility of having the automobile, vx. Third, preferences change from those given in (1) to those given in (2). The implication of (2), therefore, is that the consumer just indifferent between buying auto (P, x) has v equal to:

$$(7) \qquad \frac{P - E}{x - \gamma}$$

[6] In fact, it is clear that the length of the interval is continuous in prices, even at those prices where that length goes to zero. It is also true that product i's demand function is concave across the point at which product $i+1$ is dominated out of the market. Thus price equilibrium always exists in "quality" product differentiation models like this one. In "location" models like that of Hotelling [1929], the continuity and concavity are absent, leading to potential nonexistence.

This has exactly the same form as (4), so that the demand function for the lowest-quality good is:

(8) $$q_1 = \delta\left[\frac{P_2 - P_1}{x_2 - x_1} - \frac{P_1 - E}{x_1 - \gamma}\right]$$

It is exactly as if there were some other "product" below the lowest-quality product. This hypothetical "product" is most plausibly interpreted as a used car, as our data refer only to new-car purchases.

That completes specification of the demand side of the model. The demand function for products 1 to n are:

(9) $$q_1 = \delta[v_{12} - vm](P_1, x_1) = \delta\left[\frac{P_2 - P_1}{x_2 - x_1} - \frac{P_1 - E}{x_1 - \gamma}\right]$$

(10) $$q_i = \delta[v_{ij} - v_{hi}] = \delta\left[\frac{(P_j - P_i)}{(x_j - x_i)} - \frac{(P_i - P_h)}{(x_i - x_h)}\right]$$

(11) $$q_n = \delta[vmu(P_n, x_n) - v_{nn-1}] = \delta\left[v_{\max} - \frac{P_n - P_{n-1}}{x_n - x_{n-1}}\right]$$

where E, γ, $v_{\max}$, and δ are the demand parameters to be estimated.

Costs and firm behavior

The cost of producing an automobile model is assumed to involve a fixed cost plus constant marginal costs at every quality level. The estimating equations come from the equilibrium conditions of the price-setting game among firms. The fixed costs are sunk at that stage; they do not affect decisions on the price-quantity margin, and so are ignored for the rest of the paper. What is of interest here is the relationship between marginal cost and product quality.

Formally, the cost function $C(x, q)$ has been restricted to the form:

(12) $$C(x, q) = A(x) + mc(x)q$$

It is clear that $mc(\cdot)$ should be increasing, so that higher quality products are more expensive to manufacture. This avoids equilibria in which only the highest quality, yet cheapest product is produced. We also assume that $mc(\cdot)$ is convex, since this restriction implies that all products for which the fixed cost is sunk are sold in positive quantity.[7] A one-parameter functional form fulfilling these conditions is the exponential:

(13) $$mc(t) = \mu e^t$$

where μ is a parameter to be estimated. The functional form is arbitrary, but

[7] Consumers trade off money and quality with a constant marginal rate of substitution. Convex costs, then, imply decreasing returns to expenditures on quality, an obvious condition to avoid degeneracies.

follows the success of hedonic models (c.f. Ohta and Griliches [1976]) in using a log linear form.

In order to calculate equilibrium prices and quantities from the vector of product qualities in the industry, only the form taken by the relations between firms remains to be described. Two assumptions about firm behavior are considered here. The collusive one has all firms setting prices to maximize the sum of all their profits, as if they were one monopolist. The competitive behavioral assumption has each firm setting the prices of its products to maximize its own profit, taking the prices of all other firms' products as given. These two solution concepts will be abbreviated C (Collusion) and B (Bertrand–Nash equilibrium with prices as strategic variables).

The profit function for a typical product is:

$$\pi_i = P_i q_i - mc(x_i) q_i - A(x_i) \tag{14}$$

Recall from (9)–(11) that the q_i are linear in P_i and in the prices of one or two neighboring products. The profit functions are therefore quadratic in prices, and the solution of any simultaneous profit-maximization problem will be linear in prices. We now construct the linear equations defining the equilibrium prices, showing their dependence on the behavioral assumptions.

The assumptions about firm behavior enter the determination of prices through the relations between neighboring products, since only neighbors have any interdependence on the demand side. Products more distant (than adjacent) in the quality scale have zero cross-price elasticities of demand. The neighboring products can either be cooperating (as all are under (C), or those of the same firm under (B)) or competing.

First consider a one-product firm which is not colluding with its neighbors. Since it is assumed to take their prices as given, it maximizes profit by setting the own-price derivative of the profit function to zero

$$\pi_i' = q_i + (P_i - mc(x_i)) \frac{\partial q_i}{\partial P_i} = 0 \tag{15}$$

If, instead, products i and $i+1$ are manufactured by the same firm or by different firms under (C), the first-order condition with respect to the ith price is changed to:

$$\pi_i' = q_i + (P_i - mc(x_i)) \frac{\partial q_i}{\partial P_i} + (P_{i+1} - mc(x_{i+1})) \frac{\partial q_{i+1}}{\partial P_i} = 0 \tag{16}$$

The distinction is this: when the two products are cooperating, they maximize the sum of their profits. The extra term in (16) is the effect of i's price on $i+1$'s profit. If the market is characterized by a high degree of substitution (products closely spaced) this extra term will be large. Then the effect of changing hypotheses about competition will be substantial.

Of course, computation of equilibrium prices and quantities requires the specification and simultaneous solution of the first-order maximizing conditions for all products.

To specify these relations, let H be the matrix representing the state of cooperation, with elements defined by

$$H_{ij} = \begin{cases} 1 & \text{if products } i \text{ and } j \text{ are cooperating} \\ 0 & \text{otherwise.} \end{cases} \tag{17}$$

For example, in a hypothetical three-product industry where products 1 and 2 are produced by General Motors (GM), product 3 by Chrysler, the Bertrand H would be:

$$\begin{matrix} 1 & 1 & 0 \\ 1 & 1 & 0 \\ 0 & 0 & 1 \end{matrix} \tag{18}$$

since the first two products are presumed to cooperate, the third not. Under the collusive behavioral assumption, the H for the same industry would be:

$$\begin{matrix} 1 & 1 & 1 \\ 1 & 1 & 1 \\ 1 & 1 & 1 \end{matrix} \tag{19}$$

since all products are presumed to cooperate.

In this notation, the first-order condition for a typical product takes the form:

$$0 = q_i + (P_i - mc(x_i))\frac{\partial q_i}{\partial p_i} + H_{ii+1}(P_{i+1} - mc(x_{i+1}))\frac{\partial q_{i+1}}{\partial P_i} + H_{ii-1}(P_{i-1} - mc(x_{i-1}))\frac{\partial q_{i-1}}{\partial p_i} \tag{20}$$

The effect of the behavioral assumptions on equilibrium prices can be seen in (20). An important determinant of $P_i - mc_i$ is the extent to which the single-product demand curve for i has slope ($q_i - (\partial q_i/\partial P_i)^{-1}$ in (20)). If the same firm produces the neighboring products, or if the firm is colluding with its neighbors, $P_i - mc_i$ is further increased. This follows from $(P_{i+1} - mc_{i+1})(\partial q_{i+1}/\partial P_i)$, P_i's impact on the neighbor's net revenue. It is easy to show that changing $H_{i,i+1}$ from zero to one for any i increases $P_k - mc_k$ for all k.

The equilibrium prices and quantities can be calculated by simultaneously solving the demand system (9)–(11) and all of the firm first-order conditions (20). The equilibrium price and quantity vectors are written:

$$\begin{aligned} p &= p^*(x, H, \gamma, V_{\max}, \delta, \mu) \\ q &= q^*(x, H, \gamma, V_{\max}, \delta, \mu) \end{aligned} \tag{21}$$

In the econometric specification described in the next section, the errors are additive in the reduced form.

To see the central intuition of the model, consider the example given in Figure 2. In the example, Firm One sells products 2, 4, and 5. Firm Two sells product 3. The prices of products 1 and 6 are held fixed—these products are sold by some third firm. In Figure 2(b), the equilibrium prices are shown under the assumption that Firms One and Two are *not* tacitly colluding. Note that the prices of products 2 and 3 are very near MC. This is because the products are nearly perfect substitutes and the solution concept is Nash in

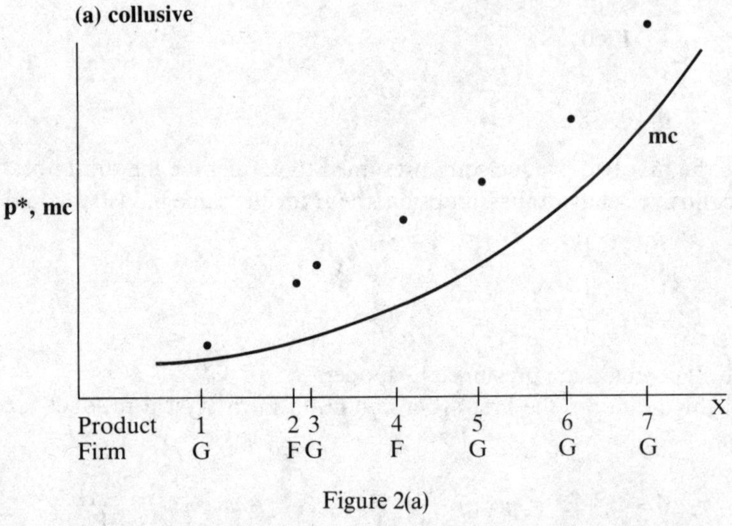

Figure 2(a)

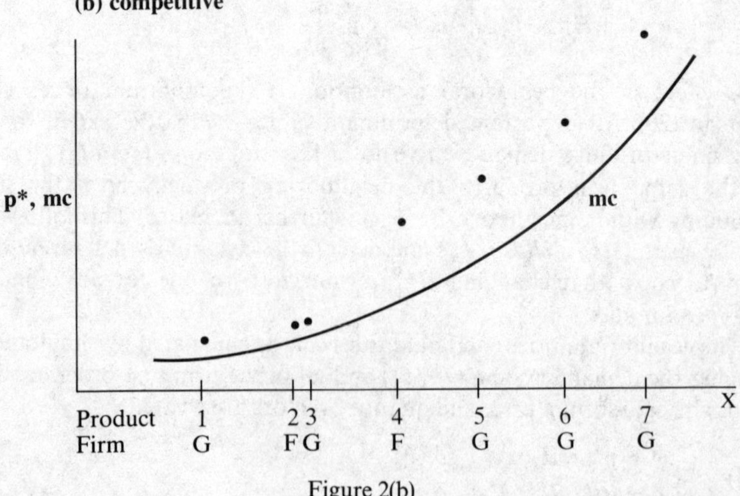

Figure 2(b)

Prices (Bertrand). In Figure 2(a), Firms One and Two are assumed to collude. The prices of products 2 and 3 are substantially above *MC*; that they are close substitutes is much less relevant when the firms maximize joint profits.

Products 4 and 5 change much less when the solution concept changes. Competition lowers their prices, of course, but it is distant rather than close competition. The intuition of the model is that product-space regions with many firms in them are quite different under competition and collusion. Product-space regions with only a few firms in them are similar under the two solution concepts, since there will be substantial market power even if firms compete.

In the mid-fifties automobile industry, the region like that around products 4 and 5 is the large-car end of the product spectrum. GM produced most of the cars sold in that segment. The region around products 1 and 2 is like the smaller-car segments; Ford, Chrysler, GM (and, to a lesser extent, the fringe and AMC are all present. Thus, for this industry, one should expect the methods developed in this section to have (statistical) power. In a product-differentiated industry where every producer had a full line, these methods might be less revealing. I shall return to this point in the concluding section.

II. ECONOMETRIC SPECIFICATION

Three main topics remain before estimation: proxies for quality, the data, and the error structure with its associated likelihood function.

Proxies for quality

The discussion of price equilibrium presumed that the quality of every product was known. In actuality, physical characteristics must be used as proxies. The interpretation of the proxy relationship comes from the hedonic price model of Rosen [1974]. Consumers are assumed to have preferences over the physical characteristics, z. Firms can produce automobiles at costs which depend on z. The proxy relationship is then interpreted as the expansion path of efficient (cost-minimizing) z's.

It is here arbitrarily assumed to take the square-root form:

$$x(c) = \sqrt{\beta_0 + \sum_j z_j \beta_j} \tag{22}$$

where β are parameters to be estimated. The interpretation of β is clouded by the fact that it contains information about both tastes and technology.

It is now possible to lay out the steps used in computing predicted prices and quantities from the parameters β, γ, μ, δ and $V_{\max}$ and the exogenous variables Z.

1. Each product is assigned a quality depending on the parameters β and its physical characteristics, z, using equation (22):

2. The products are ordered from highest to lowest, so that the product whose quality is i^{th} is assigned the index i:
3. The product qualities from step 1 and the rankings from step 2 plus the remaining parameters are used to solve (9)–(11) and (20) simultaneously for predicted values P^* and Q^*. The predicted values as a function of the parameters are then plugged into the likelihood function as described below.

Examination of (9) suggests that the demand for the lowest-quality good is overparameterized. The parameters E and γ were not easily distinguishable in data, so that the restriction $E = mc(\gamma)$ was imposed after some initial experimentation.

The data: A quantity aggregation problem

Data on prices, quantities and physical characteristics are nearly all from contemporary trade publications. A more precise version of their definition and collection is in Appendix A. Since the prime determinant of demand elasticities in the model is the difference in quality of automobile products, the definition of what constitutes a separate product is central to the data-handling part of this study. The model-naming conventions of the automakers are not useful in this regard. They vary widely across both time and firms.[8] The data used in this paper award an automobile model status as a separate product only if it is physically distinct from all others. This yields about 80–85 models each year, whereas the finest possible disaggregation might yield 140–150.

The level of disaggregation used in this paper is finer than the detail in which automobile manufacturers reported the quantities produced. For example, in the 1954 model year production data, Chrysler reports production for V-8 Desoto. But both Firedome and Fireflite models were sold with the V-8 engine. The solution to this problem is to aggregate predicted quantities up to the level of the data. In the example, the predicted quantities for the two V-8 models are summed; the difference between that sum and the reported quantity is the residual.

Since the coarseness of quantity aggregation varies over the sample, a problem of heteroskedasticity arises. It is assumed that the underlying quantity variance is $\sigma^2 q$ and that a predicted quantity formed as the sum of k products has variance $k\sigma^2 q$. If q_j is an observed quantity, we define I_j as the set of indices on the products making up q_j:

(23) $i \in I_j$ if product i is to be aggregated to quantity j

$k_j = \text{card}(I_j)$ is the number of products so aggregated.

[8] "Independent" manufacturers sometimes doubled the number of model names offered for sale in the period with only trivial expansion in the set of physical products offered. This was usually a warning sign of impending exit.

Prices are list prices as of mid-April in the model year. The physical characteristics are those used in the Ohta and Griliches [1976] hedonic study: length, weight, horsepower, engine type and a body-type dummy.

The likelihood function

The predicted prices and quantities, P^* and Q^*, defined as functions of the parameters and the exogenous variables, z, are subject to additive, independent normal error. Quantity and price errors are independent. The price errors all have variance $\sigma^2 p$ while the quantity error j has variance $k_j\sigma^2 q$. Then the likelihood function is given by:

$$(24)\qquad \prod_{i=1}^{N_p} \frac{1}{\sqrt{2\pi^2 p}} \exp\left[-\frac{(P_i - P_i^*)^2}{2\sigma^2 p} \right]$$

$$* \prod_{j=1}^{N_q} \frac{1}{\sqrt{2\pi k_j \sigma^2 q}} \exp\left[-\frac{(q_j - \sum q^* k, kI_j)^2}{2k_j\sigma^2 q} \right]$$

where N_p and N_q are the price and quantity equation sample sizes. Since P^* and Q^* are computed only in terms of the parameters and the exogenous variables, this is fully a reduced-form error structure.

The likelihood function suffers a serious irregularity—it is not continuous in the parameters.[9]

All estimation was done by (numerical) maximum likelihood. The irregularities of the likelihood function could be expected to be troublesome here as well, since a discontinuous function cannot be concave.[10]

Other specifications estimated

In order to provide tests of the Collusive and Nash-competitive models, two other models are introduced.

The hedonic-price model has been given an interpretation as the perfectly competitive equilibrium of a continuously differentiated market by Rosen [1974]. Other authors have used the hedonic price approach in the presence of oligopoly, adding firm dummies as a proxy for "market power". We will estimate such a model, the loglinear price and quantity empirical hedonic model introduced by Cowling and Cubbin [1971] with UK automobile market data. This version of the hedonic model has predicted prices and

[9] Predicted prices are everywhere continuous, but there are discrete points in the parameter space where predicted quantities are discontinuous. The points of discontinuity are those β at which two products (including γ) are equal in quality. These are unlikely to be true parameter values, so that the limiting statistical inference goes through.

[10] One might expect numerical difficulties arising from local maxima. However, none were encountered. The points of discontinuity themselves are typically local minima because they involve extreme predicted quantities.

quantities in a recursive structure:

$$(25)\qquad P_i^* = \exp\left[\alpha_0 + \sum_j \alpha_j z_{ij}\right]$$

and

$$(26)\qquad q_j^* = \exp[\lambda_0 + \lambda_1(P_j - P_j^*)]$$

This model is endowed with precisely the same error and quantity aggregation structure as the oligopoly models. The hedonic model or something like it should hold if automobile list price data are set in some nonmaximizing way.

The justification for introducing the hedonic model for test purposes lies in its radical differences from the oligopoly models. Another way to test those models might be to specify an alternative that is very much like them. This is the justification for the "products" specification. This model follows exactly the theoretical development of the oligopoly models, except that each automobile product is treated as if it were manufactured by a separate firm. The matrix C for this specification is an identity matrix, since no two products are presumed to cooperate.

Neither the hedonic nor the "products" model is an appealing economic story of the automobile industry. But the test results of the next section show these two models to be extremely useful in rejecting false specifications among the oligopoly models.

III. EMPIRICAL RESULTS

This section presents likelihood-ratio (Cox) tests of each model against all the others. Discussion of the estimates and an analysis of the residual follows for those models not rejected in the test section.

Hypothesis tests

Although the models estimated here are not nested, the results of Cox [1961] and Pesaran and Deaton [1978] allow explicit hypothesis testing.[11] In Cox's framework, the hypothesis to be tested is confronted with the data and with an alternative, nonnested hypothesis. The likelihood ratio of the two hypotheses is the central statistic. Its mean and variance are computed under the assumption that the maintained hypothesis is true. If the difference of the likelihood ratio from its mean, divided by its standard deviation, is significantly different from zero, the maintained hypothesis is rejected. One attractive feature of the test statistic so obtained is that it is known to be asymptotically a standard normal under the maintained hypothesis, so that

[11] The Pesaran–Deaton nonlinear regression Cox-test formulae have been slightly altered to take account of the aggregation of quantities. See Appendix B.

TABLE III
COX TEST STATISTICS

Hypotheses	*C*	*N–C*	*'p'*	*H*
a—1954				
Collusion	—	0.8951	0.9464	−1.934
Nash-Competition	−2.325	—	−0.8878	−2.819
"Products"	−3.978	3.029	—	−1.604
Hedonic	−12.37	−10.94	−13.02	—
b—1955				
Collusion	—	−10.36	−9.884	−13.36
Nash-Competition	−1.594	—	1.260	0.6341
"Products"	−0.7598	−4.379	—	−1.527
Hedonic	−3.353	−8.221	−5.950	—
c—1956				
Collusion	—	1.227	0.8263	1.629
Nash-Competition	−2.426	—	−4.586	0.8314
"Products"	−3.153	0.9951	—	4.731
Hedonic	−5.437	−9.671	−11.58	—

one knows what a significant difference is. It is also possible for each of two models to be rejected against the other. This is the rationale for the introduction of the "products" and hedonic models. If the oligopoly models survive against these added alternatives, it will increase one's certainty that they are correct.

The test results are summarized in Table III. The nature of the Cox test is that one model, H_0, is assumed true and then contrasted with another model (H_1) and the data. The intuition of the tests is this: if the residuals under H_0 can be explained (to a statistically significant extent) by H_1, then H_0 is rejected. In Table III, the row stub gives the hypothesis being tested, the column header the alternative being used to test it. Values of the test statistic (asymptotically a standard normal) significantly different from zero lead to rejection.

The 1954 results show the hedonic model rejected against every other hypothesis. "Products" is rejected against each of the other two oligopoly models, though not against the hedonic model.[12] Nash-Equilibrium is rejected against the Collusive and Hedonic models. Only the Collusive model escapes rejection against any alternative.

The 1956 results clearly resemble those of 1954. No specification but Collusion escapes rejection, while Collusion is not rejected against any other model.

[12] Note that the Cox test is two tailed. "Products" is rejected in one instance because its likelihood is too large.

TABLE IV
PARAMETER ESTIMATES 1954–56, MAINTAINED SPECIFICATION

Parameters	*1954*[a]	*1955*[b]	*1956*[a]
Physical Characteristics			
Quality Proxies			
Constant	47.91	48.28	50.87
	(32.8)	(43.2)	(29.4)
Weight #/1000	0.3805	0.5946	0.5694
	(0.332)	(0.145)	(0.374)
Length "/1000	0.1819	0.1461	0.1507
	(0.128)	(0.059)	(0.146)
Horsepower/100	2.665	3.350	3.248
	(0.692)	(0.535)	(0.620)
Cylinders	−0.7387	−0.9375	−0.9639
	(0.205)	(0.115)	(0.186)
Hardtop Dummy	0.9445	0.4531	0.4311
	(0.379)	(0.312)	(0.401)
Demand/Supply			
μ—*Marginal Cost*	0.1753	0.1747	0.1880
	(0.024)	(0.020)	(0.035)
γ—*Lower Endpoint*	4.593	3.911	4.441
	(1.49)	(2.08)	(1.46)
V_{max}—*Upper Endpoint*	1.92*E*+7	2.41*E*+7	2.83*E*+7
	(8.44*E*+6)	(9.21*E*+6)	(7.98*E*+6)
δ—*Taste Density*	0.4108	0.4024	0.4075
	(0.138)	(0.184)	(0.159)

Notes: Figures in parentheses are asymptotic standard errors.
[a] Estimated using the Collusion specification.
[b] Estimated using the Nash-Competition specification.

The 1955 estimates are very different. Collusion is rejected against all three alternatives, while Nash-Competition is not rejected against any. Despite this reversal, the remaining hypotheses are rejected in this year as in the other two.

Overall, the test statistics tell the story of a dramatic reversal in the 1955 automobile year. Supply side behavior was clearly much more competitive in 1955 than in the adjacent years.[13] The coincidence of these test results with the expansion in production that year is striking. It is important to emphasize that the tests results and the overall expansion are independent evidence. In the absence of cross-year restrictions, for example on the location of the automobile demand curve, there is no particular reason for the competitive model to be selected in the high quantity year. The reliability of the test

[13] The period 1954–56 is not entirely arbitrary. The Korean war price and quantity controls were lifted in February/March 1953. Foreign competition of any consequence begins with Volkswagen's entry in 1957. No labor-based work stoppages lasted more than ten days within the period.

results is also demonstrated by their robustness to the introduction of the two always-rejected specifications, the hedonic and "products".

The estimates

Table IV reports estimated parameters for those hypotheses not rejected in the tests of hypothesis. The 1954 and 1956 results come from the Collusion specification, the 1955 estimates from the Nash-competition specification. The similarity of the columns of Table IV is striking; the distinct features of the 1955 model year are captured by a change in behavioral assumption rather than by changes in the estimated parameters.

Tables V, which report parameter estimates for all years by specification, lack this consistency. When a single behavioral assumption is maintained throughout, the parameter estimates must provide the empirical explanation of 1955. In Table V(i), the results for the Collusive specification, the 1955 column departs from its neighbors. Note in particular that the 1955 estimate of μ is an order of magnitude larger, that for δ an order of magnitude smaller, than in the surrounding years. Further, length has a negative coefficient in 1955.

Table V(ii) which reports estimates from the Nash-Equilibrium specification, is similarly chaotic. 1954 shows the only negative value for the hardtop dummy estimated in any year for any specification. And the 1955 demand

TABLE V(i)
PARAMETER ESTIMATES 1954–56, COLLUSIVE SPECIFICATION

Parameters	*1954*	*1955*	*1956*
Constant	47.91	−23.37	50.87
	(32.8)	(24.5)	(29.4)
Weight	0.3805	0.0103	0.5694
	(0.332)	(5.43*E*−2)	(0.374)
Length	0.1819	−2.88*E*−3	0.1507
	(0.128)	(0.102)	(0.146)
Horsepower	2.665	0.1165	3.248
	(0.692)	(0.106)	(0.620)
Cylinders	−0.7387	−1.309	−0.9639
	(0.205)	(1.52)	(0.186)
Hardtop	0.9445	1.468	0.4311
	(0.379)	(1.08)	(0.401)
μ	0.1753	1.344	0.1880
	(0.024)	(0.151)	(0.035)
γ	4.593	1.604	4.441
	(1.49)	(4.83)	(1.46)
V_{max}	1.92*E*+7	1.46*E*+8	2.83*E*+7
	(8.44*E*+6)	(6.74*E*+6)	(7.98*E*+6)
δ	0.4108	5.75*E*−2	0.4075
	(0.138)	(8.28*E*−2)	(0.159)

Note: Figures in parentheses are asymptotic standard errors.

TABLE V(ii)
PARAMETER ESTIMATES 1954–56, BERTRAND SPECIFICATION

Parameters	*1954*	*1955*	*1956*
Constant	31.64	48.28	33.23
	(29.9)	(43.2)	(17.8)
Weight	0.9311	0.5946	$6.23E-3$
	(0.210)	(0.145)	$(8.73E-4)$
Length	0.1474	0.1461	0.1605
	(0.038)	(0.059)	(0.149)
Horsepower	4.962	3.350	$2.972E-2$
	(0.676)	(0.535)	$(1.47E-2)$
Cylinders	−0.8846	−0.9375	−0.9078
	(0.194)	(0.115)	(0.256)
Hardtop	−0.2474	0.4531	0.5282
	(0.464)	(0.312)	(0.249)
μ	0.2518	0.1747	0.2902
	(0.074)	(0.312)	(0.249)
γ	6.352	3.911	1.204
	(3.54)	(2.08)	(3.19)
V_{max}	$9.81E+5$	$2.41E+7$	$1.03E+6$
	$(8.78E+6)$	$(9.21E+6)$	$(8.90E+6)$
δ	5.04	0.4024	7.334
	(1.21)	(0.184)	(2.46)

Note: Figures in parentheses are asymptotic standard errors.

TABLE V(iii)
PARAMETER ESTIMATES 1954–56, HEDONIC SPECIFICATION

Price Equation	*1954*	*1955*	*1956*
Constant	5.294	4.469	5.239
	(2.52)	(0.230)	(0.371)
Weight	0.6117	0.4098	0.6537
	(0.093)	(0.068)	(0.023)
Horsepower	−0.7760	−0.3891	−0.8121
	(0.574)	(0.605)	(0.125)
Cylinder	0.0417	0.0442	0.0976
	(0.086)	(0.082)	(0.087)
Hardtop	2.438	3.171	2.381
	(0.224)	(0.379)	(0.257)
GM Dummy	−0.445	−0.0563	−0.0783
	(0.024)	(0.024)	(0.024)
Ford Dummy	−0.0191	0.7706	−0.0435
	(0.044)	(5.31)	(0.045)
Quantity Equation	***1954***	***1955***	***1956***
Constant	6.386	6.814	6.332
	(2.96)	(3.58)	(2.11)
Price	−3.742	−1.312	−3.322
	(0.640)	(0.787)	(0.715)

Note: Figures in parentheses are asymptotic standard errors.

parameters show tastes distributed at one tenth the density over ten times the range in the population as in the surrounding years. Table IV, which is after all constructed from these two tables, tells a much more consistent story of the underlying market than they. Indeed, no set of maintained hypotheses other than that left unrejected by the data, no other conceivable Table, could tell that consistent story. It is change of behavioral assumption, not change of parameter values, that provides a reasonable empirical explanation of 1955.

The parameter estimates in Table IV can be conveniently discussed in two groups. First are the quality-proxy parameters, β. In sign and absolute value, they are what one would expect from a hedonic regression. The one counter-intuitive sign, the negative "cylinders" coefficient, is also familiar from hedonic analyses. The econometric interpretation is that "horsepower" and "cylinders" are highly collinear. The economic interpretation is that the "cylinders" variable captures the fall in the cost of horsepower after the introduction of the V-8 engine.

The rest of the parameters require more discussion. The two central demand parameters, $V_{\max}$ and δ, tell a story of quite diverse tastes for automobile quality. Recall that δ is the density of the distribution of tastes in the population, $V_{\max}$ its upper limit. The eight million 1955 buyers then had v distributed over the interval $(4.24E+6, 2.4E+7)$. In other words, the distribution of tastes among buyers was 20 million wide and 0.4 deep (with 20 million times 0.4 giving the eight million buyers). This finding may be an artifact of the constant density assumption. The other demand parameter, γ, represents the quality of the hypothetical used car into which new-car nonbuyers substitute. It is estimated to be around 4 in each year; the lowest quality auto has quality just around 9. Thus, new and used cars are not very close substitutes. The final parameter, μ, serves only to correct the units of quality to those of money in the marginal-cost relation.

A simple calculation can clarify the role of shifts in demand versus changes in form behavior in explaining the 1955 expansion. What prices and quantities would have been observed if collusion had reigned in 1955 as well? To answer this question, we calculate equilibrium predicted values using the 1955 parameter estimates (which were estimated under the Bertrand specification) and the collusive solution concept. This calculation leads to an *increase* of 1955 prices over each of the surrounding years—about one-half of one percent over the average of 1954 and 1956. It also leads to predicted 1955 unit sales of 7.1 million units—25.5%, not 40.4%, higher than the 1954/56 average. One way to interpret this is in light of the demand for autos literature. The largest residual in Chow's [1960] demand system comes in the 1955 data. It is +0.6 million units. This is clearly comparable to the change implied by the supply side of 0.8 (7.9 − 7.1) million units.

One surprise is that the 1955 purchases do not seem to have depressed 1956 demand. In Table IV, both δ and $V_{\max}$ are greater in 1956 than in 1955, but the increases are not great. More significant is the high value of γ in 1956. This

TABLE V(iv)
PARAMETER ESTIMATES 1954–56, "PRODUCTS" SPECIFICATION

Parameters	*1954*	*1955*	*1956*
Constant	57.95	17.32	46.06
	(26.1)	(27.6)	(26.6)
Weight	$5.478E-3$	$7.98E-3$	$6.221E-3$
	$(3.44E-2)$	$(4.63E-2)$	$(8.62E-3)$
Length	0.1731	0.8984	0.1926
	(0.529)	(0.576)	(0.390)
Horsepower	0.0520	−1.003	0.0287
	(0.056)	(0.089)	(0.076)
Cylinders	−0.5267	0.3799	−0.9456
	(0.894)	(0.699)	(0.587)
Hardtop	0.2811	0.5656	0.4075
	(0.511)	(0.534)	(0.687)
μ	0.1334	0.1507	0.1748
	(0.415)	(0.224)	(0.245)
γ	6.894	1.482	1.270
	(2.86)	(4.48)	(2.99)
V_{max}	$4.21E+7$	$1.61E+8$	$1.05E+6$
	$(8.57E+6)$	$(8.38E+6)$	$(8.71E+6)$
δ	0.9648	$5.01E-2$	7.174
	(0.552)	$(8.09E-2)$	(2.27)

Note: Figures in parentheses are asymptotic standard errors.

indicates considerable competition from the used-car market. On the other hand, 1954 and 1956 have very similar demand parameters. Thus, it is difficult to argue that the 1956 estimates reflect the previous year's high quantity sold.

The residuals and some simple generalizations

Table VI gives part of the intuition behind the formal test results. The reversal between the Collusion/Bertrand models shows up here as a general reversal

TABLE VI
PRICE AND QUANTITY,* EQUATION R^2

	1954		*1955*		*1956*	
Model	P	q	P	q	P	q
Collusion	0.94	0.62	0.92	0.58	0.96	0.61
Bertrand	0.91	0.62	0.96	0.64	0.93	0.62
"Products"	0.90	0.62	0.88	0.59	0.92	0.61
Hedonic	0.89	0.71	0.88	0.73	0.88	0.71

* Quantity equation R^2 is defined as a fraction of explained variance because of the heteroskedasticity problem. That is, $R_q^2 = (s_q^2 - \hat{\sigma}_q^2)/s_q^2$, where s_q^2 is the second raw moment of the quantity data, estimated under the same heteroskedastic variance structure as used in the econometric models.

TABLE VII
BIG THREE VS. ALL OTHERS AVERAGE RESIDUALS

	1954[a]	*1955*[b]	*1956*[a]
a—Prices			
GM	20.92	28.80	21.48
Ford	−12.33	−6.28	−11.02
Chrysler	−13.16	−9.33	−17.19
b—Quantities			
GM	−99.6	−82.86	−68.73
Ford	60.2	22.97	19.06
Chrysler	96.89	64.47	11.94

Notes: Figures are: average residual for firm named minus average for all other firms (including other two big-three firms). Price figures have dollar units; quantity figures, number of cars.
[a] Estimated from Collusive specification.
[b] Estimated from Nash-Competitive specification.

in R^2. In each year, the model not rejected explains more variance in both equations. A somewhat more surprising result is the consistently better fit of the hedonic model in the quantity equation. Since this does not lead to rejection of the structural oligopoly models against the hedonic alternative, I conclude that the price equation is providing most of the power for the hypothesis tests.[14]

Table VII compares the average residuals (from the unrejected specification) for each of the big three automakers to residuals for all other firms. Since "all other firms" for Ford and Chrysler includes GM, I conclude that the clearest message from this table is about GM. The oligopoly models consistently overpredict GM prices by \$30 (out of the \$1500 price of a typical car) and underpredict GM sales by 100 units (out of typical sales of around 60 000). These figures arc not large enough to be alarming, but they do suggest that GM enjoyed either a cost or quality advantage over other producers. Two slightly more general specifications were estimated (for each oligopoly model) as a result. In one, a GM dummy was added to z, to capture superior quality. In the other, GM got a separate marginal cost parameter μ. Neither β_{GM} nor μ_{GM} was significant in any unrejected hypothesis. No Cox-test result was reversed in the broader specifications. Inclusion of either GM-specific parameter does make Table VII look much more like zeros, however.

The economic hypotheses tested in the last section depend in a crucial way on the assignment of imputed qualities, x_i, to each auto i. The tests depend crucially on which products are neighboring. Small errors in the prediction of x_i, for example, could change the *ordering* of the products, and thus change

[14] The problem here is that the models introduced in this paper have no constant in the quantity equation. See (9)–(11). For prices, *mc* explains much of the cross-section variance, so R^2 would be high even if not much of the markup were being explained.

the extent to which products produced by the same firm are neighboring or not. This can clearly have a large effect on the predicted values.[15] This problem can be minimized with a simple generalization. Following Bresnahan [1981], the quality-proxy relationship is rewritten as observed with error

$$x(z) = \sqrt{\beta_0 + \varepsilon_j \beta_j Z_j} + \varepsilon_x$$

Since x is not (directly) observable, ε_x must be integrated out of the likelihood function. This has an imporant effect on the nature of substitution across products. When ε_x has zero variance, each product is predicted to be a substitute for only two others. As the variance of ε_x increases, there is greater and greater probability of demand-side interaction with less similar products. Thus, this expansion of the specification "smears" the demand equations, significantly reducing the importance of very similar products. Unfortunately, I do not know how to construct Cox tests for this broader specification. The likelihoods of the broader specification, however, show that the Bertrand model fits best in 1955 and the Collusive model in the other years. There is, therefore, no reason to believe that the test results are an artifact of the quality-proxy.

The third simple generalization is designed to test a glaring shortcoming of the specification—that automobiles are treated as a flow good rather than a durable. This is accomplished by expanding the specification to

$$P_i = P_i^*(\cdot) + \lambda S_i + \varepsilon_p$$

and

$$q_i = q_i^*(\cdot) + \theta S_i + \varepsilon_q$$

S_i is defined as the stock of used cars "like" model *i*. Here "like" means within ten percent in weight, and used cars are assumed to depreciate at 15 percent per year. This is *ad hoc*, but should show something of the results are an artifact of the nondurability assumption. In fact, both λ and θ differ significantly from zero, but the Cox test results of Table III are unaltered.[16]

The primary results of this paper have been subjected to two kinds of tests: the simple increases in parameterization in this section and the tests against the hedonic and "products" specification in the last. I conclude first that the highly structured oligopoly models estimated here do not tell all of the story the data have to tell. I conclude second that the conclusions about firm behavior appear nonetheless to be robust.

IV. CONCLUSION

The 1955 auto model year had three anomalous features: price fell during a macroeconomic expansion, quantity increased well out of proportion to

[15] Professor Robert Masson made this argument, which is clearly a possible problem.
[16] The results were rerun only for the collusive and Bertrand specifications.

experience, and the share of the basic transportation segment in total auto sales increased. The hypothesis that tacit collusion among the automakers broke down in 1955 explains these anomalies. Like any supply-shift story, it explains the aggregate quantity and price-index movements. It rationalizes the segment shift because of differences in the nature of competitive interaction across auto market segments. The effect of increased competition on prices and quantities should have been largest in the small-car segment, where every company's products have close substitutes sold by competitors. The price war hypothesis thus explains the aggregate data as well as standing up well in econometric tests. These tests are based on the fine structure of automobile prices and quantities in cross-section.

There are two classes of methods available for empirical studies of market power. One class looks for explicit indicators of market power, for example price-cost margins. The difficulty here lies in the use of accounting data as a proxy for economic variables. The issues raised in section I about the allocation of capital costs over time strongly suggest that these methods are unsuitable for studies of single industries. A second class of method specifies and estimates structural demand and supply equations. In the presence of market power, the supply equation includes a term for the demand elasticity. Econometric detection of market power then depends on estimation of this term. This was the kind of method used in this paper. In a product-differentiated industry like automobiles, a crucial determinant of the demand elasticities is the "distance" between products in quality space. Under non-cooperative oligopoly solution concepts, such as the Bertrand model used here, it matters a great deal whether the same firm or different ones produce close substitutes. In the former case, the marginal revenue term in the imperfectly competitive supply equation is substantially larger. This distinction disappears under collusion. Thus by focussing on the structural supply equation, the econometric methods used here can discriminate between competition and collusion.

TIMOTHY F. BRESNAHAN,
Economics Department,
Stanford University,
Stanford, CA,
USA.

APPENDIX A

Data sources and handling

In this paper's empirical work, the economic variables price, quantity and product characteristics are observed as list price, model-year production and engineering specifications. One source of these data is contemporary trade publications: *Ward's,*

Automotive Industries, and *Automotive News*. The other source is Heasley [1977], based on interviews with automobile executives made between 1972 and 1974.

In general, two sources were available for every number in the data. These and precise descriptions of data provenance follow; this paragraph gives a thumbnail sketch. (1) Model specifications and list price data were copied, except for minor error checking. (2) Model-year production figures were used when reported. Otherwise the figures were constructed from monthly production data and the dates of the model year. (3) The decision as to what constitutes a separate model was independent of maker's model naming conventions. Physical distinctness led to classification as different models.

List prices are reported in tables in all three trade journals and in the Company Pages of *Ward's*. The *Ward's* and *Automotive News* tables failed to match on about two percent of all prices; recourse to the other two sources led to a three-way match in every case. No "dealer discount" correction was made since the discount was constant across models before 1959. The prices used are Ohta and Griliches [1976] "PA" Options are excluded, except heaters where the information is available. Power steering and power brakes are included only if standard.

Model specifications are available in all three trade journals in tables. The *Ward's-Automotive Industries* check yielded a nonmatch rate of over five percent. *Automotive News* resolved all of the nonmatches but one, which could be found in a contemporary brochure. The characteristics were:

Length: Bumper to bumper length in thousands of inches;
Weight: "Curb Weight", full trim included, but unloaded in thousands of pounds;
Horsepower: Advance maximum brake horsepower, in hundreds;
Cylinders: Number;

and

Hardtop: A body type dummy, one for hardtop models.

Model-year production is reported in incomplete tables in *Automotive-News*, *Ward's*, and Heasley [1977] and, also incompletely, in the Company Pages of *Ward's*. Monthly production data are also available, somewhat less incompletely, in all three trade journals. The match rate for the following procedure was 100 percent. Incomplete model year tables were filled in using the monthly data. Although model years rarely begin on the first of the month, the model changeover was always revealed (by the work-stoppage tables) to have encompassed the first. This permitted exact calculation. Heasley [1977] figures were usually the second source to confirm the constructed data, since the trade journal tables were usually all incomplete in exactly the same way.

Production data, rather than sales or registrations, have the advantage that they can be tied very precisely to the model year. Thus it is clear what physical product was sold in these data. On the other side, production data do not clearly correspond to a market definition. In particular, neither fleet sales nor end of model year bargains can be adequately treated.

The empirical definition of an automobile model is crucial to this study. Models were construed distinct in the data if they: (1) were of different makes (Pontiac and Chevrolet are different makes for this purpose even though both are GM manufactured); (2) had different engines, frames or body types. Only the hardtop and 4-door sedan (replaced by 2-door for those models with no 4-door) body types are included; or (3) differed in weight or length by over one percent.

APPENDIX B

Cox test statistics

The models estimated in this paper differ from the general regression models of Pesaran and Deaton [1978] in two ways. First, the price-quantity error covariance is here constrained to be zero, and second, there has been aggregation in the quantity equation. These two differences do not alter the nature of the test statistics in any important way, but it is necessary to allow for them in the computational formulae.

First define

(B.1) $\quad s^2jp \equiv$ estimated price variance under H_j

and

(B.2) $\quad s^2jq \equiv$ estimated quantity variance under H_j

Now consider this phony-data regression. Take the predicted values from H_0. Use these as if they were data in specification H_1. Call the estimated variances from the regression ϕ^2p and ϕ^2q. Now define:

(B.3) $\quad s^2 10p \equiv s^2 0p + \phi^2 p$

(B.4) $\quad s^2 10q \equiv s^2 0p + \phi^2 q$

Then the numerator of the Cox test statistic, which is the difference between the $H_0 H_1$ log-likelihood ratio and its expected value when H_0 is true, is given by:

(B.5) $$T_0 = \frac{Np}{2}\log\left[\frac{s^2 1p}{s^2 10p}\right] + \frac{Nq}{2}\log\left[\frac{s^2 1q}{s^2 10q}\right]$$

where Np and Nq are the price and quantity equation sample sizes.

The denominator of the test statistic is the (asymptotic) variance to T_0. To compute it requires another regression. Take the residuals from the phony-data regression above and regress them (linearly) on the derivatives of the predicted values with respect to the parameters under H_0. Call the estimated variances in that regression ϕp and ϕq. Then:

(B.6) $$V_0(T_0) = Np\phi p\left[\frac{s^2 0p}{s^4 10p}\right] + Nq\phi q\left[\frac{s^2 0q}{s^4 10q}\right]$$

The ratio of $T_0/V(T_0)$ is asymptotically a standard normal if H_0 is true. As with all asymptotic statistics in this paper, that asymptotic normality is unproven, since the likelihood function does not meet the regularity conditions for nonlinear regression. The hedonic-price model does not come under this caveat. Its rejection in this paper is statistically quite clean.

REFERENCES

Automotive News Almanac, 1954–57 (Slocum Publishing Company, Detroit).

BRESNAHAN, T. F., 1980, 'Three Essays on the American Automobile Oligopoly', unpublished Ph.D. Dissertation, Princeton University.

BRESNAHAN, T. F., 1981, 'Departures from Marginal-Cost Pricing in the American Automobile Industry', *Journal of Econometrics*, 17, pp. 201–227.

CAGAN, PHILLIP, 1971, 'Quality Changes and the Purchasing Power of Money', in Z. GRILICHES (ed.), *Price Indexes and Quality Change* (Harvard University Press, Cambridge, Mass.).

CHILTON CORPORATION, 1954–57, *Automotive Industries, Annual Statistical Issue*, Philadelphia.

CHOW, G. C., 1960, 'Statistical Demand Functions for Automobiles and Their Use for Forecasting', pp. 149–178 in A. C. HARBERGER (ed.), *Demand for Durable Goods* (University of Chicago Press).

COWLING, K. G. and CUBBIN, J., 1971, 'Price, Quality and Advertising Competition: An Econometric Investigation of the U.K. Car Market', *Economica*, pp. 378–394.

COX, D. R., 1961, 'Tests of Separate Families of Hypotheses', *Proceedings of the Fourth Berkeley Symposium on Mathematical Statistics and Probability*, Vol. 1, pp. 105–123 (University of California Press, Berkeley).

GRILICHES, ZVI, 1964, 'Notes on the Measurement of Price and Quality Changes', in *Models of Income Determination*, Studies in Income and Wealth, Vol. 28 (National Bureau of Economic Research, New York).

HEASLEY, J., 1977, *The Production Figure Book for U.S. Cars* (Motorbooks International, Osceola, Wis.).

HOTELLING, H., 1929, 'Stability in Competition', *Economic Journal*, Vol. 39 (March), pp. 41–57.

Moody's Industrial Manual, annual, various issues.

OHTA, M. and GRILICHES, Z., 1976, 'Automobile Prices Revisited: Extensions of the Hedonic Hypotheses', in N. E. TERLECKYJ (ed.), *Household Production and Consumption*, NBER Studies in Income and Wealth, Vol. 40 (Columbia University Press, New York).

PESARAN, M. H. and DEATON, A. S., 1978, 'Testing Non-Nested Nonlinear Regression Models', *Econometrica*, 46, pp. 677–694.

PRESCOTT, E. C. and VISSCHER, M., 1977, 'Sequential Location Among Firms with Foresight', *The Bell Journal of Economics*, 8(2), Autumn, pp. 378–393.

ROSEN, S., 1974, 'Hedonic Prices and Implicit Markets', *Journal of Political Economy*, 82 (January/February), pp. 34–55.

SHAKED, A. and SUTTON, J., 1983, 'Natural Oligopolies', *Econometrica*, 51, 5 (September), pp. 1469–1484.

US DEPARTMENT OF LABOR, BUREAU OF LABOR STATISTICS, *Handbook of Labor Statistics, 1967*.

US DEPARTMENT OF COMMERCE, BUREAU OF THE CENSUS, *Statistical Abstract of the United States*, annual, various issues.

US DEPARTMENT OF COMMERCE, BUREAU OF ECONOMIC ANALYSIS, *The National Income and Product Accounts of the United States, 1929–1974*.

Ward's Automotive Yearbook, 1954–57 (Powers and Company, Detroit).

WHITE, L. J., 1971, *The Automobile Industry Since 1945* (Harvard University Press, Mass.).

NONPARAMETRIC TESTS OF MARKET STRUCTURE: AN APPLICATION TO THE CIGARETTE INDUSTRY*

ORLEY ASHENFELTER AND DANIEL SULLIVAN

In this paper the revealed preference approach is used to construct a nonparametric test of the monopoly model and some simple generalizations of it, and the test is applied to data for the cigarette industry. The test exploits the maintained hypothesis that variations in the excise tax charged on a package of cigarettes allow us to assess seller reactions to common exogenous variations in product marginal cost. These easily implemented nonparametric tests indicate that the monopoly hypothesis and other simple models that do not embody at least a moderate amount of competition serve as poor predictors of the effects of excise tax changes on cigarette prices, sales, and revenues. We also find some evidence that excise tax increases do not consistently act to increase prices and decrease sales, which calls into question many other hypotheses about firm behavior in the industry.

ELEMENTARY textbooks, taking a cue from the Greek etymology, often define a monopoly as a market with one seller. The typical pattern is to argue that profit maximization requires that the monopolist set a price that equates marginal cost with marginal revenue. With a downward sloping demand curve, marginal revenue is necessarily less than price, and so monopoly must result in an inefficiently low level of output. The potential desirability of regulation or antitrust legislation is the immediate conclusion. The pattern of this discussion is by now so conventional that what it omits is hardly noticed. How might the monopoly model be tested? That is, what are the positive predictions of the model and what kind of data could be used to check their accuracy?

Even in the professional literature, the question of how to test models of market structure in a non-experimental setting has only lately been given much formal attention. Panzar and Rosse [1987] have derived a test of the model based on its comparative statics. Shaffer [1982] has used the same test to investigate the banking industry and Sullivan [1985], using a closely related methodology, obtained a lower bound on a measure of non-competitive behavior in the cigarette industry. In addition, there is a growing literature on the measurement of conjectural variations and measures of monopoly power. (See Geroski, Phlips, and Ulph [1985] for a survey.)

As is the case with virtually all econometric work, tests of the monopoly hypothesis have relied on techniques for fitting one or several equations of a particular functional form to a set of data and then testing whether the fitted

* We are grateful to the editors for their helpful comments.

equations are consistent with the proposed model. This paradigm has been criticised by Varian, among others. In the context of tests of the theory of consumer behavior, he notes, "This procedure suffers from the defect that one is always testing a joint hypothesis: whatever one wants to test plus the maintained hypothesis of functional form."[1] The implication is that we do not know whether to reject the model or just the functional form used to represent it. To this drawback could be added another: the econometric approach offers so much room for alternative parametric setups that the results often appear so susceptible to specification error as to be unconvincing.

Afriat [1967], [1976], Varian [1982], [1983] and others have offered a set of nonparametric techniques for dealing with some of the traditional questions of consumer and producer theory that provide simple and illuminating empirical analyses that serve as useful benchmarks for non-experimental econometric work. These techniques, which are based on revealed preference arguments, make use of only the observed data and do not rely on any assumptions about the functional forms of underlying utility or production functions.

In this paper the revealed preference approach is used to construct a nonparametric test of the monopoly model. This test is based on a finite difference form of a comparative static result given in differential form in Sullivan [1985] and exploits the hypothesis first advanced by Sumner [1981] that variations in the excise tax charged on a package of cigarettes allow us to assess the monopolist's reaction to exogenous variations in product marginal cost.[2] In addition we extend the test to allow the assessment of the validity of some less extreme oligopoly models.

The excise tax experiment is in several respects especially well suited to the nonparametric approach. Whereas constantly rising real income and relatively little variation in relative prices imply that nonparametric tests have little ability to detect departures from utility maximization in consumption data, the large changes which occur in excise taxes make for powerful tests of the monopoly model. Moreover, the vector nature of goods prices necessitates a relatively complicated algorithm for computing the transitive closure of the revealed preferred relation in consumer theory. The excise tax experiment, on the other hand, yields a separate prediction for every tax change. This not only greatly eases the computational burden, but it makes possible the calculation of a percentage of correct predictions for a model and thus allows us to distinguish a prediction which fails as a rule from one which is only occasionally incorrect. While not a perfect substitute for a true

[1] Varian [1983, p. 99]. There are also a number of possible responses to this criticism. First, the choice of functional form is not entirely arbitrary. A great many useful techniques exist for allowing the data to help choose the formulation. Secondly, formal specification tests which can be expected to detect gross violations of model assumptions are becoming increasingly available.

[2] Panzar and Rosse [1987] also exploit the comparative statics of shifts to marginal cost. Bresnahan [1982], on the other hand, considers the comparative statics of shifts to demand elasticity.

stochastic framework,[3] this is certainly more informative than the output of applications of nonparametric techniques to consumer theory where one obtains the all or nothing result that the data either is or is not consistent with utility maximization. However, it will also become clear that the nonparametric approach lacks some of the flexibility of parametric techniques in dealing with shifts in the structural equations of the model.

Section I contains the derivation of the tests and some related results. Section II applies the tests to the data on the cigarette industry. Finally, section III summarizes our conclusions on both the monopoly model as a description of the cigarette industry and on the nonparametric approach to tests of models of market structure based on the experience we have to date.

I. THE TESTS

Consider an industry with upward sloping total cost function $C(q)$ and downward sloping demand function $P(q)$, where $C(q) > C(r)$ and $P(q) < P(r)$ if $q > r$. If the industry is a monopoly and q is the level of output chosen, then any other level of output, $q+\Delta q$, cannot be more profitable. That is, for all Δq

$$(1) \qquad (q+\Delta q)P(q+\Delta q)-C(q+\Delta q) \leqslant qP(q)-C(q)$$

which can also be written as

$$(2) \qquad \Delta qP(q+\Delta q)+q[P(q+\Delta q)-P(q)] \leqslant C(q+\Delta q)-C(q)$$

The tests presented in this paper are designed to explore the implications for monopoly output and price of an exogenous change in marginal cost. In particular, we exploit the assumption that changes in an excise rate (t) are equivalent to a change in marginal cost, so that the cost function can be written as $C(q) = C_0(q)+tq$, where C_0 is an increasing function of q.

To continue, let t_0 be the lower of two tax rates, $t_0 < t_1$; let q_0 and q_1 be the corresponding profit maximizing levels of output, and let $p_0 = P(q_0)$ and $p_1 = P(q_1)$ be the corresponding monopoly price levels. When the excise tax rate is t_0, (2) implies that

$$(3) \qquad (q_1-q_0)p_1-q_0(p_1-p_0) \leqslant t_0(q_1-q_0)+C_0(q_1)-C_0(q_0)$$

Likewise, when the excise tax rate is t_1, (2) implies that

$$(4) \qquad (q_0-q_1)p_0-q_1(p_0-p_1) \leqslant t_1(q_0-q_1)+C_0(q_0)-C_0(q_1)$$

Adding (3) and (4) gives

$$(5) \qquad 0 \leqslant (t_0-t_1)(q_1-q_0)$$

Since $t_0 < t_1$, it follows that

$$(6) \qquad q_1 \leqslant q_0$$

[3] The lack of any convenient way in which to incorporate stochastic variation is one of the most frequently mentioned drawbacks to the use of nonparametric techniques.

and since we have assumed a downward sloping demand function,

(7) $$p_1 \geqslant p_0$$

Thus, the monopoly price must increase, and monopoly output must decrease, as a result of an increase in an excise tax. These are clearly testable propositions, though hardly unique to the monopoly model, and we offer empirical tests of them below.

Using (6), and the assumption that C_0 is increasing, (3) implies that

(8) $$p_1(q_1-q_0)+q_0(p_1-p_0) \leqslant t_0(q_1-q_0)$$

which is the main testable prediction of the monopoly model. Condition (8) is very simple and has many alternative interpretations. It implies, for example, that

$$p_1q_1-p_0q_0 \leqslant t_0(q_1-q_0)$$

The revenue loss from producing q_1 when the tax rate is t_0 must be less than the decreased tax payments associated with the lower output level; otherwise the monopolist would have done better to produce q_1 when the tax rate was t_0.[4] Alternatively, (8) may be written as

(9) $$\frac{-(q_1-q_0)p_0}{(p_1-p_0)q_0} \geqslant \frac{p_0}{p_1-t_0}$$

or as

(10) $$\frac{-(p_1-t_0)(q_1-q_0)}{(p_1-p_0)q_0} \geqslant 1$$

Expression (9) is an extension of the familiar rule that a monopolist will not produce on the inelastic portion of the demand curve. A generalization of (10) is given below.

If, rather than behaving as a monopoly, the industry in question were perfectly competitive, price would be taken as exogenous by market participants, and q would be selected so that

$$(q+\Delta q)P(q+\Delta q)-C(q+\Delta q) \leqslant qP(q+\Delta q)-C(q)$$

It follows that

(11) $$\Delta qP(q+\Delta q) \leqslant C(q+\Delta q)-C(q)$$

for all Δq. Inequality (11) may be written as

$$P(q+\Delta q) \leqslant [C(q+\Delta q)-C(q)]/\Delta q$$

[4] Panzar and Rosse [1987] test is also based on the response of total revenue to shifts in factors affecting marginal cost. Their results imply that if all input prices increase then total revenue must fall under monopoly. In the present case of an increase in the excise tax a stronger inference is possible: Not only is the change in total revenue less than zero, it is less than a certain negative number. This is because we not only can assume that marginal cost is positive, which is the basis for the Panzar–Rosse [1987] result, but also that marginal cost is greater than the tax rate.

making it clear that (11) is merely an extension of the familiar rule that price equals marginal cost under perfect competition.

Comparing (11) with (2) suggests the introduction of an index of monopoly behavior analogous to that considered in Bresnahan [1982]. That is, the industry may be said to have monopoly index β if

$$\Delta q P(q+\Delta q)+\beta q[P(q+\Delta q)-P(q)] \leqslant C(q+\Delta q)-C(q) \tag{12}$$

for all Δq.[5] The case $\beta = 0$ evidently corresponds to perfect competition and the case $\beta = 1$ to monopoly, while intermediate values index less extreme oligopoly equilibria.

In the special case of the two excise taxes t_0 and t_1 (12) implies

$$p_1(q_1-q_0)+\beta q_0(p_1-p_0) \leqslant t_0(q_1-q_0)+C_0(q_1)-C_0(q_0) \tag{13}$$

For β strictly between 0 and 1 it does not seem to be possible to demonstrate that $q_1 \leqslant q_0$ and $p_1 \geqslant p_0$, but this is certainly the most plausible case. When $q_1 \leqslant q_0$ and $p_1 \geqslant p_0$ do hold (13) implies that

$$\beta \leqslant \frac{-(p_1-t_0)(q_1-q_0)}{(p_1-p_0)q_0} \tag{14}$$

which is a generalization of (10). Inequality (14) shows which values of the monopoly index β are consistent with the data corresponding to any two tax rates and therefore provides a nonparametric way to bound that index.[6]

It is instructive to relate inequality (14) to the bound on the departure from competition given in Sullivan [1985] in the context of the conjectural variations model. Thus let there be n firms with increasing cost functions $C_1(q_1),\ldots,C_n(q_n)$ and let industry price be given by $P(q_1+\ldots+q_n)$ where $P(q)$ is a decreasing function and $q_1,\ldots,q_n$ are the outputs of the firm. Then in the case of an excise tax t, the firms' first order conditions imply that

$$q_i(t)p'(t)+(p(t)-t)q'(t)/(1+\alpha_i(t)) \geqslant 0$$

where

$$\alpha_i = \sum_{j\neq i} dq_j/dq_i$$

is the ith firm's conjectural variation. Summing these over the firms implies that

$$q(t)p'(t)+(p(t)-t)q'(t)n(t) \geqslant 0 \tag{15}$$

[5] Alternatively, assume the differentiability of $P(q)$ and $C(q)$ and let β be defined by $P(q)+\beta qP'(q) = C'(q)$. Integrating this expression from q to $q+\Delta q$ and making approximations as in the derivation given below of (18) implies inequality (12).

[6] The inferences to be drawn from (14) are one sided in the sense that values of the index can only be rejected in favor of more competitive values. Thus, for example, since the right hand side of (14) should always be positive, we cannot test perfect competition. This is analogous to the situation in Panzar and Rosse [1987] where the key expression was signed for monopoly but not for competition.

where the quantity $n(t) = \sum_i 1/(1+\alpha_i(t))$ can be thought of as the numbers equivalent of firms since, in the Cournot case where all α_i are zero, it reduces to n.

If $t_1 > t_0$ then (15) implies that

$$\int_{t_0}^{t_1} [q(t)p'(t)+(p(t)-t)q'(t)n(t)]\,dt \geqslant 0 \tag{16}$$

If $p'(t) \geqslant 0$ and $q'(t) \leqslant 0$ for all t then, since $0 \leqslant q(t) \leqslant q_0 = q(t_0)$ and $0 \leqslant p_0 - t_1 = p(t_0) - t_1 \leqslant p(t) - t$ for t between t_0 and t_1, we have

$$\int_{t_0}^{t_1} [q_0 p'(t)+(p_0-t_1)q'(t)n(t)]\,dt \geqslant 0 \tag{17}$$

Thus the mean value theorem implies that for some $\tilde{t}$ between t_0 and t_1

$$n(\tilde{t}) \geqslant \frac{q_0(p_1-p_0)}{(q_1-q_0)(p_1-t_0)} \tag{18}$$

The right hand side of (18) is a finite difference form of the lower bound on the numbers equivalent estimated in Sullivan [1985]. Below, it will be used to identify which conjectural variations models are consistent with data from the cigarette industry. Since the right hand side of (18) is equal to the reciprocal of the right hand side of (14), if the data imply the rejection of conjectural variations models with numbers equivalents less than some number N, then they also imply the rejection of models with monopoly index β greater than $1/N$.

II. EVIDENCE

The cigarette industry, with only six major firms, is one of the most highly concentrated of US industries. According to recent estimates, the two largest firms accounted for 66% and the four largest for 90% of total cigarette production.[7] The major firms have, moreover, maintained virtual list price identity for the last thirty years and twice this century have been convicted of violating the antitrust laws.[8] Thus, it is not inconceivable that the monopoly or perfect cartel model could provide an adequate description of the industry, although other oligopoly equilibria may be more plausible descriptions.

The data used in this study are the same as in Sullivan [1985] and are taken from the Tobacco Tax Council's publication, *The Tax Burden on Tobacco*. They consist of the excise tax rate, the average *per capita* consumption, and the average retail price of a package of cigarettes in each of 45 states between the years 1955 and 1982. The consumption figures are

[7] Maxwell Report [1983].

[8] For some history of the cigarette industry, see Nicholls [1951], Telser [1962], and Schmalensee [1972].

cumulative totals for the state and year in question and are obtained indirectly from data on state tax receipts.[9] The price variable, on the other hand, reflects the results of a survey taken in November of each year. The tax variable is the sum of the state and federal taxes for the state and year in question. In years in which the rate changed, the weighted average (with weights proportional to the length of time the rate was in effect) tax rate was used. The two dollar denominated variables were converted to real terms by dividing by the national consumer price index. It is a relatively straightforward matter to check the sensitivity of our results to these details of how the data were handled, and we do so below.

The prediction of the simple monopoly model summarized in expression (8) is straightforward to check. Nevertheless, in its derivation we maintained the hypotheses that the same demand and cost functions applied to both points considered. Although we began our investigation with the prior view that the cigarette industry was a good candidate for maintaining these hypotheses, failure of the prediction for two given points can always be attributed to either a failure of the monopoly model (for at least one of the points) or to a shift in the demand or cost functions. Since the focus of this paper is on the monopoly model, and since it is therefore desirable to be able to interpret failures of the predictions as failures of the model, we have taken considerable care in choosing to which pairs of points to apply the tests.

In the case of the cigarette data, it seems possible that the same cost and demand conditions may not have prevailed in all of the states. For this reason, the predictions checked below are only for pairs of points corresponding to the same state. Moreover, patterns of cigarette consumption have changed greatly over the years, albeit slowly, so that attention is also confined to pairs of points at most two years apart. Fortunately, even with these restrictions, the data are rich enough to yield an ample supply of testable predictions.

Consider first all pairs of consecutive years within the same state. The accuracy of the model is in this case truly poor. Of the 1178 changes, the monopoly prediction (8) was correct only 432 times or 37% of the time.

On the face of it this is strong evidence against the monopoly hypothesis. It might be objected, however, that due to the possibility of measurement errors, not all pairs of consecutive years should be considered. In the majority of the cases considered above the change in the real tax rate was due entirely to changes in the consumer price index. Many of these changes were quite trivial and the index is not, after all, perfect. Thus perhaps a cleaner test would be to restrict the tests of the predictions to some subgroup of points where there were more significant changes. The second row of Table I displays the results for subgroups where there was an increase in the real tax

[9] Thus, since a few of the states did not have cigarette taxes in the early part of the sample period, no data is available for several state-year pairs.

TABLE I
TESTS OF THE PREDICTIONS OF THE MONOPOLY MODEL ABOUT CHANGES IN QUANTITY, PRICE, AND REVENUE

Data From	*Number Cases*	*Percentage Predictions Correct*				
		$\Delta q \leqslant 0$[a]	$\Delta p \geqslant 0$[b]	(6)–(7)[c]	(8)[d]	(6)–(8)[e]
Consecutive Years	1178	70.8	75.3	54.6	36.7	14.9
Consecutive Years— Real Increases	216	74.1	83.8	68.1	17.1	6.0
Consecutive Years— Real Decreases	962	70.1	73.4	51.6	41.1	16.8
Consecutive Years— Statutory Changes	288	69.8	81.9	62.5	22.9	9.7
Consecutive Years— No Statutory Change	890	71.1	73.2	52.0	41.1	16.5
Skip Year Changes[f]	1133	71.8	85.0	62.0	27.4	15.1
Skip Year Changes— Flat-Jump-Flat[g]	199	68.8	94.0	66.8	13.6	10.6

Notes: [a] Prediction tested is expression (6): Quantity consumed will decline.
[b] Prediction tested is expression (7): Price will increase.
[c] Test of the joint prediction that quantity declines and price increases.
[d] Prediction tested is expression (8): Total revenue will fall by more than the product of the lower tax rate and the change in quantity.
[e] Test of the joint prediction that quantity, price and revenue all change in accordance with the monopoly model.
[f] Pairs of data points separated by one year.
[g] Statutory rates constant for both data points and a statutory increase during the intervening year.

rate (from the earlier year); the third row displays results where there was a decrease in the real tax rate (to the later year), and the fourth and fifth rows display results where there was an actual change in the average statutory tax rate, and where there was no change in the statutory rate.[10] In all cases, the performance of the monopoly model's prediction is again poor. Indeed, when attention is restricted to those changes where measurement errors are likely to be less significant, the predictions of the monopoly model are even more likely to be erroneous. Thus the evidence against the monopoly model (with the maintained hypothesis of stable costs and demand) is indeed quite strong.

Before going on to use (18) to see whether or not other, less extreme, oligopoly models are consistent with the data, it is necessary to check (6) and (7), since these are assumed in its derivation. Recall that (6) and (7) which are also predictions of the monopoly model, simply state that when the tax rate increases, the quantity consumed should fall and the price should rise. The results, given in the first three columns of Table I, are quite disturbing. For the entire set of 1178 changes, the two predictions are both correct only 55% of the time. In contrast to prediction (8), the results for the subgroups where there was a real or statutory increase are more consistent with the predictions,

[10] When changes in the statutory rate occur in the middle of the year, the weighted average tax rate changes for two years in a row. We call both of these statutory changes.

but there are still many violations. The last column of Table I shows how seldom all three of the monopoly model's predictions are correct.

The failures of (6) and (7) are, of course, more surprising than that of (8) since they are almost certain to be predictions of any reasonable economic model that assumes a downward sloping demand curve. Indeed, these results suggest to us that it may be desirable to eliminate possible cases of measurement error. One possible source of error is the treatment of the tax rate in years in which more than one prevailed. In such cases, the weighted average tax rate has been used, but that choice was hardly inevitable.

In order to see whether or not the averaging of the tax rates was a major reason for the apparent failure of (6) and (7), pairs of points separated by one year were considered. Although this procedure allows any instability in cost or demand functions to more heavily influence the results, it does remove measurement error from the tax data. The last two rows of Table I give the results for all of these "Skip Year Changes" and also for a subset of these where in the first year the rate was constant, in the second year (not used in the tests) the rate jumped, and in the third year the rate was again flat. This last category of points should be relatively immune to measurement error. Yet, as the Table shows, (6) and (7) are still violated in the data, although the violations of (7) are considerably fewer. The monopoly prediction (8), on the other hand, has even less success with these relatively clean data.

Table II shows how the monopoly predictions (6)–(8) fair according to the size of the change in the tax rates. As can be seen, as the magnitude of the tax change increases, (6) and (7) tend to be more often correct. Indeed, when the tax change is greater than 2 cents (in 1967 dollars), both predictions are

TABLE II

TESTS OF THE PREDICTIONS OF THE MONOPOLY MODEL ABOUT CHANGES IN QUANTITY, PRICE, AND REVENUE: DISAGGREGATION BY SIZE OF TAX CHANGE

Data From	*Number Cases*	*Percentage Predictions Correct*				
		$\Delta q \geqslant 0$[a]	$\Delta p \geqslant 0$[b]	(6)–(7)[c]	(8)[d]	(6)–(8)[e]
Skip Year Changes[f] Δt[g] < 1	467	69.2	76.9	53.5	42.0	23.1
Skip Year Changes $1 < \Delta t < 2$	444	69.1	86.9	61.0	23.0	11.9
Skip Year Changes $\Delta t < 2$	222	82.9	98.2	81.5	5.9	4.5

Notes: [a] Prediction tested is expression (6): Quantity consumed will decline.
[b] Prediction tested is expression (7): Price will increase.
[c] Test of the joint prediction that quantity declines and price increases.
[d] Prediction tested is expression (8): Total revenue will fall by more than the product of the lower tax rate and the change in quantity.
[e] Test of the joint prediction that quantity, price and revenue all change in accordance with the monopoly model.
[f] Pairs of data points separated by one year.
[g] Change in tax rate in 1967 cents.

TABLE III
TESTS OF THE PREDICTIONS OF ALTERNATIVE OLIGOPOLY MODELS

Numbers Equivalent	Percent Consistent With Numbers Equivalent[a]	
	Skip Year Changes $\Delta q \leqslant 0$ $\Delta p \geqslant 0$ (702 Cases)	*Jump-Flat-Jump* $\Delta q \leqslant 0$ $\Delta p \geqslant 0$ (133 Cases)
$n = 1$	24.4	15.8
$n = 2$	45.2	39.8
$n = 3$	60.4	55.6
$n = 4$	69.7	70.7
$n = 5$	75.1	76.7
$n = 6$	79.3	81.2
$n = 7$	82.9	83.5
$n = 8$	85.2	85.7
$n = 9$	86.5	88.0
$n = \infty$	100.0	100.0

Note: [a] Consistency denotes that expression (18):

$$n \geqslant q_0(p_1 - p_0)/(q_1 - q_0)(p_1 - t_0)$$

holds for the indicated value of n and thus that the changes in quantity and price are consistent with that value for the numbers equivalent of firms.

correct 82% of the time. Prediction (8), on the other hand, has less success as the tax change becomes larger, predicting correctly only 6% of the time when the change in the rate exceeds 2 cents (in 1967 dollars).

The pattern seems clear: Tax increases are usually associated with cigarette price increases and are often associated with cigarette sales decreases when the change in the tax rate is a significant one. On the other hand, expression (8), which is the distinctive prediction of the monopoly model, is only rarely correct when the tax change is most likely to be free of significant measurement errors.

Table III exhibits the extent to which other oligopoly models with higher numbers equivalents are consistent with the "Skip Year Changes" and "Flat-Jump-Flat" data. Since the assumptions that quantity falls and price rises when the excise tax rate increases were assumed in the derivation of (18), the test has only been applied to pairs of years in which these conditions held. The Table shows that only models with numbers equivalents in excess of 5 or 6 are consistent with the bulk of this data. Moreover, 12% to 13% of the data points can only be rationalized by models with numbers equivalents larger than 9. The conclusion to be drawn is that simple conjectural variations models can be rejected unless they embody at least a moderate amount of competition.

This conclusion must be qualified to the extent that the not infrequent failures of (6) and (7) call into question the entire framework of the analysis. For this reason it is worth further considering some possible reasons for these failures. First, it should be noted that the model of the cigarette industry we have presented is an extremely simple one that omits many potentially important aspects of reality, any one of which could cause violations of (6) and (7). Thus we assume away advertising and possible adjustment lags in the cost and demand functions. Nor does our model incorporate any of the details of the cigarette market place such as the use of vending machines which might make it more difficult to charge certain prices. Finally, we have assumed that firms and customers care about relative prices and that uncertainty about the price level can be ignored. There is evidence that this last point may be of some importance: When we adopt the opposite extreme assumption and work with nominal prices, (7) is correct in 196 out of the 199 "Flat-Jump-Flat" cases.[11]

Another natural explanation for the failures of conditions (6) and (7) is that the demand and cost functions cannot be taken as fixed even over short periods. Indeed, of the 1133 "Skip Year Changes", 371 had quantity and price changes in the same directions, indicating a definite shift in the demand curve. Eliminating these cases necessarily improves the percentage of correct quantity and price predictions with the rates going to 92% for both. On the other hand, the monopoly prediction (8) is correct in only 26% of these cases where there was no obvious shift in the demand curve.

Suppose, because of factors not included in our model, that if q_0 and p_0 represent the initial year's quantity and price in some state, it may be expected that even without a tax change, next year's quantity and price will be $q_0+\Delta q'$ and $p_0+\Delta p'$. In this situation it is natural to consider testing the hypothesis that an excise tax increase will result in a smaller change in sales than $\Delta q'$ and a greater change in price than $\Delta p'$, so that

(6′) $$q_1 \leqslant q_0+\Delta q' \quad \text{and}$$

(7′) $$p_1 \geqslant p_0+\Delta p'$$

Strictly speaking, in order to implement such a test, it is necessary to know $\Delta q'$ and $\Delta p'$ for each state and year. This is, of course, not possible. However, a number of plausible methods of estimating these quantities clearly exist. Perhaps the simplest procedure is to make use of the longitudinal nature of the data and use as $\Delta q'$ and $\Delta p'$ the mean change in these variables for the year for all states not altering their statutory tax rate. This procedure assumes that the changes in price and quantity that would have occurred would be the same as the average change in the price and quantity in states where an excise tax change did not occur.[12] The results of these tests are displayed in the first two rows of Table IV. For the set of all statutory changes between consecutive years, the performance of (6′) and (7′) is slightly worse than the performance

[11] Of course, since the Consumer Price Index is rising over the sample period, the success rate of (7) is guaranteed to be higher when calculated in nominal terms.

[12] This procedure of using the non-treatment state-years as a control for the treatment state-years is a familiar method in the statistical program evaluation literature. See, for example, Ashenfelter [1978].

TABLE IV
TESTS OF THE PREDICTIONS OF THE MONOPOLY MODEL ABOUT CHANGES IN QUANTITY AND PRICE RELATIVE TO EXPECTED LEVELS

Data From	*Type Fit*	*Number Cases*	*Percentage Predictions Correct*		
			$\Delta q \leqslant 0$[a]	$\Delta p \geqslant 0$[b]	(6′)–(7′)[c]
Consecutive Years—Statutory Changes	Simple[d]	288	68.4	80.9	60.1
Skip Year Changes—Flat-Jump-Flat	Simple	199	68.8	92.0	65.3
Consecutive Years—Statutory Changes	Two-Way[e]	288	77.8	79.2	68.4
Skip Year Changes—Flat-Jump-Flat	Two-Way	199	85.9	97.0	83.9

Notes: [a] Prediction tested is expression (6′): Quantity consumed will be less than otherwise expected.
[b] Prediction tested is expression (7′): Price will be greater than otherwise expected.
[c] Test of the joint prediction that quantity consumed will be less than and price greater than otherwise expected.
[d] Simple fit indicates that expected changes were taken to be the mean of the changes of the states with constant tax rates that year.
[e] Two-Way fit indicates that expected changes were obtained from a two-way fit to all state-year pairs with constant tax rates.

of (6) and (7) shown in Table I. For the set of "Flat-Jump-Flat" changes, the performance of the quantity prediction (6′) and (6) are identical, while for the price predictions, (6′) again does slightly worse than (6).

A slightly more sophisticated procedure is to fit by least squares a model with state effects in addition to year effects to the set of all changes in quantity and price not accompanied by a change in the statutory tax rate and then use the estimated model to predict what the changes would have been in the states which did change their tax rates. This allows for state specific linear time trends in the deviation from the aggregate year to year time pattern of price and quantity levels. The results of the tests applied to $\Delta q'$ and $\Delta p'$ estimated in this way are shown in the last two rows of Table IV. As can be seen, the accuracy of (6′) is considerably improved and to a lesser extent so is that of (7′) for the "Flat-Jump-Flat" data. This improvement reflects the shift in relative consumption of cigarettes in the various states. For instance, in the early part of the sample period, Southern states had relatively low levels of consumption but by the end of the period, consumption was as high or higher there as elsewhere in the country.

The results of this last empirical procedure, while giving results more consistent with predictions (6′) and (7′), still indicate that in 15% of the cases, quantity and price do not both move in the direction expected. We have, moreover, moved a considerable distance from the nonparametric approach with which we started.

Another possible explanation for the failure of (6) and (7) is that excise tax changes ought not to be identified as the equivalents of exogenous changes in

TABLE V

TEST OF THE INDEPENDENCE OF THE SIGN OF CURRENT TAX CHANGES FROM THE SIGNS OF LAGGED PRICE AND QUANTITY CHANGES CONDITIONAL ON THE SIGN OF LAGGED TAX CHANGES

$\Delta \text{Tax}_{-1} \leqslant 0$[a]	$\Delta P_{-1} \leqslant 0$[b] $\Delta Q_{-1} \leqslant 0$[c]	$\Delta P_{-1} \leqslant 0$ $\Delta Q_{-1} > 0$	$\Delta P_{-1} > 0$ $\Delta Q_{-1} \leqslant 0$	$\Delta P_{-1} > 0$ $\Delta Q_{-1} > 0$	*Total*
$\Delta \text{Tax} \leqslant 0$[d]					
expected[e]	34.7	118.2	221.6	418.4	
actual	31	114	226	422	793
$\Delta \text{Tax} > 0$					
expected	7.3	24.8	46.4	87.6	
actual	11	29	42	84	166
$\%\Delta \text{Tax} > 0$	26.2	20.3	15.7	16.6	17.3

Pearson Chi Square Statistic for $\Delta \text{Tax}_{-1} \leqslant 0$ *Table*[f] *3.9*

$\Delta \text{Tax}_{-1} > 0$	$\Delta P_{-1} \leqslant 0$ $\Delta Q_{-1} \leqslant 0$	$\Delta P_{-1} \leqslant 0$ $\Delta Q_{-1} > 0$	$\Delta P_{-1} > 0$ $\Delta Q_{-1} \leqslant 0$	$\Delta P_{-1} > 0$ $\Delta Q_{-1} > 0$	*Total*
$\Delta \text{Tax} \leqslant 0$					
expected	6.8	12.6	104.3	44.4	
actual	4	13	105	46	168
$\Delta \text{Tax} > 0$					
expected	0.2	0.4	3.7	1.6	
actual	3	0	3	0	6
$\%\Delta \text{Tax} > 0$	42.8	0.0	2.8	0.0	3.5

Pearson Chi Square Statistic for $\Delta \text{Tax}_{-1} > 0$ *Table*[g] *34.9*

Overall Pearson Chi Square Statistic[g] *38.8*

Notes: [a] Upper table is for $\text{Tax}_{t-1} - \text{Tax}_{t-2}$ less than or equal to zero and the lower table is for $\text{Tax}_{t-1} - \text{Tax}_{t-2}$ greater than zero where Tax refers to the nominal rate in effect at the end of the year.

[b] Indicates $\text{Price}_{t-1} - \text{Price}_{t-2}$ less than or equal to zero or greater than zero where Price is the nominal value observed at the time of the survey.

[c] Indicates $\text{Quantity}_{t-1} - \text{Quantity}_{t-2}$ less than or equal to zero or greater than zero where Quantity is the *per capita* consumption inferred from tax collections.

[d] Indicates $\text{Tax}_t - \text{Tax}_{t-1}$ less than or equal to zero or greater than zero where Tax is the nominal rate in effect at the end of the year.

[e] "Expected" denotes the fitted value of the count under the assumption of the conditional independence of the lagged price and quantity sign changes from the current sign change in the tax rate. "Actual" denotes the actual count.

[f] Chi Square statistics are for the null hypothesis of conditional independence. The degrees of freedom are three for the two four by two contingency tables and six for the overall statistic.

[g] The Chi Square approximation to the distribution of the statistic for the $\Delta \text{Tax}_{-1} > 0$ table and for the overall statistic may be poor due to the low expected counts for several cells.

the cigarette industry's marginal costs. After all, some political or other process is determining the level and timing of excise tax changes, and it is conceivable that this process must be treated explicitly in order to make sense of the history of cigarette prices and sales.[13]

Table V investigates the possible dependence of statutory tax changes on previous changes in prices and quantities. To keep the analysis nonparametric we use only the sign (plus or minus) of the relevant changes and, to avoid

[13] Strictly speaking, without an explicit stochastic setting, it does not make sense to discuss "simultaneity bias", but something of that nature may be important to understanding the data.

issues of measurement error, we present calculations using nominal prices and the statutory tax rates at the end of the period.[14] Since increases in the statutory rate are considerably less likely immediately after a previous increase, the analysis is carried out conditional on the sign of the tax change in the previous period. The top table compares the actual counts of observations in the various categories to those expected under the hypothesis that the signs of tax changes in the current period are independent of the signs of price and quantity changes in the previous period, conditional on there not having been a tax increase in the previous period. The bottom table does the same conditional on there having been a tax increase.

The results of these comparisons, which are in the spirit of Granger style tests of causality, are mixed for the conditional independence hypothesis. As can be seen, the fit for the table conditioning on no increase is very good and this is reflected in the Pearson Chi Square statistic of 3.9 which is less than the usual critical values for three degrees of freedom. Casual inspection of the table conditioning on an increase in the rate also suggests a reasonably good fit, but the Chi Square statistic of 34.9 says otherwise. However, the expected counts for several of the cells are low enough to make the usual approximate critical values suspect. Moreover, virtually the whole value of the statistic is contributed by the two cells for which price and quantity both fall. If just two more of these changes had not been followed by a tax increase, the Chi Square statistic for the lower table and for the conditional independence hypothesis as a whole would have been in the acceptable range. We conclude that despite the nominal significance of the tests we need to look elsewhere for an explanation of the failures of price and quantity to move as expected.

III. CONCLUSION

As we have seen, our nonparametric tests indicate that the monopoly hypothesis serves as a poor predictor of the effect of excise tax changes on cigarette prices, sales, and revenues. Likewise, simple conjectural variations models are consistent with the data only if they embody at least a moderate amount of competition. These conclusions are similar to those of Sullivan [1985] where it was found using parametric statistical techniques that industry behavior was not consistent with a numbers equivalent any less than two or three.

Our failure to uniformly find that excise tax increases (decreases) act to increase (decrease) cigarette prices and to decrease (increase) cigarette sales is especially disturbing and calls into question virtually any hypothesis about firm behavior in this industry. One explanation for these anomalies that we have investigated thoroughly attributes them to measurement error. Indeed,

[14] This differs from our previous use of weighted averages in years in which the rate changed. We adopt the present definitions in order to focus more clearly on occurrences of actual changes in the statutes. Similar results were obtained, however, using other definitions of price and tax.

more careful measurement does tend to confirm that tax increases *are* typically associated with price increases and, to a lesser extent, sales decreases. However, more careful treatment of the data leads to even stronger evidence against the monopoly model.

We also investigated the possible dependence of the timing of tax increases on previous changes in price and quantity using nonparametric methods. Though the usual cautions about interpreting the results of causality tests apply, we did not find any pattern in the data suggestive of an explanation of the frequent failure of price and quantity to move in the expected direction that could be based on the endogeneity of tax rates.

Perhaps our prior expectation that cost and demand conditions are likely to be stable enough to ensure the usefulness of the nonparametric approach is simply wrong. We have shown how the nonparametric approach can be modified to admit some flexibility regarding the other determinants of cigarette consumption by using state-year observations where no tax change takes place as a comparison group. However the flexibility thereby gained may be insufficient and so there may be no alternative in appraising market structure in the cigarette industry to using the parametric approach and all the untestable assumptions it embodies.

It seems that the nonparametric approach to appraising the nature of market structure needs more empirical testing. The nonparametric tests are so easily derived, explained, and implemented that they deserve more attention than they have received.

ORLEY ASHENFELTER,
Princeton University,
Princeton, New Jersey,
USA.

DANIEL SULLIVAN,
Northwestern University,
Evanston, Illinois,
USA.

REFERENCES

Afriat, S., 1967, 'The Construction of a Utility Function from Expenditure Data', *International Economic Review*, 8, pp. 67–77.

Afriat, S., 1976, *The Combinatorial Theory of Demand* (Input–Output Publishing Company, London).

Ashenfelter, O., 1978, 'Estimating the Effect of Training Programs on Earnings', *Review of Economics and Statistics*, 60 (1), pp. 47–57.

Bresnahan, T., 1982, 'The Oligopoly Solution Concept is Identified', *Economic Letters*, 10, pp. 87–92.

Geroski, P., Phlips, L. and Ulph, A., 1985, 'Oligopoly, Competition and Welfare: Some Recent Developments', *The Journal of Industrial Economics*, 33 (June), pp. 369–387.

MAXWELL, J., 1983, 'The Maxwell Report' (Lehman Brothers Kuhn Loeb Research).

NICHOLLS, W., 1951, *Price Policies in the Cigarette Industry* (Vanderbilt University Press, Nashville).

PANZAR, JOHN C. and ROSSE, JAMES N., 1987, 'Testing for "Monopoly" Equilibrium', *Journal of Industrial Economics*, this issue.

SCHMALENSEE, R., 1972, *The Economics of Advertising* (North-Holland, Amsterdam–London).

SHAFFER, S., 1982, 'A Nonstructural Test for Competition in Financial Markets', in *Proceedings of a Conference on Bank Structure and Competition* (Federal Reserve Bank of Chicago).

SUMNER, D., 1981, 'The Measurement of Monopoly Power: An Application to the Cigarette Industry', *The Journal of Political Economy*, 98 (October), pp. 1010–1019.

SULLIVAN, D., 1985, 'Testing Hypotheses About Firm Behavior in the Cigarette Industry', *The Journal of Political Economy*, 93 (June), pp. 586–598.

TELSER, L., 1962, 'Advertising and Cigarettes', *The Journal of Political Economy*, 70 (October), pp. 471–499.

TOBACCO TAX COUNCIL, 1985, *The Tax Burden on Tobacco*, vol. 20 (Washington DC).

VARIAN, H., 1982, 'The Nonparametric Approach to Demand Analysis', *Econometrica*, 50, pp. 945–973.

VARIAN, H., 1983, 'Non-parametric Tests of Consumer Behaviour', *Review of Economic Studies*, 50, pp. 99–110.

INTERFIRM RIVALRY IN A REPEATED GAME: AN EMPIRICAL TEST OF TACIT COLLUSION*

MARGARET E. SLADE

Rivalry in the Vancouver retail gasoline market is modeled as a repeated game. Service-station demand, cost, and reaction functions are estimated from daily data on individual station prices, costs, and sales. These functions are then used to calculate noncooperative and cooperative solutions to the constituent game and the actual outcome of the repeated game. The actual outcome is found to be substantially less lucrative than the monopoly solution. Nevertheless, all stations are better off than if they played their noncooperative strategies in every period. In addition, the continuous supergame strategies associated with reaction functions are found to provide a better model of the price-war dynamics than alternative discontinuous strategies, where price wars are reversions to Nash behavior.

I. INTRODUCTION

THIS PAPER uses a unique data set to test for the degree and to discriminate among models of tacit collusion. The market investigated is the Vancouver, British Columbia retail gasoline market. The players are service stations who meet daily to compete. Station operators choose price, and the quantity of gasoline sold at each station each day depends on the prices chosen by all.

Oligopolistic interaction is modeled as a repeated game. In an earlier paper (Slade [1985]) I derive a method of producing price wars in price-setting supergames. The method is illustrated with two examples: one where firms use discontinuous strategies in the spirit of Friedman [1971] and the other where strategies are continuous as in Kalai and Stanford [1985].

The present paper attempts to distinguish between these two supergame price-war models. The object of the paper is to examine the behavior of firms during wars. Because many punishment strategies can support the same collusive outcome, it is of interest to determine what strategies firms actually use in a particular situation. To anticipate results, weak support is given to the continuous-reply model, where small deviations lead to small punishments, over its discontinuous alternative.

The exercise is very different from the Porter (1983b) empirical work, where

* This research was supported by a grant from the Canadian Social Sciences and Humanities Research Council. I would like to thank the ten oil-company regional marketing managers and the thirteen service-station operators that were involved in the data collection. Without their cooperation, this study would not have been possible. I would also like to thank Charles Blackorby, Timothy Bresnahan, Paul Geroski, Jonathan Hamilton, Louis Phlips, and Richard Schmalensee for thoughtful and constructive comments on an earlier draft.

tests are made for the occurrence and timing of price wars. In this market, it is obvious to all customers, dealers, and observers when a war is occurring. Cooperative periods in the industry are characterized by identical prices for all firms which are constant over time. Such data are therefore useless for empirical purposes. For this reason, my data do not include stable periods.

The data set, which I collected, pertains solely to a price-war period. It consists of daily price, sales volume, and cost figures for three types of gasoline sold at thirteen service stations in a submarket of Vancouver. The data are therefore extremely rich, making it possible to estimate demand, cost, and reaction functions at a very micro level. These estimated functions are then used to calculate various solutions to the game—noncooperative and cooperative solutions to the one-shot game and the actual outcome of the repeated game. By comparing solutions, it is possible to see if firms in fact do better through repeated play than they would if they played the game only once. In addition, it is possible to test the explanatory power of various price-war models.

II. THE MODEL

II(i). *Background*

The game that is described in this section is noncooperative. Overt collusion is ruled out because, at least in North America, binding agreements on price or output are illegal. Nevertheless, when a game is repeated many times, solutions that have a collusive flavor can emerge.

In a companion paper (Slade [1985]) I derive a method of generating price wars in supergame models. The market considered is one where oligopolists produce a differentiated product and use price as a strategic variable. Prices are posted and can be observed by all. In addition, rival sales can be monitored. There is thus little uncertainty or scope for secret price cutting.[1] Nevertheless, price wars occur. Many real-world markets which are plagued by price wars fit this description—retail gasoline and airline-seat sales are just two examples.

In the Slade model, price wars are information-gathering devices. Demand is subject to periodic but infrequent random shifts. After a demand shift has occurred, unless firms change prices they cannot know the new demand conditions. Incentives are such that considerable price cutting and undercutting occurs before the market settles down to the new equilibrium.

The method of generating price wars is illustrated with two examples. The first involves discontinuous or "grim" strategies in the spirit of Friedman (1971). With a grim strategy, punishment for any deviation from the collusive

[1] Price-war models such as that of Green and Porter [1984] and Porter [1983a] rely on unobservability of choice variables and inability to detect cheating to produce wars.

outcome involves reversion to Nash behavior for the one-shot game. The second uses continuous strategies as in Kalai and Stanford [1985]. With a continuous strategy, small defections trigger small punishments and large defections trigger large punishments. The price-war dynamics inherent in the two examples have much in common. There are, however, testable differences as described below.

II(ii). *The constituent game*

Suppose that N firms in a market produce a differentiated product. Suppose additionally that the N firms can be partitioned into M strategic subgroups, where all members of a group face similar demand conditions and exhibit similar responses to rival actions. All members of a group are then considered to be identical and the players in the game are the strategic groups.

This does not mean that players within groups collude to choose their strategies. What it means is that, because all members of a group are identical and because each member chooses its actions optimally, the actions chosen will be the same for like players.

To identify the groups, the set of integers from one to N is partitioned into M subsets, where the ith member of this partition indexes the firms in strategic group i. Denote the ith set by N_i, which has M_i members.

Assume that M demand equations are known, one for each group, where the quantity sold by a given firm depends on the prices posted by all firms. Let these demand equations be approximated by linear functions

$$q^i = a_i + b_i p^i + c_i \sum_{\substack{j \in N_i \\ j \neq i}} w_j^{ii} p^j + \sum_{\substack{h=1 \\ h \neq i}}^{M} d_{hi} \sum_{k \in N_h} w_k^{ih} p^k + g_i(z), \qquad i = 1, \ldots, M, \tag{1}$$

where

q^i	is the quantity sold by a firm from group i,
p^i	is the price charged by this firm,
p^j	is a price charged by another firm from group i,
p^k	is a price charged by a firm from a different group,
w^{ih}	is a vector of weights of unit norm, $h = 1, \ldots, M$, and
z	is a vector of exogenous variables that shift demand.

Note that, even though in equilibrium the prices charged by firms in the same group will be equal, in this specification of the demand equations, each price is allowed to move independently. Equation (1) will be estimated to obtain the demand parameters $a_i, \ldots, d_i$, $i = 1, \ldots, M$.

Strategies for the constituent game consist of the choice of prices, p^i, one for each group. The payoff for each firm is its profit, $\pi^i(p)$, where p is a vector of M prices. If marginal cost is constant, then the profit for a firm from group i can be written as

(2) $\pi^i(p) = (p^i - mc^i)q^i(p)$

where

π^i is the profit earned by a representative firm from group i, and
mc^i is that firm's marginal cost.

Each firm's objective is to choose price so as to maximize profit,

(3) $$\max_{p^i} \pi^i(p)$$

First-order conditions for this maximization are

(4) $$d\pi^i/dp^i = (p^i - mc^i)dq^i/dp^i + q^i = 0, \qquad i = 1, \ldots, M$$

Different assumptions about the way in which firms respond to each other determine dq^i/dp^i. And, when expressions for dq^i/dp^i are substituted into the first-order conditions, they determine different solutions to the constituent game.

For example, suppose that each firm plays Bertrand–Nash. Then dp^j/dp^i is zero for j not equal i and $dq^i/dp^i = b_i$. When b_i is substituted for dq^i/dp^i in (4), we have M linear equations in M unknown prices, which can be solved for the unique vector of Nash prices p_n. Corresponding quantities and profits, q_n and π_n, can then be obtained from equations (1) and (2).

More generally, suppose that players have linear reaction functions with slopes $dp^j/dp^i = R^{ji}$, $R^{ji} \in I_R = [-1, 1]$. Then dq^i/dp^i is

(5) $$dq^i/dp^i = b_i + c_i R^{ii} + \sum_{\substack{h=1 \\ h \neq i}}^{M} d_{hi} R^{hi}$$

and the first-order conditions (4) become

(6) $$d\pi^i/dp^i = (p^i - mc^i)\left(b_i + c_i R^{ii} + \sum_{\substack{h=1 \\ h \neq i}}^{M} d_{hi} R^{hi}\right) + a_i + b_i p^i$$
$$+ c_i \sum_{\substack{j \in N_i \\ j \neq i}} w_j^{ii} p^j + \sum_{\substack{h=1 \\ h \neq i}}^{M} d_{hi} \sum_{k \in N_h} w_k^{hi} p^k + g_i(z) = 0,$$
$$i = 1, \ldots, M$$

Given any matrix of reactions R, if we assume that prices are the same for firms in the same group, the system of M linear equations (6) can be solved for the unique vector of M prices, p_R, corresponding to R. It is easy to show that many sets of prices, including all those between Bertrand and monopoly, can be obtained through appropriate choices of R.

Bertrand–Nash behavior corresponds to a particular choice of R, R_n identically equal to zero. We wish to consider another special matrix R_b

corresponding to the single-period best replies. Consider equation (6), firm i's first-order condition. Suppose that firm j in group i initiates a price change. Because optimal behavior satisfies the first-order conditions, firm i's best response, $R_b^{ii} = dp^i/dp^j$ for j in N_i, is the one that restores the first-order condition to zero. Differentiating (6) with respect to p^j results in

$$\pi_{ji}^i = d^2\pi^i/dp^j dp^i = R^{ii}\left(b_i + c_i R^{ii} + \sum_{\substack{h=1\\h\neq i}}^{M} d_{hi}R^{hi}\right) + b_i R^{ii} \tag{7}$$

$$+ c_i\left(w_j^{ii} + \sum_{\substack{l\in N_i\\l\neq i\\l\neq j}} w_l^{ii}R^{ii}\right) + \sum_{\substack{h=1\\h\neq i}}^{M} d_{hi}R^{hi} = 0$$

Using the same technique, all M^2 equations of the form of $\pi_{jk}^k = 0$, $k, j = 1, \ldots, M$, can be obtained. The result is M^2 quadratic equations in M^2 unknowns R^{jk}, which can be solved for the best-reply matrix R_b. When R_b is substituted into equation (6), best-reply prices p_b are found. Corresponding quantities and profits, q_b and π_b, can then be calculated from equations (1) and (2).

Finally, we wish to consider a cooperative solution to the constituent game. Suppose that instead of each firm maximizing its own profit, given rival reactions, the firms in the market collude to maximize joint profit.[2] Joint profit can be expressed as

$$\Pi(p) = \sum_{h=1}^{M} M_h(p^h - mc^h)q^h(p) \tag{8}$$

A vector of prices p^h, $h = 1, \ldots, M$, is chosen to maximize (8) subject to the demand constraints (1).[3] First-order conditions for this maximization are

$$\partial\Pi/\partial p^i = M_i(p^i - mc^i)\partial q^i/\partial p^i + M_i q^i + \sum_{\substack{h=1\\h\neq i}}^{M} M_h(p^h - mc^h)\partial q^h/\partial p^i = 0, \tag{9}$$

$$i = 1, \ldots, M$$

Differentiating the demand equation to obtain $\partial q^j/\partial p^i$, substituting into (9) and rearranging, we have

$$M_i\{(2p^i - mc^i)(b_i + c_i) + a_i + g_i(z)\} + \sum_{\substack{h=1\\h\neq i}}^{M} M_h M_i\{(d_{hi} + d_{ih})p^h \tag{10}$$

$$- d_{ih}mc^h\} = 0, \qquad i = 1, \ldots, M$$

[2] Because firms are asymmetric and because there are no sidepayments, joint-profit maximization is not the expected outcome of successful collusion. This calculation is performed in order to get a reasonable upper bound for prices.

[3] Additional constraints that all profits be nonnegative or that the solution be individually rational can also be imposed.

The M linear equations of the form of (10) can be solved for the unique joint-profit-maximizing price vector p_m. Corresponding quantities and profits, q_m and π_m, can be found in the obvious fashion. p_m is a cooperative solution to the constituent game. It is, however, not a noncooperative equilibrium. The problem is that when $M-1$ groups play cooperatively, the Mth group can unilaterally improve its profit by cutting price. When all deviate, however, all are worse off. As discussed in the next section, p_m and many reaction-function price vectors p_R can be stationary noncooperative equilibria for the repeated game.

II(iii). *The repeated game*

The repeated game consists of playing the constituent game an infinite number of times. A strategy for the ith player in the repeated game is a choice of price to play in every period $(p_0^i, p_1^i, \ldots)$, where p_t^i can depend on the history of play. Payoffs in the repeated game take the form

$$(11) \qquad \Gamma^i = \sum_{t=0}^{\infty} \delta^t \pi^i(p_t), \qquad i = 1, \ldots, M, \qquad 0 < \delta < 1,$$

where

Γ^i is the payoff to a firm from group i in the repeated game, and
$\delta = 1/(1+\rho)$ is the discount factor (ρ is the discount rate).

In the Slade [1985] model, demand shocks trigger the punishment strategies which support the collusive outcomes that are observed during stable periods. With example one, during wars firms aim at the expected values of their Bertrand–Nash prices, p_n^i, for the new (post demand-shock) one-shot game. Expectations about the new demand conditions are updated in each period as new price-quantity combinations are observed. Behavior during wars is thus described by

$$(12) \qquad \Delta p_t^i = \Delta E(p_n^i | \Omega_t) + \eta_t^i, \qquad i = 1, \ldots, M$$

where

Δ denotes a first difference,
E is the expectation operator,
Ω_t is the information available at time t, and
η is a random disturbance.

If demand and cost conditions are similar for firms in different groups, contemporaneous price changes will be correlated as players use the same information to update their expectations. Players may thus appear to be moving in tandem. However, they will not react to rival previous-period price changes.

With example two, in contrast, firms follow their intertemporal reaction functions during wars. Their behavior is thus described by

$$\text{(13)} \qquad \Delta p_t^i = \sum_{h=1}^{M} R^{ih}\left(\sum_{\substack{k \in N_h \\ k \neq i}} w_k^{ih} \Delta p_{t-1}^k\right) + \eta_t^i, \qquad i = 1, \ldots, N$$

With this example, R^{ih} is the response of a player in group i to previous-period price changes initiated by players from group h. The R's are thus slopes of intertemporal reaction functions.

Given any reaction matrix $R = (R^{ih})$ there is a unique fixed point for the mappings (12) which is a stationary Nash equilibrium for the supergame with payoffs given by (11).[4] This vector, which we denote p_R, will be observed during stable periods. During price wars, however, prices will be below p_R. In these periods, firms move along their reaction functions.

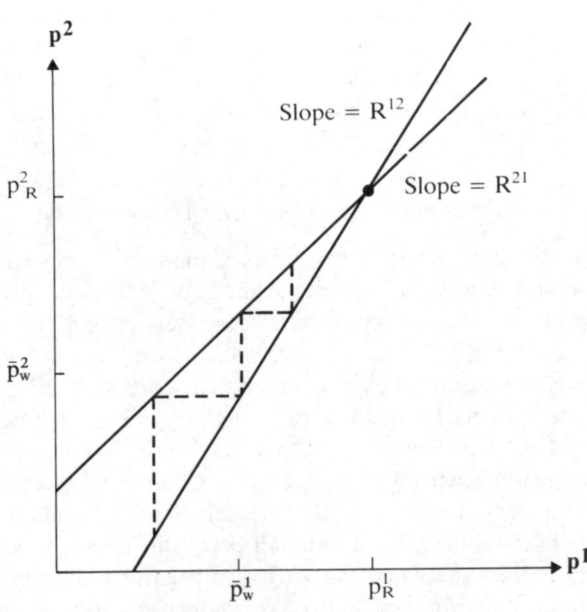

Figure 1
Intertemporal Reaction Functions.

This situation is illustrated in Figure 1 for the case of two players. In the figure, $\bar{p}_w^i$ is the average price charged by player i during a war and p_R^i is the price that the same firm will charge when the war is over.

An equation for price changes that nests these two examples can be

[4] Slade [1985] demonstrates this for the case of symmetric duopolists.

written as

$$\Delta p_t^i = \sum_{h=1}^{M} \left\{ \alpha_{ih} R^{ih} \sum_{\substack{k \in N_h \\ k \neq i}} w_k^{ih} \Delta p_t^k + (1-\alpha_{ih}) R^{ih} \sum_{\substack{k \in N_h \\ k \neq i}} w_k^{ih} \Delta p_{t-1}^k \right\} + \eta_t^i, \tag{14}$$

$$i = 1, \ldots, N, \qquad 0 \leqslant \alpha_{ih} \leqslant 1$$

The R's have different interpretations, depending on the example. With example one, R is a matrix of contemporaneous price-change correlations whereas with example two, it is a matrix of slopes of intertemporal reaction functions.

A test for example one is $\alpha_{ih} = 1$. Here, the R matrix may or may not be zero. A test for example two, in contrast, is $R^{ih} > 0$ and $\alpha_{ih} = 0$.

These hypotheses can be assessed statistically if demand and price-change equations have been estimated. In addition, Bertrand–Nash, best-reply, and monopoly prices, p_n, p_b, and p_m can be calculated and compared to the prices observed both during and after the price war. Finally, equilibrium reaction-function prices p_R can be compared to the stable prices that were observed when the war was over. In this way, it can be seen if the estimated reaction-function strategies are capable of supporting the prices that were the outcome of the war.

III. THE VANCOUVER RETAIL GASOLINE MARKET

Prior to 1981, the retail gasoline market in Canada was very stable. Prices and sales rose in a steady and orderly fashion, price dispersion was almost nonexistent, and discounts for type of service (self service or cash transactions, for example) were small.[5]

Recently, a combination of excess refining capacity and softening world-wide petroleum markets have led to radical changes in Canadian gasoline-marketing practices. The last several years have been characterized by some degree of price instability in all urban centers of Canada. One key change that occurred in the early 1980s was the reversal of the Canadian–American relative price. Traditionally, the Canadian price was lower. It continued to rise, however, at the time when the US price began to fall and eventually gasoline became cheaper in the US. Because many Canadians live within easy driving distance of the American border, buying gasoline in the US became a regular activity. This shift in demand seems to have been largely unanticipated and has left the industry with unwanted excess capacity. The result has been instability and price wars.

With the exception of periodic demand shifts, there is little uncertainty in this market. Prices are posted and posted prices are the same as transactions

[5] Between 1972 and 1979, despite price increases, Canadian consumption of gasoline grew at a steady rate of four percent per year. In 1980, consumption leveled off. Then in 1981, it dropped by four percent, to be followed by a ten-percent decline in 1982.

prices. In addition, rival sales can be monitored by counting rival customers. This market, therefore, seems to conform closely to the theoretical model of Slade [1985].

The specific marketing area studied is a heavily traveled five-mile strip that is known as the Kingsway region of Vancouver. Stations along the Kingsway strip are well connected but are only loosely connected to other regions of the city. The area contains stations owned by most of the major and independent oil companies active in British Columbia as well as stations owned by the government. Ten companies and thirteen retail outlets are involved.

The product sold, gasoline, is relatively homogeneous. Differentiation exists, however, for two reasons. First, stations are differentiated by type of ownership and service offered, the characteristics that determine the strategic groups. And second, stations are differentiated by location, the characteristic that determines the weights used to average prices within groups.

The strategic groups remain to be specified. Service stations are characterized by type of ownership—major, independent, or government; type of service offered—self or full serve; and by extent of horizontal and vertical integration. Not all of these characteristics, however, are important determinants of producer and consumer behavior (that is, of the demand facing the station and of the station's reactions to rival price changes).

A priori, one might expect to find three distinct groups of stations: those owned by major integrated firms, those owned by small independent marketers, and those owned by the government. In an earlier study (Slade [1984]), however, only two distinct groups were identified: majors and independents.[6] The behavior of the government firm was seen to be indistinguishable from that of a private firm.

The government firm, Petro-Canada, owns two types of stations in the area. Some stations market under the name Petro-Canada and display the characteristic red maple leaf. The behavior of these stations was seen to be indistinguishable from the behavior of the integrated privately owned majors.

Petro-Canada has acquired most of its assets through purchase rather than through construction. When it purchases independent retail outlets, it may decide not to rebrand these outlets. Instead it may operate the stations as second or "fighting" brands, a practice that is common for the majors as well. Second-brand stations maintain their independent "personalities".[7] The behavior of the government second brand, PayNSave, was seen to be indistinguishable from that of the independents.

[6] A third class of station was identified in Slade [1984]. These were denoted mid-tier. Unfortunately, there is only one mid-tier station in the sample, Husky, To avoid publishing numbers that can be identified with a particular station, therefore, Husky was dropped from the sample.

[7] A representative of Petro-Canada, in describing the decision to rebrand or not, stated that it depends on many factors. The stations that are operated as second brands tend to be older, have outdated equipment, and/or be run by operators with "independent" personalities.

For these reasons, the Petro-Canada stations were included with the majors whereas PayNSave stations were included with the indepenents.

IV. DATA CONSTRUCTION AND ESTIMATION TECHNIQUE

IV(i). *The data*

The data set used in this study was collected by the author in the summer of 1983. It consists of observations on price, variable cost, and sales volume for three types of gasoline at each of the thirteen service stations in the Kingsway region. Data were collected over a three-month price-war period.

Prices are posted at each station and are therefore public knowledge. In order to collect sales and cost data, however, it was necessary to obtain the cooperation of the ten regional-marketing managers and the thirteen station operators. All were very accommodating in releasing this information. The one stipulation that they made was that when results were presented, stations be identified by number and not by name or brand.

For each station there are three variables to specify, p^i, q^i, and mc^i, as well as the weights, w^{ih}. The variable p^i is constructed as a Divisia price index for the three types of gasoline sold. q^i is then constructed as the implicit Divisia quantity index corresponding to p^i. Price is measured in cents per liter and quantity in 100 liters.

The construction of marginal cost requires several assumptions. It is clear that capital is fixed in the short run. It is additionally assumed that labor is fixed. At least one person must be employed to sell gasoline and, for many modern stations, only one person is required. Even when more than one person is employed or when a single employee spends only a fraction of his time selling gasoline, the number of people at a given station varies little with the quantity sold. Marginal cost is therefore assumed to be the cost of purchasing wholesale gasoline, which is also measured in cents per liter.

The weights w_k^{ih} used to average prices charged by stations within a group are inversely proportional to distance. That is, if d_{ik} is the distance between station i and station k, where $k \in N_h$, then w_k^{ih} is proportional to $1/d_{ik}$.

Finally, the exogenous demand-shift variables are chosen to be six dummy variables that distinguish the days of the week plus two dummies for the two holidays that occurred during the period of data collection.

IV(ii). *Estimation*

When additive disturbance terms have been appended to the N demand equations of the form of (1), they are estimated as a simultaneous seemingly unrelated system using iterative three-stage least squares. Correction for autocorrelation is performed when indicated. Coefficient restrictions are imposed so that parameters for stations in the same group will be equal.

The R matrix must also be assessed. This is accomplished by estimating N equations of the form of (14) as a simultaneous system. For the estimation, prices are calculated net of marginal cost so that price changes include only those not due to cost changes.[8] Again, iterative three-stage least squares is used, correction for autocorrelated errors is performed when appropriate, and coefficient restrictions are imposed so that stations in the same group will have the same parameters. The estimated response matrix is denoted R_a.

With both sets of equations, p_t^i and q_t^i are endogenous variables. The instruments used in the estimation of (1) and (14) are the station and firm characteristics discussed in Slade [1984], the demand-shift variables, and lagged values of the endogenous variables.

A problem arises in interpreting the estimated α's and therefore in discriminating between the two examples. The period of data collection does not necessarily correspond to the response period. In practice, reaction times are very short in this market. Obtaining an α close to one, therefore, may not be evidence against example two, the reaction-function example. A large value of α may just mean that stations change prices more often than once a day. Obtaining a value of $1-\alpha$ that is significantly nonzero, in contrast, is evidence against example one, the discontinuous-strategy example. With short reaction times, it is highly unlikely that contemporaneous price changes occur a day apart.

V. EMPIRICAL RESULTS

V(i). *The demand equations*

There are only two groups N_i and N_m with M_i and M_m members respectively. Let p^i be a price charged by an independent and let v^m be a price charged by a major. Define

$$(15) \qquad \bar{p}(i) = \sum_{\substack{j \in N_i \\ j \neq i}}^{N} w_j^{ii} p^j$$

and

$$(16) \qquad \bar{p}(m) = \sum_{j \in N_i} w_j^{im} p^j$$

For independent station i, $\bar{p}(i)$ is the inverse-distance-weighted average of rival independent prices, and for major station m, $\bar{p}(m)$ is the inverse-distance-weighted average of rival independent prices. $\bar{v}(m)$ and $\bar{v}(i)$ are defined similarly.

[8] Many of the cost changes during the year were due to tax changes or to the introduction or removal of dealer supports as described in Slade [1984]. For this reason, it seems reasonable to assume that players know rival costs.

TABLE I
EMPIRICAL ESTIMATES
ESTIMATED DEMAND EQUATIONS

Group	Coefficients			
	a_1	b_1	c_1	d_1
Independents	73.55	−12.96 (−4.9)*	0.67 (0.23)	11.86 (4.9)*
	a_2	b_2	c_2	d_2
Majors	149.10	−12.44 (−8.3)*	9.75 (3.7)*	0.80 (0.40)

ESTIMATED RESPONSE MATRICES

Group	Coefficients			
	R_a^{ii}	α^{ii}	R_a^{im}	α^{im}
Independents	0.81 (11.0)*	0.80 (17.6)*	0.55 (11.9)*	0.56 (13.0)*
	R_a^{mm}	α^{mm}	R_a^{mi}	α^{mi}
Majors	0.56 (12.2)*	0.71 (17.3)*	0.73 (5.6)*	0.61 (7.8)*

* Denotes significance at the 99 percent level of confidence.

Using this notation, the demand equations are

$$q_t^i = a_1 + b_1 p_t^i + c_1 \bar{p}(i)_t + d_1 \bar{v}(i)_t + g_1(z_t) + \varepsilon_t^i \tag{17}$$

and

$$q_t^m = a_2 + b_2 v_t^m + c_2 \bar{v}(m)_t + d_2 \bar{p}(m)_t + g_2(z_t) + \varepsilon_t^m \qquad i \in N_i, \qquad m \in N_m \tag{18}$$

where g_1 and g_2 are linear functions of the demand-shift dummy variables.

Equations (17) and (18) were estimated by the method described in the previous section. Table I shows the estimated demand parameters. In the table, t-statistics are shown under the corresponding estimated coefficients.

An inspection of Table I shows that own-price effects are negative and significant. Rival-price effects are positive, both for members of the same group and for members of the opposite group. What is surprising is that pricing by the independents, other than an independent's own price, has little effect on demand. Both c_1 and d_2 are small and statistically insignificant.

In the middle of the period of data collection, there was a temporary lull in pricing activity. It is therefore possible that what we have is two price wars occurring back to back. To test this hypothesis, the sample was divided into two subperiods and separate demand equations were estimated for each.[9] Quasi-likelihood-ratio tests (Gallant and Jorgenson [1979]) were then calculated to see if demand was stable over the entire period or whether there were two distinct demand regimes. The quasi-likelihood ratio (QLR) is distributed asymptotically χ_r^2, where r equals the number of independent restrictions.

Calculated QLR's are 7.3 for the independent demand equations and 1.2 for the major demand equations. Stability of demand over the entire period therefore cannot be rejected at any reasonable level of confidence. The test thus gives support to the idea of a single price war.

V(ii). *The estimated response matrices*

To estimate the response matrices used in the repeated game, prices are calculated net of marginal cost. Net prices are denoted by capital letters. That is, $P^i = p^i - mc^i$ is a net price for an independent firm and $V^m = v^m - mc^m$ is a net price for a major. $\bar{P}(i)$ and $\bar{P}(m)$ are then defined as in equations (15) and (16) with p^j replaced by P^j. $\bar{V}(m)$ and $\bar{V}(i)$ are defined similarly.

Using this notation, equations (14) become

$$\text{(19)} \qquad \Delta P_t^i = \alpha_{ii} R_a^{ii} \Delta\bar{P}(i)_t + (1-\alpha_{ii}) R_a^{ii} \Delta\bar{P}(i)_{t-1} + \alpha_{im} R_a^{im} \Delta\bar{V}(i)_t + (1-\alpha_{im}) R_a^{im} \Delta\bar{V}(i)_{t-1} + \eta_t^i$$

$$\text{(20)} \qquad \Delta V_t^m = \alpha_{mm} R_a^{mm} \Delta\bar{V}(m)_t + (1-\alpha_{mm}) R_a^{mm} \Delta\bar{V}(m)_{t-1} + \alpha_{mi} R_a^{mi} \Delta\bar{P}(m)_t + (1-\alpha_{mi}) R_a^{mi} \Delta\bar{P}(m)_{t-1} + \eta_t^m$$

If the estimated α's do not equal one, the matrix $\hat{R}_a$ is an estimate of the intertemporal responses for the repeated game. This response is distributed over two periods. In contrast, if the estimated α's equal one, $\hat{R}_a$ is an estimate of contemporaneous price-change correlations.

The second half of Table I shows the estimated R's and α's. Asymptotic t-statistics are shown under each estimated coefficient.[10]

V(iii). *Solutions to the game*

Given the demand and cost parameters, calculation of the various outcomes for the constituent game requires numerical solution of systems of equations. For example, calculation of the best-reply matrix R_b is accomplished by solving the M^2 quadratic equations of the form of (7) for the M^2 unknowns R_b^{kj}.

[9] The first subperiod consists of observations 1 through 40 whereas the second consists of observations 41 through 92.

[10] Equations (19) and (20) are nonlinear in the structural parameters. The asymptotic t-statistics are therefore really the square root of a chi-squared variable with one degree of freedom. The distribution of that statistic, however, is almost the same as a two-tailed t-statistic for large samples.

TABLE II
SOLUTIONS TO THE GAME

		Responses			
		ii	*mi*	*im*	*mm*
Nash	R_n	0.0	0.0	0.0	0.0
Best Replies	R_b	0.03	0.02	0.14	0.13
Actual	R_a	0.81	0.73	0.55	0.56
	α	0.80	0.61	0.56	0.71
Test for		t-*statistics*			
$R_a = R_n$		11.0*	5.6*	11.9*	12.2*
$R_a = R_b$		10.6*	5.4*	8.9*	9.4*
$(1-\alpha) = 0$		4.4*	5.0*	10.2*	7.1*

	Prices and Profits		
	Independent Price, p	*Major Price, v*	*Industry Profit, Π*
Model			
$p_n \Pi_n$	44.6	45.1	277 628
$p_b \Pi_b$	44.9	45.6	303 011
$p_{R_a} \Pi_a$	50.0	48.8	419 948
$p_m \Pi_m$	55.1	64.9	1 032 010
Observed			
Price War	44.7	45.2	282 369
Stable Outcome	50.0	50.0	428 678

* Denotes rejection at the 99 percent level of confidence.

Responses R^{kj}, where k and j take on the values i for independent and m for major, are shown in the first half of Table II. Three response matrices appear: Nash, best-reply, and actual (or econometrically estimated). Under the actual replies the parameters α_{kj} are listed. The α's distinguish between same-day and previous-day price-change correlations as discussed earlier.

The table also shows t-statistics that test the hypotheses $R_a^{kj} = R_n^{kj}$ and $R_a^{kj} = R_b^{kj}$. It can be seen that both uncorrelated Bertrand–Nash and one-shot best-reply behavior are resoundingly rejected.

t-statistics that test the hypotheses $(1-\alpha_{kj}) = 0$ are also shown. These hypotheses are also rejected, which can be interpreted as evidence against the discontinuous-strategy example and in favor of the continuous-strategy alternative. Unfortunately, given the data, it is not possible to test the continuous-reaction-function example directly. Indirect tests, however, are discussed below.

Table II shows certain empirical regularities. Consider the best replies for the constituent game. Reactions to price changes initiated by independents

(R_b^{ii} and R_b^{mi}) are very small. This is not very surprising, given that analysis of the estimated demand equations revealed that prices charged by independent rivals are not significant determinants of sales. In contrast, reactions to price changes initiated by majors are moderate but not large.

The actual responses R_a are very different from R_b and from R_n. It is in general true that

$$R_a > R_b > R_n \tag{21}$$

Repeated play is thus associated with more "punishment" in the form of price-matching behavior than is associated with single-period solutions. In addition, actual responses to price changes initiated by independents are larger than actual responses to major-price changes. It seems that the independents are being punished more than the majors.

There is a possible explanation for this behavior. Price uniformity appears to be a goal of the majors.[11] When interviewed, marketing managers spoke of not "allowing" independents to charge lower prices than the majors charge. In equilibrium, the price that a firm chooses is inversely related to its own price elasticity of demand and directly related to rival responses to price changes that it initiates. The independents face more elastic demand than the majors (Slade [1984]).[12] Price uniformity therefore requires that responses to their price changes be larger.

The second half of Table II shows price and profit combinations for various solutions to the game. The first four rows show estimated single-period prices and profits for various solution concepts. The monopoly solution shown was calculated subject to a constraint of individual rationality. That is, joint profits were maximized subject to the constraint that each group do as well as in the single-period Bertrand–Nash equilibrium.[13]

The calculation of prices and profits corresponding to the intertemporal reaction functions with slopes R_a involves the discount factor δ. For the solution shown, δ was set equal to one and equations (7) were used.[14] Given the speed of reaction in this market, the approximation should be reasonable.

It can be seen that

$$\Pi_m > \Pi_a > \Pi_b > \Pi_n \tag{22}$$

Through repeated play, therefore, stations do better than they would if they played the noncooperative game only once. Profit, however, is far short of the monopoly profit.

Finally, Table II shows average prices observed during the price war and

[11] It is not clear why the majors desire uniformity but it is clear that uniformity is a goal.

[12] Demand elasticities can be calculated from Table 1 as $\varepsilon_j = -\hat{b}_j\bar{p}_j/\bar{q}_j$, where $j = i, m$ and a bar over a variable denotes its mean. The two $\hat{b}$'s and $\bar{p}$'s are nearly equal. $\bar{q}_m > \bar{q}_i$ therefore implies that $\varepsilon_i > \varepsilon_m$.

[13] In the unconstrained monopoly solution, some firms earn negative profits.

[14] When $\delta = 0$, response is immediate and therefore the value of α is irrelevant.

the stable prices that prevailed when the war was over.[15] These correspond to $\bar{p}_w$ and p_R in Figure 1. Two features of these prices are of interest. First, average prices observed during the price war are indistinguishable from Nash prices. If one had only aggregate data on prices and quantities, therefore, it would be difficult to reject Nash behavior during the war. When we observe how stations respond to one another, however, one-shot Nash behavior is easily rejected.

Second, during stable periods prices don't change. It is therefore impossible to estimate response matrices for these periods. We can, however, perform a weaker test. It is possible to check if the equilibrium prices p_{R_a} corresponding to the estimated response matrix R_a are close to the prices observed when the war was over, as example two would predict. A glance at Table II reveals that these two price vectors are very close, a fact that gives further credence to the continuous-reaction-function example.

A final test of the reaction-function example is performed—the stability of the estimated response matrix is investigated. With example two, these functions are institutional regularities that determine the equilibrium price vector. Lack of stability of this matrix would therefore be evidence against the example.

As with the demand equations, the sample was divided into two subperiods and separate response matrices estimated for each. Likelihood ratios that test for stability are as follows:

Response	R^{ii}	R^{mi}	R^{im}	R^{mm}
QLR	5.6	3.4	9.5*	2.6

In general, the responses are stable. Only the stability of the response of independents to major-price changes is rejected at the 95 percent level of confidence. With this response, there is a trend over time. In the first subperiod, the response is 0.46 whereas in the second, the response increases to 0.69. The average over the entire period is 0.55.

It is also possible that near the end of each subperiod, when prices are approaching stability, reactions change. For each response and each subperiod, an additional test was performed to assess if the last ten observations in the period belong to a different regime. With this test, stability of responses was never rejected.

VI. SUMMARY AND CONCLUSIONS

The existence of a very large number of solutions to a repeated game leads one naturally to an empirical assessment of the outcome that in fact results in a given game. This is one object of the present paper. It is possible, using data

[15] After the price war, the period of price stability lasted for nearly a year until the summer of 1984.

on service stations in the Vancouver retail gasoline market, to calculate and compare cooperative and noncooperative solutions to the constituent game and the actual outcome of the repeated game.

The actual outcome turns out to be substantially less lucrative than the cooperative solution to the one-shot game. It is, however, more profitable for all players than noncooperative single-period solutions. The possibility of punishing undesirable behavior that arises through repeated play is therefore a threat that enables firms to move in the direction of the cooperative outcome.

A second object of the paper is to model the price-war dynamics in such a way that tests of alternative supergame strategies are possible. In particular, discontinuous punishment strategies are assessed versus the alternative of continuous reaction-function strategies. With reaction-function strategies, firm price changes are related to previous-period rival-price changes. With discontinuous strategies, in contrast, price wars are periods of reversion to Nash behavior.

With example one, in each period firms charge prices close to the expected value of their Bertrand–Nash prices for the one-shot game. If demand and cost conditions are not too different across firms, therefore, Nash prices may be similar and contemporaneous price changes may appear to be correlated as players update their expectations. With example two, in contrast, firms react to rival previous-period price changes.

Definitive tests that distinguish between the two examples are not possible. The problem arises because the period of data collection is longer than the response time. Nevertheless, the evidence seems to point to the reaction-function example as the most appropriate for this market.

After the price war came to an end, prices were stable for nearly a year. Without any price variation, it is impossible to estimate response matrices. A weaker test of the reaction-function model, however, was performed. The equilibrium prices associated with the response matrix that was estimated from the price-war data were calculated and compared to the stable prices that were observed at the end of the war. These two price vectors were seen to be almost equal.

Stability of the reaction functions was not rejected by most of the tests performed. There is some evidence, however, of a trend in the response parameters for the independents. This raises the possibility of allowing firms to update their expectations about rival responses to the changes that they initiate. Such investigations will be pursued in the future.

MARGARET E. SLADE,
Department of Economics,
The University of British Columbia,
Vancouver, BC,
Canada, V6T 1Y2.

REFERENCES

Friedman, J., 1971, 'Noncooperative Equilibria for Supergames', *Review of Economic Studies*, 38 (January), pp. 1–12.

Gallant, R. and Jorgenson, D. W., 1979, 'Statistical Inference for a System of Simultaneous Equations in the Context of Instrumental-Variable Estimation', *Journal of Econometrics*, 11 (October/December), pp. 275–302.

Green, E. J. and Porter, R. H., 1984, 'Noncooperative Collusion Under Imperfect Price Information', *Econometrica*, 52 (January), pp. 87–100.

Kalai, E. and Stanford, W., 1985, 'Conjectural Variations in Accelerated Cournot Games', *International Journal of Industrial Organization*, 3 (June), pp. 133–152.

Porter, R. H., 1983a, 'Optimal Trigger-Price Strategies', *Journal of Economic Theory*, 29 (April), pp. 313–338.

Porter, R. H., 1983b, 'A Study of Cartel Stability: The Joint Executive Committee, 1880–1886', *The Bell Journal of Economics*, 14 (Autumn), pp. 301–314.

Slade, M. E., 1984, 'Conjectures, Firm Characteristics, and Market Structure', Department of Economics Working Paper No. 84–25, UBC, forthcoming in *International Journal of Industrial Organization.*

Slade, M. E., 1985, 'Price Wars in Price-Setting Supergames', Department of Economics Working Paper No. 85–35, UBC, Vancouver, BC.

INFORMATION, RETURNS, AND BIDDING BEHAVIOR IN OCS AUCTIONS: 1954–1969*

KENNETH HENDRICKS, ROBERT H. PORTER AND BRYAN BOUDREAU

This paper examines federal auctions for leases on the Outer Continental Shelf (OCS) in the light of the predictions of the first-price, sealed bid, common values model of auctions. We find that the data strongly support the model for auctions in which one bidder is better informed than the other bidders. The evidence for auctions in which bidders have noisy but qualitatively similar information is less conclusive, but is consistent with a model in which each bidder does not know either the actual or potential number of bidders on a lease.

I. INTRODUCTION

THIS PAPER provides a preliminary statistical analysis of bidding and returns data for the US government auctions of oil and gas leases for the Outer Continental Shelf (OCS) from 1954 through 1969. We have two objectives. One is to document the relationships between information, competition and profits, and the other is to examine whether the assumptions and predictions of the theoretical bidding models are consistent with these data.

As Weaver *et al.* [1973] document, by 1970 16.7 per cent of US domestic oil and lease condensate production, and 15 per cent of marketed gas production, came from offshore wells. These shares have since increased. Through the end of 1970, 7.1 million offshore acres had been auctioned off by the federal government, for a total of $5607.8 million (in constant 1972 dollars) in bonus bids, royalty payments and rental fees. Of course, leases auctioned off in this period continued to contribute royalty payments after 1970. By the end of 1980, 22 million acres had been auctioned. In short, these auctions have involved an increasing fraction of US domestic hydrocarbon production, and are an important source of revenue to the federal government.

The oil lease auctions are also an excellent source of data on the strategic behavior of firms in situations of imperfect and asymmetric information. In recent years, there has been a great deal of theoretical and experimental work on this issue, particularly in the context of auctions, but almost no work using field data has been done. This is unfortunate, since the predictions of the theoretical models often rely upon the assumption that each agent is able to correctly predict the behavioral rules adopted by the other agents in his

* This research was funded by NSF Grant No. SES-8511068. It and related research were presented at the 1985 Winter meetings of the Econometric Society in New York, and at a number of universities. We are indebted to the participants in these sessions, and to T. Bresnahan, T. McGuire, P. Milgrom and R. Schmalensee for helpful comments.

decision environment. It is important to verify whether this assumption is valid empirically. This paper takes a small step toward answering this question by evaluating whether the common values model of auctions (see Wilson [1975]), or some modification of it, provides an appropriate description of bidding behavior in oil lease auctions.

We begin in section II with a description of the auction mechanism. Section III describes the data set. In addition to detailed bidding information, we have post-auction production and drilling data. From these latter series, we construct estimates of the *ex post* profitability and social value of each lease. Some summary statistics are then provided, together with a cross-tabulation which succinctly describes the joint distribution of bids and *ex post* (or the realization of) profits.

In section IV we document individual firm participation rates and returns. There is substantial interfirm variation in the return figures, part of which may be attributable to luck. To identify other causes, we conduct two experiments. The first compares the profits which each firm earned to the profits it would have earned, had it won every tract on which it bid at the price it submitted. This reveals whether there were any biases in the firms' evaluations of tracts. The second experiment consists of proportionately varying all bids by a particular firm, holding constant the bids of all other firms, and computing the change in returns associated with these bid variations. This determines whether, given the set of leases which the firm chose to bid on, and given the bids of all other firms, the firm's bidding strategy maximized its *ex post* net returns. The results of these experiments indicate that a few firms did not behave optimally, and that, in at least one case, a firm consistently overestimated the value of tracts. Most firms seemed aware that their valuations of tracts they win are biased upward, although a subset of the firms may have underestimated the extent of this bias. Furthermore, there is little evidence of collusion in bidding.

In section V we examine several hypotheses about the joint distribution of firm valuations and *ex post* profits. The evidence suggests that there is significant variation in this distribution across geographical areas and across sale dates, but not across firms. The variation in firms' profitability appears to be primarily due to differences in their criteria for determining which tracts to explore and bid on. Furthermore, the factors accounting for these differences are not area- or sale-specific, but are common to all of the firms' bidding decisions.

In section VI we examine the drilling decisions of firms and the impact of (local) information externalities on these decisions. We find that firms adopt sequential drilling programs in which they first drill leases that are viewed *ex ante* as being more valuable. Twenty-seven percent of all leases were allowed to expire without any wells being drilled. We also find that there is a sharp distinction between leases in new geographical areas and those which are adjacent to previously sold leases. In the former case, the probability of a tract being productive does not depend on when the tract is drilled. Thus, the acquisition of information from drilling outcomes appears to be sufficient to offset the decline in the average quality of the tracts. In the latter case, those leases drilled earliest are more likely to be productive, and the winning firm captures a higher percentage of social rents, as much as 37 per cent, versus 26 per cent for all leases. This probably represents a return for superior information.

The penultimate section categorizes leases according to the number of bidders and examines the effect of competition on bidding and returns. Our most important finding is that bidding and return patterns are qualitatively different on leases adjacent to previously explored areas than on leases in *de novo* areas. In the former case, some firms are likely to be better informed, since they had won neighboring leases in previous sales. For these leases, we find that the *ex post* profits on tracts which receive no informed bids is substantially lower than on tracts which receive an informed bid; that the average net return on tracts won by uninformed firms is zero; that informed firms won about half of the tracts; and that the informed firms earn very high returns, which are independent of the number of uninformed bids. These facts match the predictions of theoretical work on auctions with asymmetrically informed bidders (e.g. Engelbrecht–Wiggans *et al.* [1983] and Milgrom and Weber [1982a]). We also note that very few leases received more than one informed bid, an outcome which is not due to informed firms forming joint ventures. Indeed, if there is any collusion in these auctions, it probably only arises via bid rotation schemes. Such schemes are unlikely to be effective in these auctions, because of the infrequency of lease sales.

Our analysis of the effect of competition in *de novo* areas is less definitive. Consistent with theoretical predictions, both winning bid and the difference between the two highest bids, or "money left on the table", increase with the number of bidders, and the ratio of money left on the table to the winning bid falls. In addition, higher value tracts attract more bidders. However, *ex post* profits net of bids are a decreasing function of the number of bidders, and are even negative when this number is seven or greater. The difficulty with establishing whether or not this pattern is consistent with the common values model is that the number of bidders is not the correct measure of competition on tracts. It is clearly an endogenous variable, since active firms with sufficiently low valuations of a tract do not submit bids.

An explanation of the return pattern which is *not* consistent with the common values model is that firms do not adequately account for the "winner's curse". That is, they may fail to recognize that, when the number of bidders increases, the firm with the highest *ex ante* evaluation of lease profitability is increasingly more optimistic relative to the true lease value, and so should reduce its bid accordingly. (See, for example, Capen, Clapp, and Campbell [1971].) An equally plausible explanation, which is consistent with the common values model, is based on the assumption that firms did not know the number of competitors on a lease. In that case, its prior estimate of the value of the tract conditional on winning is on average too low if the realized number of competitors is below average, and it is too high if the number is above average. To discriminate between these explanations, one needs to develop and estimate an explicitly parametric econometric model of bidding strategies. This is what we intend to do in our future research.

We conclude with a brief discussion of some implications of our findings.

II. DESCRIPTION OF THE AUCTION MECHANISM

The federal government transfers the production rights to oil and gas deposits on offshore public lands to the private sector by means of a sequence of lease sales. The organization of a lease sale begins when the government makes a particular area available for exploration and invites nominations from the oil industry as to which tracts should be offered for sale. A tract typically consists of 5000 or 5760 acres. The firms are permitted to gather information about the tracts using seismic surveys and off-site drilling, but they are not allowed to drill any on-site wells. After the firms make their nominations, the government constructs a final list of tracts, which it then offers to the public through the first price, sealed bid auction procedure described below.

There are two kinds of lease sales. A wildcat sale consists of tracts whose geology is not well-known, and only seismic exploration precedes these sales. The wells which are drilled on such tracts are called *wildcat* wells, since they involve searching for a new deposit. In contrast, a *drainage* sale consists of tracts which are adjacent to tracts on which a deposit has been discovered. Wells drilled on these tracts are, for the most part, developmental, rather than exploratory, wells.

A sale consists of the simultaneous auction of the nominated tracts. In our sample, the average number of tracts sold in wildcat and drainage sales were 132 and 27, respectively. A firm which participates in a sale submits a separate bid on each tract that it is interested in acquiring. A bid is a dollar figure which the firm promises to pay to the government at the time of the sale if it is awarded the tract. This payment is called the *bonus*. The firm submitting the highest bonus is awarded the tract. The results of the bidding on all tracts, as well as the identities of the bidders and the values of their bids, are announced at a public meeting.

When a firm wins a tract, it has 5 years to explore it. If no work is done during this period, ownership of the lease reverts to the government, which may subsequently auction off the tract in some future sale. In our sample, a nominal rental fee of $3 per acre on wildcat tracts, and $10 per acre on drainage tracts, is paid by the firm each year until either the lease expires or production begins. If oil and/or gas is discovered in sufficient quantities so that the firm begins production, the lease is automatically renewed for as long as it takes the firm to extract the hydrocarbons. A fixed fraction of the revenues from any oil and/or gas extracted, 1/6th throughout our sample, accrues to the government. This sum is paid on an annual basis and is called the *royalty* payment. There is virtually no incidence in our sample of tracts being resold from one firm to another after the auction is held. There was little or no motive for speculative purchases of leases, since real wellhead prices were constant for practical purposes in the US until 1973.

The government may enter the auction as a bidder in two ways. In our sample, it announced a reservation price of $15 or $25 per acre on wildcat leases and $25 on most drainage leases. (The reservation prices varied from sale to sale.) In addition, it retains the right to reject the high bid on a tract if it believes the bid is too low. The usual basis on which it makes this judgment is its private estimate of the value of the tract. These estimates may be based in part upon the geological and seismic reports which the firms are required to submit. For sales in our sample, the high bid was rejected on 7 per cent of the wildcat tracts, and on 15 per cent of the drainage tracts..

III. DATA DESCRIPTION

Our study focuses on the federal lands off the coasts of Louisiana and Texas which were leased between 1954 and 1969. During this period, the government held 8 wildcat sales and 8 drainage sales, in which it auctioned off 1056 wildcat tracts and 144 drainage tracts. (These numbers do not include the 81 wildcat and 25 drainage tracts on which the high bid was rejected.) There were also several wildcat sales off the Florida and the Pacific Coasts in this period. We have dropped these sales from our sample because of their relatively low level of post-auction drilling activity, and because they are in geologically distinct areas.

Our data set, which we obtained from the Department of the Interior, contains the following information for each tract: the date it was sold; its location, water depth, and acreage; which firms bid and the value of their bids; the number and date of any wells that were drilled; and its annual production through 1980 if any oil or gas was extracted. The drilling and production data were used, together with the annual survey of drilling costs conducted by the American Petroleum Institute, to calculate *ex post* value for each tract.

Our projected production profile for each tract was constructed as follows. Each productive well potentially yields four separate commodities: oil, condensate, natural gas, and other hydrocarbons. For each of these commodities, if the tract had stopped being productive by 1980, we assumed that production had terminated on that tract. (It is not inexpensive to cap and reopen an offshore well.) If production was still continuing in 1980, we determined the year of peak production for that commodity on that tract, and then filled in the missing values of the production path for 15 years after the peak production year by using a 25 per cent per annum decline in the rate of production, where the base is the production in the peak year. Production more than 15 years after the peak year was assumed to be zero. This production model describes the terminated production profiles in our sample quite closely.

In order to convert these four output sequences into revenues, we noted that real wellhead prices in the US were virtually constant from 1950 until 1973, and assumed that the expectations of the bidders in our sample would be for this pattern to continue. Accordingly, we took the real wellhead price of each of the four commodities received in the year the tract was auctioned off, in 1972 dollars (adjusted by the GNP deflator), and multiplied that price times production of that commodity for each productive year. This real revenue sequence was discounted at a 5 per cent per annum rate to the year of the tract sale to obtain the present discounted value of revenues. Formally, the real revenue, R, from a tract sold in year t is calculated as:

$$R = \sum_{s=0}^{\infty} \beta^s \left(\sum_{i=1}^{4} p_{i,t} \cdot q_{i,t+s} \right) \tag{1}$$

where $\beta = \exp(-0.05)$ is the discount factor, $p_{i,t}$ is the real price of commodity i in year t, and $\{q_{i,t+s}\}_{s=0}^{\infty}$ is the actual and projected sequence of production of commodity i. Again, note that, for each i, $p_{i,t}$ is almost constant.

Our construction of discounted costs is similar to that of Mead *et al.* [1980]. We consider only the cost of drilling and equipping wells. Each well drilled on a tract is classified according to four criteria: (1) its location, whether it is offshore Texas or offshore Louisiana, (2) its spud year, (3) its depth, on the basis of which it is assigned to one of eleven categories, and (4) its production status. A well is called an oil well if the majority of its revenue was from oil and condensate; all other productive wells are called gas wells. Unproductive wells are called dry, and are less costly, since some drilling and equipping costs are avoided.[1] Given this four-way classification, we rely upon the annual Joint Association Survey of the American Petroleum Institute to impute a cost per foot for each well drilled on each tract.[2] Well costs are then discounted back to the auction year according to the 5 per cent rate, and then

[1] For productive tracts, we designated wells as productive or dry according to the following formula. Of the first 11 wells drilled on a tract, 65 per cent were assumed to be productive; of the next five wells drilled, 77.5 per cent were assumed to be productive; and of any additional wells drilled, 90 per cent were assumed to be productive. This scheme, also used by Mead *et al.*, is roughly consistent with offshore experience, and accounts for the fact that later wells are more likely to be productive.

[2] Cost estimates for 1957 and 1958 were unavailable, and their values were estimated by interpolation of estimated costs in adjacent years. Additional interpolation and extrapolation was also necessary for some categories of wells in early years or when there were small sample sizes.

TABLE I
LIST OF VARIABLES

N :	number of bidders	B :	bid
A :	tract acreage	$B1$:	winning bid
R :	*ex post* value of revenues	π :	*ex post* gross profits
C :	*ex post* value of drilling costs	$\pi - B1$:	*ex post* net profits
V :	discounted social value, or rent	$B1 - B2$:	"money left on table"
$B2$:	second highest bid, or if there is one bidder, the government reservation price.		

summed to yield the estimated discounted value of costs for that tract, also in 1972 dollars, which we denote by C.

Table I lists some of the variables. All monetary variables are denominated in millions of 1972\$. We denote bids by B, winning bid by $B1$, and the second highest bid by $B2$. If there is only one bidder, $B2$ equals the announced government reservation price. Our estimate of the *ex post* discounted social value of a tract is $R - C$, which we shall refer to as *rent* and denote by V. Our estimate of the *ex post* discounted gross profit, which is net of royalty payments, but not the bonus bid, is $\pi = (5/6)R - C$. Finally, our measure of *ex post* net profits is $\pi - B1 = (5/6)R - C - B1$.

These measures of *ex post* returns ignore costs associated with presale exploration, bid preparation and other overhead costs, as well as some post-auction costs. As a result, our *ex post* profit and rent figures are best thought of as a residual comprised of omitted costs, together with *ex post* profit or rent. We have tried to control for most variable costs, so that omitted costs should be relatively constant across tracts, particularly within a given sale. We should point out, however, that most of the omitted costs are pre-sale geophysical expenditures, which are sunk when the bidding decisions are made. Hence, they should not affect the bidding behavior of the firms. It is also important to note that our measures of profit and social rent will understate realized profits and rent on productive tracts, since our projections of real prices are significantly lower than realized prices, especially from 1973 through 1985. Recall that our measures of returns are constructed so that their distribution best approximates the actual distribution of *ex post* value, conditional on plausible forecasts of future prices at the auction date (i.e., an approximately constant sequence of real wellhead prices).

Note that these numbers represent before-tax returns. We have not taken into account any of the special tax treatments afforded offshore drilling activity. Finally, these numbers will be biased if we have selected an incorrect discount factor, or if this factor has varied over the sample period. However, the comparison of return figures across tracts and firms is not altered significantly when alternate discount factors are employed.

Table II provides several statistics on some of the more important variables. Note that, except for B/A, the relevant sample is defined as the set of tracts, rather than the set of bids. The latter is a much larger set. For this

TABLE II
SUMMARY STATISTICS OF MAJOR VARIABLES*

Variable	*Mean*	*St. Dev.*	*Minimum*	*Maximum*
(i) Wildcat				
N	3.46	2.81	1	14
π/A	793.7	6323.1	−153 231	59 638
B/A	443.9	874.6	18.98	22 913.6
$B1/A$	607.2	1235.1	21.4	22 913.6
$(B1-B2)/A$	287.9	712.4	0.24	16 348.4
(ii) Drainage				
N	2.73	2.09	1	14
π/A	4863.8	11 740.2	−5036.3	79 854
B/A	1846.1	3310.1	23.96	33 196.1
$B1/A$	2377.2	3853.0	40.94	33 196.1
$(B1-B2)/A$	1254.9	1908.3	0.66	11 976.1

	Correlation Coefficients		
	N	π/A	$B1/A$
(i) Wildcat			
π/A	0.03		
$B1/A$	0.56	−0.32	
$(B1-B2)/A$	0.31	−0.41	0.87
(ii) Drainage			
π/A	0.20		
$B1/A$	0.31	0.52	
$(B1-B2)/A$	0.06	0.52	0.78

* All dollar figures are in $1972 per acre.

table, we normalize by dividing by the number of acres, to obtain a dollar per unit area figure. This exercise does not alter the coefficient of variation of the bid variable (i.e., the ratio of the standard deviation to the mean in the sample) very much.

The table reveals important differences between wildcat and drainage tracts. Both gross profits and bids were much higher on drainage tracts, and net profits ($(\pi - B1)/A$) higher still. However, the average number of bidders on a tract was lower on drainage tracts. For both wildcat and drainage tracts, money left on the table ($(B1-B2)/A$) is about half the winning bid on average. Note that all of these variables have relatively large standard deviations.

The correlation coefficients show that winning bid, money left on the table and the number of bidders are positively correlated for both wildcat and drainage tracts. While this is also true of gross profits on drainage tracts, it is not true for wildcat tracts. This latter finding is a consequence of the relatively large number of wildcat tracts which are never drilled, as the next table demonstrates.

TABLE III
JOINT DISTRIBUTION OF BID PER ACRE AND GROSS PROFITS PER ACRE*

	π/A					
B/A	*< 0*	*0*	*0–1500*	*1500–5000*	*> 5000*	*Total*
(i) Wildcat						
0–50	351 9.6	232 6.3	88 2.4	64 1.8	48 1.3	783 21.4
50–100	390 10.7	173 4.7	71 1.9	46 1.3	55 1.5	735 20.1
100–200	397 10.9	128 3.5	65 1.8	53 1.5	50 1.4	693 19.0
200–500	328 9.0	87 2.4	71 1.9	50 1.8	66 1.8	602 16.5
> 500	499 13.7	47 1.3	91 2.5	88 2.4	119 3.3	844 23.1
Total	1965 53.8	667 18.2	386 10.6	301 9.2	338 9.2	3657 100.0
(ii) Drainage						
0–200	35 8.9	10 2.5	11 2.8	8 2.0	7 1.8	71 18.1
200–500	30 7.6	7 1.8	9 2.3	14 3.6	21 5.3	81 20.6
500–1000	35 8.9	5 1.3	11 2.8	7 1.8	17 4.3	75 19.1
1000–2000	25 6.4	5 1.3	12 3.1	9 2.3	17 4.3	68 17.3
> 2000	22 5.6	1 0.3	13 3.3	4 1.0	58 14.8	98 24.9
Total	147 37.4	28 7.1	56 14.3	42 10.7	120 30.5	393 100.0

* The number in the upper left corner of each cell is the number of tracts in that category, and the other number expresses this figure as a percentage of all wildcat or drainage tracts. π/A and B/A are expressed as \$1972 per acre.

Table III provides a cross-tabulation of the joint distribution of bid per acre and *ex post* gross profits per acre, for the entire set of bids. We compute two such tables, one for wildcat tracts and one for drainage tracts. The bid per acre categories approximately correspond to quintiles for each type of tract. Again, note that bids are much higher on drainage tracts. Tracts with zero *ex post* gross profits were never drilled. Note that tracts with higher bids

TABLE IV
INDIVIDUAL FIRM RETURNS

Firm	# Bids	# Wins	# Tries	# Hits	$\pi - B1$	$\pi - B1$/ # Wins	$\pi - B$/ # Bids	θ^*	$R(\theta^*)$
1. *Shell*	426	164	105	58	533.3	3.25	5.09	0.85	557.4
2. *SOCAL*	398	125	93	56	195.9	1.57	5.76	0.30	358.4
3. *SONJ*	293	94	66	31	341.1	3.63	2.78	0.90	382.4
4. *Gulf*	142	64	51	31	289.5	4.52	4.64	0.75	373.1
5. *Forest*	142	57	46	29	−9.9	−0.17	3.81	1.10	42.9
6. *Sunoco*	182	54	17	4	−25.2	−0.47	1.61	1.20	76.8
7. *Texaco*	128	44	38	13	−373.9	−8.50	−1.18	0.15	1.6
8. *SOInd*	140	20	13	6	−6.5	−0.32	2.18	1.65	59.8
9. *Tenneco*	117	38	33	23	186.2	4.90	5.97	1.00	186.2
10. *Union*	117	30	20	11	186.3	6.21	6.32	0.60	231.6
11. *Murphy*	99	13	12	4	23.2	1.79	1.99	0.95	23.6
12. *Phillips*	128	33	25	11	−91.0	−2.76	2.56	0.00	0.0
13. *SOCONY–Mobil*	207	74	57	31	94.7	1.28	3.77	1.15	188.5
14. *C/C/A/G**	488	132	91	49	287.3	2.18	3.62	0.45	387.3
15. *La. Land/Hess*	87	22	21	9	9.1	0.41	2.18	0.35	22.6
16. *Texaco/SOInd*	137	43	40	26	72.6	1.69	9.53	1.05	77.3
17. *Misc. Joint*	154	40	31	17	68.0	1.70	0.96	0.25	122.6
18. *Fringe*	665	153	113	63	168.2	1.10	3.24	0.60	275.0
Total	4050	1200	872	472	1951.2	1.63	3.76	na	na

* Continental/Cities/Arco/Getty.

are more likely to be drilled, since the tracts with zero gross profits receive lower bids on average than tracts with negative or positive profits. This result implies that the correlation coefficients for gross profits per acre and the other variables in Table II are somewhat misleading. Also, high value tracts receive higher bids. This indicates that while firms' information is imperfect, it is nevertheless correlated with tract gross profitability.

IV. INDIVIDUAL FIRM RETURNS

In this section we examine the bidding performances of the main participants in the oil lease auctions. We first document the bidding activity and returns of the individual firms. Both are shown to differ widely across firms. We then conduct two experiments to determine whether part of the variation in returns is explained by behavioral differences among firms, and find affirmative evidence. Some firms did not behave optimally, and in at least one case, a firm consistently overestimated the value of tracts.

A large number of firms participated in the OCS auctions. Table IV provides a list of the main participants together with some information summarizing their activity and returns. In constructing this classification of firms, we treated subsidiaries of a parent firm as belonging to the same firm. A "fringe" firm is defined as one which bid on fewer than 99 tracts. The first 12 bidding units were all firms which bid on at least 99 tracts either as a solo bidder or jointly with a fringe firm. The thirteenth bidding unit consists of all bids involving Socony-Mobil, a firm which bid mostly with other "large" firms, and only occasionally by itself or with a fringe firm. In addition, there were three consortia of firms which bid on a large number of tracts. For our current purposes, it is notable that, for almost all sales, the member firms of each consortium rarely bid against one another in sales where the consortium was active. This suggests that we can aggregate the participating firms and treat them as a single unit. Joint ventures among the 16 main bidding units constitutes the residual category.

The gross profit columns of Table IV, $\pi - B1$ and $(\pi - B1)/(\#\text{wins})$, show that there is significant variation in returns across firms, even when one controls for the number of tracts won. However, there is little variation in hit rates (number of productive tracts per number of tracts drilled), or in the ratio of number of tries (i.e. tracts drilled) to number of wins. An exception is Sunoco, whose low returns are attributable both to a low hit rate, and to a low try rate. The low returns of some firms, and the relatively high returns of other firms, are less readily explained, and so we examined each firm's bidding behavior more closely to see whether it was possible to identify the causes.

Our first test examines whether the variation in net profits can be explained by the fact that some firms were better at evaluating tracts and identifying the productive ones. The test consists of computing the average net profits which a firm would have earned, had it won every tract that it bid on at the price that it submitted. If the firm's estimates are unbiased, this figure should be positive. Furthermore, "winner's curse" considerations imply that the number should not be small relative to the value of the bid. The average bid is $2.26 million. The results of these calculations are reported in the $(\pi - B)/(\#\text{Bids})$ column of Table IV. In almost all instances the average return that the firm would have earned exceeds $2 million per tract. The exception is Texaco, which would have lost $1.18 million per tract. Texaco's low returns were not due to poor site selection, since average gross profits were positive for both the set of tracts won and the set of tracts bid on. The problem was that it consistently overestimated the value of tracts, and as a consequence, overbid on most of them.

A comparison of the $(\pi - B)/(\#\text{Bids})$ column and the $(\pi - B1)/(\#\text{Wins})$ column reveals a strong correlation between the return figures in these two columns. This suggests that luck is not the only determinant of the variation in net profits. Differences in the firms' evaluation procedures and/or bidding strategies are also important. It is apparent from these columns that the average value of $(\pi - B)$ for each firm is substantially lower on the set of tracts which it wins than on the set of tracts which it bids on. This fact is consistent with the common values model of auctions, which predicts that the estimates of a firm on the tracts it wins are biased upward. In the independent values model, this result would occur only if firms bid more aggressively when their valuations are high. However, given the magnitude of the differences in returns in Table III, this is an unlikely explanation.

Our second test of the firms' bidding behavior consists of calculating the revenues which a firm would have earned had it rescaled all its bids by a factor of θ, holding constant the bids of all other firms. More formally, for any firm i, let K_i denote the set of tracts on which firm i submitted a bid. We will index these tracts by k, and denote the bid of firm i by b_{ik}. Let $\bar{B}_{ik}$ represent the maximum bid submitted by all other firms on that tract or, if firm i was the only bidder, the stipulated minimum acceptable bid. Now suppose that firm i varies all its bids by a factor θ, holding constant the vector $(\bar{B}_{ik})_{k \in K_i}$ and holding constant the set K_i of tracts bid on. If π_k is the discounted value of *ex post* gross profits on tract k (net of royalty payments, but not the bonus bid), then the expected net return associated with bid variation strategy θ is

$$(2) \qquad R_i(\theta) = \sum_{k \in K_i} (\pi_k - \theta b_{ik}) I_{\{\theta b_{ik} - \bar{B}_{ik}\}}$$

where $I_{\{x\}} = 1$ if $x \geqslant 0$ and $I_{\{x\}} = 0$ if $x < 0$. Thus, I is an indicator function which equals one when firm i wins tract k.

Our experiment consisted of varying the value of θ on the interval $(0, 2)$, employing a step size of 0.05 and holding K_i fixed for each firm. The outcomes of these experiments are reported in the last two columns of Table IV.

They give, for each firm i, the value of θ which maximizes $R_i(\theta)$ and the value of $R_i(\theta)$ evaluated at this point. Note that $R_i(1)$ is just the *ex post* net profit of firm i displayed in the $(\pi - B1)$ column of the Table. Similarly, $R_i(2)$ represents the net profits that firm i would have earned had it doubled all the bids it submitted, holding constant the bids of all other firms. Obviously, firm i would not have known either π_k or $\bar{B}_{ik}$ at the time it submitted its bid. However, by summing over all the tracts in K_i, we can examine broadly the appropriateness of firm i's bidding strategy.

If firms pursue a mark-down strategy, with bids being proportional to their estimates of π_k, as is suggested by anecdotal evidence and by the model of Rothkopf [1969], and if all firms choose their bid factors according to risk-neutral Nash equilibrium behavior, then θ^* should equal one. Since we are examining realizations of net returns, values of θ^* close to one are also acceptable. However, Table IV reveals that the value of θ^* for most firms is significantly less than one, so they would have been better off had they bid less. By significant, we mean that a large increase in net returns was possible with a relatively small decrease in θ. (Compare $R_i(\theta)$ with $\pi - B1$.) This result suggests that some firms may have systematically overvalued the tracts and/or failed to fully anticipate the impact of the "winner's curse".

Another possible explanation for this finding is that firms are risk-averse. In his survey paper, Milgrom [1985, pp. 272–273] points out that in auctions where each firm's valuation is certain and independent of the valuations of other firms, risk averse firms bid more than they would have if they were risk neutral and maximizing net profit. It is not clear, however, that this result extends to oil lease auctions, since the distribution of income which a firm faces in making a bid does not have all of its mass concentrated at two values (that is, 0 if it loses, and $\pi_i - B_i > 0$ if it wins, where π_i denotes firm i's valuation). Uncertainty about the value of the tract, and in particular, the fact that this value is negative on at least 60 per cent of the wildcat tracts, may cause a risk-averse firm to bid more cautiously than a risk-neutral firm in oil lease auctions.

In any event, there is little evidence of collusion in bidding, which presumably would entail some firms jointly reducing their bids, and so imply gains to unilaterally increasing one's bid (that is, θ^* would be greater than one). Collusion is not a likely explanation for the low returns of firms with θ^* greater than one, since they lost money. Of course, it is possible that some firms colluded through a bid rotation mechanism or joint venture activity on some tracts.

In conducting the two experiments, it was apparent that the number of wins was frequently not large enough to eliminate all of the idiosyncratic noise in the relationship between a firm's bids and profits. For example, there were a few instances in which the optimal value of θ^* was somewhat sensitive to the outcomes on one or two tracts. The presence of randomness reinforces the suspicion that some firms, such as Forest, may have done poorly because they were unlucky. Forest appears to have pursued a relatively good bidding strategy. Its average value of $(\pi - B)$ was higher than over half of the other firms, and its bid factor was only slightly below its optimal value. Nevertheless, its net profits per tract were among the lowest, which suggests that it may have been in the wrong place at the wrong time. Some firms, such as Texaco and Phillips, appear to have pursued inappropriate bidding strategies. For these firms, there are essentially no values of θ which would have resulted in positive net profits.

A final caveat is in order. Our comparisons of returns across firms, as well as our calculations of optimal bidding factors, necessarily rely on the assumption that the *ex post* gross profit of a tract is independent of the identity of the firm which wins the tract. Thus, we are implicitly assuming that firms have identical or similar cost functions. Since the hit rate and the ratio of tries to tracts won is relatively constant across firms, this assumption may be acceptable. In any case, it is unlikely that all the observable differences in returns and bidding can be attributed either to heterogeneity in costs, or to luck.

V. INFORMATION AND THE BIDDING DECISION

In this section we examine several hypotheses about the joint distribution of valuations and gross profits on wildcat tracts by analyzing the joint distribution of bids and gross profits. The statistical evidence indicates that there is significant variation in the joint distribution of values and gross profits across geographical areas and across sale dates, but not across firms. We suggest that the differences in these distributions across areas and sale dates are mostly due to the differences in the drilling histories of the areas. This result is crucial for estimating bidding strategies, since it means that the econometrician can use the history of an area to obtain information about the firms' unobserved prior valuations, and hence about whether and how much they will bid.

We also suggest that differences in the distributions of bids across firms are caused primarily by differences in the firms' participation rates across areas and sales, and not by differences in their bidding strategies. Furthermore, the factors which account for most of the variation in participation rates are not area- or sale-specific, but are common to all of the firms' bidding decisions. Thus, factors such as the quality of the firm's geologists or its budget constraints are likely to be more important than factors such as area-specific components of the firms' private information about tracts in a sale.

We first examine whether the underlying distributions of gross profits per acre on wildcat tracts varies across sales and areas. We restrict our attention to wildcat tracts, where the quality of the firms' information is similar. The tracts in our data are drawn from 26 separate geographical areas off the coast of Louisiana, and 7 areas off the coast of Texas. Since the tracts from many of these areas are, for practical purposes, within the same region, we have reduced this classification to 14 categories, 10 off Louisiana and 4 off Texas. We also grouped three early sales and aggregated the 1962 sales, leaving 5 sale dates. We first regressed gross profit per acre on a set of sale and area dummies. The F-statistic for this regression was 2.57 with (17, 1039) degrees of freedom, which establishes that area and sale effects are jointly significant at the one per cent level. (The R^2 of this regression was 0.038.) We then alternately set each set of coefficients equal to zero to test whether that set has significant explanatory power. The F-statistics were 4.74 for the sale dummies and 2.28 for the area dummies with (4, 1039) and (12, 1039) degrees of freedom, respectively. These statistics are significant at the one per cent level. Of course, these results may simply reflect differences in the selection rules determining which tracts are to be auctioned in each area. In any event, it is apparent that there are some differences between areas and sales in the set of tracts auctioned.

We then ask whether the distribution of bids on wildcat tracts possesses a firm-, area-, and sale-specific component. Since bid per acre is approximately lognormally distributed, we regressed the logarithm of this variable, using the entire sample of wildcat bids, on the set of firm-, area-, and sale-specific dummies. (The R^2 is 0.18 for this regression.) We then alternately set each set of coefficients equal to zero in order to test whether that set has significant explanatory power. The F-statistics were 14.3 for the firm dummies, 13.4 for thd area dummies, and 63.0 for the sale dummies, with (17, 3623), (12, 3623), and (4, 3623) degrees of freedom, respectively. These results provide evidence in support of firm, area, and sale effects on the distribution of bids.

The significance of area and sale effects on bids can be explained in part by the differences in the average gross profits across areas and sales. However, this cannot be the entire story since both of these factors appear to be more important for bids than for gross profits. The probable cause is the importance of area- and sale-specific information that is publicly available at the time of the sale. To test this implication we regressed gross profit per acre minus bid per acre ($(\pi - B)/A$) on firm-, area-, and sale-specific dummies. In this way, we attempted to control for any differences in the underlying distribution of gross profits across areas and sales. We find that the sale and area effects remain highly significant, lending support to the hypothesis that firms share common area- and sale-specific information that is imperfectly correlated with *ex post* gross profits. The F-statistics measuring the marginal contributions of these two sets of dummies were 27 and 15.5, with (4, 3623) and (12, 3623) degrees of freedom respectively.

Somewhat surprisingly, the firm effects in these regressions were not significant. The F-statistic for the firm dummies was 0.74, with (17, 3623) degrees of freedom. From the evidence in Table IV, which we discussed in the previous section, we know that average net returns do vary significantly across firms. Apparently, area and sale effects can account for most of this variation. This suggests that there must be significant interfirm differences in participation rates across areas and sales.

To pursue this point somewhat further, we regressed the logarithm of bid per acre on the firm dummies for each (area, sale) pair separately and compared the sum of the *SSE* of these regressions to the *SSE* of the regression for all areas and sales together. This comparison tests whether there is significant variation in bids by individual firms across (area, sale) pairs. The F-statistic for this test was 2.73, with (334, 3455) degrees of freedom, which is marginally significant at the one per cent level of significance. This is only weak evidence of between (area, sale) variation in firm-specific bids. Thus, the variation in bids across firms is greater than the variation of individual firm bids across areas or sales. The interpretation of this finding is that the firm-specific factors which are common to all of a firm's bidding decisions (e.g. the quality of its geologists) are much more important in explaining differences between the firms' bids than the firm-specific factors which vary across (area, sale) pairs (e.g. the private information which a firm possesses about an area in a sale).

In summary, the statistical evidence presented in this section suggests that, as a first approximation, one can make the following distributional assumptions in developing a model of bidding for oil leases on wildcat tracts in OCS auctions: (1) that the joint distribution of valuations and tract values differs across areas and sales, but not across firms; (2) that the information which firms share about the different areas prior to obtaining private seismic reports appears to have a significant impact on their valuations; (3) that the private reports of firms are individually informative, but provide quite noisy estimates of the value of tracts. The substantive differences between firms lies in their criteria for selecting which tracts to explore and bid on. Our future research on bidding functions will attempt to identify these differences and the significant area- and sale-specific factors, and to determine whether they remain significant when one appropriately accounts for other factors (i.e. the number of bidders) that are likely to affect firms' bids.

VI. INFORMATION AND THE DRILLING DECISION

This section provides some evidence on drilling decisions and the impact of local information externalities on these decisions. We establish that firms adopt sequential drilling programs in which the tracts that are believed to be of higher value are drilled first. Overall 27 per cent of the leases were allowed to expire without any wells being drilled. We also provide some evidence that firms which have won only a few tracts in an area delay drilling their tracts until after the firms which have won more tracts in that area have drilled some of their tracts.

Table V provides a decomposition of tracts according to the number of years after the date of acquisition that the first well is drilled. Year 0

TABLE V
DECOMPOSITION OF TRACTS BY LEASE YEAR IN WHICH FIRST WELL IS DRILLED

	Number of Years After Acquisition That First Well Is Drilled							
	0	*1*	*2*	*3*	*4*	*5*	*Never*	*Total*
(i) Wildcat								
No. of Tracts	234	138	93	109	116	58	308	1056
No. of Hits	122	71	51	54	53	34	0	385
Average B1	6.56	3.21	2.23	1.67	1.07	1.42	0.80	2.67
Average B1 − B2	2.93	1.54	1.25	0.86	0.53	0.80	0.34	1.31
Average π − B1	2.18	1.58	1.37	4.05	1.27	1.50	−0.80	1.22
Average V	11.75	6.66	4.95	7.65	3.31	3.77	0	5.27

	0	*1–5*	*Never*	*Total*
(ii) Drainage				
No. of Tracts	90	34	20	144
No. of Hits	68	18	0	86
Average B1	8.13	2.13	1.27	5.76
Average B1–B2	3.88	1.25	0.99	2.86
Average π − B1	7.46	0.60	−1.27	4.63
Average V	20.22	3.71	0	13.51

represents the 12 month period immediately following the *month* in which the tract was purchased, Year 1 represents the next 12 month period, and so on. The Year 5 column is comprised mainly of tracts which received their first well in the sixth or seventh year of the lease, but where exploration presumably began previously. This column also includes about 10 productive tracts which were never drilled, and about 5 tracts in which production began prior to recorded drilling. In both cases, some production may have resulted from drilling in adjacent tracts, so these tracts are not necessarily misclassified. As a result, the Year 5 column is best viewed as a residual category for the tracts that were drilled.

Table V reveals several interesting facts. First, the firms clearly use sequential drilling programs. These programs have the property that 29 per cent of the wildcat tracts and 14 per cent of the drainage tracts are never drilled. This suggests that firms acquire post sale information about tracts which causes them to choose not to drill certain tracts. Furthermore, the likelihood of acquiring such information is higher on wildcat tracts than on drainage tracts. Second, the average winning bid of a tract is a decreasing function of the time until the first well is drilled. This indicates that tracts which are expected to be more valuable, as reflected by the firms' bids, are drilled before the lower value tracts. Third, with the exception of drainage tracts that are drilled immediately, the hit rate is independent of when the tract is drilled and of whether it is a drainage or a wildcat tract, and it is slightly above 50 per cent. This invariance with respect to the date of drilling may be attributed either to the acquisition of information from prior drilling that offsets the decline in the average quality of the tracts, or to the fact that geologists are better at predicting the amount of oil on a tract, conditional on the tract containing an oil deposit, than at predicting whether a tract contains an oil deposit. However, evidence presented in a later table suggests that the latter explanation is not correct.

Two other facts are worth noting. In all categories the ratio of "money left on the table" to the winning bid is about 50 per cent. Also, net profit on drainage tracts drilled in Year 0 is a great deal higher than on any other tracts, as is the percentage of social rents which accrue to the winning firm (that is, $(\pi - B1)/V$). In our sample, social rents on the 1056 wildcat tracts totalled \$5.57 billion (in 1972\$), and the firms' share was \$1.28 billion. Thus, the winning firms on wildcat tracts captured an average of 23 per cent of total social rents. This figure is similar to Smiley's [1979] estimates for some sales in the 1970s, which were computed by a different method. On the 144 drainage tracts, social rents totalled \$1.95 billion, and the firms' share was \$0.67 billion, or 34 per cent. This higher share accrues primarily to firms which drill immediately, and, as we shall see in the next section, it is a rent which is captured by firms which own leases on adjacent tracts.

It is important to recall that these numbers are biased for two reasons. First, as mentioned previously, some costs are omitted, which will bias the firm share upward. However, these costs should be relatively constant across tracts, so that comparisons of shares is a valid exercise. Second, we are using a predicted price sequence which is much lower than actual prices. This will bias these share numbers downward. This is especially important for the later sales in our sample. Since these tended to be drainage sales, we have probably understated the difference in realized firm shares between wildcat and drainage sales.

The presence of information externalities implies that firms have an incentive to delay drilling their tracts in order to free ride on the information generated by the drilling outcomes of other firms. To examine this implication, we compared the drilling programs of firms which had won different numbers of tracts in an (area, sale) pair. The hypothesis being tested is that the probability that a particular tract is drilled in year v of the lease depends on the number of tracts which its leaseowner won in that area. The reasoning is as follows. If the drilling decisions of firms are independent of the information generated by the exploration activity of other firms, then a firm which won only one or two tracts in an area should drill these tracts immediately. It gains nothing by waiting, and to delay is costly. Firms which won many tracts, however, may choose to delay drilling a particular tract until after it obtains information from the drilling outcomes of other tracts in its portfolio.

We compute the frequency of tracts drilled in year v for each firm with a portfolio of m tracts in a particular (area, sale) pair. Aggregating over (area, sale) pairs, let $n_{v,m}$ denote the total number of tracts that were drilled in

TABLE VI
COMPARISON OF DRILLING PROGRAMS OF FIRMS WITH DIFFERENT TRACT HOLDINGS IN AN (AREA, SALE) PAIR*

	Number of Years After Acquisition That First Well Is Drilled								
m	*0*	*1*	*2*	*3*	*4*	*5*	*Never*	*No. of Tracts*	*Av. Rent*
1	0.25	0.21	0.08	0.07	0.16	0.05	0.18	76	5.83
2	0.27	0.13	0.13	0.09	0.12	0.06	0.21	120	9.51
3	0.21	0.15	0.16	0.15	0.14	0.01	0.17	66	6.64
4	0.18	0.17	0.09	0.14	0.09	0.03	0.30	88	5.55
5	0.24	0.15	0.04	0.12	0.19	0.12	0.15	75	5.92
6–9	0.20	0.14	0.14	0.14	0.14	0.07	0.18	199	6.07
⩾ 10	0.24	0.12	0.09	0.12	0.16	0.05	0.26	218	7.54

* The number of tracts won by a leaseowner in a particular (area, sale) pair is denoted by m. The entries of the table are, for each value of m, the fraction of the leaseowner's tracts in that area drilled each year after the sale date. Thus the first 6 columns of each row sum to one, modulo rounding errors.

lease year v and whose leaseowners had won m tracts in an (area, sale) pair. Let $n_m = \sum_{v=0}^{6} n_{m,v}$ denote the total number of tracts whose leaseowners won m tracts in the (area, sale) pair that the tract is sold. Here v equals six for tracts which are never drilled. The frequency ratio is then given by $(n_{v,m}/n_m)$. Table VI reports these ratios for lease years $v = 0$ through 5 and the category "never drilled", and for area portfolio sizes $m = 1, \ldots, 5$, 6–9, and greater than 9.

The striking feature of this table is that the probability that a particular tract is drilled in year v does not depend on the value of m. In the case of solo winners, for example, only 40 per cent of the tracts were drilled in the first two years of the lease. Over half of these tracts were either drilled in the later years of the lease or not drilled at all. A similar story holds for values of m greater than one. Thus, firms frequently delay their drilling decisions on tracts, even when no new information may be forthcoming from its own drilling activity. Furthermore, as the last column shows, the values of the tracts were similar across categories. This suggests that the reason why firms may be waiting is because they intend to free ride on the information generated by the drilling outcomes of other firms. In particular, the firms which possess a relatively large portfolio of tracts cannot afford to wait too long to begin drilling their tracts, or they will run into the five year lease tenure constraint. Firms with smaller holdings can exploit the information generated by this drilling activity. We therefore conclude that firms appear to behave strategically in deciding when to drill marginal tracts.

There are two important implications which follow from these results. First, it means that a firm's evaluation of a tract depends in part on the potential of neighboring tracts, and the probability that the firm will win these tracts. Winning tracts which are dispersed within an area is not as valuable as winning the same number of tracts when they are adjacent to each other. It is worth noting that the optimal bidding strategies for these kinds of auctions have not been studied in detail. Second, the government must be concerned with exploration incentives when designing an auction, since there is a strong possibility that a tract may not be drilled. For example, in auctions where the bidding variable is the royalty rate rather than the bonus payment, the number of wells drilled is likely to be smaller, since the expected marginal revenue to a firm from drilling a well is lower when it has to share more of the revenues with the government.

VII. INFORMATION, COMPETITION, AND RETURNS

In this section we examine the effects of competition on bids and profits. A complete analysis of this relationship requires the estimation of bidding strategies, which is the subject of a subsequent paper. Nevertheless, a number of theoretical predictions about bidding behavior and the pattern of returns can be tested by simply examining variable means conditional on the number of bidders. In particular, we find that the differences between the returns on drainage leases and those on wildcat leases can be explained in terms of asymmetries in the quality of information among bidders on drainage tracts. We identify which bidders possess better information on drainage leases, and contrast their behavior and returns with those of relatively uninformed bidders.

Only a fraction of the set of potential bidders typically choose to submit bids in any auction. In some instances, the absence of a bid from a firm is the result of that firm's decision not to be active in the auction, but in other instances it is because the firm's valuation of the tract following its seismic survey would lead it to bid below the reservation price. Consequently, the number of bidders is likely to be a crude measure of both the quality of the tract and the level of competition.

Table VII decomposes wildcat and drainage tracts according to the number of bidders. Both the percentage of tracts that are drilled and the value of the social rent are increasing functions of the number of bidders, with both sequences being significantly higher on drainage tracts than on wildcat tracts. Evidently, firms are more likely to bid on high value tracts, and are more likely to drill these tracts. This follows from Table V, which shows that high value tracts are on average drilled before low value tracts. This confirms our hypothesis that the number of bidders is positively correlated with the value of a tract.

Somewhat surprisingly, the hit rate on wildcat tracts is virtually constant at 50 per cent. This is also true of drainage tracts with one or two bidders, although the hit rate increases to 80 per cent when there are 3 or more bidders. Since the number of bidders is correlated with tract value, this

TABLE VII
DECOMPOSITION OF TRACTS BY NUMBER OF BIDDERS

	Number of Bidders					
	1	*2*	*3*	*4*	*5–6*	*≥7*
A. Wildcat						
No. of Tracts	339	213	106	103	126	169
No. of Tries	183	135	81	83	109	156
No. of Hits	86	75	39	42	51	92
Average B1	0.49	1.03	1.70	2.35	3.47	9.32
Average B1 − B2	0.40	0.72	1.11	1.46	1.63	3.32
Average π − B1	1.64	1.68	0.87	3.95	2.55	−2.66
Average V	2.87	3.64	3.65	8.37	8.04	9.21
Average V|Hit	12.20	11.09	11.21	22.05	21.50	18.34
	1	*2*	*3*	*4*	*≥5*	
B. Drainage						
No. of Tracts	49	32	24	21	18	
No. of Tries	33	29	24	21	17	
No. of Hits	22	13	20	18	14	
Average B1	2.01	3.08	8.03	10.07	12.69	
Average B1 − B2	1.94	2.25	4.43	3.52	3.57	
Average π − B1	3.50	1.74	4.08	8.60	8.93	
Average V	7.08	6.27	16.01	24.07	28.24	
Average V|Hit	16.14	16.69	19.43	21.87	36.64	

implies that firms which win tracts with a small number of bidders delay their drilling decision until after the drilling outcomes on the high value tracts are known. As a result, the try rate on lower value tracts is lower, thereby offsetting the decline in the quality of the tracts and leading to a hit rate which is more or less constant. Notice, however, that the expected value of social rent conditional on a hit is not constant (Average $V|Hit$). For both wildcat and drainage tracts, it is almost twice as high on tracts with many bidders as on tracts with one or two bidders. This indicates that the geological data which firms acquire on a tract yields information about both the probability of a hit and the size of the deposit conditional on a hit.

Both winning bid and money left on the table are increasing functions of the number of bidders.[3] However, the ratio of money left on the table to the winning bid is a rapidly decreasing function. On wildcat tracts, it falls from 0.81 when N equals one to 0.36 when N exceeds six. On drainage tracts, it falls

[3] For tracts with one bid, money left on the table is the difference between that bid and the stipulated minimum bid. On drainage sales with no minimum bid, we continued to use as a lower bound $25 per acre, the minimum bid on the other drainage sales. Our justification is that firms probably expected the government would reject any bid that was below $25 per acre. In any case, no bids in these drainage sales were less than this figure.

from 0.96 when N is one to 0.28 when N exceeds four. This is consistent with the model of Wilson [1975], in which this ratio falls monotonically to zero as the number of bidders increases. (In that model, firms know the number of actual bidders.) By this measure, auctions with more bidders are more competitive, for both wildcat and drainage tracts.

Net profits on wildcat tracts are (roughly) a decreasing function of the number of bidders, and more so when expressed as a fraction of social rents. Indeed, when there are seven or more bidders, net profits are *negative*, even though the tracts themselves are quite valuable. For these results to be consistent with the Wilson model, one would have to assume that our measure underestimates net profits and that the number of *active* firms is positively correlated with the number of bidders. However, if the latter condition is true, one would have to explain why competition varies across tracts. Arbitrage would seem to imply that the number of active firms should be constant across tracts, for otherwise the *ex ante* expected profits from bidding on different tracts are not equalized.

A more plausible explanation for this result centers on firm uncertainty about the number of firms which are active on a given tract. Recall that a firm is denoted as active on a tract if it conducts or purchases a seismic survey on that tract prior to the sale. Now suppose that a firm's decisions to survey tracts are private. Then, in calculating the expected value of a tract conditional on its own information and on winning the tract, a prospective bidder needs to distinguish between the valuations of inactive and active firms, since the latter are more informative. But if the number of active firms is random and unobservable, then each firm's estimate of the magnitude of the "winner's curse" is biased downward on tracts where there are relatively many active firms, and is biased upward on tracts where there are relatively few active firms. In that case, one would expect profits to decline as the actual number of bidders increases, and it would be increasingly likely that average profits are negative when the number of bidders is very large.

Another explanation is, of course, that firms did not adequately account for the "winner's curse" in their bidding strategies. The analysis of section IV suggests that this may be true of a subset of the major participants. Yet another possible explanation is that firms collude via some type of bid rotation mechanism, and on tracts with fewer bidders earn higher profits. However, it is not obvious why they should choose to collude on less valuable tracts. Nor can these results be explained by lack of experience. When we classified tracts by sale, net profits in the later sales were significantly lower for tracts with many bidders, relative to tracts with few bidders.[4]

The problem in trying to test these explanations is that one needs to

[4] It is worth noting that gross profits were generally lower in the later wildcat sales. Consequently, it may be the case that firms bid relatively conservatively in earlier sales, saw that their net returns were high, and then bid too aggressively in the sales of the late 1960s. It would be interesting to see whether this trend persisted or reversed itself in the sales of the 1970s.

compute variable means conditional on the number of active firms rather than the number of bidders. The latter is an endogenous variable, as is clear from the fact that the number of bidders increases with tract value. Hence, more sophisticated econometrics is required to discriminate between the different behavioral hypotheses. This is the subject of our next paper.

In contrast, net profit on drainage tracts increases with the number of bidders. The obvious explanation for this finding, as well as other differences in the pattern of returns between wildcat and drainage leases, is the presence of asymmetric information on drainage tracts. Firms which own adjacent tracts are better informed, in the sense of more precise priors, than other firms. Theory (see Milgrom and Weber [1982b]) then predicts that uninformed firms should bid more cautiously, lest they be afflicted with the winner's curse, and informed firms should shade down their bids accordingly, thereby earning an information premium. Indeed, Milgrom and Weber show that this premium does not vanish in the limit, but that an informed bidder will earn positive profits even as the number of uninformed bidders increases without bound.

To verify the asymmetric information story, we partitioned drainage tracts according to whether the winning bid was submitted by an informed firm or an uninformed firm. A bidder is designated as informed if it won the lease on an adjacent *federal* tract in a previous auction. The largest possible number of informed bidders is eight, since each tract has at most eight neighbors. In many cases, this number was smaller because some of the tracts adjacent to a drainage tract were on state lands, for which we had no information. When this is the case, we may have misidentified some informed bids as uninformed. These would be bids that were submitted by a firm which had won one of the adjacent state leases and no adjacent federal lease. In addition, we classified bids by fringe firms as uninformed. In what follows, therefore, we may be understating the true differences between the returns to informed and uninformed firms.

Twenty-eight leases had to be dropped from the sample, since they possessed no informed firms by our definition. All but two of these leases were on the boundary of state leases. Of the 116 remaining leases for which we were able to identify at least one informed firm, 26 received no bids by informed firms, 76 received one informed bid, 13 received two informed bids, and only one lease received more than two informed bids. Of the 90 leases with at least one informed bid, 61 were won by an informed bidder. This is a remarkably high figure, given the likelihood that our list of informed firms on many of these tracts is incomplete. Nevertheless, informed bidders won 61 of these 116 drainage leases. This is consistent with the theory of auctions with asymmetric information, which would predict that the relatively uninformed bidders should win half of the tracts. This conclusion is valid for any specification of the underlying distributions. (See, for example, Milgrom and Weber [1982b].)

TABLE VIII
INFORMED VS UNINFORMED BIDDING ON DRAINAGE TRACTS
DECOMPOSITION BY NUMBER OF BIDDERS

	Number of Bidders			
	1	*2*	$\geqslant 3$	*Total*
A. Informed Winner				
No. of Tracts	31	10	14	55
No. of Tries	19	10	14	43
No. of Hits	13	7	13	33
Average B1	2.41	3.91	16.87	6.36
Average B1 – B2	2.34	2.62	5.88	3.29
Average $\pi - B1$	5.32	8.88	11.41	7.52
Average V	9.72	16.20	36.98	17.84
B. Uninformed Winner				
No. of Tracts	12	17	32	61
No. of Tries	11	15	31	57
No. of Hits	8	3	24	35
Average B1	1.34	2.43	7.78	5.02
Average B1 – B2	1.25	2.11	2.62	2.21
Average $\pi - B1$	–1.98	–3.15	3.23	0.43
Average V	–0.27	–0.58	14.57	7.43

Table VIII separately considers drainage tracts won by informed bidders and uninformed bidders, and provides for each set of tracts a decomposition of returns by number of bidders. The results are clearly in accord with the predictions of the theoretical models of asymmetrically informed bidders. Both social rents and net profits are much higher on tracts won by an informed bidder. For both variables, the amounts increase with the number of bidders. (To avoid small sample problems, we restrict our attention to only 3 categories for the number of bidders.) Uninformed bidders which won on tracts receiving one or two bids obviously suffered from an acute attack of the winner's curse. Notice, however, that average net profits on all drainage tracts won by uninformed firms are zero. Thus, the uninformed firms won profitable tracts often enough to keep them interested in participating in the drainage auctions. These results on returns are consistent with those of Mead *et al.* [1984], who calculated internal rates of returns for informed and uninformed bidders on OCS drainage sales from 1959 to 1969.

The basic message of this table seems to be that it pays to be better informed.[5] On tracts won by informed firms, 42 per cent of social rents accrue as profits to the firms. This is in contrast to 6 per cent on drainage tracts won

[5] Notice that, while it is true that economies of scale in production is consistent with some of these findings (e.g. the fact that neighboring firms are more likely to win drainage tracts when they bid), it does not explain why average net profits to the non-neighboring firms are zero.

by uninformed firms, and 23 per cent on wildcat tracts. Note that this implies that we may be understating the true return on wildcat tracts, since firms may earn large profits on the subsequent sale of adjacent tracts. As a practical matter, this is unlikely to be important, since the number of wildcat tracts that turn out to be adjacent to tracts that are later auctioned off as drainage tracts is quite small. Furthermore, it is clear that the number of bidders is not a very good measure of competitiveness on drainage leases, since it is usually not a good proxy for the number of informed bidders. One task which we will pursue in future research is a detailed investigation of the bidding behavior of informed versus uninformed bidders on drainage tracts.

An important question prompted by the findings on differential returns to informed and uninformed firms is the extent to which joint venture activity on drainage leases represent collusion, or at least information sharing, by informed firms. To study this question, we decomposed the joint venture bids on drainage tracts according to the information status of the member firms. Of the forty-nine joint venture bids submitted, twenty-four were by joint ventures whose member firms were not informed. Of the remaining twenty-five informed bids, four were submitted by joint ventures with one informed member, and twelve were submitted by joint ventures which had won an adjacent tract in a previous sale. Thus, there were only 9 instances of winning firms of adjacent tracts forming a joint venture on drainage tracts. Since there were 75 tracts on which such an event could have taken place, this does not provide strong evidence for collusive joint venture activity. Of course, we may be understating the actual number of informed firms, as we noted previously.

The results of this section suggest that the government ought to adopt a different auction mechanism for drainage sales. Since the probability of drilling a drainage tract is close to unity, the government does not need to worry as much about the moral hazard problem. The optimal auction literature (see, for example, Riley and Samuelson [1981] and McAfee and McMillan [1986]) suggests that a higher royalty rate is warranted for drainage sales.

VIII. CONCLUDING REMARKS

The statistical analysis of the preceding sections provides considerable support for the common values model as a description of the bidding behavior of firms in OCS oil and gas auctions. We find that the data are consistent with both the assumptions and predictions of the model, or at least some variant of it. One extension of the theoretical model which needs to be investigated is to allow for interdependencies in the valuations of tracts due to economies of scale in exploration.

In many respects, however, our analysis is only suggestive, and not definitive. A detailed econometric analysis of the bidding behavior of participant firms is clearly needed to provide more precise answers to some of the questions posed in this paper. This is the subject of some of our related research projects, where we estimate auction participation decisions, bidding strategies, the determinants and effects of joint venture formation, and post-auction drilling decisions. This econometric work is intended to determine whether the statistical regularities documented in this paper are indeed consistent with existing theoretical models, or whether they can be otherwise explained.

KENNETH HENDRICKS, ROBERT H. PORTER
AND BRYAN BOUDREAU,
State University of New York at Stony Brook,
Stony Brook,
USA.

REFERENCES

CAPEN, E. C., CLAPP, R. V. and CAMPBELL, W. M., 1971, 'Competitive Bidding in High-Risk Situations', *Journal of Petroleum Engineering*, 23 (June), pp. 641–653.

ENGELBRECHT-WIGGANS, R., MILGROM, P. R. and WEBER, J., 1983, 'Competitive Bidding and Proprietary Information', *Journal of Mathematical Economics*, 11 (April), pp. 161–169.

MCAFEE, R. P. and MCMILLAN, J., 1986, 'Auctions', University of Western Ontario, mimeo.

MEAD, W. J., MOSEIDJORD, A. and SORENSON, P. E., 1984, 'Competitive Bidding Under Asymmetrical Information: Behavior and Performance in Gulf of Mexico Drainage Lease Sales, 1959–1969', *Review of Economics and Statistics*, 66 (August), pp. 505–508.

MEAD, W. J., SORENSON, P. E., JONES, R. D. and MOSEIDJORD, A., 1980, *Competition and Performance in OCS Oil and Gas Lease Sales and Development, 1954–1969*, Final Report to US Geological Survey, Reston, Virginia.

MILGROM, P. R., 1985, 'The Economics of Competitive Bidding: A Selective Survey', in L. HURWICZ, D. SCHMEIDLER and H. SONNENSCHEIN (eds.), *Social Goals and Social Organization*, pp. 261–289 (Cambridge University Press).

MILGROM, P. R. and WEBER, R. J., 1982, 'A Theory of Auctions and Competitive Bidding', *Econometrica*, 50 (September), pp. 1089–1122.

MILGROM, P. R. and WEBER, R. J., 1982, 'The Value of Information in a Sealed Bid Auction', *Journal of Mathematical Economics*, 10 (June), pp. 105–114.

RILEY, J. and SAMUELSON, W., 1981, 'Optimal Auctions', *American Economic Review*, 71 (June), pp. 381–392.

ROTHKOPF, M., 1969, 'A Model of Rational Competitive Bidding', *Management Science*, 15, pp. 362–373.

SMILEY, A. K., 1979, *Competitive Bidding Under Uncertainty: The Case of Offshore Oil* (Balinger, Cambridge, Mass.).

WEAVER, L. K., JIRIK, C. J. and PIERCE, H. F., 1973, 'Offshore Petroleum Studies: Historical and Estimated Future Hydrocarbon Production From U.S. Offshore Areas and the Impact on the Onshore Segment of the Petroleum Industry', U.S. Department of the Interior, Bureau of Mines, Information Circular 8575.

WILSON, R., 1975, 'A Bidding Model of Perfect Competition', *The Review of Economic Studies*, 44 (October), pp. 511–518.

FIRM SIZE AND R & D INTENSITY: A RE-EXAMINATION*

WESLEY M. COHEN, RICHARD C. LEVIN AND DAVID C. MOWERY

Using data from the Federal Trade Commission's Line of Business Program and survey measures of technological opportunity and appropriability conditions, this paper finds that overall firm size has a very small, statistically insignificant effect on business unit R & D intensity when either fixed industry effects or measured industry characteristics are taken into account. Business unit size has no effect on the R & D intensity of business units that perform R & D, but it affects the probability of conducting R & D. Business unit and firm size jointly explain less than one per cent of the variance in R & D intensity; industry effects explain nearly half the variance.

I. INTRODUCTION

TWO SETS of well-known hypotheses are associated with the later work of Joseph Schumpeter. The first concerns the effects of market concentration on research and development investment and on innovative performance. The second bears on the effects of firm size on R & D and innovation. In a recent paper (Levin, Cohen, and Mowery [1985]), we re-examined the first set of hypotheses. Simple regressions at the line of business level replicated the established findings that both R & D intensity and innovative performance first increase and then decrease as industrial concentration rises. The effect of concentration, however, was sharply attenuated when we controlled for inter-industry differences in technological opportunity and in the appropriability of returns from new technology. Our results suggested that it is probably unwarranted to conclude that market concentration favors R & D investment and innovation.

In this paper we investigate the Schumpeterian hypothesis that large size is conducive to R & D investment. This relationship has been studied at least as intensively as the link between concentration and R & D, but our approach is novel in two respects. First, using data collected by the Federal Trade

* The research reported in this paper was supported by the Division of Policy Research and Analysis of the National Science Foundation. We wish to thank Joe Cholka, George Pascoe, and Mike Dodman of the Federal Trade Commission for their assistance in computing, and we thank Tim Bresnahan, Zvi Griliches, Vassilis Hajivassiliou, Mark Kamlet, Steve Klepper, Ariel Pakes, Peter Reiss, Richard Schmalensee, Andrea Shepard and Larry White for valuable suggestions.

The representations and conclusions presented herein are those of the authors. They have not been adopted in whole or in part by the Federal Trade Commission, its Bureau of Economics, or any other entity within the Commission. The FTC's Disclosure Avoidance Officer has certified that the data included in this paper do not identify individual company line of business data.

Commission's Line of Business Program, we are able to distinguish scale effects associated with the business unit from those associated with the size of the firm as a whole. Second, survey data collected by Levin, Klevorick, Nelson, and Winter [1984] and used in our previous paper allow us to control for previously unmeasured differences in technological opportunity and appropriability across lines of business.

We find little support for Schumpeter. Without close attention to the data it would appear that the size of the firm as a whole, though not the size of the business unit, has a significant but small positive effect on the R & D intensity of business units. When a mere handful of outliers is removed from the sample, we find that controlling for interindustry differences eliminates the apparent influence of firm size. Business unit and firm size jointly explain only a negligible fraction of the variance in R & D intensity among business units that perform R & D. Fixed industry effects, however, explain nearly half the variance in R & D intensity, and, in turn, measured industry characteristics explain about half the variance explained by these industry effects. Only one size-related effect withstands scrutiny. Although neither measure of size influences the behavior of R & D performers, business unit size does affect the probability of conducting R & D.

II. MOTIVATION

The hypothesis set forth rather imprecisely by Schumpeter [1950] and more sharply by Galbraith [1957] is that in a mature capitalist economy large firms generate a disproportionately large share of society's technological advances. Several arguments have been offered in support of this hypothesis. One claim is that capital market imperfections confer an advantage on large firms in securing finance for risky R & D projects, because size is correlated with the availability and stability of internally-generated funds. A second claim is that there are scale economies in the technology of R & D. Another is that the returns from process R & D are higher where the innovator has a large volume of sales over which to spread the fixed costs of innovation. Finally, R & D is alleged to be more productive in large firms as a result of complementarities between R & D and other nonmanufacturing activities (e.g. marketing and financial planning) that may be better developed within large firms.

Each of these claims depends on assumptions about the nature and magnitude of transaction and adjustment costs that are rarely tested. Two other objections, however, are more germane to an assessment of the validity of the empirical evidence.

First, the arguments supporting Schumpeter's hypothesis are usually offered without adequate attention to the appropriate unit of analysis. The argument about capital market imperfections, for example, predicts a relationship between innovation and overall *firm* size. The fixed cost argument, by contrast, concerns the volume of a particular product or product line and hence predicts a relationship more likely to be observed at the level of the *business unit*. The R & D scale economies and the complementarity arguments may be applicable at either the firm or the business unit level, or both, depending on the nature of the relevant economies of scale and scope.

Second, the relationship between size and innovation may vary across industries with different technologies and market conditions, a possibility largely ignored by the arguments advanced in support of Schumpeter. Interindustry differences in technological opportunities and in the appropriability of returns from R & D investment may, for example, influence the degree to which size confers advantages or disadvantages. Indeed, a spurious statistical connection between R & D and size may arise as a consequence of failure to take adequate account of interindustry differences.

These two shortcomings—inadequate attention to the unit of analysis and to industry effects—pervade the extensive empirical literature on the relationship of size and R & D investment. In nearly all the studies reviewed by Scherer [1980] and Kamien and Schwartz [1982], both size and R & D have been measured at the firm level. When industry characteristics have been studied, the multiproduct character of large firms has been commonly ignored. Typically each firm is assigned to a "primary" industry and assumed to face conditions in all product markets identical to those prevailing in its primary industry.

Despite these methodological problems, there existed until recently a tentative "consensus" on the stylized facts concerning size and R & D. As summarized by Scherer and by Kamien and Schwartz, this consensus view held that firm size is associated with increasing R & D intensity up to some threshold (near the bottom of the Fortune 500). Among larger firms, R & D intensity does not increase, and it may even decline, with the possible exception of firms assigned to the chemical industry.

Recent work has cast doubt on the basis for this consensus. Employing data from the Federal Trade Commission's Line of Business Program for 1974, Scherer [1984] found "mild support" (p. 233) for the position that business unit R & D intensity increases with business unit size. A different dissenting note was sounded by Bound *et al.* [1984]. Using a larger and more comprehensive sample of American firms than any previously employed to study the size–R & D relationship at the firm level, and implicitly assuming firms to be single product entities, they found that R & D intensity first falls and then rises with firm size. Thus, both very small and very large firms appeared to be more R & D intensive than those intermediate in size.[1]

This paper does not provide a definitive test of Schumpeter's hypothesis concerning innovative performance and size. We have data on R & D invest-

[1] Cremer and Sirbu [1978], and Pavitt *et al.* [1987] have obtained results similar to those of Bound *et al.* Cremer and Sirbu used data on French firms; Pavitt studied British firms.

ment only and no adequate measure of innovative output (see Fisher and Temin [1973]). Our primary purpose is descriptive; we seek to establish more clearly whether size is systematically related to R & D intensity by examining the effects of both business unit size and firm size, and by controlling for interindustry differences in market structure, demand conditions, technological opportunity, and appropriability. An ancillary purpose is to assess whether available measures of industry conditions—recently augmented by the survey research of Levin *et al.*—explain a substantial fraction of interindustry variation in R & D intensity.[2]

III. THE DATA

Data on R & D expenditures, business unit size, and firm size were obtained from the Federal Trade Commission's Line of Business program. Our sample includes 2494 business units in 244 manufacturing lines of business operated by 345 firms. We excluded all firms in the FTC database that operate mainly in regulated industries, and we excluded firms with obvious intertemporal inconsistencies in reporting methods or other obvious reporting errors.[3] All business units operating outside the manufacturing sector, and those that were not continuously active during the period 1974–1977, were excluded as well.

The FTC data have certain limitations. Foreign activities of the sample firms are not reported, distorting our measure of R & D intensity for business units that do disproportionate amounts of their worldwide R & D in the United States. The FTC sample is drawn almost entirely from the 1000 largest firms in the economy, as measured by domestic sales of manufactured products. Nonetheless, the data have overwhelming advantages for our purposes. They represent the only available, reliable, disaggregated data on R & D expenditures,[4] and they allow us to distinguish between business unit size and firm size. Although large firms are overrepresented, the sample contains business units of all sizes.[5]

[2] Although we attempt to control for industry effects, we do not consider the influence on R & D intensity of firm-specific variables other than size. These may be important; an analysis of covariance done by Scott [1984] indicates that firm effects explain roughly as much variance in business unit R & D intensity as do two-digit industry effects. In a related effort, Cohen and Mowery are exploring this issue.

[3] See Cohen and Mowery [1984, Appendix V] for a detailed discussion of the screening procedures used to check the validity of the FTC's Line of Business Program R & D data.

[4] Cohen and Mowery [1984, Appendix VI] compare the coverage and representativeness of the FTC's R & D data with the NSF's R & D data, which is reported at a higher level of aggregation. The coverage of the FTC data is just over 60% of that of the NSF, and the representativeness of the FTC data, judging from the similarity of overall and industry mean R & D intensities, is excellent.

[5] Although firms had the option of consolidating all business units with revenues below ten million dollars, many did not exercise it.

The three variables of primary interest were taken from the FTC data: (1) company-financed R & D expenditures (*RDI*) expressed as a percentage of business unit sales and transfers over the period 1975 through 1977, (2) business unit sales and transfers (*BUSALES*), measured in billions of dollars and averaged across 1974–1976, and (3) firm sales (*FIRMSALES*), also measured in billions of dollars and averaged across 1974–1976. Averages were employed to control for differences in the impact and timing of business cycles across industries. The size variables were lagged one year to reflect the fact that R & D funds are usually budgeted many months before they are spent.

Data on industry conditions were drawn from several sources. As in our 1985 paper, we use variables intended to capture three dimensions of technological opportunity: closeness to science, the importance of external sources of technical knowledge, and industry maturity. Using the Levin *et al.* [1984] survey, we measure closeness to science with responses to questions concerning the relevance of eleven fields of basic and applied science.[6] We calculate for each line of business the mean of the responses (on a seven-point Likert scale) for each field of science.[7] We summarize this information with the variable, *SCIENCEBASE*, which represents for each line of business the maximum of the mean scores received (on a seven-point Likert scale) by a field of science. The survey also asked respondents to evaluate the importance (on a seven-point scale) of the contributions of various external sources to technical progress within each line of business. We consider four such sources here: upstream suppliers of raw material and equipment (*MATERIALTECH* and *EQUIPTECH*, respectively), downstream users of the industry's products (*USERTECH*), and government agencies and research laboratories (*GOVTECH*). Industry maturity may also affect opportunity conditions. A variable intended to reflect the relative maturity of an industry's technology, *NEWPLANT*, measures the percentage of an industry's property, plant, and equipment installed within the five years preceding 1977, as reported to the FTC's Line of Business Program.

[6] The basic sciences listed in the survey questionnaire are biology, chemistry, geology, mathematics, and physics. The applied sciences are agricultural science, applied math/operations research, computer science, materials science, medical science, and metallurgy.

[7] There are numerous statistical problems associated with the use of Likert-scale survey responses as independent variables in regressions. The most fundamental is whether responses along a semantic continuum can be treated as if they were interval data. In the absence of adequate alternative measures of technological opportunity and appropriability, we assume that such treatment is reasonable. Given this assumption, there remain several potential sources of measurement error. One is that individual respondents may differ in their use of the seven-point scale. In related work Levin is exploring the importance of interrater differences in mean responses and in the variance of responses. Preliminary results indicate that the ranking of industry mean responses to particular questions is reasonably insensitive to correction for these individual effects. Another form of measurement error is introduced by using industry means instead of individual responses. We attempt to control for this type of error by including the number of survey responses per industry among the variables used to correct regression results for heteroscedasticity.

Appropriability conditions are measured with two indices derived from the Levin *et al.* survey. Respondents were asked to rate (on a seven-point scale) the effectiveness of six mechanisms used by firms to capture and protect the competitive advantages of new processes and new products.[8] *APPROPRIABILITY* is the maximum of industry mean scores received by any one of these mechanisms for either process or product innovations. The survey also asked respondents to report for their line of business the range of imitation costs and time lags for major and minor, process and product, and patented and unpatented innovations. These measures tend to be highly correlated with one another, though they are not highly correlated with *APPROPRIABILITY*. We use here the average number of months required to duplicate a patented, major product innovation (*IMLAG*).

In the absence of an explicit structural model, prior expectations about the effects of the opportunity and appropriability variables are ambiguous. Greater opportunity should increase innovative output. To the extent that the contributions of external science, upstream suppliers, downstream users, and the government substitute for a firm's own R & D effort, however, these opportunity variables may be inversely related to R & D intensity. Appropriability may also have ambiguous effects on R & D incentives, as recent theoretical work has emphasized (Cohen and Levinthal [1986]).

Many previous studies of R & D have attempted to control for demand conditions, on the assumption that market growth increases the returns to investment in R & D. Typically, sales growth is used as an unsatisfactory proxy for growth in demand. We represent industry demand conditions with estimates developed by Levin [1981] of price elasticity (*PELAS*), income elasticity (*INCELAS*), and a time shift parameter (*DGROWTH*). These estimates were derived from consumer demand functions estimated by Almon *et al.* [1974] and the input–output tables.[9] We expect demand growth and income elasticity to be positively associated with R & D intensity, but the expected impact of price elasticity is ambiguous. Elastic demand should provide a

[8] These mechanisms are patents to prevent duplication, patents to secure royalty income, secrecy, lead time, moving quickly down the learning curve, and complementary sales and service efforts.

[9] Almon *et al.* estimated demand functions for 56 input–output sectors in which the predominant share of output goes to personal consumption expenditures. For each sector a constant price elasticity, a constant income elasticity, and a parameter representing the annual percentage shift in the demand curve were estimated using time series data from 1947 to 1970. Using these parameters and the 1972 *Input–Output Tables for the United States*, Levin [1981] calculated demand elasticities for each of the remaining disaggregated input–output sectors in manufacturing. For the handful of consumer goods sectors for which Almon *et al.* found zero price elasticities, alternative estimates were found by a search of the empirical literature. Where necessary, these derived elasticities were aggregated to the line of business level using sales-weighted averages.

The procedure requires some very strong, and obviously counterfactual, assumptions: a fixed coefficient technology and an input–output structure that can be partitioned into intermediate and final goods sectors. Nonetheless, the procedure produced only a few anomalies, and the relative magnitudes of the elasticities across industries accord reasonably well with intuition.

TABLE I
NUMBER OF FIRMS AND BUSINESS UNITS BY SAMPLE

	All Business Units		*R&D Performers Only*	
	All LBs	*Survey LBs*	*All LBs*	*Survey LBs*
Business Units	2494	1719	1797	1302
Firms	345	318	317	297

positive incentive to investment in cost-reducing process R & D, since the returns from lowering cost are greater if demand is elastic. On the other hand, inelastic demand should encourage product R & D by magnifying the returns to a rightward shift in the demand curve.

Market structure is measured with four-firm concentration ratios at the four-digit SIC level taken from the 1977 *Census of Manufactures.* When necessary, these concentration ratios are aggregated to the LB level using the value of shipments as weights.

Our effort to control for measurable interindustry differences in opportunity, appropriability, demand, and market structure restricts the size of our sample. The Levin *et al.* survey data are available for only a subset of the lines of business included in the FTC database. For much of the work reported in this paper, therefore, our sample is reduced from 2494 business units, representing 345 companies in 244 lines of business, to 1719 business units, representing 318 companies in 151 lines of business.

Within both of these samples, a significant minority of business units reported no R & D expenditures in at least one year from 1975 through 1977. As explained in the next section, for some purposes we employ samples containing only business units that performed R & D over the entire period. Table I indicates the composition of each of the samples that we used, and Table II presents descriptive statistics on the size and R & D variables for each sample. Firms and business units tend to be somewhat larger, and R & D intensity somewhat higher in the lines of business covered in the Levin *et al.* survey. Also, business units performing R & D are on average larger than those that do none, and tend to be operated by larger parent firms.

IV. SPECIFICATION AND ESTIMATION

We begin by estimating simple regressions of business unit R&D intensity on size. We then proceed to control for interindustry differences using fixed industry effects and, subsequently, measured industry characteristics.

Since business unit sales are a component of the sales of the firm, our benchmark specification is:

TABLE II
DESCRIPTIVE STATISTICS ON R & D INTENSITY, BUSINESS UNIT SALES AND FIRM SALES BY SAMPLE

	R & D Intensity (percent)*				*Business Unit Sales ($ billion)*				*Firm Sales ($ billion)*			
	All Business Units		*R & D Performers Only*		*All Business Units*		*R & D Performers Only*		*All Business Units*		*R & D Performers Only*	
	All LBs	*Survey LBs*	*All LBs*	*Survey LBs*	*All LBs*	*Survey LBs*	*All LBs*	*Survey LBs*	*All LBs*	*Survey LBs*	*All LBs*	*Survey LBs*
Mean	1.59	1.81	2.12	2.31	0.20	0.25	0.25	0.30	2.31	2.46	2.44	2.57
Median	0.68	0.81	1.16	1.30	0.06	0.07	0.07	0.08	1.14	1.23	1.23	1.31
*Minimum***	0.00	0.00	0.00	0.00	0.00	0.00	0.00	0.01	0.11	0.11	0.12	0.12
*Maximum***	22.35	22.35	22.35	22.35	16.04	16.04	16.04	16.04	34.13	34.13	34.13	34.13

* Business unit R & D spending as a percentage of business unit sales and transfers.

** To preserve the confidentiality of responding firms, we report the mean values of the four smallest and largest business units or firms, respectively.

$$RDI = \alpha_1 + \alpha_2 BUSALES + \alpha_3 OTHERSALES + e \quad (1)$$

where *OTHERSALES* is defined as the difference between *FIRMSALES* and *BUSALES*. With this specification we can test all hypotheses of interest. If business unit size alone affects R & D intensity, then we should be able to reject the hypothesis that $\alpha_2 = 0$, but should not reject $\alpha_3 = 0$. If the size of the firm as a whole is all that matters, then $\alpha_2 = \alpha_3$, but we should be able to reject the hypothesis that these coefficients are jointly equal to zero. If business unit and firm size have independent effects on R & D, we should be able to reject the hypotheses that $\alpha_2 = 0$, that $\alpha_3 = 0$, and that $\alpha_2 = \alpha_3$. If neither business unit nor firm size affects R & D intensity, then $\alpha_2 = \alpha_3 = 0$. Finally, if the scale of a firm's activities outside the business unit influences R & D intensity, but business unit size does not, then we should be able to reject both $\alpha_3 = 0$ and $\alpha_2 = \alpha_3$, but not $\alpha_2 = 0$.[10] By a straightforward extension, we can estimate the quadratic variant of specification (1) by squaring each variable and adding an interaction term. We can then test all hypotheses concerning the possible nonlinearity of size effects.

Two statistical issues required attention: the boundedness of the dependent variable and the possible heteroscedasticity of the disturbances.

As Table II indicates, only 72 per cent of the business units in our unrestricted sample and 76 per cent of those in our restricted sample performed R & D throughout the period 1975–77. If we follow the prevailing practice in the literature on Schumpeter's hypothesis and estimate specification (1) and its variants on samples that include only performers of R & D,[11] the truncation of the error term will bias the resulting parameter estimates. The Tobit model (Tobin [1958]) avoids this problem at the cost of restricting the way in which the explanatory variables simultaneously determine the probability of engaging in R & D and the amount of R & D spending. We thus present Tobit estimates of (1) using all available observations in each of our samples. To permit comparison of our results with prior studies, we also report OLS results for R & D performers only.

Reported Tobit and OLS coefficient estimates are not directly comparable. As McDonald and Moffitt [1980] demonstrate, a Tobit coefficient can be interpreted as a weighted average of two effects: (1) the effect of an increase in an independent variable on the probability that the dependent variable exceeds the limit (in our case, that R & D is greater than zero) and (2) the effect on the expected value of the dependent variable, given that it is above the limit. The magnitude of these effects depend on the values of the independent variables; as they grow large, the second effect converges to the value of the

[10] Although the reader may be concerned with possible collinearity between *BUSALES* and *OTHERSALES*, the correlation between these variables is only 0.13. The large number of observations in our sample further mitigates concern over the effect of multicollinearity.

[11] A notable exception to this common practice is the work of Bound *et al.* [1984]. They find that estimates of the effect of firm size on R & D obtained on a sample of firms reporting R & D are essentially unchanged by correcting for selectivity bias in reporting.

Tobit coefficient and the first effect goes to zero. OLS regression on a sample restricted to observations above the limit provides an estimate of the second effect, but OLS imposes a constant slope where the Tobit model implies a nonlinear response. Moreover, the OLS estimate is biased because the expected value of the truncated error term is positive. We can, nonetheless, assess the extent of this bias by using the decomposition of the Tobit coefficients proposed by McDonald and Moffitt.

A problem arises when we wish to control for industry effects using the Tobit estimator. We have 2494 observations distributed over 244 industries. The average number of observations per industry is small, reflecting in many cases a characteristic of the population as well as a characteristic of the sample. In principle, we would like to obtain estimates of the coefficients on the size variables that are consistent as the number of industries tends to infinity, holding the number of observations per industry fixed. In the linear regression framework, least squares estimates of the fixed effects model have this consistency property. As Chamberlain [1980] has shown, however, in a nonlinear probability framework (such as the Tobit model), maximum likelihood estimates of the fixed effects model are inconsistent.

This problem could potentially undermine our efforts to explore the robustness of the size–R & D relationship to the inclusion of industry effects, as well as our efforts to compare the performance of measured industry characteristics against fixed effects. We can, however, use the Tobit model to obtain consistent estimates for specifications including measured industry

TABLE III
THE EFFECTS OF SIZE ON R & D INTENSITY
R & D PERFORMERS ONLY

		Regression Coefficient (Standard Error)			
		All LBs		*Survey LBs*	
Parameter	*Variable/ Hypothesis*	(*1*)	(*2*)	(*3*)	(*4*)
α_1	*Intercept*	1.957** (0.076)	a	2.165** (0.096)	a
α_2	*BUSALES*	−0.024 (0.067)	0.049 (0.073)	−0.043 (0.072)	0.054 (0.076)
α_3	*OTHERSALES*	0.058** (0.013)	0.045** (0.011)	0.052** (0.016)	0.043** (0.013)
	$H_0: \alpha_2, \alpha_3 = 0$	F(2,1794) 9.86**	F(2,1551) 9.13**	F(2,1299) 5.21**	F(2,1149) 5.90**
	$H_0: \alpha_2 = \alpha_3$	F(1,1794) 1.39	F(1,1551) 0.002	F(1,1299) 1.59	F(1,1149) 0.02
	R^2	0.011	0.473	0.008	0.480
	n	1797	1797	1302	1302

a LB level fixed effects suppressed.
** Significant at the 0.01 level.

characteristics, although it remains to determine whether measured industry characteristics are a reasonable substitute for fixed industry effects. Decomposing the Tobit coefficients, we can assess the direction and magnitude of bias in least squares estimates obtained from the sample of R & D performers. This information should yield insight concerning the validity of inferences drawn from comparing the performance of fixed effects and measured characteristics in the least squares framework.

Breusch–Pagan tests revealed no heteroscedasticity in specifications that included only size measures. When measured industry characteristics were included among the explanatory variables, however, we typically rejected the hypothesis of homoscedasticity. After some experimentation, we found the error structure in these specifications to be best described by the model of "multiplicative heteroscedasticity", in which the logarithm of the error variance is a linear function of the exogenous variables and the number of respondents to the Levin *et al.* survey questions in the relevant industry. We thus followed the procedure suggested by Harvey [1976] to obtain asymptotically efficient GLS estimates of the parameters.[12] Breusch–Pagan statistics were calculated for each specification estimated by GLS, and in no case could we reject homoscedasticity at the 0.05 level.

V. RESULTS: THE EFFECTS OF SIZE ON R & D INTENSITY

For comparability with previous findings, we first report results obtained using two samples of R & D-performing business units. The first sample contains all R & D performers in our full set of 244 manufacturing lines of business; the second sample is limited to R & D performers in the 151 lines of business covered by the Levin *et al.* survey. Columns (1) and (3) of Table III display the results of simple regressions of R & D intensity on our two size variables. Columns (2) and (4) present the results of regressions of R & D intensity on the two size variables and industry fixed effects. Comparing columns (1) to (3), and (2) to (4), we see that the two samples produce very similar ordinary least squares estimates for comparable specifications.

The results in columns (1) and (3) support rejection of the hypothesis that α_2 and α_3 are jointly zero, but the hypothesis of equality of these two coefficients cannot be rejected. This pair of tests indicates that the size of the firm as a whole, but not business unit size, affects R & D intensity. Although

[12] Specifically, where Breusch–Pagan test revealed the presence of heteroscedasticity, the logarithm of the squared residuals from OLS estimation was regressed against first and second order size terms. For specifications involving industry characteristics, the industry variables were also included at this stage, along with the number of respondents from the industry to the Levin *et al.* survey. The primary specification was then weighted by the square root of the antilog of the predicted values from this auxiliary equation. The number of survey respondents per industry (*NRESP*) was included in the auxiliary equation to control for possible measurement error in the survey variables. In no instance, however, did *NRESP* have a statistically significant effect on the size of the residuals from the R & D equations.

the joint effect of both size measures is statistically significant, only one per cent of the variance in business unit R & D intensity is explained. Moreover, the magnitude of the firm size effect is small. The coefficient of *OTHERSALES* reported in column (1) implies that firm size must increase by 17 billion dollars to increase R & D intensity by one per cent of sales. Alternatively, doubling the size of the mean firm in our sample would produce an increase in R & D intensity of less than two-tenths of one per cent. There is no evidence of a nonlinear size–R & D relationship.[13]

The hypothesis that firm size alone influences business unit R & D intensity is further supported in the fixed effects regressions reported in columns (2) and (4) of Table III. The coefficient of *OTHERSALES* falls somewhat when fixed industry effects are included, but it remains statistically significant in both samples. The coefficient of *BUSALES* remains insignificant, but it becomes positive and moves much closer to the *OTHERSALES* coefficient, strengthening the conclusion that the size of the firm as a whole (*BUSALES* plus *OTHERSALES*) affects R & D intensity. Nevertheless, industry effects appear to be far more important than firm size; they explain nearly half the remaining variance in business unit R & D intensity.

To test the sensitivity of the results in Table III to outliers, we excluded those observations with large absolute residuals. Over a wide range of cutoff values, this procedure produced no change in our qualitative conclusions and only small changes in the estimated coefficients.

We also tested for systematic differences in the size–R & D relationship across industries. Since many lines of business contain few observations, estimation of separate slopes for each industry at the FTC line of business (LB) level was infeasible. Instead, while retaining LB-level fixed effects, we estimated separate size-related slopes for each two-digit industry.[14] The hypothesis of the homogeneity of the slopes across two-digit industries could not be rejected in either sample. In only six industries, however, was the influence of *OTHERSALES* on R & D intensity statistically significant in one or both samples. These six industries were printing and publishing (SIC 27), stone, clay, glass and cement (SIC 32), fabricated metal products (SIC 34), machinery (SIC 35), electrical equipment (SIC 36), and motor vehicles (SIC 37). The apparent absence of significant size effects in two-thirds of the two-digit industries suggested that our new "stylized fact" was fragile.

To probe further we looked carefully for outliers within each of these two-digit industries. A distinctive pattern appeared. Five of the six industries

[13] When second order terms were added to our benchmark specifications in columns (1) and (3), the coefficients were individually and jointly insignificant, and their magnitude implied that R & D intensity rises almost linearly throughout the range of firm sizes in our sample. The second order terms contributed virtually no explanatory power, and the qualitative inferences about the significance of size were unaffected. These conclusions hold for all least squares estimates reported in this paper.

[14] Our more inclusive sample contains observations from 19 two-digit industries; the lines of business covered by the Levin *et al.* survey are drawn from only 16 two-digit industries.

contained a total of seven outlier observations with a common characteristic. In each case a very large firm, much larger than typical for the particular line of business, had an uncharacteristically high R & D intensity. These firms were among the very largest in the manufacturing sector, and although the specific business units involved were not especially large for the relevant lines of business, the value of *OTHERSALES* was in each instance at least $2.78 billion above the mean for the line of business. There were three such observations in fabricated metals (SIC 34), and one each in SICs 27, 32, 35, and 36. Although the particular reasons for the exceptionally high R & D intensity differed, some form of measurement error is suggested in each instance. Two of the outliers appear to be the artifact of an excessively broad four-digit industry definition; these two business units manufacture products that are quite distinct from those supplied by others in the same line of business. Two other outlying business units produce inputs to downstream products manufactured by their parent companies. Their atypically high R & D intensities may result from understated transfer prices or from the method of allocating R & D between intermediate and final product. A similar case seems to involve the allocation of R & D among complementary final products. Finally, the two remaining outliers represent business units that sell military products. Their atypically high company-financed R & D expenditures may reflect the common practice of including "independent R & D" (IR & D) funds reimbursed by the Pentagon, or they may, alternatively, result from the behavior

TABLE IV
THE EFFECTS OF SIZE ON R & D INTENSITY
R & D PERFORMERS ONLY
OUTLIERS REMOVED

		Regression Coefficient (Standard Error)			
		All LBs		*Survey LBs*	
Parameter	*Variable/ Hypothesis*	(1)	(2)	(3)	(4)
α_1	*Intercept*	1.999**	a	2.206**	a
		(0.075)		(0.095)	
α_2	*BUSALES*	−0.002	0.074	−0.024	0.077
		(0.065)	(0.070)	(0.071)	(0.074)
α_3	*OTHERSALES*	0.032*	0.016	0.027	0.017
		(0.013)	(0.011)	(0.016)	(0.013)
	$H_0: \alpha_2, \alpha_3 = 0$	F(2,1787)	F(2,1544)	F(2,1294)	F(2,1144)
		2.90	1.85	1.45	1.54
	$H_0: \alpha_2 = \alpha_3$	F(1,1787)	F(1,1544)	F(1,1294)	F(1,1144)
		0.25	0.63	0.48	0.61
	R^2	0.003	0.484	0.002	0.492
	n	1790	1790	1297	1297

a LB level fixed effects suppressed.
* Significant at the 0.05 level.
** Significant at the 0.01 level.

described by Lichtenberg [1986], where government contractors signal their ability to perform by privately financing R & D.

Deleting these seven observations from our sample of 1797 (and deleting the five of these that appear in our restricted sample of 1302 observations) dramatically altered the results. The statistical significance of *OTHERSALES* vanished within each of the five two-digit industries from which outliers were omitted, despite the fact that only one observation was deleted from four of these industries. Furthermore, across all two-digit industries, tests of the joint significance of the size-related coefficients produced F-statistics below 1.0, as did tests on the homogeneity of the slopes across all two-digit industries.[15]

Table IV displays the results of deleting these few outliers and re-estimating the specifications reported in Table III. In each case the coefficient of *OTHERSALES* is approximately halved, and it remains significant at the 0.05 level only in the larger sample prior to the inclusion of industry effects. Even in this last instance, however, the hypotheses that α_2 and α_3 are jointly zero cannot be rejected at the 0.05 level. Moreover, the modest share of the variance in R & D intensity that is explained by the two size variables falls to less than one-third of one per cent when the outliers are removed.[16]

Table V displays maximum likelihood estimates of the Tobit specification of our simple benchmark equation with the outliers removed. Using a Tobit estimator, and adding nearly 700 observations on business units with no reported R & D, does not alter the qualitative results. Though insignificant, the coefficient of *BUSALES* turns positive, presumably reflecting the fact that R & D-performing business units within this sample are slightly larger on average than nonperformers. The coefficient of *OTHERSALES* remains statistically significant in the more inclusive sample and insignificant in the smaller sample.

From a decomposition of the Tobit coefficient estimates, we find that, at the sample means of *BUSALES* and *OTHERSALES*, less than one-half of the total response of R & D to an increase in *OTHERSALES* is attributable to an increase of R & D by business units above the threshold; the remainder is attributable to an increased probability of performing R & D. To be more precise, at the means of both size variables in our more inclusive sample, the R & D intensity of performers rises by 0.018 per cent per billion dollars of *OTHERSALES*. The OLS estimate from column (1) of Table IV of this same response is 0.032.

[15] Dropping one observation alone was sufficient to render the coefficient on *OTHERSALES* insignificant in the restricted sample.

[16] Although the degree to which our results are sensitive to a mere handful of observations in a large sample is surprising, the deleted observations are, after all, precisely those which might be expected to have the largest effect on the coefficient of *OTHERSALES*. We therefore proceeded to check the robustness of the results reported in Table IV by deleting all observations for which the value of *OTHERSALES* exceeded its LB-level industry mean by at least $2.78 billion, the smallest deviation among our seven outliers. In this way, we selected on the independent variable alone. This required us to drop 169 observations from our larger sample and 126 observations from our restricted sample. The results were qualitatively identical and quantitatively very similar to those reported for each of the four equations in Table IV.

TABLE V
TOBIT REGRESSIONS OF R & D INTENSITY ON SIZE

Parameter	Variable/ Hypothesis	Regression Coefficient (Standard Error) All LBs (1)	Survey LBs (2)
α_1	*Intercept*	1.141**	1.451**
		(0.091)	(0.118)
α_2	BUSALES	0.126	0.083
		(0.076)	(0.104)
α_3	OTHERSALES	0.038**	0.026
		(0.014)	(0.017)
	$H_0: \alpha_2, \alpha_3 = 0$	$\chi^2(2)$	$\chi^2(2)$
		11.62**	3.53
	$H_0: \alpha_2 = \alpha_3$	$\chi^2(1)$	$\chi^2(1)$
		1.21	0.28
	σ	2.778	2.955
	Log-likelihood	−5440	−3938
	n	2487	1714

** Significant at the 0.01 level.

Thus, there appears a modest upward bias in our OLS estimates of the effect of firm size on R & D intensity within the sample of R & D-performing business units. The robustness of this last inference is confirmed when we calculate the Tobit estimate of the R & D response of business units above the threshold at values of *OTHERSALES* that bracket the vast majority of observations in our sample. Maintaining *BUSALES* at its sample mean and allowing *OTHERSALES* to vary from one per cent of its sample mean to ten times its mean, we find that estimates of the R & D response of performers range from 0.0175 to 0.0215. We conclude that over the relevant size range our OLS results overstate the effect of firm size on R & D intensity among R & D performers.

We next consider how the use of measured industry characteristics affects our conclusions about the size–R & D relationship. We defer discussion of the performance of these industry characteristics to the next section and focus here on the coefficients of the two size variables. Table VI presents Tobit, OLS, and GLS results for the smaller of our two samples. In this sample, once outliers were removed, size effects were absent in both the simple and fixed effects specifications.

The OLS estimates in column (2) of Table VI contain no evidence of size effects in the sample of R & D performers. Indeed, the coefficients of *BUSALES* and *OTHERSALES* are almost identical to the fixed effects estimates reported in column (4) of Table IV. The coefficient of *OTHERSALES*, however, is sensitive to the heteroscedasticity correction in the sample of R & D performers, as shown in column (3) of Table VI. The coefficient of *OTHERSALES* more than doubles,

TABLE VI
THE EFFECTS OF SIZE AND INDUSTRY CHARACTERISTICS ON R & D INTENSITY

Parameter	Variable/ Hypothesis	Regression Coefficient (Standard Error) Tobit (1)	OLS (2)	GLS (3)
α_1	*Intercept*	−7.572**	−8.348**	−3.240**
		(1.264)	(1.362)	(0.980)
α_2	BUSALES	0.163*	0.074	−0.024
		(0.071)	(0.063)	(0.049)
α_3	OTHERALES	0.017	0.018	0.041**
		(0.014)	(0.014)	(0.012)
α_4	SCIENCEBASE	0.267	0.358**	0.232**
		(0.139)	(0.126)	(0.071)
α_5	GOVTECH	0.309**	0.363**	0.182**
		(0.068)	(0.071)	(0.055)
α_6	MATERIALTECH	−0.110	−0.077	0.087
		(0.089)	(0.094)	(0.066)
α_7	EQUIPTECH	−0.446**	−0.310**	−0.501**
		(0.103)	(0.104)	(0.066)
α_8	USERTECH	0.571**	0.455**	0.279**
		(0.093)	(0.090)	(0.064)
α_9	APPROPRIABILITY	0.535**	0.540**	0.338**
		(0.160)	(0.154)	(0.116)
α_{10}	IMLAG	0.100*	0.102*	0.060*
		(0.041)	(0.042)	(0.031)
α_{11}	PELAS	−0.282**	−0.301**	−0.165**
		(0.080)	(0.059)	(0.036)
α_{12}	INCELAS	1.471**	1.450**	0.794**
		(0.158)	(0.149)	(0.121)
α_{13}	DGROWTH	0.171	0.198*	0.074
		(0.096)	(0.084)	(0.046)
α_{14}	NEWPLANT	0.051**	0.059**	0.030**
		(0.007)	(0.008)	(0.006)
	$H_0: \alpha_2, \alpha_3 = 0$	$\chi(2)$	F(2,1283)	$\chi(2)$
		7.62*	1.73	5.67*
	$H_0: \alpha_2 = \alpha_3$	$\chi(1)$	F(1,1283)	$\chi(1)$
		3.95*	0.70	1.56
	H_0: *Opportunity* = 0	$\chi(5)$	F(5,1283)	$\chi(5)$
	$(\alpha_4, \alpha_5, \alpha_6, \alpha_7, \alpha_8 = 0)$	99.76**	18.12**	22.51**
	H_0: *Appropriability* = 0	$\chi(2)$	F(2,1283)	$\chi(2)$
	$(\alpha_9, \alpha_{10} = 0)$	18.79**	9.77**	6.45**
	H_0: *Demand* = 0	$\chi(3)$	F(3,1283)	$\chi(3)$
	$(\alpha_{11}, \alpha_{12}, \alpha_{13} = 0)$	93.85**	35.90**	15.55**
	R^2		0.236	
	n	1714	1297	1297

* Significant at the 0.05 confidence level.
** Significant at the 0.01 confidence level.

and it becomes significant at the 0.01 level. This anomaly results from the heteroscedasticity correction. The size variables receive little weight in the auxiliary equation. Instead, the survey variables reflecting technological opportunity, notably *SCIENCEBASE*, receive the greatest weight because the largest residuals occur disproportionately in industries with very high technological opportunity. Observations from high opportunity industries thus receive less weight in the GLS equation, and firm size becomes significant. The result hints that if firm size matters at all, it matters in low opportunity industries.[17]

The Tobit results in column (1) of Table VI reinforce the conclusion that the effect of *OTHERSALES* is insignificant. At the sample means of all variables, just over half of the reported Tobit coefficients represents the effect of the independent variables on the R & D intensity of performers. Thus, the insignificant OLS coefficient once again overestimates the effect of firm size on R & D intensity.

Contrary to all previously reported results, *BUSALES* has a significant positive effect in column (1) of Table VI. At the means of the independent variables, the estimated response of R & D performers to *BUSALES* is, however, identical to the comparable OLS coefficient estimate in column (2).[18] This suggests that the significance of *BUSALES* in the Tobit specification may be attributable to its influence on the probability of conducting R & D. To explore this possibility, we estimated probit equations using the explanatory variables from both our simple specification and the specification including the measured industry characteristics.[19] The effect of business unit size on the probability of conducting R & D was positive and significant at the 0.01 confidence level in both specifications. The coefficient of *OTHERSALES* was insignificant.

VI. FURTHER RESULTS: FIXED EFFECTS VS. MEASURED INDUSTRY CHARACTERISTICS

Table VI reveals that measured industry characteristics perform well as substitutes for industry fixed effects. In the OLS specification estimated on the restricted sample of R & D performers, industry characteristics explain 23.4% of the variance in business unit R & D intensity beyond that explained by size alone. This represents 48% of the incremental variance explained by industry fixed effects, with great economy in the use of parameters (11 instead

[17] We explored this possibility by restricting our sample to lines of business with values of *SCIENCEBASE* below its sample mean of 6.2 (on a scale of 7.0) and, alternatively, below 6.0. The results were sensitive to the cutoff level. In the first case firm size had a significant but small effect on R & D intensity. In the second case, it did not.

[18] Whether or not it is significant, the quantitative effect of *BUSALES*, given R & D performance, is minute. An eleven billion dollar increase in business unit sales is required to increase R & D intensity by one per cent.

[19] We estimated the probit specifications with two forms of our dependent variable. We defined the dependent variable to equal one if the business unit conducted R & D in any one of the three years, 1975–1977, and, alternatively, to equal one if R & D was conducted in all three years, 1975–1977. The qualitative results were insensitive to this variation in the dependent variable.

of 151). In addition, about 50% more variance is explained by measured industry characteristics than by fixed two-digit industry effects.

TABLE VII
THE EFFECTS OF SIZE AND INDUSTRY CHARACTERISTICS ON R & D INTENSITY IN SELECTED 2-DIGIT INDUSTRIES
R & D PERFORMERS ONLY
(ADJUSTED FOR HETEROSCEDASTICITY)

Parameter	Variable/ Hypothesis	Regression Coefficient (Standard Error)			
		SIC 20 (Food)	*SIC 28 (Chemicals)*	*SIC 35 (Machinery)*	*SIC 36 (Electrical)*
α_1	*Intercept*	1.145	−24.436**	−17.293**	−5.135
		(3.536)	(6.461)	(5.037)	(7.469)
α_2	*BUSALES*	−0.430*	−0.033	0.738**	1.374
		(0.179)	(0.293)	(0.280)	(0.911)
α_3	*OTHERSALES*	0.019	0.013	0.024	0.029
		(0.029)	(0.007)	(0.019)	(0.017)
α_4	*SCIENCEBASE*	−0.261	0.637	1.183**	0.672
		(0.239)	(0.704)	(0.453)	(0.755)
α_5	*GOVTECH*	0.020	1.226**	0.959**	−0.234
		(0.114)	(0.324)	(0.316)	(0.226)
α_6	*MATERIALTECH*	0.136	1.010**	0.987**	−1.144*
		(0.131)	(0.363)	(0.284)	(0.494)
α_7	*EQUIPTECH*	0.097	−0.821*	−0.896**	1.467*
		(0.091)	(0.394)	(0.241)	(0.650)
α_8	*USERTECH*	−0.091	1.958**	0.120	1.098**
		(0.129)	(0.384)	(0.253)	(0.324)
α_9	*APPROPRIABILITY*	−0.107	0.199	0.786	−0.086
		(0.368)	(1.277)	(0.529)	(0.576)
α_{10}	*IMLAG*	0.053	0.371**	−0.182	−0.533**
		(0.043)	(0.120)	(0.145)	(0.148)
α_{11}	*PELAS*	−0.191	1.978	−0.511	−1.176
		(0.257)	(1.101)	(0.385)	(0.910)
α_{12}	*INCELAS*	0.678	2.643**	2.197**	1.110
		(0.426)	(0.878)	(0.523)	(1.236)
α_{13}	*DGROWTH*	0.113	−2.453**	−0.316	0.767
		(0.084)	(0.834)	(0.342)	(0.771)
α_{14}	*NEWPLANT*	0.012	0.156**	0.096**	−0.003
		(0.009)	(0.042)	(0.023)	(0.043)
	$H_0: \alpha_2, \alpha_3 = 0$	$\chi^2(2)$	$\chi^2(2)$	$\chi^2(2)$	$\chi^2(2)$
		3.59	1.88	5.73	2.21
	$H_0: \alpha_2 = \alpha_3$	$\chi^2(1)$	$\chi^2(1)$	$\chi^2(1)$	$\chi^2(1)$
		6.52*	0.025	6.21*	2.19
	H_0: *Opportunity* = 0	$\chi^2(5)$	$\chi^2(5)$	$\chi^2(5)$	$\chi^2(5)$
	$(\alpha_4, \alpha_5, \alpha_6, \alpha_7, \alpha_8 = 0)$	1.02	12.02*	7.96*	14.46*
	H_0: *Appropriability* = 0	$\chi^2(2)$	$\chi^2(2)$	$\chi^2(2)$	$\chi^2(2)$
	$(\alpha_9, \alpha_{10} = 0)$	0.79	8.70*	1.62	6.51*
	H_0: *Demand* = 0	$\chi^2(3)$	$\chi^2(3)$	$\chi^2(3)$	$\chi^2(3)$
	$(\alpha_{11}, \alpha_{12}, \alpha_{13} = 0)$	2.90	12.45**	6.33	0.68
	R^2(OLS)	0.076	0.369	0.440	0.309
	n	142	254	217	115

* Significant at the 0.05 confidence level.
** Significance at the 0.01 confidence level.

Most of the industry characteristics are individually significant at conventional levels. In the OLS version, only the contribution of raw material suppliers (*MATERIALTECH*) is insignificant. The remaining opportunity variables are significant at the 0.01 level in all three equations, with the exception of *SCIENCEBASE* in the Tobit variant. The appropriability variables have a substantial impact on R & D intensity. Our demand growth measure performs rather poorly, but the price and income elasticity terms are significant in all three equations. Wald tests of the joint significance of the vectors of opportunity, appropriability, and demand variables each compel rejection of the null hypothesis by all three methods of estimation.[20]

One widely employed industry characteristic, seller concentration, is excluded from the specification estimated in Table VI. As in Levin *et al.* [1985], the coefficient of this variable is statistically insignificant in nearly all specifications reported in this paper. It is always insignificant when concentration appears along with our size measures as the only industry characteristic. All principal results concerning the significance and importance of size and industry characteristics hold whether or not concentration is included in the specification.

There are insufficient degrees of freedom to test the homogeneity of the coefficients of the industry characteristics across two-digit industry groups, since there are not enough lines of business in most two-digit industries. Nonetheless, we investigated the performance of the measured industry characteristics within those two-digit groups with enough lines of business to support the specification. These include food (SIC 20), chemicals (SIC 28), machinery (SIC 35), and electrical equipment (SIC 36). These four two-digit industries respectively contain 21, 16, 24, and 16 lines of business. Together, they account for 77 of the 151 lines of business and 728 of the 1297 R & D-performing business units in the restricted sample. The groups differ markedly in their opportunity and appropriability conditions. Food processing industries tend to score relatively low on survey measures of both opportunity and appropriability. Chemical industries score relatively high on both. Electrical equipment has high opportunity, but appropriability is average or below average. The machinery industries are more difficult to summarize; there is considerable heterogeneity within the two-digit group.

As noted previously, fixed effects regressions within each of these industrial groups produced no evidence of size effects after outliers were removed. Substituting measured industry characteristics for fixed effects, we estimated a Tobit equation for all business units within each two-digit group, and OLS

[20] It should be noted that tests on the joint significance of the technological opportunity variables include only the five opportunity measures drawn from the Levin *et al.* survey and exclude *NEWPLANT*, a measure of the age of the industry's physical plant and equipment. We adopt this approach because we are particularly interested in assessing the value of the survey data. Dropping *NEWPLANT* from the estimating equation, here and in Table VII, produces virtually no change in the remaining coefficients, and alters none of our qualitative conclusions.

and GLS equations on the R & D-performing business units. With the exceptions noted below, the qualitative results on the influence of the two size variables were insensitive to the estimation technique. The Tobit estimates of the coefficients of the measured industry characteristics were generally less significant than the GLS or OLS estimates, but tests of the joint significance of each category of industry characteristics were largely identical.[21] Thus, we confine attention to the GLS estimates presented in Table VII.

Table VII indicates that firm size is insignificant in all four two-digit industries. Business unit size is however, negatively related to R & D intensity in the food processing industries. This result, however, is not robust; *BUSALES* is insignificant in the OLS and Tobit equations for food processing. Business unit size appears to be positively related to R & D intensity in the machinery industries (although not in the OLS estimates), but this result is driven by the historical anomaly of classifying electronic computing equipment as nonelectrical machinery. When a dummy variable is substituted for measured characteristics in the computer industry alone, the coefficient on *BUSALES* becomes insignificant.

The measured industry characteristics perform best in the chemical industries, where the vectors of opportunity, appropriability, and demand variables are each jointly significant at the 0.05 level or better. The opportunity variables do reasonably well in machinery and electrical equipment, but most of the appropriability and demand variables fare poorly outside the chemical

TABLE VIII
COMPARISON OF PERCENT CONTRIBUTIONS TO EXPLAINED VARIANCE IN R & D INTENSITY MEASURED INDUSTRY CHARACTERISTICS V. FIXED INDUSTRY EFFECTS

	Sample				
	All Industries	*SIC 20*	*SIC 28*	*SIC 35*	*SIC 36*
(1) *Percent of variance explained by size measures*	0.2	1.5	0.4	6.6	0.2
(2) *Additional variance explained by measured industry characteristics*	23.4	6.1	36.5	37.4	30.7
(d.f.)	(11)	(11)	(11)	(11)	(11)
(3) *Additional variance explained by fixed industry effects (d.f.)*	49.0	12.1	46.9	44.8	35.8
	(151)	(21)	(16)	(24)	(16)
(4) (2) ÷ (3)	0.48	0.50	0.78	0.83	0.86

[21] Of the twelve joint significance tests (three categories of industry characteristics by four industry groups) the only two exceptions were the appropriability variables in SIC 28, which were insignificant in the Tobit specification, and the demand variables in SIC 35, which were significant in the Tobit specification.

industries. One exception is electrical equipment where short imitation lags appear to spur R & D investment.

Table VIII summarizes our results concerning the explanatory power of size, fixed industry effects, and measured characteristics. Both within and across two-digit industries, firm and business unit size explain very little of the variance in business unit R & D intensity. In chemicals, machinery, and electrical equipment, as well as across industries, both measured industry characteristics and fixed effects explain a substantial fraction of additional variance. Across all industries, the 11 measured industry characteristics capture nearly half the variance explained by 151 fixed effects, and capture between 78 and 86 per cent of the variance explained by fixed LB-level industry effects within the two-digit chemical, machinery and electrical equipment sectors.

The performance of measured industry characteristics may also be judged by how well they explain the between-industry variation in business unit R & D intensity. By regressing the LB-level means of R & D intensity against measured industry characteristics, we explain about one-third of this between-industry variation, whether or not we control for the effects of size. If we restrict attention to the 80 lines of business in which there were at least three responses to the Levin *et al.* survey questionnaire, thus reducing the likely magnitude of measurement error in the survey variables, industry characteristics account for 56 per cent of the between-industry variation in business unit R & D intensity.

VII. CONCLUSIONS

Our investigations of the FTC Line of Business data reveal that, among business units that perform R & D, there is no significant relationship between size and R & D intensity once care is taken to separate the influence of business unit and firm size, to control for interindustry differences in the R & D investment environment, and to remove outliers from the data. Once outliers are removed, a simple regression of R & D intensity on size measures alone suggests that the size of the firm is positively associated with business unit R & D intensity, although the effect is quite small. This result, however, appears only in the larger of our two samples, and it vanishes entirely once we control for industry effects. Moreover, the magnitude of the effect of either firm size or business unit size upon the R & D intensity of R & D performing business units is always minute, regardless of the associated significance level, or the sample or estimation technique employed. We also find that although business unit size exercises no influence on the R & D conducted by R & D performers, it does influence the probability of engaging in R & D.

Our results also suggest that previous findings supporting the connection between overall firm size and R & D intensity in samples of R & D performers may have resulted from inadequate attention to outliers and industry effects, and not from inappropriate estimation technique. Tobit regressions produce conclusions concerning the effect of size on R & D performers that are qualitatively identical to those based on OLS estimates derived from censored samples of the type used in most prior literature. On the other hand, we find that least squares results were somewhat sensitive to corrections for heteroscedasticity.

Taken together, the research reported in this and a previous paper provides little support for the much-tested Schumpeterian hypotheses that firm size and market concentration influence R & D intensity. Our inquiry also yields constructive results, however, suggesting that industry effects have a very important influence on R & D, and that industry effects can be reasonably well represented by measures of demand conditions, and by survey-based measures of technological opportunity and appropriability.

These findings do not, of course, rule out the possibility, supported in the work of Scott [1984], that there are characteristics of firms that influence R & D intensity. Our results suggest that firm size is not one such characteristic, at least not within the size range we observe. In this connection, it is important to recall that though our data include many small business units, all are drawn from firms that are among the largest in the US manufacturing sector.

WESLEY M. COHEN AND DAVID C. MOWERY,
Carnegie-Mellon University,
Pittsburgh, Pennsylvania,
USA.

ACCEPTED DECEMBER 1986

RICHARD C. LEVIN,
Yale University,
New Haven, Connecticut,
USA.

REFERENCES

ALMON, C., *et al.*, 1974, *1985: Interindustry Forecasts of the American Economy* (Lexington Books, Lexington, Mass.).

BOUND, J., CUMMINS, C., GRILICHES, Z., HALL, B. and JAFFE, A., 1984, 'Who Does R & D and Who Patents?', in Z. GRILICHES (ed.), *R & D, Patents, and Productivity* (University of Chicago Press, Chicago).

CHAMBERLAIN, G., 1980, 'Analysis of Covariance with Qualitative Data', *Review of Economics Studies*, 47, 1 (January), pp. 225–238.

COHEN, W. M. and LEVINTHAL, D., 1986, 'The Endogeneity of Appropriability and R & D Investment', Mimeo, Carnegie-Mellon University.

COHEN, W. M. and MOWERY, D. C., 1984, 'The Internal Characteristics of the Firm and the Level and Composition of Research & Development Spending: Interim Report, NSF grant PRA 83-10664', Mimeo, Carnegie-Mellon University.

CREMER, J. and SIRBU, M., 1978, 'Une analyse économetrique de l'effort de recherche et développement de l'industrie Francaise', *Revue Economique*, 29, 5 (September), pp. 940–954.

FISHER, F. M. and TEMIN, P., 1973, 'Returns to Scale in Research and Development: What Does the Schumpeterian Hypothesis Imply?', *Journal of Political Economy*, 81, 1 (January/February), pp. 56–70.

GALBRAITH, J. K., 1957, *American Capitalism: The Concept of Countervailing Power* (M. E. Sharpe, White Plains, NY).

HARVEY, A. C., 1976, 'Estimating Regression Models with Multiplicative Heteroscedasticity', *Econometrica*, 44, 3 (May), pp. 461–465.

JUDGE, G. G., GRIFFITHS, W. E., HILL, R. C., LUTKEPOHL, H. and LEE, T., 1985, *The Theory and Practice of Econometrics*, 2nd ed. (John Wiley and Sons, New York).

KAMIEN, M. I. and SCHWARTZ, N. L., 1982, *Market Structure and Innovation* (Cambridge University Press, Cambridge).

LEVIN, R. C., 1981, 'Toward an Empirical Model of Schumpeterian Competition', Working Paper, Yale School of Organization and Management, Series A, No. 43.

LEVIN, R. C., COHEN, W. M. and MOWERY, D. C., 1985, 'R & D Appropriability, Opportunity, and Market Structure: New Evidence on Some Schumpeterian Hypotheses', *American Economic Review*, 75, 2 (May), pp. 20–24.

LEVIN, R. C., KLEVORICK, A. K., NELSON, R. R. and WINTER, S. G., 1984, 'Survey Research on R & D Appropriability and Technological Opportunity: Part 1', Mimeo, Yale University.

LICHTENBERG, F., 1986, 'Private Investment in R and D to Signal Ability to Perform Government Contracts', National Bureau of Economic Research, Working paper No. 1974.

McDONALD, J. and MOFFITT, R., 1980, 'The Uses of Tobit Analysis', *Review of Economics and Statistics*, 62, 2 (May), pp. 318–321.

PAVITT, K., ROBSON, M. and TOWNSEND, J., 1987, 'The Size Distribution of Innovating Firms in the UK: 1945–1983', *Journal of Industrial Economics*, 35, 3 (March), pp. 297–316.

SCHERER, F. M., 1980, *Industrial Market Structure and Economic Performance*, 2nd ed. (Houghton Mifflin, Boston).

SCHERER, F. M., 1984, *Innovation and Growth: Schumpeterian Perspectives* (MIT Press, Cambridge, Mass.).

SCHUMPETER, J. A., 1950, *Capitalism, Socialism, and Democracy*, 3rd ed. (Harper & Row, New York).

SCOTT, J. T., 1984, 'Firm versus Industry Variability in R & D Intensity', in ZVI GRILICHES (ed.), *R & D, Patents, and Productivity* (University of Chicago Press, Chicago).

TOBIN, J., 1958, 'Estimation of Relationships for Limited Dependent Variables', *Econometrica*, 26, 1 (January), pp. 24–36.

THE RELATIONSHIP BETWEEN FIRM GROWTH, SIZE, AND AGE: ESTIMATES FOR 100 MANUFACTURING INDUSTRIES

DAVID S. EVANS*

The study uses a sample of all firms operating in 100 manufacturing industries to examine some aspects of firm dynamics. It finds that firm growth, the variability of firm growth, and the probability that a firm will fail decrease with firm age. It also finds that firm growth decreases at a diminishing rate with firm size even after controlling for the exit of slow-growing firms from the sample. Gibrat's Law therefore fails although the severity of the failure decreases with firm size.

I. INTRODUCTION

THIS ARTICLE examines some dynamic aspects of firm behavior for all firms that operated in a sample of 100 manufacturing industries between 1976 and 1980. It examines the relationship between three aspects of industry dynamics—firm growth, firm dissolution, and the variability of firm growth—and three key characteristics of a firm—its size, its age, and the number of plants it operates. It presents estimates of these relationships based on data pooled across all industries. It then presents a summary of the relationships found for each of the industries.

A number of studies have examined the relationship between firm growth and firm size. Hart and Prais's [1956] pioneering study of the growth of British companies was followed by studies by Hymer and Pashigian [1962], Mansfield [1962], and Hall [1987] for the United States and Singh and Whittington [1975] and Kumar [1985] for the United Kingdom. This paper makes three contributions to this literature.

First, it examines the relationship between firm age and firm dynamics. Except for my earlier paper [1987] and Brock and Evans [1986], previous studies have not examined the lifecycle aspects of firm growth. Second, it relies on a larger and more comprehensive sample of firms and reports results for more detailed industry groups than have previous studies. With the exception of Mansfield [1962], researchers have relied on samples of publicly

* I would like to thank Timothy Bresnahan and Richard Schmalensee for helpful comments. My research was supported by SBA Contract No. SBA-8575-AER-84 to CERA Economic Consultants, Inc. and by the C.V. Starr Center for Applied Economics at New York University where I was a Visiting Scholar. An earlier version of the paper was presented at the Fifth World Congress of the Econometric Society, Cambridge, Mass., August 1985. I retain full responsibility for the contents of this paper.

traded (and therefore generally large) companies and have not disaggregated these samples below the 2-digit industry level. This paper uses data on the complete size distribution of firms in the manufacturing industries considered and summarizes results for separate 4-digit industries. Third, unlike previous studies except for Hall [1987] and myself, it controls for sample selection bias and heteroskedasticity. Little hinges, however, on the statistical novelties.

The study finds several interesting relationships. First, firm growth decreases with firm size and firm age at the sample mean and for most of the firms in the interindustry sample. The negative relationship between growth and size holds for 89 percent of the industries and the negative relationship between growth and age holds for 76 percent of the industries. Second, the probability of firm survival increases with firm size and firm age at the sample mean and for most of the firms in the interindustry sample. The positive relationship between survival and size holds for 81 percent of the industries and the positive relationship between survival and age holds for 83 percent of the industries. Third, the variability of firm growth decreases with firm age at the sample mean and for most of the firms in the interindustry sample. The negative relationship holds for 85 percent of the industries. The relationship between the variability of firm growth and firm size is less clear. There is a negative relationship between variability and size for 80 percent of the industries. However, there is some evidence from the interindustry sample that the sign of the relationship between variability and size varies with age and with the number of plants operated by the firm.

The study therefore finds that firm age is an important determinant of firm growth, the variability of firm growth, and the probability of firm dissolution. Notably, the age relationships found are broadly consistent with the predictions of Jovanovic's theory of firm growth in which entrepreneurs learn about their abilities over time.[1] Further empirical and theoretical work on the lifecycle dynamics of firms may hold some promise.

Gibrat's Law that firm growth is independent of firm size is rejected for this sample. The departures from Gibrat's Law decrease as firm size increases. Mansfield [1962] reached a similar finding and speculated that it was due to the exit of slow-growing small firms from the sample. The departures found here remain, however, after controlling for sample censoring arising from firm exit. This finding is of interest because several theories either assume or imply Gibrat's Law for the full size range of firms in homogeneous-product industries.[2]

Section II describes the data used in this study. Section III presents the statistical framework. Section IV reports the estimates. Section V summarizes the major results.

[1] See Evans [1987] and Brock and Evans [1986] for more on this point.

[2] See the models developed by Lucas [1967], [1978] and special cases of the model developed by Jovanovic [1982].

II. THE DATA

The sample of firms analyzed in this study was drawn from the Small Business Data Base (SBDB), which was constructed by the Office of Advocacy of the US Small Business Administration from information originally collected by Dun and Bradstreet.[3] Data are available on firm employment, age, the 4-digit SIC code in which the firm primarily operates, and the number of plants.[4] The dataset includes most manufacturing firms with employees.

The fact that a firm has data on a file for a particular year does not necessarily mean that the data apply to that year. Because of reporting and collecting delays, the data for some firms are older than the data for other firms. Generally, current data are available for most larger and older firms. In order to examine firm dynamics over roughly the same phase of the business cycle and for roughly the same amount of time, observations for which data were more than two years old in the relevant years were deleted.[5]

Firm age is reported by year for firms that were six years old or younger in 1976. Firm age is reported for four age intervals for firms that were seven years or older in 1976: 7–20, 21–45, 46–95, and 96+. Estimates are reported separately for young firms and for old firms. For old firms, age is measured by an estimate of the average age of firms in the interval.[6] Separate estimates are reported for firms six years old or younger in 1976—hereafter referred to as young firms—and firms seven years or older—hereafter referred to as old firms.

There are several other drawbacks to this dataset. First, no data on mergers or acquisitions are available.[7] Second, although firms are identified by 4-digit SIC codes, such identification is problematic for diversified (usually large) firms. Third, as of this time no systematic comparison of the SBDB data with alternative data sources has been made. But the number of firms identified by SBDB as operating in an industry differ, sometimes greatly, from the corresponding Census figures. Given the amount of judgement that is required to determine the industry classification of a firm, this disparity is disconcerting but not surprising.[8]

[3] See Executive Office of the President [1983, pp. 405–428] for further details. Interested researchers can obtain a copy of the data from the Office of Economic Research of the Small Business Administration.

[4] In the ensuing results the number of plants includes the headquarters of the company.

[5] Because the variability of firm growth is calculated from observations on firm growth for three two-year periods, observations for which data were more than one year old were deleted for the variability analysis.

[6] The estimate is based on fitting a lognormal distribution to the age data. The estimates are 13 years for firms between 7 and 20, 27 years for firms between 21 and 45, 63 years for firms between 46 and 95, and 103 years for firms older than 95 years.

[7] This problem afflicts all previous studies of industry dynamics with the exception of the recent study by Kumar [1985].

[8] See Evans [1986b] for details.

The SBDB is relied upon here because it is the most comprehensive micro dataset on firms and the only dataset that contains age information.[9] On the one hand, the results reported here are sufficiently promising to warrant the development of more refined panel datasets containing financial information as well as age data. On the other hand, given the potential problems with these data, considerable caution in evaluating the findings is advisable until they have been replicated on more refined datasets.

A sample of 100 4-digit manufacturing industries was selected randomly from the population of 450 4-digit industries. The 100 industries comprise 22.2 percent of all 450 manufacturing industries. They contribute 24.2 percent of value added and account for 25.9 percent of employment. The ratio of capital to sales was 0.33 for the sample and 0.35 for all manufacturing industries. Thus the sample is reasonably representative of the manufacturing sector. For a list of the industries included and summary information see Evans [1986b].

Data on all firms operating in these 100 industries were extracted from the SBDB. There were 105 186 firms operating in the sample of industries in 1976. The vast majority of these firms have fewer than 20 employees. In order to reduce the amount of data to be analyzed, only 25 percent of these small firms were included in the study.[10] Two industries had unusually large numbers of firms—SIC Code 2752 had 23 132 firms and SIC Code 3599 had 18 425 firms. In order to reduce the amount of data and in order to prevent these two industries from dominating the interindustry regression results, only 25 percent of the firms in these industries were included. These exclusions together with the ones discussed below reduced the sample to 42 339 firms.

Because the economy was in a severe recession in 1982, growth and dissolution were examined between 1976 and 1980.[11] Firm growth is defined as

$$\text{Growth} = \text{Ln}\,[S_{t'}/S_t]/[t'-t]$$

where S is employment size, t' is the date to which the 1980 data apply, t is the date to which the 1976 data apply, and $t'-t$ is the number of years between these two dates. Observations were excluded if t' was less than 1978 or if t was less than 1974. Growth can only be calculated for firms that did not dissolve between 1976 and 1980. About a third of the young firms and about 15 percent of the old firms dissolved. The sample available for estimating the determinants of growth is therefore censored, a problem that will be dealt

[9] Other generally available datasets, such as Compustat or the Longitudinal Establishment File of the Census Bureau, do not have age information.

[10] General results are similar when these firms are included. The main difference is that nonlinearities in the relationships become less pronounced.

[11] The results are consistent, however, with the results for 1976–1982 reported by Evans [1987].

with below. No information is available on mergers. Thus, there is no way to distinguish between internal growth and growth through mergers.

Firm survival was coded as a 1 if a firm was on the dataset in both 1976 and 1980 and as a 0 if a firm was on the dataset in 1976 but not in 1980. The fact that a firm is not on the dataset in 1980 may mean several things. It may have failed (i.e. filed for bankruptcy), it may have voluntarily dissolved itself, it may have merged with another firm, or it may have been acquired by another firm. It is impossible to distinguish between these possibilities with the SBDB. Although information on some mergers and acquisitions could be obtained from auxiliary datasets, the large number of firms and industries included in the sample and limited resources precluded such an undertaking. An analysis of firms in the food manufacturing industries by MacDonald [1986] found that mergers and acquisitions accounted for approximately 13 percent of all dissolutions on the SBDB for firms with more than 20 employees. Mergers and acquisitions are probably less frequent for firms with fewer than 20 employees. Thus, while the data for the survival analysis may be contaminated with some "false" dissolutions, the degree of contamination is probably not too severe.[12]

In order to estimate the variability of firm growth the growth rate was calculated for 1976–1978, 1978–1980, and 1980–1982 and the standard deviation of these three growth rates was calculated. While the variability of firm growth is estimated imprecisely for each firm, there is some hope that the large number of observations available will enable reasonably precise estimates of the effect of size and age on this variability. Observations were deleted if the data were more than a year old in any one of the years. Because of dissolutions and lack of current data, an estimate of the variability of firm growth was available for only half of the firms that were on the dataset in 1976. The sample for estimating the determinants of variability is censored, a problem considered below.

Table I reports summary information on the variables used in the statistical analysis. Further details are in Evans [1986b].

III. STATISTICAL FRAMEWORK

This section outlines the estimation framework.[13] Firm growth is represented by the following regression equation.

$$[\ln S_{t'} - \ln S_t]/d = \ln g(A_t, S_t, B_t) + u_t \qquad (1)$$

where A, S, and B denote age, size, and the number of plants respectively, $t' > t$, $d = t' - t$, g is a growth function which we shall approximate by taking

[12] This contamination poses no problem for the sample selection correction so long as the sample-inclusion equation is otherwise correctly specified.

[13] The interested reader may consult my earlier paper [1987] for details.

TABLE I
SUMMARY STATISTICS ON VARIABLES USED IN REGRESSION ANALYSIS

Variable	Mean (Standard Deviation) *Survival*	*Growth*	*Variability*
Young Firms			
Survival	0.671 (0.470)	—	—
Growth	—	0.029 (0.149)	—
Log [Standard Deviation of Growth]	—	—	−1.749 (1.015)
Log [Employment]	2.261 (1.144)	2.351 (1.159)	2.605 (1.160)
Log[Age]	1.258 (0.571)	1.301 (0.557)	1.319 (0.549)
Log[Plants]	0.067 (0.268)	0.073 (0.285)	0.090 (0.323)
Number of Observations	13 735	9221	6195
Old Firms			
Survival	0.848 (0.359)	—	—
Growth	—	−0.101 (0.012)	—
Log [Standard Deviation of Growth	—	—	−2.220 (0.930)
Log [Employment]	3.224 (1.251)	3.304 (1.230)	3.510 (1.146)
Log [Age]	2.982 (0.491)	2.299 (0.494)	3.014 (0.502)
Log [Plants]	0.199 (0.552)	0.207 (0.565)	0.231 (0.596)
Number of Observations	28 604	24 244	19 569

Growth is measured as the annual logarithmic growth rate between 1976 and 1980. The standard deviation of growth is based on three observations of annual logarithmic firm growth between 1976 and 1982.

a second-order expansion in the logs, and u is a normally distributed disturbance term with mean zero and possibly nonconstant variance across observations.

Growth is observed only for firms that are in the sample in both t' and t. The probability that a firm will survive from t to t' is represented by the following probit equation. Let $I = 1$ if a firm survives and 0 if it fails. The conditional expectation of I given the initial age, size, and number of plants is

$$E[I \mid A_t, S_t, B_t] = \Pr[e_t > -V(A_t, S_t, B_t)] \\ = F[V(A_t, S_t, B_t)] \tag{2}$$

where V can be thought of as the value (in excess of opportunity cost) of remaining in business, e_t is a normally distributed disturbance with mean zero and unit variance, F is the cumulative normal distribution function with unit variance. Equation (2) is a standard probit regression.[14] V is approximated by a second-order logarithmic expansion.

Equations (1) and (2) form a standard sample-selection model. (See, e.g., Amemiya [1984].) It is possible to obtain consistent estimates of the parameters of the regression functions g and V using maximum likelihood. It is also possible to obtain consistent estimates of the standard errors of these parameters in the face of heteroskedasticity in the disturbance term of the growth equation using the procedure suggested by White [1982].[15]

The variability of growth equation is represented by

$$\text{LnStdDev}(g) = \ln h(A_t, S_t, B_t) + w \tag{3}$$

where StdDev(g) is the estimate of the standard deviation of growth described in the previous section, h is a regression function which will be approximated by a second-order expansion in the logs, and w is a mean-zero error term with possibly non-constant variance. The sample upon which (3) is estimated is censored because, for a variety of reasons including failure, the variance of firm growth is not observed for part of the sample. In order to correct for this problem, we can posit a probit equation similar to (2) for the probability of sample inclusion and estimate (3) and the sample-inclusion equation jointly using maximum likelihood. The sample-inclusion equation is *ad hoc* and has no economic interpretation.

IV. STATISTICAL TESTS AND ESTIMATION RESULTS

Second-order logarithmic expansions of the growth function, survival function, and variability of growth functions were estimated separately for young firms (for which continuous age information was available) and old firms (for which age was imputed from categorical age information). As discussed below, some of the higher-order regressors were dropped because they were highly insignificant or because multicollinearity hindered convergence of the maximum-likelihood function.

[14] See Amemiya [1984] for further discussion. The unit-variance assumption is a simple normalization that arises from the fact that the value function V (and the regression coefficients) are identified only up to a constant of proportionality.

[15] A critical assumption here is that the disturbance term of the probit equation is homoskedastic. If it is not, standard errors and coefficient estimates of both equations are inconsistent. As an informal test of misspecification I compared the regular and White standard errors for the probit equation. The fact that they differ by less than one percent suggests that heteroskedasticity is not a problem here. A difficult problem that arises in this sort of study is identifying sample selection from nonlinearities. I [1987] discuss this problem in more detail and present evidence that suggests that the main relationships between growth, size, and age are not an artifact of sample selection.

TABLE II
FIRM SURVIVAL, GROWTH, AND VARIABILITY OF GROWTH—YOUNG FIRMS[a]

Variable	*Survival*	*Growth*	*Variability of Growth*
	1976–1980		*1976–1982*
Size	0.1779***	−0.0721***	−0.0402
	[0.0437]	[0.0071]	[0.0311]
Age	−0.0262	−0.0341***	−0.1724***
	[0.0741]	[0.0118]	[0.0495]
Size^2	−0.0203***	0.0054***	—
	[0.0071]	[0.0012]	
Age^2	0.0762*	−0.0560	—
	[0.0320]	[0.0485]	
Size Age*	0.0351*	0.0142***	0.0195
	[0.0176]	[0.0029]	[0.0203]
Plants	—	0.0860***	0.3605
		[0.0255]	[0.1951]
Plants^2	—	0.0423	—
		[0.0375]	
*Plants * Size*		−0.0252***	−0.0997***
	—	[0.0057]	[0.0328]
*Plants * Age*	—	0.0197	0.2196*
		[0.0148]	[0.1041]
Constant	−0.0349	0.1687***	−2.2510***
	[0.0629]	[0.0117]	[0.1453]
Sigma	—	0.1453***	0.9451***
		[0.0020]	[0.0389]
Correlation	—	0.0189	0.5997***
		[0.0144]	[0.0730]
Observations	13 735	9221	5493
Log-Likelihood[a]	—	−3843.5	−15 407.2

[a] The first log-likelihood is for the survival-growth system. The second log-likelihood is for the variability of growth system. The selection equation for the variability of growth equation is available from the author upon request. All regressors are measured in logs. Thus size is the log of employment, age is the log of age, branch is the log of the number of branches. White standard errors are in brackets.

* Significant at the 5 percent level.
** Significant at the 1 percent level.
*** Significant at the 0.1 percent level.

Table II reports the results for young firms. Table III reports the values of the partial derivatives of the survival, growth, and variability of growth functions with respect to size, age, the number of plants at the sample mean and over the sample. The results show that the probability of survival increases with size and age.[16] At the sample mean, a 1 percent change in firm size leads to a 7 percent change in the probability of survival; a 1 percent change in age leads to a 13 percent change in the probability of survival. The positive coefficient on the product of size and age implies that the probability

[16] Preliminary results found that the number of plants was always insignificant. Consequently, the plant variables were excluded from the final estimates.

TABLE III
THE EFFECTS OF FIRM SIZE, AGE, AND NUMBER OF PLANTS ON FIRM DYNAMICS —YOUNG FIRMS

Partial Derivative of[a] *with Respect to*		*Survival*	*Growth*	*Variability of Growth*
Size				
	Mean	0.047	−0.032	−0.022
	Standard Deviation	0.019	0.016	0.028
	Fraction Positive	0.990	0.023	0.000
	Fraction Negative	0.010	0.977	1.000
Age				
	Mean	0.084	−0.142	−0.133
	Standard Deviation	0.030	0.064	0.060
	Percent Positive	0.990	0.028	0.066
	Percent Negative	0.010	0.972	0.934
Plants				
	Mean	—	0.060	0.087
	Standard Deviation	—	0.033	0.155
	Percent Positive	—	0.961	0.733
	Percent Negative	—	0.039	0.267

[a] Partial derivative of the regression function on the horizontal with respect to the logarithmic value of the variable on the vertical.

of survival increases with size more rapidly for older firms and that the probability of survival increases with age more rapidly for larger firms.[17]

Firm growth decreases with size and age. In order to characterize the relationship between firm growth and firm size and age it is useful to look at the elasticity of ending-period size with respect to beginning-period size and beginning-period age.[18]

The estimates imply at the sample mean that over a ten year period, a 1 percent increase in beginning-period size leads to a 0.68 percent increase in ending-period size. Thus firm growth is considerably less than proportionate to firm size at the sample mean. The departure from Gibrat's Law decreases with size and age. The negative coefficient on the crossproduct of the number of plants and firm size indicates that the departure from Gibrat's Law is greater the more plants operated by the firm. This result is consistent with a negative relationship between growth and size at the plant level: smaller plants grow more rapidly than larger plants so that firms whose size is split among more plants grow more rapidly than firms whose size is split among fewer plants.

The estimates also imply that over a ten year period, a 1 percent increase in

[17] The probability of firm survival was found not to depend upon the number of plants in preliminary work and these variables were consequently deleted to make the maximum likelihood estimation easier.

[18] Let g_s and g_a denote the partial derivatives of growth with respect to log size and log age respectively. Then the elasticity of ending-period size with respect to beginning period size is $1+dg_s$ and the elasticity of ending-period size with respect to beginning age is dg_a where d is the length of time considered.

beginning-period age leads to a 1.42 percent decrease in ending-period size. Thus firm growth is smaller for older firms. The results also show that firm growth increases with the number of plants operated by the firm, although this growth is smaller for larger firms.

Firm growth increases with the number of plants holding firm size and age constant at the sample mean. A 1 percent increase in the beginning-period number of plants leads to a 0.6 percent increase in ending-period size. Thus firm growth is greater when firm size is spread across a larger number of plants.

The positive correlation coefficient for the growth and survival equations indicates, as one would expect, that failures tend to have unusually low

TABLE IV
FIRM GROWTH AND SURVIVAL—OLD FIRMS 1976–1980

Variable	*Survival*	*Growth*	*Variability of Growth*
	1976–1980		*1976–1982*
Size	0.2767***	−0.0327***	−0.0385
	[0.0451]	[0.0064]	[0.0487]
Age	0.6470**	−0.0754***	−0.2004***
	[0.2291]	[0.0199]	[0.0608]
Size^2	−0.0334***	0.0009	0.0145**
	[0.0043]	[0.0010]	[0.0055]
Age^2	−0.1219***	0.0078*	—
	[0.0377]	[0.0034]	
*Size * Age*	0.0496**	0.0052*	−0.0005
	[0.0160]	[0.0022]	[0.0166]
Plants	—	0.0006***	0.3922***
		[0.0001]	[0.0915]
Plants^2	—	0.0085***	—
		[0.0018]	
*Plants * Size*	—	−0.0198***	−0.0817***
		[0.0029]	[0.0128]
*Plants * Age*	—	0.0597	0.0685*
		[0.0470]	[0.0299]
Constant	−0.6816	0.1853***	−2.2821***
	[0.3549]	[0.0304]	[0.1667]
Sigma	—	0.1453***	1.0720***
		[0.0020]	[0.0096]
Correlation	—	0.0193	0.6871***
		[0.0144]	[0.0143]
Observations	28 604	24 244	16 155
Log-Likelihood[a]	—	4049.8	−39 454.10

[a] The first log-likelihood is for the survival-growth system. The second log-likelihood is for the variability of growth system. The selection equation for the variability of growth is available from the author upon request. All regressors are measured in logs. Thus size is the log of employment, age is the log of age, branch is the log of the number of branches. White standard errors are in brackets.

* Significant at the 5 percent level.

** Significant at the 1 percent level.

*** Significant at the 0.1 percent level.

growth rates. But the correlation coefficient is small and not statistically significant. This result is consistent with my previous work (Evans [1987], Evans [1986a], and Brock and Evans [1986]) and with the study by Hall [1987].

The results for the variability of growth should be viewed with some caution. The dependent variable for these regressions is based on just three firm-growth observations and is therefore measured very imprecisely. Moreover, the dependent variable is missing for more than half of the cases. The delicacy of the correction for sample-selection in these kinds of models should make us circumspect in giving the results recorded below too much weight.

The variability of firm growth decreases with firm age.[19] A 1 percent increase in firm age leads to a 0.13 percent decrease in the standard deviation of firm growth. For single-plant firms—most of the firms in our sample of young firms—there is little evidence that firm growth depends upon firm size: the coefficients on the size variables are small and not statistically significant. For multiple-plant firms there is evidence that the variability of firm growth decreases with firm size and that the rate of decrease is greater for firms with more plants.[20]

Table IV reports the results for old firms. Table V summarizes the relevant partial derivatives. Results are generally similar to those for young firms, although there is some evidence that the relationships deteriorate for very old firms. A 1 percent change in firm size leads to a 6 percent increase in the probability of firm survival and a 1 percent increase in firm age leads to a 2 percent increase in the probability of firm survival. The probability of survival decreases with firm size for very old firms (about 21 percent of the sample).[21]

Firm growth is roughly independent of age at the sample mean. Firm growth decreases with firm age for younger firms (about 75 percent of the sample of old firms) but then eventually increases with firm age for older firms (about 25 percent of the sample of old firms). Firm growth decreases with firm size at the sample mean and for almost all of the sample. Over a ten year period, a 1 percent increase in beginning-period firm size leads to a 0.85 percent increase in ending-period size at the sample mean. The departure from Gibrat's Law decreases with size and with age and increases with the number of plants. As with young firms, firm growth increases with the number of plants. A 1 percent increase in the initial number of plants leads to a 1.18 percent increase in ending-period size over a ten year period.

[19] I was unable to obtain convergence when the quadratic terms in age and plants were included.

[20] Previous studies have found that the variability of firm growth decreases with firm size. Because these studies did not consider age or the number of plants—both of which are positively correlated with firm size—the results found here are consistent with these studies. See Mansfield [1962] and Hymer and Pashigian [1962].

[21] While this finding might reflect senescence of firms, it might also reflect an increased probability of acquisition.

TABLE V
THE EFFECTS OF FIRM SIZE, AGE, AND NUMBER OF PLANTS ON FIRM DYNAMICS—OLD FIRMS

Partial Derivative of[a] *with Respect to*		*Survival*	*Growth*	*Variability of Growth*
Size				
	Mean	0.049	−0.015	0.037
	Standard Deviation	0.032	0.010	0.047
	Fraction Positive	0.993	0.001	0.852
	Fraction Negative	0.007	0.999	0.148
Age				
	Mean	0.016	0.000	−0.188
	Standard Deviation	0.025	0.038	0.038
	Percent Positive	0.790	0.251	0.992
	Percent Negative	0.210	0.749	0.008
Plants				
	Mean	—	0.118	0.333
	Standard Deviation	—	0.033	0.097
	Percent Positive	—	0.998	0.999
	Percent Negative	—	0.002	0.001

[a] Partial derivative of the regression function on the horizontal with respect to the logarithmic value of the variable on the vertical.

The same caveat as above applies to the variability of growth equation. The variability of firm growth decreases with firm age. At the sample mean a 1 percent increase in firm age leads to a 0.19 percent decrease in the standard deviation of firm growth. The variability of firm growth increases slightly with firm size. A 1 percent increase in firm size leads to a 0.04 percent increase in the standard deviation of growth at the sample mean. The rate of increase is smaller the larger the number of plants operated by the firm. This result is not consistent with previous studies which have found that firm growth decreases with firm size. It is also not consistent with the separate industry results reported below.

In order to summarize the relationships for each industry first-order logarithmic expansions of the growth, survival, and variability of growth functions were considered.[22] No corrections were made for sample selection. Thus the results for variability of firm growth should be viewed with caution. The probability of survival results are based on ordinary least squares estimates of the linear probability model. The significance tests are based on a five percent level using the regression standard errors.[23]

Table VI summarizes the results for size and age. Results at the industry level are imprecisely estimated for most industries. This lack of precision may reflect the poor quality of the data, including industry misclassification, or the

[22] The lack of precision at the industry level and the high collinearity between the first and second-order terms made the inclusion of the second-order terms pointless.

[23] Resource constraints prevented me from correcting the standard errors for heteroskedasticity. The significance results should therefore be viewed with considerable caution.

TABLE VI
SUMMARY OF INDUSTRY REGRESSIONS[a]

Independent Variable		*Dependent Variable*					
		Growth		*Survival*		*Variability of Growth*	
		Number of Industries with Coefficient Sign					
Age		+	−	+	−	+	−
	Significant	4	31	48	1	1	26
	Insignificant	20	45	35	15	17	54
	Total	24	76	83	16	18	80
Size							
	Significant	1	61	37	3	1	26
	Insignificant	10	28	44	15	12	59
	Total	11	89	81	18	13	85

[a] Estimates based on a regression of the dependent variables described in the text against the log of age, size, and the number of plants. There were insufficient observations to perform the regression for 1 industry for survival and 2 industries for the variability of growth. Significance level is 5 percent.

collinearity between age, size, and the number of plants at the industry level. Nevertheless, the directions of the relationships are broadly consistent with the interindustry results reported above. Firm survival increases with firm size for 81 percent of the industries and with firm age for 83 percent of the industries. Firm growth decreases with size in 89 percent of the industries and with firm age in 76 percent of the industries. The variability of firm growth decreases with firm age for 80 percent of the industries and with firm size for 85 percent of the industries.

V. CONCLUSIONS

The first key finding of this study is that firm age is an important determinant of firm dynamics. The probability of firm failure, firm growth, and the variability of firm growth decrease as firms age. The importance of age is consistent with the predictions of the learning model developed by Jovanovic [1982].[24]

The second key finding is that firm growth decreases at a diminishing rate with firm size even after controlling for the selection of firms out of the sample. Gibrat's Law fails. The departures from Gibrat's Law are severe for small firms but become less severe for larger firms. This pattern is broadly consistent with previous studies which tend to show severe departures from Gibrat's Law for small firms—e.g. Mansfield [1962]—and no or less severe departures for large firms—e.g. Hymer and Pashigian [1962], Hall [1987], Kumar [1985], and myself [1986a].

[24] Note, however, that these relationships appear to break down for very old firms in the interindustry results. Jovanovic's model predicts that the probability of firm survival increases with size but the survival-age relationship is ambiguous.

The importance of these departures from Gibrat's Law depends upon the use to which this Law is put. Gibrat's Law is not an unreasonable assumption for the very large firms which do, at any point in time, contribute most industrial output. The departures from Gibrat's Law found by studies using recent data are around 10 percent over a ten-year period.[25]

A theory that seeks to explain short-run changes in the growth and size distribution of the largest firms in the economy may not go too wrong by maintaining Gibrat's Law. But many of our industrial organization theories are meant to apply to the complete size distribution of firms in narrowly defined industries, not to interindustry samples of large firms. Gibrat's Law is not a reasonable assumption for the smaller firms which account for the vast majority of firms in most industries and from which the large firms of the future will come.

The data behind these findings are crude. Replication of these results with more refined datasets is crucial before they are accepted. Nevertheless, this study (along with related work by Evans [1987] and Brock and Evans [1986] that yield similar results) provides a starting point for further theoretical and empirical work on industry dynamics. For theoretical work, it suggests that theories that incorporate age hold some promise. It also indicates caution in maintaining Gibrat's Law for theories, such as Lucas [1978], that are meant to apply to the complete size distribution of firms. For empirical work, it suggests the importance of age as a factor in determining industry dynamics. Longitudinal datasets containing experience information on firms (and on the managers and entrepreneurs associated with the firms) should be developed. Such datasets would help researchers disentangle the effects of alternative forms of learning from each other and from the effects of capital accumulation.

DAVID S. EVANS,
Department of Economics,
Fordham University,
Bronx, NY 10458,
USA.

[25] Kumar [1985] using net assets finds that the departure over a 10-year period is about 10 percent based on United Kingdom data for 1960–1976. See Kumar [1985, Table II and note 10, p. 333]. Using book value of assets, I [1986a, Table 4) also find that the departure is about 10 percent based on Fortune 500 data for the United States for 1958–1984. Hall [1987] using employment finds that the departure is also about 10 percent over a 10-year period based on Compustat data for the United States for 1976–1983. Studies based on data for the late 1940s and 1950s show a positive relationship between growth and size while studies based on pre-1940 data typically show a negative relationship. See Hymer and Pashigian [1962], Singh and Whittington [1975], and the summary in Prais [1975, Table D.2, p. 205]. None of these studies, with the exception of Hall [1987] and myself, tests for nonlinearities in the growth-size relationship. The differing estimates may depend partly on having different size ranges in the samples.

REFERENCES

AMEMIYA, T., 1984, 'Tobit Models: A Survey', *Journal of Econometrics*, 11 (February), pp. 1–45.

BROCK, W. A. and EVANS, D. S., 1986, *The Economics of Small Businesses* (Holmes and Meier, New York).

EVANS, D. S., 1986a, 'Firm Growth, Gibrat's Law, and the Fortune 500', unpublished, (February).

EVANS, D. S., 1986b, *The Determinants of the Growth and Size Distribution of Firms* (Small Business Administration, Washington, DC).

EVANS, D. S., 1987, 'Tests of Alternative Theories of Firm Growth', *Journal of Political Economy*, forthcoming.

EXECUTIVE OFFICE OF THE PRESIDENT, 1983, *The State of Small Business: Report of the President* (Government Printing Office, Washington, DC).

HALL, BRONWYN H., 1987, 'The Relationship between Firm Size and Firm Growth in the US. Manufacturing Sector', *Journal of Industrial Economics*, this issue.

HART, P. E. and PRAIS, S. J., 1956, 'The Analysis of Business Concentration: A Statistical Approach', *Journal of the Royal Statistical Society*, 119, pt. 2, pp. 150–191.

HYMER, S. and PASHIGIAN, P., 1962, 'Firm Size and the Rate of Growth', *Journal of Political Economy*, 70 (December), pp. 556–569.

KUMAR, M. S., 1985, 'Growth, Acquisition Activity and Firm Size: Evidence from the United Kingdom', *Journal of Industrial Economics*, 33 (March), pp. 327–338.

JOVANOVIC, B., 1982, 'Selection and Evolution of Industry', *Econometrica*, 50 (May), pp. 649–670.

LUCAS, R. E., 1967, 'Adjustment Costs and the Theory of Supply', *Journal of Political Economy*, 75 (August), pp. 321–334.

LUCAS, R. E., 1978, 'On the Size Distribution of Business Firms', *Bell Journal of Econonmics*, 9 (August), pp. 508–523.

MACDONALD, JAMES, 1986, 'Entry and Exit on the Competitive Fringe', *Southern Economic Journal*, 52 (January) pp. 640–652.

MANSFIELD, E., 1962, 'Entry, Gibrat's Law, Innovation, and the Growth of Firms', *American Economic Review*, 52 (December), pp. 1031–1051.

PRAIS, S. J., 1975, *The Evolution of Large Industrial Firms* (Cambridge University Press, Cambridge, England).

SINGH, AJIT and WHITTINGTON, GEOFFREY, 1975, 'The Size and Growth of Firms', *Review of Economic Studies*, 52 (January), pp. 15–26.

WHITE, H., 1982, 'Maximum Likelihood Estimation of Misspecified Models', *Econometrica*, 50 (May), pp. 1–25.

THE RELATIONSHIP BETWEEN FIRM SIZE AND FIRM GROWTH IN THE US MANUFACTURING SECTOR*

BRONWYN H. HALL

Using panel data on the publicly traded firms in the US manufacturing sector in the recent past, I find that most of the change in employment at the firm level in any given year is permanent, that year-to-year growth rates are largely uncorrelated over time or with prior characteristics of the firm, and that there is almost no measurement error. Gibrat's Law is weakly rejected for the smaller firms in my sample and accepted for the larger firms. This finding remains when I control for the effect of selection (attrition) on estimates obtained from this sample.

I. INTRODUCTION

THE PRESENT paper is a first step in an investigation of the dynamics of firm growth in the US manufacturing sector during the recent past.[1] It updates work by earlier researchers on the relationship between firm size and growth using a more comprehensive dataset and modern econometric techniques to attempt to correct for some of the problems in estimating such a relationship. The question addressed here is "Do small to medium-sized publicly traded manufacturing firms grow faster than large ones?" If they do, is it because of the way they are selected into our sample, or because of a difference in the rate and direction of innovative activity, or simply because the economy is finite and diminishing returns set in eventually? I do not claim to be able to distinguish clearly among all these alternatives, or even that only one must be true, but I do explore the implications of each for the data.

Stochastic models of firm growth have been subjected to two kinds of empirical tests: the first posits a growth model that is stationary over time and then looks at the implications of this model for the equilibrium size distribution of firms. Various authors, beginning with Gibrat, have shown that the simplest version of a growth model, in which growth rates are

* I am indebted to Zvi Griliches for numerous helpful discussions and to Tim Bresnahan, Peter Reiss, Sherwin Rosen, David Evans, Tom MaCurdy, and members of the Stanford University Industrial Organization seminar for comments. The current version of the paper owes much to the careful reading by the editors, Tim Bresnahan, Dick Schmalensee, and Larry White. Joy Mundy provided extremely able research assistance and Clint Cummins programmed the sample selection models in TSP. Parts of this research were supported by a National Science Foundation Grant (PRA 81-08635), the National Bureau of Economic Research and a Sloan Foundation Dissertation Fellowship.

[1] A longer version of this paper, including three appendices, appeared as National Bureau of Economic Research paper Number 1965, April 1986.

independent of size, generates a log normal size distribution, albeit with an increasing variance over time. Mandelbrot [1963] provides a survey of this and other models, in which he shows the conditions under which the equilibrium size distribution is a stable Pareto distribution. Boundary conditions on exit and entry are required in order to achieve a stable distribution in most cases. Size distributions have been investigated empirically by Simon and coworkers (e.g., Ijiri and Simon [1977], Simon and Bonini [1958]), Quandt [1966], and Hart and Prais [1956]. Typically, the size distribution conforms fairly well to log normal, with possibly some skewness to the right. The power of this kind of test is low, since the relationship of growth rates to size is not explicitly investigated. However, several of the existing theories, such as those of Lucas [1978] and the stochastic theory of Simon and Bonini have as their main implication these static distributions.

The other approach to empirical work in this area is to investigate the relationship of growth rates and size in a panel of firms. This work is exemplified by Hymer and Pashigian [1962] and Mansfield in the sixties, and the more recent work by Birch, Armington and Odle [1982], and Evans [1985] using the Dun and Bradstreet files (as cleaned by Brookings Institution for the Small Business Administration) and by Evans using Fortune 500 firms. Except for Evans, none of these researchers attempted to correct econometrically for biases induced by sample selection and measurement error. One of the purposes of this paper is to investigate whether such biases have an appreciable effect on the results.

The first econometric problem is the phenomenon of regression to the mean: If the dependent variable in question is the growth rate, measured as size in a final period less size in an initial period, and the independent variable is size in the initial period, measured with error, then firms that have transitorily low size due to measurement error will on average seem to grow faster than those with transitorily high size. With yearly observations from a panel of firms it is possible to control for this kind of random measurement error with instrumental variable techniques (see Griliches and Hausman [1985]).

The second problem is somewhat more serious: Measuring growth with a panel of firms requires that data on size will be available for every firm in both the beginning and the end period. But small firms that have slow or negative growth are more likely to disappear from the sample than are large firms, yielding the well-known problem of sample selection bias. In addition, some of the most rapidly growing and successful small firms may not be present at the beginning of the period, which will produce biases in the other direction. In section IV of the paper I present estimates of a model that attempts to control for sample selection.

The plan of the paper is as follows: First I describe the data and present preliminary results on the role of measurement error in the size-growth relationship. This is followed by an exploration of the time series behavior of employment growth, with the issue of selection bias set aside temporarily. Then I develop an econometric model of sample attrition and discuss the problems that arise in estimating such a model in the presence of heteroskedasticity and the absence of adequate information to identify separately the probability of firm survival. Finally, I investigate the relationship of investment, both in physical capital and research and development, to firm growth, using the sample selection model to control for attrition. The main conclusion of the paper is that the previously observed negative relationship between size and growth for smaller firms is robust to corrections for selection bias and heteroskedasticity, although this conclusion is clouded by the difficulties of separating nonlinearity from selection bias in the presence of size-related heteroskedasticity.

II. DESCRIPTION OF THE DATA

In this paper I confine my analysis to data on publicly traded manufacturing firms, drawn from the Compustat files. These data cover approximately ninety percent of the employment in the manufacturing sector in 1976, although they account for only about one percent of the firms in this sector.[2] Thus the study is really about the relationship of growth and size across firms that have already reached a certain minimum size, large enough to require outside capitalization. We would argue that these are the firms of interest, since their relative sizes are the main determinants of concentration in most markets. (This argument applies mainly to the manufacturing sector, where there are almost no privately held firms of any size.)

The universe from which I draw my sample consists of 1778 firms in the manufacturing sector in 1976[3] (see Bound *et al.* [1984] for further description of these data). I considered two different panels selected from this universe: all the firms with employment data from 1972 through 1979, and all the firms with employment data from 1976 to 1983. The first set maximizes the sample size, since the basic universe of firms is as of 1976, while the second has the advantage that it begins in the year in which the sample was chosen and hence suffers from selection bias in only one direction. There are 1349 firms in

[2] The total number of employees in our 1976 cross-section is 16.7 million, possibly including some foreign employees. The total domestic manufacturing employment reported by the Bureau of Labor Statistics for the same year is 19 million. The number of enterprises in the Census of Manufacturers in 1977 is approximately 300,000.

[3] An earlier draft of this paper was based on a sample of 2577 firms, which included all the firms on the Compustat full coverage file that were in the manufacturing sector. Further investigation of the full coverage sample has revealed that it is unsuitable for a study of growth and sample selection due to exit: many of the firms on the file are not really publicly traded and most do not have valuation information. In addition, many of them file for a year or two after a public offering, and then suspend filing because there are less than 300 shareholders on record. This is not really an exit, but we no longer can obtain data on the firm.

the first sample and 1098 in the second; 962 firms are in both samples. The remainder of the firms either entered or exited the sample during the period. A few firms participate in a merger of equals and become in effect a new firm; these observations are treated as exits (and the new entity as an entry).[4]

The overall growth rate of employment in this sample was about 2.9 percent in the 1972–79 period and 0.8 percent in the 1976–83 period. There are substantial differences across the industries, with the so-called "high tech" industries (drugs, computing equipment, communication equipment, and scientific instruments) typically growing more rapidly throughout both periods. (Details are available from the author on request.)

We first consider the possible role of measurement error in biasing a regression of changes on levels. A simple model of Markov growth with errors in variables would look like

$$y_t = X_t + w_t \tag{1}$$

$$X_t = X_{t-1} + u_t \tag{2}$$

with w and u uncorrelated white noise errors, X unobserved ("true" size) and y the observed logarithm of employment. Under this model, the true relationship between change in size and its level is

$$E(\Delta X_t | X_{t-1}) = 0 \tag{3}$$

but the estimated relationship will be

$$E(\Delta y_t | y_{t-1}) = -(\sigma_w^2/(\sigma_X^2 + \sigma_w^2))\, y_{t-1} \tag{4}$$

where σ_w^2 and σ_X^2 are variances of the error term and the unobservable size respectively. For these data, the ratio of the variance of growth rates (within a firm) to the total variance of log employment is approximately six percent. Under the simple Markov model presented above, the variance of growth rates is the sum of twice the measurement error (σ_w^2) plus the variance of the disturbance u; if we make the most extreme assumption that all the variation is measurement error so that $0.06 \approx 2\sigma_w^2/(\sigma_X^2 + \sigma_w^2)$, then the largest negative value we would expect for this coefficient is -0.03 (for year-to-year growth rates). If we compute annual growth rates over a longer period, this estimate of the coefficient would be divided by the number of years over which the employment change is computed.

In Table I, I present the results of a simple regression of growth on size for the two samples, with and without individual industry effects. The coefficient of $\log E_{72}$ in a regression of the annual growth rate from 72 to 79 is -1.14%,

[4] This is obviously an inadequate treatment of an interesting aspect of growth in the manufacturing sector, but it involves a relatively small number of firms, and it is beyond the scope of the present paper to model major merger activity. We hope to explore the extent to which this kind of growth impacts on our estimates in future work.

TABLE I
GROWTH RATE REGRESSIONS

	Annual Growth Rate in Percentage Terms			
Dependent Variable	*72–79 OLS*	*73–79 OLS*	*73–79 OLS*	*73–79 Inst. Var.*
1972–1979: 1349 Firms				
Intercept	4.0 (0.2)	2.9 (0.3)	2.9 (0.3)	3.0 (0.3)
Logarithm of Size	−1.14 (0.15)	−0.98 (0.14)	−0.92 (0.14)	−0.99 (0.14)
in Year	72	72	73	73
Standard Error	8.4	9.4	9.5	9.5
Intercept	*20 Industry Dummies*			
Logarithm of Size	−1.09 (0.13)	−0.95 (0.14)	−0.90 (0.14)	−0.97 (0.14)
in Year	72	72	73	73
Standard Error	7.6	8.7	8.7	8.7
F-*statistic for Industry Dummies*	7.20	6.36	6.44	6.44
	Annual Growth Rate in Percentage Terms			
Dependent Variable	*76–83 OLS*	*77–83 OLS*	*77–83 OLS*	*77–83 Inst. Var.*
1976–1983: 1098 *Firms*				
Intercept	1.89 (0.30)	1.07 (0.32)	1.06 (0.33)	1.13 (0.33)
Logarithm of Size	−1.06 (0.15)	−0.99 (0.16)	−0.93 (0.16)	−1.00 (0.16)
in Year	76	76	77	77
Standard Error	8.6	9.2	9.2	9.2
Intercept	*20 Industry Dummies*			
Logarithm of Size	−0.89 (0.16)	−0.79 (0.17)	−0.72 (0.17)	−0.80 (0.17)
in Year	76	76	77	77
Standard Error	8.3	8.9	8.9	8.9
F-*statistic for Industry Dummies*	4.83	5.24	5.30	5.30

Note: Figures in parentheses are standard errors.

while that of $\log E_{76}$ in the growth rate regression is -1.06%. That is, doubling a firm's size decreases its annual growth rate by about eight tenths of one percent. In the remainder of the table I try to correct for possible measurement error bias in this relationship, but it remains remarkably stable. First, the model of pure random walk with measurement error would predict an estimated coefficient of zero in the regression of the growth rate on size in the period preceding that from which the growth rate is measured, whereas in column 2 we obtain an estimate only slightly smaller in absolute value than in the previous regression. Second, in the last column we regress the growth rate on size at the beginning of the period using size one year prior to the beginning of the period as an instrument, since by assumption it is uncorrelated with the measurement error, but this regression yields almost the same result as the ordinary least squares estimate in column 5.

The addition of industry dummies does not change the coefficients much, although they are significant at conventional levels (the 1% critical level for the F-statistic is about 2.2). Since this pattern held for most of the results reported in this paper, we have not presented estimates with industry dummies in the rest of the tables; they almost invariably were moderately significant but had little or no effect on the other coefficients. The study of interindustry differences in these data appears to be warranted but is beyond the scope of this paper.

My tentative conclusion is that uncorrelated errors of measurement in employment cannot be responsible for more than about ten percent of the observed negative relationship between size and growth. From the fall in absolute value of the size coefficient in the growth equation in going from column 1 to columns 2 or 4 in Table I, we can infer a value for $\sigma_w^2/(\sigma_X^2+\sigma_w^2)$ of approximately 0.0015, or one tenth of a percent. Since the variance of the logarithm of employment is approximately 2.7 and the mean is around 0.8, this does correspond to a standard deviation of about fifteen percent of the level of employment in any one year, a not inconsiderable amount. It is simply that a measurement error of this magnitude is swamped by the large variance in size across our firm population, and it introduces very little bias in the estimating equation.

Repeating the exercise using sales produced much the same result in the growth-size regressions, although the standard deviation of the measurement error in this case could be about half again as large. For the instrumental variable estimates corresponding to column 4 of Table I, the size coefficient was -0.90 (0.21).

III. THE TIME SERIES BEHAVIOR OF EMPLOYMENT GROWTH

Since I rejected the simplest random walk with measurement error model in the previous section, the approach I take in this section is to try to discover what time series model *will* adequately describe the data, so that I can specify more fully the way in which firm growth deviates from Gibrat's Law. In an appendix to the unpublished version of this paper (available from the author on request), I present the results of a time series analysis of the three different panels of firms drawn from my sample. In this section I interpret the results of that analysis.

The fact that the coefficient of lagged size in the growth rate equation in Table I was always negative, even with a measurement error adjustment, suggests that the simple random walk model I was considering should be modified to include an autoregressive component. This is because the model in equation (2) has a coefficient on lagged size equal to unity, while the estimates imply a coefficient on lagged size which is somewhat less than one.

This expanded model can be written as[5]

(5) $X_t = \beta X_{t-1} + u_t \qquad Eu_t^2 = \sigma_t^2 \qquad EX_{t-1}u_t = 0$

(6) $y_t = X_t + w_t \qquad Ew_t^2 = \sigma_w^2 \qquad Eu_s w_t = 0, \forall s, t$

I have allowed the variance of employment growth to vary from year to year since the observed variances change considerably over time. The model above is equivalent to a standard ARMA(1, 1) model, but the latter is valid over a larger parameter space; this property turns out to be important. The ARMA(1, 1) model is written as

(7) $(1-\alpha L)\, y_t = (1-\mu L)\varepsilon_t$, where ε_t is white noise

whereas the AR(1) model with measurement error, (3), implies

(8) $(1-\beta L)\, y_t = u_t + (1-\beta L) w_t = u_t + w_t - \beta w_{t-1}$

If the disturbances are normally distributed, it is easy to show that the two models are equivalent with

$$\alpha = \beta$$
$$(1+\mu^2)\sigma_\varepsilon^2 = \sigma_u^2 + \sigma_w^2(1+\beta^2)$$
$$\sigma_w^2 = (\mu/\beta)\sigma_\varepsilon^2$$

However, the measurement error model requires that σ_w^2 be positive, which imposes the constraint that μ and α are of same sign in the ARMA(1, 1) model and restricts the parameter space. When I estimate the ARMA(1, 1) model using these data, the constraint is *not* satisfied, which implies a slightly negative σ_w^2.

Estimates for the models in this section were obtained by maximum likelihood under the assumption that the disturbances are homoskedastic and normal. The method is described in somewhat more detail in Hall [1979]. MaCurdy [1981] has shown that these estimates are consistent even if the disturbances are not multivariate normal (as seems likely in this case), although the estimated standard errors are no longer correct. Estimates for the model in equation (8) are shown in the top half of Table II. They are quite stable across the periods and are consistent with the *IV* estimates in Table I, since they imply a coefficient of $100(\beta-1) = -1.0$ percent in the growth rate equation together with a slightly *positive* measurement error bias (of the order of 0.001, or one tenth of a percent).

Since the time series analysis in the appendix shows that an ARMA(2, 1) model fits the data significantly better than an ARMA(1, 1) model, we also explore what Leonard [1984] calls a "mean-reverting" model, which is familiar from the investment literature as a flexible accelerator model. This

[5] Throughout this section, I have suppressed the i subscript (indicating the firm) on y, X, w, i, and ε for simplicity.

TABLE II
TIME SERIES BEHAVIOR OF LOG EMPLOYMENT

	1972–79	*1976–83*	*1972–83*
Autoregressive Model with Measurement Error[a]			
β	0.991 (0.001)	0.990 (0.002)	0.991 (0.001)
Var. of Meas. Error (σ_w^2)	−0.0018 (0.0004)	−0.0036 (0.0005)	−0.0027 (0.0012)
Var. of Shock (σ_u^2)[c]	0.0368 (0.0015)	0.0426 (0.0023)	0.0406 (0.0174)
Adjustment Cost Model[b]			
λ	1.745 (0.147)	0.553 (0.097)	0.878 (0.051)
Var. of Meas. Error (σ_w^2)	0.057 (0.005)	0.015 (0.004)	0.029 (0.002)
Var. of Shock (σ_u^2)[c]	0.032 (0.001)	0.057 (0.006)	0.075 (0.019)

Notes: [a] These estimates are derived from the ARMA(1, 1) estimates which were based on the covariance of the levels of log employment described in Appendix A. See the text for a definition of the model and an explanation of the negative variance estimate.
[b] These estimates are derived from the ARMA(1, 1) estimates which were based on the covariance of the first differences of log employment described in Appendix A.
[c] These are derived for a representative estimate of σ_ε^2 (about 0.035). They actually will change slightly each year.

model rests on the idea that the number of employees is a kind of stock that is not instantaneously adjustable at zero cost to the firm. For a firm with constant returns to scale that has quadratic adjustment costs, there is a linear relationship between employment changes and the current and desired levels of employment:

$$\Delta y_t = (1-\lambda)(y_t^* - y_{t-1}) + w_t, \text{ or} \tag{9}$$

$$(1-\lambda L)\, y_t = (1-\lambda)\, y_t^* + w_t \tag{10}$$

The time series process implied by this model depends on what is assumed about the process generating the desired level of employment. If $y_t^* = y_i^*$ for all t, (7) becomes

$$(1-\lambda L) y_t = \alpha_i + w_t, \quad \text{where } \alpha_i = (1-\lambda) y_i^* \tag{11}$$

Because of the short panel, this cannot be estimated consistently in levels, so I write it in first differences:

$$(1-\lambda L)\Delta y_t = (1-L) w_t$$

This is an ARMA(1, 1) process with μ constrained to be equal to one.

It seems more reasonable to assume that the desired level of employment is a Martingale process, since we might expect that the target size evolves as the firm receives random shocks each year involving demand, cost, and so forth. This implies

$$(1-L)\, y_t^* = u_t \quad \text{with } Eu_t^2 = \sigma_t^2 \tag{12}$$

and the process becomes

$$(13)\qquad (1-\lambda L)\Delta y_t = (1-\lambda)u_t + (1-L)w_t$$

which is equivalent to an ARMA(1, 1) process (4) with both α and μ free.[6] Since the estimated μ for this model is not unity, it is easy to reject the first version (constant target size). The estimates for the second version are shown in the bottom of Table II. They are unstable across the time periods. The estimates for the first period do not make much sense in the context of this model since they imply that the firm adjusts its size away from the desired level of employment ($1-\lambda = -0.745$).

I conclude the following from this time series analysis of employment growth: (1) The failure of Gibrat's Law to hold is not due to serially uncorrelated measurement error in the size variable, but rather to the fact that there is very slight tendency for large firms to become smaller and small firms to become larger; this tendency is stable over time (the autoregressive coefficient of 0.991 in all three columns of Table II). (2) The variance in growth rates across firms changes significantly from year to year (the relationship of this finding to macroeconomic effects deserves investigation in further work). (3) A simple adjustment cost model (in which employment is not adjusted freely from year to year due to such effects as labor hoarding, etc.) fits the data fairly well, but produces extremely unstable parameter estimates over the relatively short time period which I am studying. The estimates imply that adjustment costs rose between the earlier (1972 to 1979) and later periods (1976 to 1983), so that the response of firm employment to surprises in optimal size is somewhat dampened in the later sample.

IV. CORRECTING FOR SAMPLE ATTRITION

In obtaining the previous time series results, I used a balanced sample of firms, ignoring the possible biases introduced by entry into and exit from the sample during the time period. In this section I explore the consequences of sample attrition on the estimates of a growth equation. My sample is drawn from the universe of Compustat firms in 1976. Hence there is selection in both directions: small, fast-growing firms may exist in 1976 but not in 1972, and

[6] This can be shown in the same way we showed the equivalence of (4) and (5). Since the order of the AR part is the same, $\alpha = \lambda$, and we have

$$2\sigma_w^2 + (1-\alpha)^2\sigma_u^2 = \sigma_\varepsilon^2(1+\mu^2)$$

$$\sigma_w^2 = \mu\sigma_\varepsilon^2$$

which implies

$$\sigma_u^2 = \sigma_\varepsilon^2(1-\mu)^2/(1-\alpha)^2$$

where α, μ, σ_ε^2 are the parameters of the ARMA(1, 1) model.

TABLE III
GROWTH RATE REGRESSIONS WITH SELECTION CORRECTION
1778 FIRMS

	OLS and Probit		*Sample Selection*	
	Annual Growth Rate			
Dependent Variable	*76–79*	*76–83*	*76–79*	*76–83*
Number of Firms	1551	1184	1551	1184
Intercept	5.54 (0.40)* (0.33)	1.81 (0.34) (0.29)	5.54 (**) (0.69)	1.69 (0.33) (1.05)
LogE_{76}	−1.06 (0.18) (0.18)	−0.92 (0.16) (0.15)	−1.06 (**) (0.18)	−0.91 (0.15) (0.17)
Standard Error	11.7	8.6	11.7	8.6
Dependent Variable	*Probability of Survival*			
Intercept	1.10 (0.041) (0.041)	0.352 (0.034) (0.034)	1.10 (**) (0.041)	0.352 (0.034) (0.034)
LogE_{76}	0.057 (0.021) (0.024)	0.104 (0.019) (0.019)	0.057 (**) (0.024)	0.104 (0.019) (0.020)
$\hat{\rho}$	—	—	0.0 (**) (0.204)	0.022 (0.011) (0.197)
Log of Likelihood	446.3	105.1	446.3	105.1
χ^2 *for Squared and Cubic Size Terms (DF = 4)*			60.4	32.8
LM *Test for Heteroskedasticity (DF = 2)*	60.6	43.0	60.6	43.2

* The first set of numbers in parentheses are heteroskedastic-consistent standard error estimates and the second set are ordinary estimates.

** The HS-consistent standard errors are not computable since the maximum likelihood estimate of ρ is exactly zero.

some firms exit in the years after 1976. Here I consider the consequences of exit for estimates of the growth rate-size relationship in these data.[7]

Because I wish to focus on the effects of exit conditional on a complete population of firms in the initial period, I use growth rates based in 1976 for the results in this and subsequent sections of the paper. Two periods are considered: three year growth rates from 1976 to 1979 and seven year growth rates from 1976 to 1983. The comparison allows us to obtain some idea of the stability of the results over time. All growth rates are actually measured in annual terms in order to make the coefficients comparable. The first two columns of Table III (top portion) show the results of a simple growth rate on

[7] An earlier draft of this paper considered the bias induced by entry between 1972 and 1976 using a truncated Tobit model (see, for example, Maddala [1983, pp. 176–177]), but I found the estimates to be extremely imprecise due to the fact that identification of the parameters in the selection equation come only from the probability term in the denominator of the likelihood function, so I have omitted these estimates here.

size regression using these two periods. The size coefficient is approximately the same as those in Table I, about -1.0 percent per unit change in the logarithm of employment. I now consider whether this can arise because of the attrition of smaller firms during the period.

In order to measure the growth rate, I required that data be available for the firm in both the beginning and the ending period. Even if I was able to draw a sample of firms that are representative of the population in the initial period, by the time I reached the final period, the smaller and more slowly growing firms are those most likely to have dropped out of the sample.

In concrete terms, let γ_i be the growth rate of the ith firm, and let y_i and $\tilde{y}_i$ be the initial and final period logarithm of size. Then the observed growth rate is

$$(14) \qquad \Delta y_i = \tilde{y}_i - y_i = \gamma_i + u_i$$

where u_i is an i.i.d. random variable, with $E(y_i u_i) = E(\gamma_i u_i) = 0$. The probability that a firm will survive to the end of the period so that Δy_i is observed is given by a Probit model, with the latent variable a function of such firm characteristics as industry or beginning of period size. Thus the model is a standard generalized Tobit model of the form

$$(15) \qquad \begin{aligned} \Delta y_i = y_{1i} &= X_i\beta + v_{1i} && \text{if } y_{2i} > 0 \\ y_{1i} & \quad \text{not observed} && \text{if } y_{2i} < 0 \\ y_{2i} &= Z_i\delta + v_{2i} \end{aligned}$$

with a covariance matrix

$$(16) \qquad Evv' = \begin{bmatrix} \sigma_1^2 & \rho\sigma_1 \\ & 1 \end{bmatrix}$$

where I have normalized the residual variance of the unobserved latent variable y_{2i} to be unity. A discussion of this model and its estimation by the method of maximum likelihood is given in Griliches, Hall and Hausman [1978].

It is an implication of this model that a regression run on only the observed data will have the property

$$(17) \qquad \begin{aligned} E(\Delta y_i | \Delta y_i \text{ observed}) &= X_i\beta + E(v_{1i} | \Delta y_i \text{ observed}) \\ &= X_i\beta + \rho\sigma_1 \Lambda(Z_i\delta) \end{aligned}$$

where $\Lambda(\cdot)$ denotes the inverse Mills ratio $\phi(\cdot)/\Phi(\cdot)$ and $\phi(\cdot)$ and $\Phi(\cdot)$ denote the normal density and cumulative distribution respectively. That is, if the disturbances in the two equations are positively (negatively) correlated, the estimated growth rates will be biased upward (downward). In this case, if size is a predictor of survival, then $\Lambda(Z_i\delta)$ will be higher for small firms than for large, and the bias will be correspondingly larger for these firms. Note that if the disturbances of the survival equation and the growth rate equation are uncorrelated ($\rho = 0$), no bias will result even though size may still be a predictor of survival.

In the last two columns of Table III I present the results of estimation of the growth rate equations for the two periods 1976–1979 and 1976–1983 using maximum likelihood estimation of the sample selection model (the model described by equations (15) and (16)). In neither period was the sample selection correction significant; the estimated ρ is essentially zero, and the coefficients do not change between the ordinary least squares and sample selection estimates. In the case of the first period, the selection model is close to being unidentified since ρ is zero and the standard errors are not really computable. The bottom half of the table shows the estimates for the equation describing the probability of survival. We can see that survival is significantly positively related to size (a t-statistic of about 5 in column 2, for example), but because the estimated ρ is zero, this does not bias the coefficients of the growth rate equation. What this means is that the variation in growth rates across firms which remains after controlling for size is uncorrelated with the probability of survival. Big surprises in growth rates, either positive or negative, do not seem to be related to survival, at least in a way that is detectable when we look at the entire manufacturing sector.

I should note that the lack of correlation between the survival and growth rate equations holds even though I have excluded a quadratic size term from the model, so that the spurious collinearity with a Mills ratio term that the inclusion of powers of size might induce is not the problem.[8] In the table I show the $\chi^2(4)$ statistic for the inclusion of quadratic and cubic terms in both equations in the presence of correlated sample selection. There is evidence of nonlinearity in the relationship of growth and size, and in the next section I attempt to disentangle this nonlinearity from size-related heteroskedasticity coupled with sample selection.

I note in passing that adding industry dummies improved the explanatory power of the survival equation (from 76 percent correct to 84 percent correct) but did not change the size coefficient in the growth rate equation very much. The conclusion is that selection bias of this simple kind does not seem to account for the negative relationship between growth and size.

V. CORRECTING FOR HETEROSKEDASTICITY

It is well known that estimates of limited dependent variable models are not robust to departures from normality or heteroskedasticity of the disturbances.

[8] Because the variables in the growth rate equation and the survival equation are the same, the Mills' ratio term shown in equation (17) is just a nonlinear function of the X_i's (size). If a quadratic size term is included in the growth rate regression, then the estimated ρ might be insignificant even though there was selection; this would happen because the Mills' ratio was collinear with size and size squared. See Griliches, Hall and Hausman [1978] or Maddala [1983, p. 271], for a further discussion of this point.

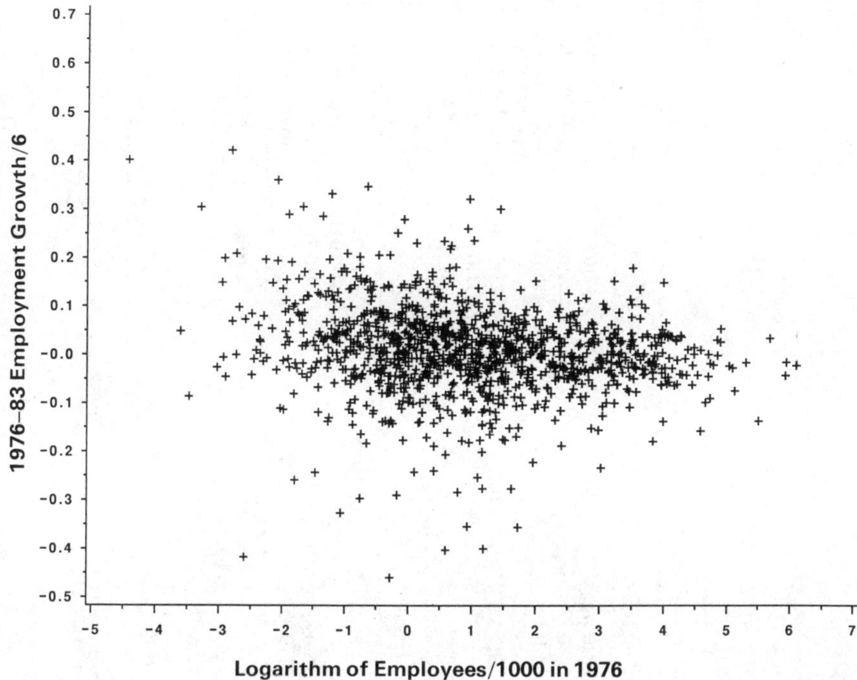

Figure 1
1976–1983 Growth Rate versus Size in 1976.

This seems likely to be a problem here from the evidence of the plot in Figure 1, which suggests that the variance of growth rates is size-related. To check this, I use a version of a Lagrange Multiplier test due to Poirier and Rudd [1983] in order to test for heteroskedasticity in the generalized Tobit model. This test consists of regressing a function of the squared residuals and the estimated correlation coefficient from the sample selection model on the variables of the model. The value of the test statistic when the heteroskedasticity is modelled as a function of size and size squared is shown in columns 3 and 4 of Table III.[9] The null hypothesis of homoskedasticity is decisively rejected in favor of size-related heteroskedasticity.

If I were willing to maintain that the error in the selection (survival) equation was homoskedastic and normally distributed, it would be possible to compute consistent estimates of the coefficients of the growth equation and their standard errors by including the estimated Mills ratio in the regression

[9] The test statistic is almost the same as that given in the first two columns, which is not surprising given the low estimated value of ρ. We would not generally expect the statistics to be the same if ρ were significantly different from zero, however.

TABLE IV
GROWTH RATE REGRESSIONS WITH CORRECTIONS FOR HETEROSKEDASTICITY AND SELECTION
1778 FIRMS

	Annual Growth Rate					
Dependent Variable	*76–79*	*76–79*	*76–79*	*76–83*	*76–83*	*76–83*
Intercept	4.51 (0.45)	6.79 (0.45)	5.73 (0.76)	0.19 (0.49)	6.37 (0.57)	6.15 (0.64)
$\text{Log}E_{76}$	−0.53 (0.16)	−1.52 (0.29)	−1.54 (0.29)	−0.48 (0.14)	−2.12 (0.30)	−2.08 (0.30)
$(\text{Log}E_{76})^2$		0.16 (0.07)	0.64 (0.14)		0.16 (0.07)	0.26 (0.16)
$(\text{Log}E_{76})^3$			−0.10 (0.03)			−0.03 (0.03)
Slope ($E = 700$)	−0.53 (0.16)	−1.64 (0.35)	−2.03 (0.37)	−0.49 (0.22)	−2.23 (0.34)	−2.28 (0.35)
Slope ($E = 17\,000$)	−0.53 (0.16)	−0.78 (0.20)	−0.14 (0.29)	−0.49 (0.22)	−1.39 (0.21)	−1.27 (0.26)
Standard Error (Wtd.)	10.7	11.1	10.9	8.32	9.65	9.62
Dependent Variable	*Probability of Survival*					
Intercept	1.26 (0.05)	1.22 (0.05)	1.26 (0.06)	0.35 (0.04)	0.33 (0.04)	0.33 (0.05)
$\text{Log}E_{76}$	−0.95 (0.02)	−0.27 (0.05)	−0.28 (0.05)	0.07 (0.02)	−0.04 (0.03)	−0.04 (0.04)
$(\text{Log}E_{76})^2$		0.07 (0.02)	0.04 (0.03)		0.04 (0.01)	0.04 (0.02)
$(\text{Log}E_{76})^3$			0.005 (0.007)			0.0001 (0.005)
$\hat{\rho}$	0.16 (0.10)	−0.50 (0.11)	−0.41 (0.22)	0.22 (0.08)	−0.74 (0.06)	−0.73 (0.06)
Log Likelihood	603.2	619.7	625.6	168.9	188.9	189.3
LM *Test for Heteroskedasticity* ($DF = 2$)	0.17	0.07	0.08	2.17	1.85	1.95

All standard error estimates are heteroskedastic-consistent estimates; they are the same as the conventional estimates to two digits.
The weights are inversely proportional to size and size squared (see the text for an explanation of the heteroskedasticity correction).

and using White's formula for heteroskedastic-consistent standard errors (Olsen [1980]). However, in spite of the fact that the probit disturbance appears to be homoskedastic, this assumption seems unwarranted here, since the selection equation itself arises from much the same process as generated the heteroskedastic disturbances in the regression equation. A more promising avenue to explore would be the modelling of the heteroskedasticity in some simple fashion depending on size.

Accordingly, I constructed a simple model for the variance σ_i^2 of the disturbances in the growth equation by regressing the estimated residuals squared on size and size squared in the initial period. A typical regression of this sort had a negative coefficient on size and a small positive coefficient on size squared. The predicted standard deviation of the growth rate disturbance fell from about 17 percent for small firms to seven percent for the larger firms. I assumed that the heteroskedasticity in the selection equation is proportional to that in the growth equation, and used these estimated σ_i^2 as weights in both equations to induce approximate homoskedasticity of the disturbances. Note that this procedure performs the estimation of the model in two stages, and the maximum likelihood estimates are no longer fully efficient, but are conditional on the model chosen for σ_i^2. It would be possible, but difficult due to the high nonlinearity involved, to estimate this new model by maximum likelihood by including the model for σ_i^2 explicitly in the denominator of the residual functions, but I have chosen not to do this in order to simplify the estimation.

The results of this procedure are shown in Table IV. Focusing for the moment on columns 1 and 4, which are comparable to the sample selection estimates in the previous table, we can see that the size coefficient has fallen by one half, and the estimate of ρ is now positive, but insignificant. The LM test for heteroskedasticity of the disturbances of the weighted model no longer rejects after the weighting has been performed. However, the results now show that size has an opposite effect on the probability of survival during the two periods, which seems highly unlikely, given that one sample is a subset of the other. This turns out to be due to a combination of the weighting scheme used and the nonlinearity of the probit index with respect to size; it shows how sensitive this type of estimate can be to weighting.

Because of this problem and because my goal in performing this test in the sample selection setting was to sort out the different effects of size-related heteroskedasticity, size-related sample attrition, and nonlinearity in the relationship of growth and size, in the other columns of Table IV I present estimates of the growth rate equation with quadratic and cubic size terms. Note first that the LM test statistic is still insignificant, so heteroskedasticity of a size-related kind is not a problem here. In the growth equation, the quadratic term is significant in both periods, and the cubic term is significant only in the first. The estimates for the probit equation imply a probability of survival which is roughly constant (about 0.88 in 1979 and 0.65

in 1983) until a size of around 10 000 employees and then rises fairly quickly to near one. This is consistent with the observed survival rates.

In both periods, the estimated ρ is quite negative. The fact that the estimate of ρ is robust to the order of the polynomial expansion of the size equation is evidence that the Mills ratio term is not simply proxying for some higher order function of size (in fact, a quartic does not enter the growth equation significantly in the presence of quadratic and cubic terms). However, a negative correlation between the disturbances of the growth equation and the survival equation does call into question the basis for my original model of exit from the sample, since it seems to imply that firms that grow faster than predicted by their size are more likely to exit from the sample, holding size constant. I will explore this puzzle further in the next section when I look at the reasons for exit from the sample.

VI. SAMPLE ATTRITION AS A FUNCTION OF TOBIN'S Q

The preceding discussion highlights a problem with the generalized Tobit approach to sample selection correction. Many previous researchers have pointed out that in the absence of exclusion restrictions in the selection equation the identification in such sample selection models comes through the nonlinearity of the Mills' ratio—i.e., the exact functional form of the disturbance distribution function (see, e.g., Bound *et al.* [1984], or Maddala [1983]). In principle, as we add higher order terms to the regression equation, these terms become increasingly collinear with the Mills ratio variable, which itself can be approximated by a polynomial expansion in the Z's. When there are additional variables in the selection equation, this collinearity disappears and it becomes possible to include nonlinear terms without necessarily having them proxy for the selection bias correction.

However, when correcting for selection related to size in a growth equation, it is extremely difficult to think of variables which belong in an equation describing the probability of survival, but not in the growth equation. One possible avenue to pursue is a more explicit modelling of the reasons for exit, about which we have some information. Of the 1778 firms in 1976, 225 exit from the sample by 1979 and another 369 exit by 1983. Both Compustat and the CRSP files (which include many but not all of these firms) contain a code giving the reason for deletion when the data for the firm is removed from the file. Using these codes, Addanki [1985] and I, in parallel work, were able to establish that approximately sixty percent of the firms were dropped due to merger or acquisition, eight percent because of bankruptcy or liquidation, and the remainder for reasons unknown. The last category includes smaller firms, many of which were probably acquired.

We hypothesize that a firm will be acquired and disappear from the sample when the existing assets of the firm are not being employed in an optimal way; a prospective buyer is willing to buy the firm at the current stock price in the hopes of producing an above average return on the stock by redeploying the assets in some way. That is, the probability of a firm's being acquired is a function of the average Tobin's Q for the firm, the ratio of the market value to the book value of the assets. The market value is assumed to be the current capitalized value of the future earnings potential of the firm's assets. The higher is Q, the less likely that the firm will be acquired and disappear from our sample. This is a fairly crude story, which leaves unexplained why the market is undervaluing the assets in this way; it simply posits that if they are undervalued, an opportunity exists for a potential purchaser. Of course, if the stock market is perfectly efficient, the Q for these firms should be driven up on the expectation that they will be acquired in the future. Therefore it is somewhat surprising that this variable turns out to be a fairly good predictor of survival, somewhat better than the pure size variable we have been using.

The assets of a firm include more than the physical assets; in particular, we are interested in the value of the assets represented by the firm's technological position, or knowledge stock, as proxied by its R & D history. Thus we would like to use a Q variable that contains a measure of R & D stock as well as physical capital in the denominator. Following Hayashi [1982], Wildasin [1984] has shown that the market value of a firm that maximizes discounted cash flow using more than one stock of capital is given by a weighted sum of the value of the capital stocks:

$$V = \sum_{i=1}^{n} \lambda_i K_i \tag{18}$$

where K_i are the capital stocks in physical units and the λ_i are the shadow prices of these stocks, which depend on taxes, depreciation, and adjustment costs and are not necessarily equal over different kinds of stocks. Unfortunately, we do not have a measure of these shadow prices, so we do not know how to weight the physical assets and R & D stock appropriately in computing Q. Denoting the physical assets by A and the knowledge stock by R, we can write Q as

$$Q = \frac{V}{\lambda_1 A + \lambda_2 R} = \frac{V}{\lambda_1 A}\left(\frac{1}{1+\gamma R/A}\right) \tag{19}$$

where γ is the ratio of the two shadow prices. Because the measured Q variable in these data exhibits a very longtailed distribution, which tends to give extreme weight to a few outliers, I chose to use the logarithm of the variable in the selection equation, so that the variable becomes

$$\log Q \approx \log(V/A) - \log(1+\gamma(R/A)) \tag{20}$$

I approximate $\log(1+\gamma(R/A))$ by $\gamma(R/A)$ since I expect $\gamma(R/A)$ to be small, so that the variables actually used in the selection equation are $\log(V/A)$ and R/A. Firms with no R & D program have an R/A stock equal to zero; the inclusion of a separate dummy for these firms in the selecting equation had no effect on the results. Because of work by Addanki [1985], who found that the valuation of a firm's R & D program at the time of acquisition differed depending on whether a firm was a patenter, I allowed for a separate coefficient on R/A for those firms that filed successful patent applications in 1976.

As a measure of the Q of physical assets, V/A, I use the total market value of the firm (common stock, debt, and preferred stock) divided by the sum of net capital stock, inventories, and other assets (including subsidiaries). The value of the components of both V and A have been adjusted for the effects of inflation using the methodology of Brainard, Shoven, and Weiss [1980]; the computations are more fully described in Cummins, Hall, Laderman, and Mundy [1984].[10]

The estimates for a probability of survival equation using these variables are shown in Table V, along with growth rate equations augmented by the two investment variables (these will be discussed later). What the probit equations show is that both the V/A and R/A variables are more important in predicting survival than the raw size variable, employment, although the R/A variable has a large standard error.[11] At the sample means these estimates imply that a doubling of employment increases the probability of survival to 1983 by 0.03, a doubling of Q increases the probability 0.10, and a doubling of R & D increases it 0.03 for non-patenters and 0.01 for patenters, *ceteris paribus.* Firms with a larger portion of their assets in R & D are less likely to disappear from the sample, while having patents makes them somewhat more likely to exit than firms with R & D and no patents. This last result is consistent with Addanki [1985], who found that the R & D expenditures of firms that have a record of patenting are more highly valued than those of firms that hold no patents.

The use of these variables to help predict the probability of survival has had some effect on the estimates of the growth rate equation. The size coefficient has increased substantially in absolute value over the estimates in columns 1 and 4 of Table IV, and the estimated correlation between the residuals of the selection equation and the growth rate equation is quite negative. The results are not sensitive to the exact specification of the selection equation. Inclusion of the Q variable as a predictor seems to be enough to produce a rather anomalous result: a firm that grows faster than predicted by its size and level of investment is somewhat *more* likely to exit from the sample, controlling for size and Q. This implies that the average

[10] For comparison, I also used an unadjusted Q based solely on the raw numbers on the Compustat files. In 1976, the value of this Q was lower, and the dispersion less. The qualitative results of the Probit equation were unchanged, and the coefficients were more significant, suggesting that the process of adjusting for inflation bias also introduces more measurement error into the variable.

[11] The other variables in the growth equation were also included in the selection equation, but they had insignificant coefficients so the estimates reported do not include them.

growth rate for the smaller firms is underestimated and hence that the size coefficient in the growth rate equation is biased towards zero when we do not correct for selection.

VII. INVESTMENT AND FIRM GROWTH

This section reports on some descriptive regressions that relate the firm growth rates to the level of investment, both physical and R & D, in 1976. These results reported in this section are in no sense derived from a structural model; we are merely documenting the magnitude of the correlation between investment and growth in the manufacturing sector.

In Table V we have added three variables to the standard growth rate equation: the logarithm of capital expenditures in 1976, the logarithm of R & D investment in 1976, and a dummy equal to one for those firms who do no or negligible R & D. Both of the expenditure variables have been scaled by

TABLE V
GROWTH RATE REGRESSIONS WITH Q
1753 FIRMS

	OLS and Probit		*Sample Selection*	
	Annual Growth Rate			
Dependent Variable	*76–79*	*76–83*	*76–79*	*76–83*
Number of Firms	1529	1171	1529	1171
Intercept	6.68 (0.46)	2.59 (0.38)	8.38 (0.51)	6.78 (0.44)
$\text{Log}E_{76}$	−1.08 (0.16)	−1.14 (0.13)	−1.46 (0.18)	−1.94 (0.15)
$\text{Log}(I/E)_{76}$	1.26 (0.28)	1.22 (0.24)	1.41 (0.29)	1.36 (0.24)
$\text{Log}(R/E)_{76}$	1.31 (0.35)	1.33 (0.20)	1.26 (0.35)	1.09 (0.23)
$D(R = 0)$	−3.50 (0.62)	−2.30 (0.53)	−2.71 (0.63)	−0.80 (0.51)
Standard Error (Wtd.)	10.3	7.74	11.0	9.32
	Probability of Survival			
Dependent Variable	*1979*	*1983*	*1979*	*1983*
Intercept	1.18 (0.06)	0.26 (0.05)	1.10 (0.06)	0.20 (0.04)
$\text{Log}E_{76}$	−0.09 (0.02)	0.08 (0.02)	−0.06 (0.03)	0.08 (0.02)
$\text{Log}Q_{76}$	0.17 (0.07)	0.29 (0.05)	0.25 (0.07)	0.36 (0.04)
$(R/A)_{76} \cdot (Patents = 0)$	0.28 (0.49)	0.29 (0.41)	0.82 (0.52)	0.61 (0.36)
$(R/A)_{76} \cdot (Patents > 0)$	0.26 (0.42)	0.16 (0.35)	0.37 (0.34)	0.37 (0.35)
$\hat{\rho}$	—	—	−0.61 (0.09)	−0.81 (0.03)
Log Likelihood	631.3	269.2	646.2	306.9
LM *Test for Heteroskedasticity* $(DF = 4)$			20.6	0.43

All standard error estimates are heteroskedastic-consistent estimates.
Estimates are obtained by maximum likelihood of the sample selection model with the disturbances weighted to correct for heteroskedasticity.

subtracting the logarithm of 1976 employment so that the total size effect still appears in the coefficient of $\log E_{76}$. The investment coefficients are quite substantial: at the mean level of investment for these firms, an increase of four million dollars in physical investment is associated with a one percent increase in the annual growth rate from 1976 to 1979, while it takes only two million dollars of R & D investment to achieve the same effect for those firms which have R & D programs. In the second period the effects are the same, which implies considerable persistence in the correlation of growth and investment. Firms that have no R & D program grow on average about one to two percent more slowly than those which do.

Earlier work in this area (Mansfield [1962] and Hymer and Pashigian [1962]) found that two results seem to hold when firm growth is examined over a large size range of firms: (1) the variance (in logarithms) is larger at the lower end of the size distribution, and (2) Gibrat's Law is closer to holding for large firms than for small. We have already seen that the first result holds in

TABLE VI
GROWTH RATE REGRESSIONS BY FIRM SIZE

	Small Firms ($N = 1023$)		*Large Firms* ($N = 730$)	
	Annual Growth Rate			
Dependent Variable	*76–79*	*76–83*	*76–79*	*76–83*
Number of Firms	832	604	697	567
Intercept	9.11 (0.63)	7.27 (0.61)	6.92 (0.96)	6.07 (0.93)
$\text{Log}E_{76}$	−1.58 (0.56)	−1.49 (0.49)	−0.94 (0.30)	−1.76 (0.28)
$\text{Log}(I/E)_{76}$	2.74 (0.43)	1.46 (0.38)	0.86 (0.33)	1.20 (0.30)
$\text{Log}(R/E)_{76}$	2.39 (0.38)	1.27 (0.37)	1.01 (0.35)	0.84 (0.27)
$D(R = 0)$	−4.13 (0.88)	−1.72 (0.77)	−1.48 (0.81)	0.32 (0.68)
Standard Error (*Wtd.*)	11.6	6.59	7.50	5.63
	Probability of Survival			
Dependent Variable	*1979*	*1983*	*1979*	*1983*
Intercept	1.05 (0.07)	0.30 (0.07)	1.13 (0.17)	0.11 (0.18)
$\text{Log}E_{76}$	−0.19 (0.08)	−0.005 (0.08)	0.10 (0.07)	0.20 (0.07)
$\text{Log}Q_{76}$	0.16 (0.08)	0.38 (0.08)	0.56 (0.13)	0.75 (0.11)
$(R/A)_{76} \cdot (Patents = 0)$	1.48 (0.91)	1.07 (0.55)	−5.75 (2.52)	−4.05 (2.83)
$(R/A)_{76} \cdot (Patents > 0)$	0.45 (0.37)	0.52 (0.54)	−1.6 (0.97)	0.05 (0.93)
$\hat{\rho}$	−0.77 (0.06)	−0.80 (0.05)	−0.57 (0.10)	−0.83 (0.05)
Log Likelihood	313.0	292.9	593.4	507.8
LM *Test for Heteroskedasticity* ($DF = 4$)	0.60	0.05	0.49	1.97

All standard errors are heteroskedastic-consistent estimates.

Estimates are obtained by maximum likelihood of the sample selection model with the disturbances weighted to correct for heteroskedasticity.

this sample and the nonlinear estimates in Table IV suggest that the second one probably holds as well. To check this result I divided the sample into two size classes and reestimated the equations in Table V. The size cut I chose was 2500 employees in 1976. The median number of employees in 1976 is 2300 and the geometric mean is 2700 (based on the 1349 firms that survive from 1972 to 1979), so there are roughly equal numbers in each class for the observed samples.

A summary of the results for these two size classes is presented in Table VI; these estimates are also computed with corrections for heteroskedasticity and sample selection. The results for the larger firms are not especially different from those for the smaller firms, although they are somewhat attenuated. A noteworthy feature of the estimates is the substantial difference in the variance of the growth rates across the two samples: in 1979, the ratio of the mean variances (after weighting by weights normalized to be unity on the average) is about 0.4. The estimated investment coefficients are not that different from those for the whole sample, although they have larger standard errors. The finding that a dollar of R & D expenditures is a more important predictor of growth in the immediate future than is a dollar of expenditure on physical capital is robust across size classes: the ratio of the amount required to obtain an increase in annual growth rates of one percent is 1.6 for the smaller firms and three for the larger firms.

I can imagine two different interpretations of this finding. First, R & D might be more highly correlated with future success of the firm, both because it is (possibly) more forward looking, and because R & D expenditures at the firm level tend to be substantially less volatile over time than expenditures on physical capital (Hall, Griliches, and Hausman [1986]). Second, the actual rate of return to R & D expenditures may simply be higher than that to capital expenditures for the usual reason that such expenditures have more non-diversifiable risk, and investors require a higher return for holding the stock of R & D-intensive firms. There is room here for further work.

VIII. CONCLUSION

The goal of this paper was to investigate several econometric explanations that have been suggested for the finding of a negative correlation between firm size and growth and to lay some groundwork for a more careful modelling of firm dynamics. With respect to the size-growth relationship, we have negative results in the sense that neither measurement error in employment nor sample attrition can account for the negative coefficient on firm size in the growth rate equation. There are large random changes in employment at any one firm from year to year, but these changes are largely permanent and do not reflect a non-serially correlated measurement error. Substantial differences in the variance of growth rates across size classes was also observed with smaller firms having a variance at least twice as large.

With qualifications due to the difficulty of constructing an adequate model of sample attrition, it does appear that the smaller firms in the sample grow faster, with a four percentage point difference in annual growth rates between firms in the 25th and 75th percentiles in size. Because of the large element of randomness in growth rates across firms from year to year, however, this difference is not enough to cause firms to move very far in the size distribution over a ten year period.

On the whole, correcting for attrition bias had very little effect on these results; this should give us some confidence that further research on this type of panel of firms can be done, at least over fairly short time periods, without fear of large biases in the results due to those firms that exit from the sample. It needs to be emphasized that this conclusion applies to this particular set of firms, and will not necessarily hold true for firms in a very different sector or size range.

I have also found that the obvious systematic differences among firms, such as industry and the level of investment, do very little to reduce the variance of growth rates. The best I could do was a reduction in the standard error from 12.6 percent to 12.1 percent (this conclusion is based on the unweighted data, since it is difficult to interpret the standard error after weighting). At the firm level, year-to-year growth rates in employment are largely unpredictable by past characteristics of the firm.

BRONWYN H. HALL,
Department of Economics,
Stanford University,
Stanford, CA 94305,
USA.

REFERENCES

ADDANKI, SUMANTH, 1985, National Bureau of Economic Research. Mimeo.

AMEMIYA, TAKESHI, 1984, 'Tobit Models: A Survey', *Journal of Econometrics*, 24, pp. 3–61.

AMERICAN BAR ASSOCIATION, 1968, *Selected Articles on Federal Securities Laws* (R. R. Donnelly & Sons, Chicago).

ANDERSON, T. W. and HSIAO, C., 1981, 'Estimation of Dynamic Models with Error Components', *Journal of American Statistical Association*, 76, pp. 598–606.

ARMINGTON, CATHERINE and ODLE, MARJORIE, 1982, 'Sources of Job Growth: A New Look at the Small Business Role', *Economic Development Commentary*, 6, no. 3.

BOUND, J., CUMMINS, C., GRILICHES, Z., HALL, B. H. and JAFFE, A., 1984, 'Who Does R&D and Who Patents?', in Z. GRILICHES (ed.), *R&D, Patents, and Productivity* (University of Chicago Press, Chicago).

BRAINARD, W., SHOVEN, J. and WEISS, L., 1980, 'The Financial Valuation of the Return to Capital', *Brookings Papers on Economic Activity*, 2.

BROCK, WILLIAM A. and EVANS, DAVID S., 1986, *The Economics of Small Businesses: Their Role and Regulation in the U.S. Economy* (Holmes and Meier, New York).

BUREAU OF LABOR STATISTICS, 1980, *Handbook of Labor Statistics*, United States Government Printing Office, Washington, DC, Bulletin 2070.

CUMMINS, C., HALL, B. H., LADERMAN, ELIZABETH and MUNDY, JOY, 1984, 'The R & D Master File: Documentation', National Bureau of Economic Research. Mimeo.

EVANS, DAVID S., 1985, 'The Relationship between Firm Size, Growth, and Age: U.S. Manufacturing 1976–1982', Fordham University and CERA. Mimeo.

FRIEDMAN, STANLEY J., 1977, *SEC Reporting Requirements* (Practicing Law Institute, New York, NY).

GREENE, RICHARD, 1982, 'Tracking Job Growth in Private Industry', *Monthly Labor Review*, September.

GRILICHES, ZVI, 1981, 'Market Value, R & D, and Patents', *Economic Letters*, 7.

GRILICHES, ZVI and MAIRESSE, JACQUES, 1981, 'Productivity and R & D at the Firm Level', National Bureau of Economic Research Working Paper No. 826.

GRILICHES, ZVI (ed.), 1984, *R & D, Patents, and Productivity*, NBER Conference Volume (University of Chicago Press, Chicago).

GRILICHES, ZVI, HALL, B. H. and HAUSMAN, J. A., 1978, 'Missing Data and Self Selection in Large Panels', *Annals de l'INSEE*, 30–31, pp. 137–176.

GRILICHES, ZVI and HAUSMAN, J. A., 1985, 'Errors in Variables in Panel Data', *Journal of Econometrics*, 31, pp. 93–118.

HALL, BRONWYN H., 1979, Revised 1986, *MOMENTS User's Manual* (TSP International, Stanford, California.)

HALL, BRONWYN H., GRILICHES, Z. and HAUSMAN, J. A., 1986, 'Patents and R & D: Is There a Lag?', *International Economic Review*, 27, pp. 265–283.

HARRIS, CANDEE, 1982, 'Methodological Differences in Job Generations Studies of David Birch and of Catherine Armington and Marjorie Odle', Brookings Institution. Mimeo.

HART, P. E. and PRAIS, S. J., 1956, 'The Analysis of Business Concentration: A Statistical Approach', *Journal of the Royal Statistical Society*, Series A, pp. 150–191.

HAYASHI, FUMIO, 1982, 'Tobin's Marginal *q* and Average *q*: A Neoclassical Interpretation', *Econometrica*, 50, pp. 213–224.

HYMER, STEPHEN and PASHIGIAN, P., 1962, 'Firm Size and Rate of Growth', *Journal of Political Economy*, 52, pp. 556–569.

JOVANOVIC, BOYAN, 1982, 'Selection and Evolution of Industry', *Econometrica*, 50, pp. 649–670.

LEONARD, JONATHAN, S., 1984, 'On the Size Distribution of Employment and Establishments', Institute of Industrial Relations, University of California at Berkeley. Mimeo.

LUCAS, ROBERT E., 1978, 'On the Size Distribution of Business Firms', *Bell Journal of Economics*, 9, pp. 508–523.

MACURDY, THOMAS E., 1981, 'Asymptotic Properties of Quasi-Maximum Likelihood Estimators and Test Statistics', National Bureau of Economic Research, Technical Paper No. 14.

MACURDY, THOMAS E., 1985, 'A Guide to Applying Time Series Models to Panel Data', Stanford University. Mimeo.

MADDALA, G. S., 1983, *Limited-dependent and Qualitative Variables in Econometrics* (Cambridge University Press, England).

MANDELBROT, BENOIT, 1963a, 'Oligopoly, Mergers, and the Paretian Size Distribution of Firms', Research Note #NC-246 (Thomas J. Watson Research Center, Yorktown Heights, NY).

MANDELBROT, BENOIT, 1963b, 'A Survey of Growth and Diffusion Models of the Law of Pareto', Research Note #NC-253 (Thomas J. Watson Research Center, Yorktown Heights, NY).

MANSFIELD, EDWIN, 1962, 'Entry, Innovation, and the Growth of Firms', *American Economic Review*, 52, pp. 1023–1051.

MARRIS, ROBIN, 1979, *The Theory and Future of the Corporate Economy and Society* (North-Holland Publishing Company, Amsterdam).

NELSON, FORREST, 1977, 'Censored Regression Models with Unobserved Stochastic Censored Thresholds', *Journal of Economics*, 6, pp. 309–322.

OLSEN, R. J., 1980, 'A Least Squares Correction for Selectivity Bias', *Econometrica*, 48, pp. 1815–1820.

PENROSE, EDITH, T., 1959, *The Theory of the Growth of the Firm* (M. E. Sharpe, Inc., White Plains, NY).

POIRIER, DALE J. and RUDD, P., 1983, 'Diagnostic Testing in Missing Data Models', *International Economic Review*, 24, pp. 537–546.

QUANDT, RICHARD E., 1966, 'On the Size Distribution of Firms', *Econometrica*, 34, pp. 416–432.

SCHERER, F. M., 1984, *Innovation and Growth: Schumpeterian Perspectives* (MIT Press, Cambridge, MA).

SCHERER, F. M., 1980, *Industrial Market Structure and Economic Performance*, 2nd ed. (Houghton Mifflin Company, Boston).

SIMON, HERBERT A. and BONINI, CHARLES P., 1958, 'The Size Distribution of Firms', *American Economic Review*, 48, pp. 607–617.

WHITE, HALBERT, 1980, 'A Heteroskedastic Consistent Covariance Matrix Estimator and a Direct Test for Heteroskedasticity', *Econometrica*, 48, pp. 817–838.

WILDASIN, DAVID E., 1984, 'The *q* Theory of Investment with Many Capital Goods', *American Economic Review*, 74, pp. 203–210.

WILLIAMSON, OLIVER E., 1975, *Markets and Hierarchies* (The Free Press, London).

EXCESS CAPACITY AS A BARRIER TO ENTRY: AN EMPIRICAL APPRAISAL*

MARVIN B. LIEBERMAN

This paper examines excess capacity barriers to entry and investment dynamics in a sample of thirty-eight chemical product industries. Logit and log-linear models of investment behavior are estimated, and specific case examples are considered. The results show that incumbents rarely built excess capacity pre-emptively in an effort to deter entry. In general, entrants and incumbents exhibited similar investment behavior.

I. INTRODUCTION

It was not inevitable that [Alcoa] should always anticipate increases in the demand for ingot and be prepared to supply them. Nothing compelled it to keep doubling and redoubling its capacity before others entered the field. It insists that it never excluded competitors; but we can think of no more effective exclusion than to progressively embrace each new opportunity as it opened, and to face every newcomer with new capacity already geared into a great organization, having the advantage of experience, trade connections and the elite of personnel.

Judge Learned Hand,
U.S. vs. Alcoa, 1945.

DOES EXCESS capacity deter entry? And if so, under what conditions is it in the interest of incumbent firms to maintain excess capacity as an entry deterrent? The potential use of excess capacity as an entry barrier has attracted considerable attention as a theoretical issue in industrial economics. However, little empirical evidence has been available. This paper examines the role of excess capacity as an entry deterrent in 38 chemical product industries over a period of more than two decades. The extensive data sample focuses primarily on industries with high fixed costs, sizeable economies of scale, and a relatively small number of producing firms—in short, industries where excess capacity should have its most potent effects, if it proves effective at all.

The paper is organized as follows. Section II surveys the literature on excess capacity as a barrier to entry. Section III describes the chemical industry sample and the variables used in the study. Section IV summarizes the data on market growth and capacity utilization rates prior to the construction of new plants by entrants and incumbent firms. The data show

* I thank Choon-Geol Moon for research assistance and valuable comments. Timothy Bresnahan and Richard Schmalensee made numerous helpful suggestions. The Strategic Management Program at the Stanford Business School provided financial support.

that in industries with "lumpier" plants, higher rates of market growth and capacity utilization were required to elicit construction of new plants. However, entrants and incumbents had comparable decision thresholds for new plant investment. This suggests the absence of strategic investment by incumbents to deter entry. In section V, the analysis is formalized as a logit model, which is estimated for new plants constructed by entrants and incumbents. In section VI, the data sample is screened to identify specific cases where incumbents may have maintained chronic excess capacity as an entry barrier. This screening uncovers few products where excess capacity appears to have been held in an effort to deter entry, and even fewer cases where it proved effective for this purpose. Conclusions are presented in section VII.

II. THEORY AND PRIOR EMPIRICAL EVIDENCE

Recent theoretical work in industrial organization offers a rich set of predictions on the role of excess capacity in entry deterrence. However, empirical documentation has been quite sparse. The primary purpose of this study and related work (Lieberman [1986], Gilbert and Lieberman [1987]) is to assess the frequency with which the behaviors identified in theory actually arise in practice.

Firms may construct excess capacity for both strategic and non-strategic reasons. Profit-maximizing firms hold non-strategic excess capacity in markets where demand is cyclical or stochastic, or where plants are inherently lumpy or subject to economies of scale. Optimal excess capacity increases with demand variabilty under a range of structural conditions including monopoly (Smith [1969, 1970]) and perfect competition (Sheshinski and Dreze [1976]). If plants are lumpy, temporary excess capacity normally arises after new plants are constructed, particularly if prices are not completely flexible (Manne [1961], Freidenfelds [1981]). If more than one production technology is available, plants with low fixed but high variable costs may be held in reserve to serve periods of peak demand. Lieberman [1985] shows that in the chemical industry, variations in capacity utilization across products and over time stem largely from these non-strategic motives. The maintained hypothesis of this paper is that excess capacity is non-strategic in nature.

Strategic excess capacity may be built either to deter new entry or to pre-empt existing rivals. The basic entry deterrence argument (Wenders [1971], Spence [1977], Salop [1979], Eaton and Lipsey [1979], Spulber [1981], Perrakis and Warskett [1983], Lyons [1986]) is that excess capacity enables incumbents to threaten to expand output and cut prices following entry, thereby making entry unprofitable. Deterrence is achieved by intensifying the post-entry competition anticipated by the entrant. This hypothesis, that excess capacity is held by incumbents *prior* to announced entry, is the primary strategic hypothesis examined in this paper.

Several theoretical objections to this "pre-entry excess capacity" hypothesis have been raised. Dixit [1980] argues that under linear demand and cost conditions, it is not in the interest of incumbents to increase output following entry. However, Bulow, *et al.* [1985a], [1985b] show that under alternative demand assumptions it proves rational for incumbents to expand output following entry, thereby utilizing available excess capacity.

A second critique of the excess capacity argument is that when there is more than one incumbent, "free-rider" problems may reduce the incentives of incumbents to hold excess capacity, which is in effect a public good (Waldman [1983], McLean and Riordan [1985]). However, other work suggests that these free-rider problems may not be serious, or may be counterbalanced by various incentives (Gilbert and Vives [1986], Eaton and Ware [1985], Waldman [1987]). Kirman and Masson [1986] show that excess capacity may actually prove more effective as an entry deterrent when the industry is structured as a loose oligopoly, since this increases the risk that collusive pricing agreements will unravel if entry occurs.

Market growth and depreciating capital both reduce the potency of excess capacity as an entry barrier. If capital has a limited life, this shortens the post-entry period over which excess capacity can be used, thereby reducing the magnitude of the deterrent (Eaton and Lipsey [1980], [1981]). Similarly, steady demand growth erodes existing excess capacity, unless replenished by additional investment. If growth is rapid and new plants have a long construction lead time, by the date the entrant's plant is completed, excess capacity may have fallen well below its original level. Moreover, if demand growth is stochastic, a large, unanticipated upward shift in demand can absorb the excess capacity held by incumbents, thereby creating a window for new entry.

Available empirical evidence on the excess capacity hypothesis is extremely limited. Hilke [1984] regressed entry rates on excess capacity and other variables for a 16 industry sample. The excess capacity coefficient proved negative, but insignificant at standard statistical levels. Respondents to an industry questionnaire survey by Smiley [1986] indicated that excess production capacity was the least frequently chosen of a number of alternative entry deterrence strategies in industries with mature products.

Capacity built by incumbents *after* the announcement of entry may also serve entry-deterrence objectives. If incumbents have a shorter construction lead time than entrants (e.g., incumbents can expand existing plant facilities more rapidly than an entrant can build a new plant) such behavior may be equivalent to (but less costly than) excess capacity held in advance of a specific entry threat. Even if initial entry occurs, by responding aggressively, incumbents may be able to establish a predatory reputation sufficient to deter further entry (Williamson [1977], Kreps and Wilson [1982], Milgrom and

Roberts [1982]), or to deter continued growth of the entrant (Caves and Porter [1977], Fudenberg and Tirole [1983], Spence [1979]). Lieberman [1986] gives empirical evidence that such post-entry investment and pricing responses were common in concentrated markets in the chemical industry sample.

A final motive for strategic excess capacity is to pre-empt existing rivals. In growing markets, firms that make early investments may be able to deter rivals from expanding, thereby gaining an increased share of industry output and profits (Porter and Spence [1982], Ghemawat [1984], Reynolds [1986], Gilbert and Lieberman [1987]). Alternatively, pre-emptive expansion may provide a signalling mechanism which helps to coordinate industry investment behavior (Smith [1981]).

Whether market growth is captured by entrants or incumbents depends on the rate at which profit declines with the number of firms, and the magnitude of incumbent adjustment costs relative to fixed costs of entry (Hause and DuRietz [1984], Nakao [1980]). Unfortunately, adjustment and entry costs are normally unobservable in practice. In general, however, empirical studies have shown a strong link between industry demand-growth and entry (e.g., Orr [1974], Duetsch [1984], Hause and DuRietz [1984]).[1]

III. DATA SAMPLE AND COMPUTATION OF VARIABLES

The data sample covers the 38 chemical products listed in Table I. There are approximately 20 years of coverage for each product. The starting year varies by product as shown in Table I; the last full year of coverage is 1982.[2]

The chemical product industries included in the sample bear more than a passing resemblance to the stylized industries of economic theory. All products in the sample are homogeneous and undifferentiated.[3] Production capacities are well defined; chemicals with production processes involving significant joint products have been excluded, as have those where production capacity can be switched from one product to another in response to shifts in market demand. Unit variable costs for any given plant tend to be relatively constant up to the level defined by its full production capacity. However, plants for a given product may differ in operating costs, reflecting differences in technology and age of plant.

Output was often consumed captively in firms' downstream operations, but for all products at least 25 percent of industry output was sold through

[1] For a survey of the empirical entry literature, see Geroski [1983].

[2] The basic data include production capacity by product, plant, firm and year, and total industry output for each product and year. The capacity data are primarily from annual issues of the *Directory of Chemical Producers*, published by SRI International. The output data are from various US government sources, including *Synthetic Organic Chemicals*, *Current Industrial Reports*, and *Minerals Yearbook*. These sources are described in detail in Lieberman [1982].

[3] A few products such as polyethylene and polyester fibers are slightly differentiated across producers.

arms-length channels. Also, all products in the sample had positive net output growth from the earliest year of coverage through at least 1975. Thus,

TABLE I
PRODUCTS INCLUDED IN DATA SAMPLE

Product Name	*Coverage Period*	*Average Number of Firms**	*Average Number of Plants**	*Number of New Plants Constructed by:*	
				*Entrants***	*Incumbents***
Organical Chemicals					
Acrylonitrile	1956–82	5	6	2	3
Aniline	1961–82	5	7	4	1
Bisphenol A	1959–82	4	5	3	2
Caprolactam	1962–82	3	3	2	0
Carbon Disulfide	1963–82	4	5	0	0
Cyclohexane	1956–82	8	10	14	3
Ethanolamines	1955–82	5	6	0	1
Ethylene	1960–82	23	36	9	10
Ethylene Glycol	1960–82	12	15	5	5
Formaldehyde	1962–82	16	46	4	31
Isopropyl Alcohol	1964–82	4	5	1	1
Maleic Anhydride	1958–82	7	8	6	2
Methanol	1957–82	10	13	4	6
Methyl Methacrylate	1966–82	3	5	0	1
Neoprene Rubber	1960–82	2	3	1	1
Pentaerythritol	1952–82	5	6	4	2
Phenol	1959–82	11	14	7	8
Phthalic Anhydride	1955–82	10	14	8	8
Polyethylene-LD	1957–82	12	19	7	10
Polyethylene-HD	1957–82	12	14	7	7
Sorbitol	1955–82	4	4	2	1
Styrene	1958–82	11	13	7	4
1,1,1-Trichloroethane	1966–82	3	4	1	1
Urea	1960–82	31	40	26	24
Vinyl Acetate	1960–82	6	7	4	4
Vinyl Chloride	1962–82	11	15	6	5
Inorganic Chemicals					
Ammonia	1960–82	56	84	28	40
Carbon Black	1964–82	8	31	3	7
Hydrofluoric Acid	1962–82	8	12	0	2
Sodium	1957–82	3	5	0	0
Sodium Chlorate	1956–82	8	11	10	5
Sodium Hydrosulfite	1964–82	5	6	1	4
Titanium Dioxide	1964–82	6	13	0	5
Synthetic Fibers					
Acrylic Fibers	1953–82	5	6	3	1
Nylon Fibers	1960–82	15	24	18	6
Polyester Fibers	1954–82	10	15	18	12
Metals					
Aluminum	1956–82	9	27	9	6
Magnesium	1954–82	3	4	4	0

* Rounded to nearest integer.
** Excludes first three years of coverage period.

the sample represents products with growing demand, although in a few cases output declined after 1975.

While the sample products span a range of producer concentration levels, most are quite concentrated relative to typical manufacturing industries in the US. Despite high concentration and generally high fixed costs, Table I shows that over the long term, entry was seldom completely deterred—only six products show an absence of entry over the coverage period. Moreover, the table indicates that when new plants were built, they were about as likely to be constructed by new entrants as by incumbent firms.

For the statistical analysis, the detailed plant capacity data were aggregated to the industry level for each year. Variables were defined as follows:

$DENT_{i,t}$, a dummy variable set equal to 1 if new entry into product i occurred during year t;

$DINC_{i,t}$, a dummy variable set equal to 1 if one or more incumbent firms completed a new plant for product i during year t;

$DNEW_{i,t}$, a dummy variable set equal to 1 if one or more entrants or incumbents completed a new plant during year t (that is, if either $DENT_{i,t}$ or $DINC_{i,t}$ is positive);

$g_{i,t}$, the average annual growth rate of industry output for product i over the three year period between year $t-3$ and year t;

$U_{i,t}$, the average rate of industry capacity utilization for product i during year t (that is, industry output during year t, divided by the average of beginning and end of year capacity);

$N_{i,t}$, the number of plants producing product i at the start of year t;

$1/N_{i,t}$, the reciprocal of the number of plants (proxy for plant "lumpiness");

t, the last two digits of the observation year minus 1971, the mean year in the sample, and

$N/M_{i,t}$, the average number of plants per firm.

Some additional, supplementary data were collected from the trade literature on announcements of entry that were eventually cancelled or never carried out.

IV. MARKET GROWTH AND CAPACITY UTILIZATION RATES REQUIRED TO ELICIT NEW ENTRY

Rapid demand growth and high capacity utilization signal the need for investment in additional plant capacity. This section examines rates of market growth and capacity utilization that prevailed in the sample just prior to the construction of new plants by entrants and incumbents. If entrants required a higher threshold rate of market growth or capacity utilization, this

TABLE II
GROWTH RATE OF INDUSTRY OUTPUT PRIOR TO COMPLETION OF NEW PLANTS BY ENTRANTS AND INCUMBENTS*

Number of Plants Operating at Start of Year t	*All Observations*	*Observations where Entrant Completed Plant During Year t*	*Observations where Incumbent Completed Plant During Year t*
$N \leqslant 4$	8.4% (125)	15.4% (18)	19.2% (6)
$4 < N \leqslant 8$	7.5% (252)	12.3% (23)	9.7% (24)
$N > 8$	8.3% (412)	11.5% (118)	9.6% (128)

* Average annual growth rate of industry output from year $t-4$ through year $t-1$ (that is, $g_{i,t-1}$). The number of observations in each category is listed in parentheses.

is evidence that entry barriers may have been in effect, or that incumbents expanded pre-emptively at a lower threshold in an effort to deter entry.

In industries where plants are lumpy, a period of overcapacity (or price cutting) typically follows the opening of new plants. Firms that behave non-strategically might be expected to minimize this excess capacity by requiring a higher rate of market growth or capacity utilization before committing to investment in a new plant. Thus, under the maintained hypothesis, higher rates of market growth and capacity utilization would be observed prior to the construction of new plants in industries where plants are lumpy. Moreover, in the absence of strategic entry deterrence behavior, entrants and incumbents would exhibit similar thresholds for new plant investment.

Table II summarizes the data on the growth rate of output over the three-year period prior to the completion of new plants by entrants and incumbents. In the chemical industry, there is, on average, a construction lag of about two years between the date when a decision is made to construct a new plant and the date when the plant becomes operational. Thus, plants that opened in year t were committed to in year $t-2$.[4] The table shows that: (1) new plants were constructed during periods of higher than average growth; (2) relatively higher growth rates were required to elicit construction of new plants in industries with "lumpier" plants; and (3) entrants and incumbents behaved similarly. These findings are all consistent with the maintained hypothesis.

In comparing the data for entrants and incumbents it is important to recognize that even in the absence of strategic deterrence behavior their decisions to build new plants are not exactly symmetric. This is because incumbents can often expand through incremental additions to existing plant, and they may construct new plants purely as replacement investment. These two factors would bias the average growth rates shown for incumbents

[4] Inclusion of output for year $t-1$ in the growth rate assumes that firms could project industry demand accurately through at least the middle of the construction cycle.

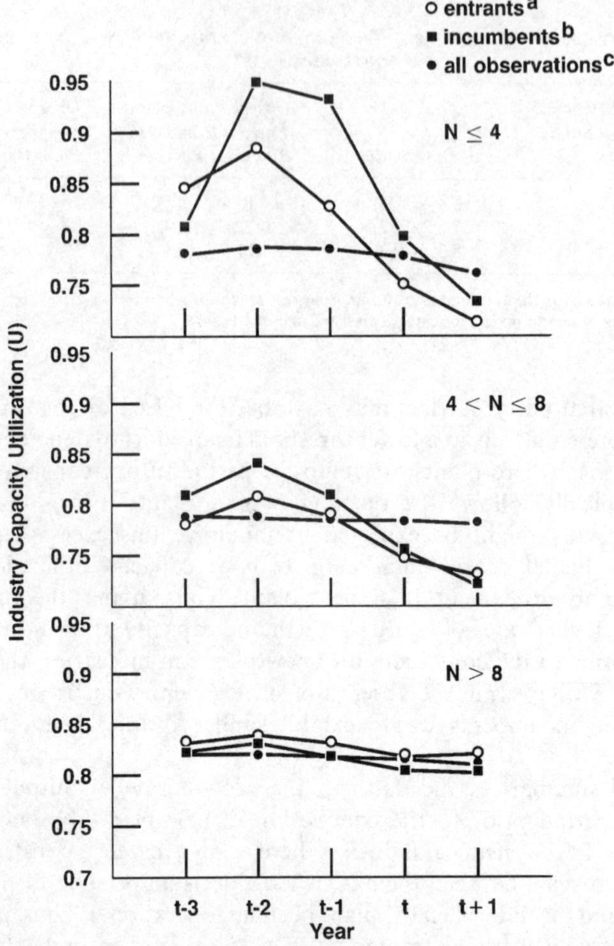

Notes: [a] Average of all industry observations where entrant completed plant during year *t*.
[b] Average of all industry observations where incumbent completed plant during year *t*.
[c] Average of all industry observations.
N equals the number of plants operating in the industry at the start of year *t*. See Table II for the number of observations in each category.

Figure 1
Relation Between Capacity Utilization and New Plant Construction by Entrants and Incumbents.

in the last column of Table II in opposite directions. The option of incremental expansion raises the threshold required by incumbents to justify construction of a lumpy new plant. The occurrence of replacement investment would lower the average growth rate shown for incumbents in Table II, since the timing of plant replacement is less sensitive to market growth. The net effect of these two influences is uncertain. Nevertheless, the table fails to show a lower expansion threshold for incumbents in highly concentrated industries ($N \leqslant 4$), where excess capacity might be expected to prove most effective as an entry deterrent.

Figure 1 traces the behavior of industry capacity utilization over a five-year period around the date when new plants were constructed. New plants became operational during year t; hence, their capacity and output are incorporated in the capacity utilization figure for half of year t and all of year $t+1$. The data show that the opening of new plants tended to depress industry capacity utilization below its mean level. This effect appears much greater in industries where plants were lumpy, as expected under the maintained hypothesis. The average capacity utilization level shown for "all observations" also declines slightly over time, reflecting the fact that mean utilization fell at about 0.003% annually in the data sample.[5]

Figure 1 also reveals that both entrants and incumbents built new plants during periods of high capacity utilization. Plant lumpiness influenced the threshold utilization level required to elicit new investment: In industries with lumpy plants, relatively large deviations from mean capacity utilization were required to trigger the construction of new plants. This is again consistent with non-strategic, profit-maximizing behavior.

Figure 1 shows that, in industries with lumpy plants ($N \leqslant 8$), incumbents set a higher capacity utilization threshold for new plant investment than did entrants. This probably reflects the fact that incumbents have the option of expanding existing plants incrementally, so they choose to build new plants only when the need for additional capacity is particularly great. In any case, there is no evidence that on average, incumbents constructed new plants at a lower threshold than entrants, as would be observed if incumbents expanded pre-emptively to deter new entry.

In addition to the data on the timing of plants actually constructed by new entrants, information was collected from the trade literature on entry that was announced but never carried out. A total of 15 such announcements were found where the existing number of plants in the industry was reasonably small, ranging from 4 to 8. Table III summarizes these data on cancelled announcements of entry.

Entry plans may have been cancelled for any number of reasons, but two main possibilities are: (1) industry growth dropped from anticipated levels soon after the announcement date, or (2) other firms pre-empted the invest-

[5] The "all observations" average capacity utilization levels shown in Figure 1 were computed as follows. The observation year t was indexed annually over the sample, starting three years after the initial year of coverage for each product, and finishing in 1981. For each observation year, the capacity utilization values for years $t-3$ through year $t+1$ were recorded; these values were then averaged for observations in each range of plant lumpiness, N. The temporal decline in utilization stems largely from the last few observations for each product, as the chemical industry fell into steep recession between 1979 and 1982.

TABLE III
INDUSTRY GROWTH AND CAPACITY UTILIZATION RATES ASSOCIATED WITH CANCELLED ANNOUNCEMENTS OF ENTRY*

	Average Industry Capacity Utilization in Each Year Following Announcement Year			
	$\hat{t}$	$\hat{t}+1$	$\hat{t}+2$	$\hat{t}+3$
*Cancelled Entry Observations**	0.822	0.818	0.782	0.767
Observations where Entry Occurred ($4 \leqslant N \leqslant 8$)**	0.822	0.795	0.746	0.737
All Observations ($4 \leqslant N \leqslant 8$)	0.785	0.779	0.776	0.772

	Average Industry Growth Rate	
	Year ($\hat{t}-3$) *through year* $\hat{t}$	*Year* $\hat{t}$ *through year* ($\hat{t}+3$)
*Cancelled Entry Observations**	11.5%	9.5%
Observations where Entry Occurred ($4 \leqslant N \leqslant 8$)**	15.6%	11.7%
All Observations ($4 \leqslant N \leqslant 8$)	8.2%	6.6%

* Sample of 15 observations where entry was announced but never completed.
** Assumes that announcement year $\hat{t}$ occurred two years prior to observed year of plant completion.

ment niche originally targeted by the announced entrant. The evidence in Table III points more strongly to the latter. For the cancelled entry sample, the mean growth rate through the announcement year was 11.5%; this is significantly above the overall sample mean but below the average for comparable observations where entry actually occurred. Growth diminished somewhat after the announcement date, but remained well above the overall sample mean. Average capacity utilization in the cancelled-entry sample fell from about 4% above the mean in the announcement year, to slightly below the mean three years later. This fall in capacity utilization, coupled with continued output growth, confirms that other firms indeed expanded capacity. Detailed inspection of the data revealed that in some instances the cancelled-entry firms were pre-empted by other entrants, and in other instances by incumbent firms. The intermediate growth rate shown for the cancelled entry sample suggests that growth may not have been sufficient to accommodate large-scale expansion by more than one or two firms.

V. LOGIT MODEL

The insights of the previous section can be formalized and extended through estimation of a logit model. We begin with a general model of new plant investment, which is then expanded to permit a comparison of entrant and incumbent investment behavior.

Consider an industry with growing demand for a homogeneous product and a well-defined minimum efficient scale that determines plant size. The industry contains N plants of equal size. As the market grows over time, at what point will an additional plant be built?

Assume, initially, that firms invest non-strategically, with the identity of the expanding firm determined in advance so that there is no pre-emptive competition over which firm has the right to build the next plant.[6] Without loss of generality, the parameters can be scaled so that current industry capacity (N plants) equals unity. Thus, an additional plant has capacity $1/N$. The unit cost function is $rk+cx$, where rk is fixed investment cost per period and c is marginal cost per unit x produced. An individual plant has fixed cost of rk/N per period. Industry price is maintained at some arbitrary level, v, above unit cost, that is, $P=rk+c+v$. Assume that demand is growing at rate g, and moreover, that any capacity currently idle is utilized before any new capacity added.

Under these conditions, a new plant will be built at the first point in time that its instantaneous profit, π, exceeds zero. If industry capacity utilization is U_0 at time t_0, then if the plant is opened at time t, its output will equal the residual demand:

$$g(t-t_0)-(1-U_0)$$

on which the firm earns margin $(rk+v)$. An additional plant is built at the first point t' where:

$$\pi=[g(t'-t_0)-(1-U_0)](rk+v)-rk/N>0 \tag{1}$$

The actual decision to build the plant is made earlier, at time $t'-t_c$, where t_c is the construction lead time. Note that the decision statistic is a positive function of g and U_0, and a negative function of $1/N$.[7]

The threshold decision structure represented by (1) can be estimated using a logit model. For each observation year t, we observe whether a new plant was completed. The underlying investment decision was made previously, in year $t-t_c$, based on rates of industry growth and capacity utilization observable at that time. (We assume that market growth is forecasted as a simple extrapolation based on g_{t-t_c}, the recent historical rate.) A new plant is completed in year t if the unobserved index, y_t' exceeds zero, where:

$$y_t'=-b_1+b_1t_cg_{t-t_c}+b_1U_{t-t_c}-b_2 1/N_t+e_t \tag{2}$$

and e_t is a random error term. The coefficients in (2) are determined only up to an arbitrary multiplicative constant: b_1 is proportional to $(rk+v)$, and b_2 is proportional to rk.

[6] If price falls when new capacity is added, or if there is pre-emptive competition among incumbents over the right to build the next plant, the timing of new plant construction is shifted somewhat but has approximately the same structure as in the simple model below. See Gilbert and Harris [1984].

[7] The decision statistic also depends on v/rk, but this ratio cannot be observed empirically.

The above model considers new investment only. Replacement investment also occurs, when old plants are replaced by new facilities. If existing plants depreciate continuously at rate b_3, the expected number of plants that must be replaced in any year equals b_3N. Thus, the logit model becomes

$$y_t' = -b_1 + b_1 t_c g_{t-t_c} + b_1 U_{t-t_c} - b_2 1/N_t + b_3 N_t + e_t \tag{3}$$

This logit model predicts whether a new plant will be constructed in a given year, but it does not distinguish between plants built by new entrants and plants built by incumbents. Assume, initially, that entrant and incumbent new plant decisions are independent and therefore can be tested in similar but separate logit equations. After estimating these separate equations we consider a more complex, log-linear model in which entrant and incumbent coefficients are estimated simultaneously, including possible interaction effects. In both models, if the growth and capacity utilization coefficients for incumbents appear significantly larger than those estimated for entrants, this is evidence that incumbent firms may have expanded pre-emptively in an effort to deter entry.

Time trend effects and multi-plant economies might also be expected to influence investment behavior. As entry occurs and the queue of potential entrants becomes depleted, the proportion of new plants that are built by entrants should decline. Thus, if a time trend, *t*, is included in the logit

TABLE IV
LOGIT ANALYSIS OF NEW PLANT CONSTRUCTION[a]

Dep. Var.	1 *DENT*	2 *DENT*	3 *DINC*	4 *DINC*	5 *DNEW*	6 *DNEW*
c	−4.08*	−4.27*	−2.29*	−3.31*	−3.05*	−3.81*
	(0.72)	(0.75)	(0.73)	(0.81)	(0.63)	(0.67)
$g_{i,t-1}$	5.57*	3.35*	3.05*	2.00**	4.90*	2.97*
	(0.86)	(0.92)	(0.96)	(1.03)	(0.83)	(0.86)
$U_{i,t-2}$	3.24*	2.95*	2.12*	1.95*	3.35*	3.14*
	(0.81)	(0.80)	(0.83)	(0.82)	(0.71)	(0.70)
$1/N_{i,t}$	−4.66*	−2.36**	−10.48*	−4.46*	−7.31*	−3.28*
	(1.04)	(1.05)	(1.43)	(1.62)	(1.02)	(1.05)
$N_{i,t}$		0.029*		0.037*		0.040*
		(0.006)		(0.007)		(0.007)
t		−0.091*		−0.055*		−0.078*
		(0.017)		(0.017)		(0.015)
$N/M_{i,t}$		−0.19		−0.06		−0.05
		(0.17)		(0.16)		(0.15)
Log Likelihood	−376.02	−351.27	−371.28	−350.46	−462.11	−431.14
Mean of Dep. Var.	0.195	0.195	0.203	0.203	0.325	0.325
No. of Obs.	839	839	839	839	839	839

[a] Numbers in parentheses are asymptotic standard errors.
* Significant at the 0.01 level, one-tailed test.
** Significant at the 0.05 level, one-tailed test.

equation for plants built by entrants, a negative coefficient should be obtained. Empirical research by Duetsch [1984] suggests that multi-plant economies of scale can create a barrier to entry favoring expansion by incumbents. This can be tested by incorporating the average number of plants per firm (N/M) as a measure of multi-plant operation in the model.

These considerations suggest the following general model:

$$y' = -b_1 + b_1 t_c g_{t-t_c} + b_1 U_{t-t_c} - b_2 1/N_t + b_3 N_t + b_4 t + b_5 N/M_t + e_t \tag{4}$$

This specification, and that described by (2), were estimated in separate logit equations for new plant investment by entrants (*DENT*), incumbents (*DINC*), and entrants and incumbents combined (*DNEW*). Results are shown in Table IV.

All coefficients in Table IV except the multi-plant measure appear with the expected signs and are significantly different from zero. More rapid market growth and higher capacity utilization served as stimuli for expansion by both entrants and incumbents. Moreover, the threshold required to elicit construction of a new plant was higher when plants were more "lumpy", as measured by $1/N$. As expected, the time trend appears negative for plants by new entrants, but it is also negative and significant for incumbents' plants.[8] The multi-plant measure proves insignificant in the entry equation, indicating the absence of multi-plant entry barriers in this particular industry sample.

The results in Table IV are consistent with the maintained hypothesis that firms made new plant investments to adjust capacity to the level required to effectively service demand. In the entry equations, the coefficients of g, U, and $1/N$ have roughly the relative magnitudes predicted by the specification in (2). In the incumbent equations, the $1/N$ coefficient appears larger than predicted (indicating that incumbents had a higher investment threshold than entrants in industries with lumpy plants, which is consistent with the data in Figure 1). However, this difference in threshold does not prove significant statistically.[9] Most importantly, the growth and capacity utilization coefficients for incumbents do not exceed those for entrants. This is evidence that incumbents did not expand pre-emptively in an effort to deter entry.

To compare the entrant and incumbent coefficients without restrictive assumptions, the two dependent variables must be estimated in the same statistical model, incorporating a common error structure and allowing for the possibility of interdependence. An extended parametrization of the log-linear model (Amemiya [1985], Goodman [1972], Nerlove and Press [1973])

[8] This arises from the fact that growth rates in the sample slowed substantially over time. This slowing growth is imperfectly proxied by the historical growth rate, g, causing the growth coefficient to decline in magnitude when the time trend is included.

[9] Several tests were performed. The $1/N$ coefficients were tested for equality between entrants and incumbents in the logit equations (assuming independence) and in the less restrictive log-linear model. Also, sums of coefficients ($1/N$ and U) were tested for equality between entrants and incumbents. None of these tests proved significant at the 0.05 level.

TABLE V
RESULTS BASED ON LOG-LINEAR MODEL[a]

	DENT	*DINC*	*INTERACTION*
c	−5.08*	−3.85*	3.10
	(0.99)	(1.00)	(1.72)
$g_{i,t-1}$	3.30*	0.90	0.06
	(1.08)	(1.54)	(2.16)
$U_{i,t-2}$	3.67*	2.84*	−3.23
	(1.06)	(1.04)	(2.03)
$1/N_{i,t}$	−2.68**	−6.46*	5.29
	(1.41)	(2.30)	(2.95)
$N_{i,t}$	0.024*	0.030*	0.011
	(0.01)	(0.008)	(0.013)
t	−0.087*	−0.050*	−0.0012
	(0.02)	(0.02)	(0.04)
$N/M_{i,t}$	−0.017	0.014	−0.42
	(0.02)	(0.18)	(0.48)
Log Likelihood			−695.08
No. of Obs.			839

[a] Numbers in parentheses are asymptotic standard errors.
* Significant at the 0.01 level.
** Significant at the 0.05 level.
One-tailed significance test used for *DENT* and *DINC* coefficients; two-tailed test used for interaction terms.

provides a suitable framework. In the extended log-linear model, independence is relaxed by incorporating a set of interaction terms which test the difference between the conditional and unconditional expansion probabilities. For example, a positive interaction constant term implies that the probability of new plant investment by incumbents, conditional on entry during the observation year, exceeded the probability of incumbent investment in the absence of entry. If incumbents accommodated entrants by withholding investment, this interaction term would prove negative, whereas if incumbents responded to entry by increasing investment, it would appear positive. Note that the interaction term provides no information on whether incumbents maintained excess capacity prior to entry. Rather, it reflects the behavior of incumbents once the intentions of entrants had been announced.

The parameterization used in Table V makes the interaction term a function of all of the explanatory variables. If the interaction coefficients all equal zero, then *DENT* and *DINC* are independent, and the log-linear model is equivalent to two separate logit models, as estimated in Table IV.

The interaction coefficients in Table V all prove statistically insignificant at the 0.05 level based on a two-tailed test. This indicates that investments by incumbents and entrants were statistically independent; i.e., the probability of new plant investment by incumbents was not influenced by the occurrence of entry during the year, and vice versa. Two interpretations are possible: (1) entrants and incumbents failed to modify investment decisions in light of announced expansions by the other group; or (2) incumbents accommodated entrants about as often as they responded to entry by increasing investment, so that the net correlation is zero. In either case, there is no evidence of any net accommodation by incumbents. If a one-tailed test is applied to the interaction coefficients, the constant and $1/N$ terms prove significant at the 0.05 level, indicating a positive correlation between entrant and incumbent investment in industries having a small number of plants. This is consistent with results in Lieberman [1986] showing that incumbents accelerated investment following entry in concentrated industries.

The non-interaction coefficients in Table V are similar in magnitude and statistical significance to the logit coefficients in Table IV. None of the individual entrant or incumbent coefficients are significantly different from each other at the 0.05 level. Thus, the hypothesis of identical behavior on the part of both entrants and incumbents cannot be rejected.

These logit and log-linear model results confirm the main conclusions of section IV, that entrants and incumbents acted similarly in their capacity expansion. There is no statistical evidence that incumbents expanded pre-emptively at a lower threshold than entrants, in an effort to deter entry.

VI. CASE EVIDENCE ON EXCESS CAPACITY HELD AS AN ENTRY DETERRENT

Lack of statistical evidence that incumbents built plants pre-emptively to deter entry does not prove that such behavior never occurred. Conceivably, excess capacity may have served as an entry barrier for only a few products in the sample and therefore cannot be detected in the statistical analysis. To check this possibility, the data sample was screened to identify specific cases where excess capacity may have been maintained as a barrier to entry. Products that exhibited chronic excess capacity were examined in detail, using information from the trade literature.

The sample was screened in the following manner. Chronic excess capacity was defined as the persistence of industry capacity utilization below the sample mean (80%) for five or more successive years. Of the sample observations that met this criterion, about a third were for years following 1973. These observations were discarded, as much of the excess capacity observed after 1973 was the result of oil price increases, which obsoleted existing plant and led to declines in industry output.[10]

Based on these criteria, ten products were classified as exhibiting chronic excess capacity. These products were examined in detail using the trade literature to help identify the reasons why excess capacity occurred. In general, these reasons appeared unrelated to strategic entry deterrence. For

[10] Capacity utilization fell below the 80% mark for 35% of the observations prior to 1973. Low capacity utilization typically stemmed from cyclical downturns; only 15% of all observations prior to 1973 were classified as chronic excess capacity.

four products,[11] excess capacity appeared to be a direct consequence of new entry. For two products,[12] excess capacity seemed to have resulted from outbreaks of investment rivalry or over-optimism among incumbent firms. For two more products,[13] excess capacity stemmed at least in part from temporary downturns in demand. However, for one of these products (magnesium) the resulting excess capacity appeared to have been used by the dominant firm as a means to deter entry. Only two products (aniline and sorbitol) exhibited continuous output growth plus evidence that excess capacity was maintained in an attempt to deter entry. These two products and magnesium are considered in greater detail below.[14]

Aniline

Aniline was produced by four firms in the early 1960s. Output grew steadily from 122 million pounds in 1961 to 263 million pounds in 1968. Industry capacity utilization fell below the 80% mark following a major expansion by DuPont in 1962, and remained below that level until 1969.

There is some evidence that incumbents held excess capacity in an unsuccessful attempt to deter entry, which was attracted by market growth. In early 1964, one new firm (Rubicon) announced plans to enter the industry, and two others were cited as potential entrants. Trade sources reported that "with Rubicon's announcement and Cyanamid's expansion, aniline capacity will be more than adequate for the next several years despite the sharp gains being recorded in consumption.... Capacity in 1965 will be 280 million pounds at a minimum, indicating an operating rate of 72% of capacity. On that basis it appears doubtful that any new producers will enter the field."[15] "Deterrents to the entry of new producers are the low price of aniline itself—

[11] Ethanolamines, high-density polyethylene, polyester fibers and urea. See, for example, "Ethanolamines: Too Much Capacity", *Chemical and Engineering News*, February 10, 1958; "High Density Polyethylene Shifts to High Gear", *Chemical and Engineering News*, December 12, 1960; "For Polyester Fibers and Films: New Patent Picture and Producers", *Chemical Engineering*, March 22, 1964.

[12] Pentarythritol and phthalic anhydride. See, for example, "PE Capacity: Running Wild?", *Chemical Week*, September 10, 1955; "PE Capacity Rises Sharply, Far Outstripping Production", *Chemical and Engineering News*, January 27, 1958; "Phthalic: Time of Plenty", *Chemical Week*, July 1, 1961; "Phthalic Anhydride Plants to Rise on Both the East and West Coasts", *Oil, Paint and Drug Reporter*, August 14, 1961; "Phthalic Woes Grow", *Chemical Week*, April 27, 1963.

[13] Sodium and magnesium. See, for example, "Sodium, Long in the Doldrums, Enjoys a Brisk Growth Rate", *Oil, Paint and Drug Reporter*, March 29, 1965; and Lieberman [1983].

[14] Capacity also played an important role with respect to entry into neoprene rubber, the most concentrated industry in the sample. The incumbent firm (DuPont) had historically been able to defend its US monopoly without maintaining substantial excess production capacity. However, in 1965 an explosion destroyed 80% of DuPont's neoprene plant. Several months later Petro-Tex announced plans for entry based on a new production process licensed from a European firm. See, "Neoprene Blast Makes Big Dent in US Capacity", *Oil, Paint and Drug Reporter*, August 30, 1965; "Neoprene: Petro-Tex to be 2nd US Maker", *Oil, Paint and Drug Reporter*, January 10, 1966.

[15] "Aniline Capacity 280 Million Pounds: That's What US–UK Effort Will Do", *Oil, Paint and Drug Reporter*, January 20, 1964.

Cyanamid made an additional 1 cent reduction last month—plus the large capital investment needed to build an aniline plant."[16] Excess capacity did not, however, forestall additional entry. A total of three new firms entered the market between 1965 and 1968.

Sorbitol

Sorbitol had capacity utilization below 70% for more than 14 years, from the beginning of sample coverage in 1955 through 1968. Atlas Powder was the sole commercial producer in the US from 1943 until 1956. (Two drug manufacturers maintained a small amount of capacity for captive use.) The sorbitol market expanded gradually from 50 million pounds in 1955 to 106 million pounds by 1968.

Trade sources suggest that excess capacity held by Atlas may have retarded the rate of entry into the sorbitol market. When the drug producer, Merck, entered in 1957, it was reported that: "Atlas was the sole commercial sorbitol producer since 1943 simply because no one chose to compete. And for a good reason: sorbitol's capacity was reported at 75 million pounds per year; selling price now runs from 15 to 17 cents a pound, depending upon amount purchased. This means that (sorbitol) is a low-unit profit item—one which calls for large capital investment and large volume production before firm gets a fair return on its venture."[17] During the course of the 1950s and 1960s, a total of only two firms entered the sorbitol market.

Magnesium

Dow Chemical dominated the US magnesium industry from World War II through the 1960s, controlling more than 80% of industry capacity and output. Over this period Dow made a number of successful attempts to deter entry, based in part on threatened utilization of excess production capacity.[18] However, Dow did not intentionally build excess capacity for entry deterrence purposes; rather, Dow's surplus plant was constructed by the US government to meet peak demand requirements during World War II, and was purchased by Dow in the late 1950s.[19]

[16] "Aniline Figures Spell Trouble, But Closer Look Reveals Trade Has Reason to be Optimistic", *Oil, Paint and Drug Reporter*, May 3, 1965, p. 3.

[17] "Merck Goes to Sorbitol", *Chemical and Engineering News*, February 11, 1957, p. 100.

[18] For a detailed account of Dow's actions relating to entry deterrence in magnesium, see Lieberman [1983].

[19] The initial postwar episode of entry deterrence by Dow involved the auction in 1957 of a large, low-cost magnesium plant which was owned by the government but operated by Dow. Several years prior to the auction, Dow began to accumulate a stockpile of magnesium ingot which by 1957 had reached a level equivalent to approximately two years of US domestic consumption. Dow proved to be the sole bidder in the auction, and purchased the plant for substantially less than the government's original construction cost. After the auction Dow closed the plant for four years in order to draw down the accumulated magnesium stockpile. (For a theoretical discussion of inventory accumulation as a strategic entry deterrent, see Ware [1985].)

By 1963, growth in magnesium demand and development of a new production process attracted the attention of a number of potential entrants. (Dow's capacity utilization rose from about 35% in 1958 to 74% in 1963.) Three firms announced specific plans to enter the industry, and others were known to be considering entry.

Dow responded to these entry threats by announcing incremental capacity increases and cost reductions. Dow's 1963 annual report stated that "process improvements boosted magnesium production capacity without expansion of our facilities, and also reduced production costs. Additional capacity gains and cost reduction are expected in 1964 and 1965." Dow made a series of additional announcements over the next few years, indicating the potential to boost capacity by 50% by reactivating and modernizing idle plant. Dow also announced plans (which it never carried out) to build a new plant at the Great Salt Lake, the site being contemplated by most potential entrants. Moreover, Dow made substantial price cuts for magnesium sold to the major aluminum companies, who used the metal for alloying purposes and were considered the most likely entrants.

These actions by Dow appear to have deterred potential entry by Kaiser Aluminum, Harvey Aluminum, Norsk Hydro, and others; and delayed entry by Alcoa and National Lead. Successful entry did not occur until the early 1970s, by which time Dow's margin of excess capacity had shrunk to virtually zero.

VII. SUMMARY AND CONCLUSIONS

The empirical evidence presented in this study suggests that the excess capacity entry barriers identified in theory are not very common in practice. While significant excess capacity was held by firms in the sample, most was maintained to accommodate demand variability and investment lumpiness. The statistical tests fail to show that incumbent firms expanded pre-emptively in an effort to deter entry. Moreover, of the 38 products in the sample, in only three cases could any evidence be found that incumbents held excess capacity for entry deterrence purposes. And in all three of these cases, some entry in fact occurred.

These findings do not imply that excess capacity cannot deter entry, but rather that its use is both rare and unlikely to be completely effective. Theory suggests that the potency of excess capacity as an entry barrier may be undercut by market growth, free-rider problems, and demand-related effects. The two products where excess capacity seems to have offered at least partial success as an entry deterrent—magnesium and sorbitol—were characterized by slow market growth, high producer concentration, and high capital intensity. Thus, excess capacity was employed and may have provided some deterrent value in two specific instances where the conditions for its effective use coincided.

Although the data provide little evidence that incumbents built strategic excess capacity in advance of announced entry, there do seem to have been numerous instances of aggressive capacity expansion once the threat of entry became tangible. Such behavior is evident in the cancelled-entry sample and in the interaction coefficients of the log-linear model, as well as in the analysis reported in Lieberman [1986]. Thus, incumbents seem to have built strategic excess capacity in a manner more consistent with "predation" and "mobility deterrence" theories than with the standard excess capacity deterrence argument.

Related empirical evidence on investment by incumbents (e.g., Gilbert and Lieberman [1987]) points to the occurrence of pre-emptive investment behavior in which firms rush to fill new investment niches as they become available. One interpretation of the results obtained here is that in industries where potential entrants are present, incumbents and entrants act to pre-empt these niches in roughly similar manner.

MARVIN B. LIEBERMAN,
Graduate School of Business,
Stanford University,
Stanford, California 94305,
USA.

REFERENCES

AMEMIYA, T., 1985, *Advanced Econometrics* (Harvard University Press, Cambridge).

BULOW, J., GEANAKOPLOS, J. and KLEMPERER, P., 1985a, 'Holding Idle Capacity to Deter Entry', *The Economic Journal*, 95 (March), pp. 178–182.

BULOW, J., GEANAKOPLOS, J. and KLEMPERER, P., 1985b, 'Multimarket Oligopoly: Strategic Substitutes and Complements', *Journal of Political Economy*, 93 (June), pp. 488–511.

CAVES, R. E. and PORTER, M. E., 1977, 'From Entry Barriers to Mobility Barriers: Conjectural Decisions and Contrived Deterrence to New Competition', *Quarterly Journal of Economics*, 91 (May), pp. 243–261.

Chemical and Engineering News, 1950–1973, various issues.

Chemical Engineering, 1950–1973, various issues.

Chemical Week, 1950–1973, various issues.

DIXIT, A., 1980, 'The Role of Investment in Entry-Deterrence', *The Economic Journal*, 90 (June), pp. 95–106.

DUETSCH, L. L., 1984, 'Entry and Extent of Multiplant Operations', *The Journal of Industrial Economics*, 32 (June), pp. 477–487.

EATON, B. C. and LIPSEY, R. G., 1979, 'The Theory of Market Pre-emption: The Persistence of Excess Capacity and Monopoly in Growing Spatial Markets', *Economica*, 46 (May), pp. 149–158.

EATON, B. C. and LIPSEY, R. G., 1980, 'Exit Barriers are Entry Barriers: The Durability of Capital as a Barrier to Entry', *Bell Journal of Economics*, 11 (Autumn), pp. 721–729.

EATON, B. C. and LIPSEY, R. G., 1981, 'Capital, Commitment, and Entry Equilibrium', *Bell Journal of Economics*, 12 (Autumn), pp. 593–604.

EATON, B. C. and WARE, R., 1985, 'A Theory of Market Structure with Sequential Entry', Working Paper, University of Toronto.

FREIDENFELDS, J., 1981, *Capacity Expansion, Analysis of Simple Models with Applications* (Elsevier, New York).

FUDENBERG, D. and TIROLE, J., 1983, 'Capital as a Commitment: Strategic Investment of Deter Mobility', *Journal of Economic Theory*, 31 (December), pp. 227–250.

GEROSKI, P. A., 1983, 'The Empirical Analysis of Entry: A Survey', Research Paper, University of Southampton.

GHEMAWAT, P., 1984, 'Capacity Expansion in the Titanium Dioxide Industry', *The Journal of Industrial Economics*, 33 (December), pp. 145–163.

GILBERT, R. J. and HARRIS, R. G., 1984, 'Competition with Lumpy Investment', *The Rand Journal of Economics*, 15 (Summer), pp. 197–212.

GILBERT, R. and LIEBERMAN, M., 1987, 'Investment and Coordination in Oligopolistic Industries', *Rand Journal of Economics*, 18 (Spring), pp. 17–33.

GILBERT, R. J. and VIVES, X., 1986, 'Noncooperative Entry Deterrence and the Free Rider Problem', *Review of Economic Studies* (forthcoming).

GOODMAN, L. A., 1972, 'A Modified Multiple Regression Approach to the Analysis of Dichotomous Variables', *American Sociological Review*, 37, pp. 28–46.

HAUSE, J. C. and DURIETZ, G., 1984, 'Entry, Industry Growth, and the Microdynamics of Industry Supply', *Journal of Political Economy*, 92 (August), pp. 733–757.

HILKE, J. C., 1984, 'Excess Capacity and Entry: Some Empirical Evidence', *The Journal of Industrial Economics*, 33 (December), pp. 233–241.

KIRMAN, W. I. and MASSON, R. T., 1986, 'Capacity Signals and Entry Deterrence', *International Journal of Industrial Organization*, 4 (March), pp. 25–44.

KREPS, D. M. and WILSON, R., 1982, 'Reputation and Imperfect Information', *Journal of Economic Theory*, 27 (August), pp. 253–279.

LIEBERMAN, M. B., 1982, 'The Learning Curve, Pricing, and Market Structure in the Chemical Processing Industries', PhD Thesis, Harvard University.

LIEBERMAN, M. B., 1983, 'The US Magnesium Industry', Stanford University business case no. S-BP-231.

LIEBERMAN, M. B., 1985, 'Capacity Utilization in the Chemical Processing Industries: Theoretical Models and Empirical Tests', Working Paper 817, Stanford Graduate School of Business.

LIEBERMAN, M. B., 1986, 'Entry, Excess Capacity, and Market Structure in the Chemical Processing Industries', Working Paper 830a, Stanford Graduate School of Business.

LYONS, B. R., 1986, 'The Welfare Loss Due to Strategic Investment in Excess Capacity', *International Journal of Industrial Organization*, 4 (March), pp. 109–120.

MANNE, A. S., 1961, 'Capacity Expansion and Probabilistic Growth', *Econometrica*, 29 (October), pp. 632–649.

MCLEAN, R. P. and RIORDAN, M. H., 1985, 'Equilibrium Industry Structure with Sequential Technological Choice', Working Paper 132, Studies in Industry Economics, Stanford University.

MILGROM, P. and ROBERTS, D. J., 1982, Predation, Reputation, and Entry Deterrence', *Journal of Economic Theory*, 27, 2 (August), pp. 280–312.

NAKAO, T., 1980, 'Demand Growth, Profitability, and Entry, *Quarterly Journal of Economics*, 94 (March), pp. 397–411.

NERLOVE, M. and PRESS, S. J., 1973, 'Univariate and Multivariate Log-Linear and Logistic Models', Research Paper R-1306-EDA/NIH, Rand Corporation.

Oil, Paint and Drug Reporter, 1950–1973, various issues.

ORR, D., 1974, 'The Determinants of Entry: A Study of the Canadian Manufacturing Industries', *Review of Economics and Statistics*, 56 (February), pp. 58–65.

PERRAKIS, S. and WARSKETT, G., 1983, 'Capacity and Entry Under Demand Uncertainty', *Review of Economic Studies*, 50 (July), pp. 495–511.

PORTER, M. E. and SPENCE, M., 1982, 'The Capacity Expansion Process in a Growing Oligopoly: The Case of Corn Wet Milling', in JOHN J. MCCALL, *Economics of Information and Uncertainty* (University of Chicago Press, Chicago).

REYNOLDS, S. S., 1986, 'Strategic Capital Investment in the American Aluminum Industry', *Journal of Industrial Economics*, 34 (March), pp. 225–245.

SALOP, S. C., 1979, 'New Directions in Industrial Organization: Strategic Entry Deterrence', *American Economic Review*, 69 (May), pp. 335–338.

SHESHINSKI, E. and DREZE, J. H., 1976, 'Demand Fluctuations, Capacity Utilization and Costs', *American Economic Review*, 66 (December), pp. 731–742.

SMILEY, R., 1986, 'Empirical Evidence on Strategic Entry Deterrence', Working Paper, Johnson Graduate School of Management, Cornell University.

SMITH, K. R., 1969, 'The Effect of Uncertainty on Monopoly Capital Stock and Utilization of Capital', *Journal of Economic Theory*, 1 (June), pp. 48–59.

SMITH, K. R., 1970, 'Risk and the Optimal Utilization of Capital', *Review of Economic Studies*, 37 (April), pp. 253–259.

SMITH, R. L., 1981, 'Efficiency Gains from Strategic Investment', *The Journal of Industrial Economics*, 30 (September), pp. 1–23.

SPENCE, A. M., 1977, 'Entry, Capacity, Investment and Oligopolistic Pricing', *The Bell Journal of Economics*, 8 (Autumn), pp. 534–544.

SPENCE, A. M., 1979, 'Investment Strategy and Growth in a New Market', *The Bell Journal of Economics*, 10 (Spring), pp. 1–19.

SPULBER, D. F., 1981, 'Capacity, Output, and Sequential Entry', *American Economic Review*, 71 (June), pp. 503–514.

SRI INTERNATIONAL, annual issues, Directory of Chemical Producers (Menlo Park, California).

US DEPARTMENT OF THE INTERIOR, BUREAU OF MINES, annual issues, Minerals Yearbook (GPO, Washington).

US DEPARTMENT OF COMMERCE, BUREAU OF THE CENSUS, annual issues, Current Industrial Reports, M28a (GPO, Washington).

US INTERNATIONAL TRADE COMMISSION, annual issues, Synthetic Organic Chemicals, US Production and Sales (GPO, Washington).

WALDMAN, M., 1983, 'Limited Collusion and Entry Deterrence', Working Paper 306, Department of Economics, UCLA.

WALDMAN, M., 1987, 'Noncooperative Entry Deterrence, Uncertainty, and the Free Rider Problem', *Review of Economic Studies* (forthcoming).

WARE, R., 1985, 'Inventory Holding as a Strategic Weapon to Deter Entry', *Economica*, 52 (February), pp. 93–101.

WENDERS, J. T., 1971, 'Excess Capacity as a Barrier to Entry', *Journal of Industrial Economics*, 20 (November), pp. 14–19.

WILLIAMSON, O. E., 1977, 'Predatory Pricing: A Strategic and Welfare Analysis, *Yale Law Journal*, 87, pp. 284–340.

INDEX